ADRIAN FORT

Nancy

The Story of Lady Astor

VINTAGE BOOKS

London

Published by Vintage 2013

2 4 6 8 10 9 7 5 3 1

Copyright © Adrian Fort 2012

Adrian Fort has asserted his right under the Copyright, Designs
and Patents Act 1988 to be identified as the author of this work

First published in Great Britain in 2012 by Jonathan Cape

Vintage
Random House, 20 Vauxhall Bridge Road,
London SW1V 2SA

www.vintage-books.co.uk

Addresses for companies within The Random House Group Limited
can be found at: www.randomhouse.co.uk/offices

The Random House Group Limited Reg. No. 954009

A CIP catalogue record for this book
is available from the British Library

ISBN 9781845951610

The Random House Group Limited supports the Forest Stewardship
Council® (FSC®), the leading international forest-certification
organisation. Our books carrying the FSC label are printed on
FSC®-certified paper. FSC is the only forest-certification scheme
supported by the leading environmental organisations, including
Greenpeace. Our paper procurement policy can be found at
www.randomhouse.co.uk/environment

Typeset in Sabon by Palimpsest Book Production Limited,
Falkirk, Stirlingshire
Printed and bound by CPI Group (UK) Ltd, Croydon, CR0 4YY

NANCY

Adrian Fort was educated at Eton and Oxford, where he was subsequently a Clarendon Fellow. He practised as a barrister and became involved with politics before pursuing a financial career. He has published many articles on financial and economic matters and has broadcast frequently on the radio. His previous books include *Prof: The Life of Frederick Lindemann* and *Archibald Wavell: The Life and Times of an Imperial Servant*.

Acknowledgements

I should like to thank the Society of Authors for their kindness in providing me with an Authors' Foundation Grant. I am also indebted to the trustees of the Royal Literary Fund for encouraging me in my research.

I am very grateful to members of the Astor and Langhorne families who, while wholly at arm's length from this book, nevertheless allowed me access to private papers and gave me helpful advice; in particular I should like to thank Viscount Astor, David Astor, Lord Astor of Hever, Bronwen Lady Astor, Alice Astor, Micky Astor, Hon. Mrs Baring and Langhorne Gibson, Jnr.

Officials, historians, archivists and librarians, both in England and America, have been greatly helpful, and I have received patient and sound advice from archivists at the University of Reading; Balliol College, New College and the Bodleian Library at Oxford; the Royal Archives; Plymouth and West Devon Record Office, and Plymouth Central Library; the Bulldog Trust; the National Archives of Scotland; Lucy Cavendish College; Churchill Archives Centre; the Liddell Hart Centre for Military Archives; Franklin D. Roosevelt Presidential Library and Museum; Hertfordshire Record Office; British Library; the Lilly Library, Indiana University; Eton College Library; The Women's Library, London Metropolitan University; the Naval and Military Club; Hatfield House Archive; Boston Athenaeum; University of Virginia Library; the National Library of Wales; New England Historic Genealogical Society; Massachusetts Archives; Massachusetts Historical Society; Museum of the Confederacy, the Baring Archive; and the University of Exeter.

In particular I should like to thank Pat Maurakis, Christine Faunch, Dr Alex May, Dr Priscilla Roberts, Guy Baxter, Nathan Williams, Nancy Fulford, Verity Andrews, Jean Rose, Charles Arkwright, Alan Borthwick, Anna Sander, Penelope Bulloch, Penny Hatfield, Robin Harcourt Williams, Sir Henry Bedingfeld Bt., Sue Briggs, Dr Geoffrey Waddington, Dr Stuart Ball, Anne Morgan, Deborah Watson, Ian Criddle, Stacey Dyer, Colette Hobbs, Graham Naylor, Karen Davies, Pamela Clark, Nicholas Connell, Ana Da Silva, Craig Finlay, John Chignoli, Joe Maldonado, Lucy McCann, Kirsten Carter, John Hannigan, Autumn Haag, Dr Graham Jones; Mary McFarland, Marit Grujis, Anita Saunders, Caroline Herbert, Lynsey Robertson,

Nicholas Robinson, Nicholas Baldwin, Haim A. Gottschalk, Lynn Shirey, Teresa Roane, Rhonda McClure, Aidan Haley, Dr David Bradshaw, Wendy Hawke, Dianne Shepherd, Sarah Charlton, Jenny Dancey, Andre Gailani, Isabel Holoway, Jane Keskar, Moira Lovegrove, John Orbell, John Lloyd, Jeremy McIlwaine, John Partington, Tessa Rawle, Jane Rawson, Sabine Schafferdt, Nicholas Scheetz, Christina Thompson, Lianne Smith, Naomi Van Loo, Prof Dr Johannes Tuchel, David Sutton, Mary Warnement.

For their invaluable help and skill I should like sincerely to thank my literary agents, Peters Fraser and Dunlop, and my publishers in England and America, Jonathan Cape and St. Martin's Press, and especially Annabel Merullo, Alex Bowler, Steven Messer, Charles Spicer, Grainne Fox, Ellah Allfrey, Allison Caplin and Laura Williams.

Others who have in their various ways been of very great help in my preparation of this book include: Anthony Brotherton-Ratcliffe, Lady Abdy, Mark Amory, Viscount Asquith, Lt. Col. Thomas Baring, Dugald Barr, Mark Barrington-Ward, Lottie Barton, David Beamish, Jurgen Becker, Dr Nils Beckman, Gill Bennett, John Bignell, Denys Blakeway, Alexandra Bolitho, Hon. Lady Bonsor, Hon. Evelyn Boscawen, Michael Bottenheim, Graham Brady, MP, Charlotte Breese, James Bristow, John Bromley-Davenport, QC, Mrs Meriel Buxton, Dame Frances Campbell-Preston, Peter Carroll, Rosemary Castle, Sir Edward and Lady Cazalet, Victor Cazalet, Lord Charles Cecil, Mrs B.Chapman, Colin Chisholm, Anthony Clarke, Michael Clayton, Richard Davenport-Hines, Martha Davidson, Dr Ralph Davison, Dowager Duchess of Devonshire, Lady Dodds-Parker, Helen Donald, Mrs Jan Douglas, Christopher Flynn, Elizabeth Fortescue, James Fox, Drusilla Fraser, Francis and Kishanda Fulford, Robin B. Gillie, Sir David Gilmour, Bt., John Gisbey, Earl of Gowrie, Amanda Gustin, Janie Hampton, Major David Hardy, Adam Healy, David Heathcoat-Amory, Nicholas Hextall, Harold and Annie Hickson, Nicholas Hiley, Gwen Hillman, Major Rex Hitchcock, Lady Holderness, Gregory Holyoake, the Reverend Hunter Miller, Christopher Hunwick, Kazuo Ishiguro, Dr Simon James, Justin Kaplan, Freddie Knox, Dr Robin Lane Fox, Victoria Legge-Bourke, Jeremy Lewis, Countess of Lichfield, Tony Lobl, Calder Loth, James Lowther, Viscountess Macmillan, Mark Grindon-Welch, Juliet Maxey, Hon. Hector McDonnell, Andrew Merriam, David Metcalfe, Anthony Mildmay-White, Tracy Murrell, Shahid Nazir, Tom Nelson, Adam Nicolson, Dowager Duchess of Northumberland, Conrad Ogrodowczyk, Anna Olatokun, David Oldrey, Lady Katherine Page, Lady Victoria Percy, Dan Pezzoni, Rachel Polonsky, Lord Ravensdale, Mrs Helen Roche, Audrey Roethenbaugh, Kenneth Rose, Hon. John Rous, Albert Roux, Robert Sackville-West, The Dowager Marchioness of Salisbury, Lady Salt, Adrian Scott Knight, Professor Robert Self, Julian Seymour, Richard Southby, James Srodes, Caroline Stanley, Christopher Sykes, Sir Tatton Sykes, Bt., Edward Synge, Lee Taylor, Ian Thorne, Heather Tylor, Rebecca Vick, Hugo Vickers, Juri Viehoff, Lyuba Vinogradova, Lady Walters, Catherine Wardroper, Earl of Wemyss, Cyril Whiting, Hon. Andrew Wigram, Lord Wigram, John T. Williams, Baroness Willoughby, Julia Wills, R. F. Wilson, Elizabeth Winn, Anne Wyndham, and Henry Wyndham.

CONTENTS

LIST OF ILLUSTRATIONS

Astor Family

John Jacob Astor [1763–1848]

William Backhouse Astor [1792–1875]

John Jacob Astor III [1822–1890] = Charlotte Augusta Gibbes

William Waldorf Astor [1st Viscount] [1848–1919] = (1878) Mary Dahlgren Paul, of Philadelphia [1858–1894]

Waldorf Astor [2nd Viscount] [1879–1952] = (1906) Nancy Witcher Langhorne Shaw [1879–1964]

William Waldorf Astor, 3rd Viscount [1907–1966]
Phyllis [1909–1975]
David [1912–2001]
Michael [1916–1980]
John Jacob [1913–2000]

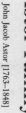

Langhorne Family

Chiswell Dabney Langhorne [1843–1919] = (1864) Nancy Witcher Keen [1848–1903]

Lizzie   Keene   Irene   Nancy = (1) (1897) Robert Gould Shaw II [1873–1930]   Phyllis   Buck   Nora
= (2) (1906) Waldorf Astor

Robert Gould Shaw III ['Bobbie'] [1898–1970]

Prologue

When Nancy Astor first came to England, a little over a hundred years ago, a divorcee from America with a young son to look after, it seemed unlikely that she would soon find her way to becoming a famous hostess near the centre of the British Empire's highest social spheres. That she would then leave a deep and lasting imprint on the whole political life of the nation was wholly unexpected. She was not even English, but instead a restless, controversial American dynamo – very different from most of those who formed the society which, without much delay, she would enter.

However, her arrival coincided with the beginning of a period of huge upheaval in British life. The changes that tore through its society in the early part of the last century were on a scale comparable only with those thrown up by the Civil War some three hundred years earlier, and before that by the Reformation, and even the Norman Conquest. Soon after 1910 the grace and ease of the condition of the ruling classes, epitomised by the tranquil luxury of the Edwardian Age, began to dissolve. Imperceptibly and then violently, the instability created first by Lloyd George's radical upheaval of long-established principles of taxation, to be sealed by the carnage of the Great War, altered beyond recognition the atmosphere of order and prosperity that had come to be perceived as permanent. At the same time, bitter constitutional conflict, unimaginable only a few short years earlier, led to the passing of the Parliament Bill of 1911, which emasculated the power of the peerage, and hastened the dilution of the long held influence of the aristocracy.

The growing turbulence also forced open the way to a profound alteration in the political status of women, as, in parallel with the dissolution of the wealth and stability of the old order, there was fought a bitter and violent battle for the rights of women, its most dramatic clash occurring perhaps on June 4, 1913, when a Suffragette ran onto the racecourse to collide, fatally, with the King's horse, Anmer, galloping towards the finishing post of the Epsom Derby.

Soon after the tragedy on the Epsom turf, women's struggles for political recognition were swamped by the cataclysm of the First World War. For a time the fight for the Cause was suspended, but its aims came suddenly close to achievement soon after the Armistice, in 1918, when the British government, conscious that millions of women had done their bit for an embattled empire, rewarded them with the vote. So, before long, women's rôle in society was increased far beyond anything seen in British history, leading in time, but inevitably, to the equality of status they enjoy today.

Almost as an afterthought, the government also agreed to a Bill allowing women to stand for Parliament. The door left ajar when a hundred years' peace ended in 1914, was opened even wider.

Into that gap, after a pause, there came a new champion. Someone entirely different to the women's leaders who had gone before: not, as had been feared and expected by men, some hard-bitten Suffragette, the survivor perhaps of imprisonment and force-feeding, or a victim of the notorious Cat and Mouse Act. Far from being a virago on the model of the rugged, tough women who had suffered for their cause, the newcomer, Nancy Astor, was young and lovely, and not even English. Coming from a famous Virginian family, she was a sister of the celebrated Gibson Girl, proud of her expatriate ancestry and ever ready to blow bracing American air into what she regarded as the stuffy corners of English life.

In further contrast to what might have been expected of a woman trying to run a stake into established political ways, she was already near the centre of the ruling society which had so long been opposed to political change. She had married, soon after her appearance in England, into the family of one of the richest men in the world, who was also American, and who had settled in England some years earlier, after his own controversial strut - on the political stage of New York.

With immense wealth harnessed to an exceptionally vibrant and colourful character, she now took English politics by storm, and after a sensational campaign, reported world wide, she was elected a Member of Parliament for Plymouth, a constituency that fittingly included the harbour from which the Pilgrim Fathers had sailed for the New World, long years before. And so, in December 1919, Nancy Astor became the first woman to take her seat in the Mother of Parliaments.

There she sat, fiercely independent, facing down the unceasing and virulent hostility of almost all the six hundred or so male members surrounding her. In those first hard years she was fortified by a determination, which she never abandoned, to do what she saw as 'good' regardless of the irritation it caused to fellow politicians – and to wide swathes of the British public, not least with her unrelenting attack on the evils of alcohol and other attendant sins so much enjoyed by the average man. Holding her own long enough for the idea of a woman in Parliament finally to become accepted, her example led others to follow the path which she had cut, successfully taking into British law rafts of legislation in support of women, children and the family, which a short time earlier would have been unthinkable.

Not as well suited to studious debate as her new-found colleagues in the House of Commons, Nancy then developed a parallel life as a political hostess of almost unchallenged prominence. With the influence created by her talents and her wealth – which enabled her personally to meet and challenge Stalin in his private den, just as her husband Waldorf was among the first British politicians to have an interview with Hitler – and deploying her masterly wit and sense of comedy, Nancy played hostess throughout the 1930s to Prime Ministers and members of the British government, to leading Americans, and to Nazis and others in the forefront of European politics as a second world war drew near.

Secure in her position high in the ranks of the social and political worlds, and with innate strength of character, Nancy expressed her opinions freely, careless of the sometimes explosive reactions that they caused. But as the Dictators grew ever more powerful her insistence that another war would be a catastrophe to be avoided at all costs brought her, and the 'Cliveden Set' which she was taken to represent, hostility and eventual vilification in the Press and among the public both in Europe and in America, as the policy of appeasement tottered and fell, to be trampled underfoot by Britain's enemies.

Yet the carefree but dogged characteristics that had darkened Nancy's once glowing image restored her reputation when the bombs began to fall. Together with her husband, as Lord and Lady Mayoress of Plymouth, Nancy stood her ground through the relentless, ferocious German Blitz on the city as, blackened and shattered, it all but disappeared in flames. With brave defiance she drew public admiration far and wide; cheerful and unbowed, she remained tireless in helping those whom she had for so long represented and loved, inspiring the masses who, at first huddled beneath the wreckage of their city, then rebuilt it and started its life anew.

The circumstances in which Nancy suddenly ended her political life exposed a hard and less becoming side to her character, heralded by her growing hostility to the spirit of the new world that was beginning to take shape as the war's end drew near. But her success in reaching Parliament, and in defying all attempts to freeze her out of it, ensured that age-old barriers against women entering public life were irreversibly dismantled, and to this day she remains a beacon, illuminating paths seemingly blocked by intransigence.

ONE

In Dixie

Nancy Astor was born into a family with no money and no certain future, in a country vanquished in war and destitute in its aftermath. Her parents were Chiswell Dabney Langhorne and Nannie Witcher Keen, and she too was christened Nannie, the name she used until, in 1904, in her early twenties, she travelled to England, when she began calling herself Nancy.

Her father, known as Chillie, or Dab to his parents and wife, was born in Lynchburg, Virginia, on 4 November 1843, the eldest of five children, two others having died in infancy. A heavy, stocky, rumbustious extrovert, he was good-looking, genial and jovial, but impulsive, his charm interspersed with fits of ungoverned temper. His ancestors on his father's side were Welsh, but in the seventeenth century one of them, Captain John Langhorne, had emigrated to Virginia. Langhorne proved himself a man of substance, and in time he acquired lucrative contracts, became a member of the Virginia House of Burgesses, and patented a valuable tract of land. His great-grandson, William Langhorne, was to be revered by future generations of the family for his service during the American Revolution. William's son, Major John Scarisbrooke Langhorne, married his first cousin, Elizabeth, daughter of his father's elder brother, Maurice. In 1828, their son, also Maurice, rented from its owner, a judge, a fine colonial house which had been built in 1815 next to what had once been a duelling ground, and which was consequently known as Point of Honor. It overlooked the James River, on whose banks, near Lynchburg, Virginia, Maurice and his younger brother Henry, Chillie's grandfather, established a flour milling business in 1831.

Chillie's father, John, Henry Langhorne's eldest son, married the daughter of Chiswell Dabney, a lawyer and the owner of a fine plantation near Lynchburg. Named Sarah Elizabeth, she was described by her grandchildren as 'one of those strong-willed Dabneys, conceited and bumptious'; even so, Chillie had an enjoyable and comfortable childhood, spending much of it on the Dabney plantation, riding, shooting and fishing, with a little work on the farm, plenty of food, and, to 'ease the scheme of living', slaves, one of whom, a 'Negro boy named Henry', was given to Chillie when he was six, a present from his grandfather.

By 1860, the Langhorne family milling business was prospering and had become one of Lynchburg's largest. From the bay windows of Point of Honor, Chillie's father could gaze out at the flowing water that turned the wheels of the mills, while his younger brother, James, managed land that he had bought in nearby Patrick County; there, as the family described it, 'crops were good, the slaves hard workers, and the Langhornes prospered'. After Henry retired, management of the mills devolved upon John, who in 1859 had formed a partnership with one Charles Scott. At first the two men had considerable success. Nurturing hopes for developing the business, they formed an ambitious plan to dam the James River and provide a new and reliable water supply for the mills and factories that were springing up along its banks.

On her mother's side, Nancy's family was Irish, originally from Donegal, from where some of her ancestors had sailed to America, eventually settling and prospering in Virginia. Nancy's mother, christened Nannie but always known as Nanaire, was born on 30 August 1848, the elder of two daughters of Mary Anne Witcher and her husband Elisha Ford Keen, a land- and slave-owner who was also a lawyer and a member of Virginia's state legislature.

Both the Keen and Witcher families were prominent in local politics. The proceeds of the sawmills and tobacco on the Keen estate at Cottage Hill, near Danville, provided a good living and sustained Elisha Keen's position as lawyer and senator. Nanaire attended a boarding school in North Carolina – Greensborough Female Institute – and gradually became an accomplished pianist, needlewoman and painter of watercolours. She was also a good gardener, rather more than just an issuer of orders for the planting and arranging of shrubs and flowers, as was then the practice for such ladies.

Living in quiet prosperity and in harmony with their surroundings, the Keens, perhaps slightly more than the Langhornes, had come to reflect the accepted image of Virginian life – gracious, affluent, slave-owning, and content in the tranquillity of the Old South. If not among the grandest Virginian families, they were not far off the top echelon of a society whose leaders, even in the mid-nineteenth century, cherished their links with an aristocratic past and still lived in almost feudal state: fox hunting, shooting and pursuing other pleasures drawn from English traditions. On their land they created and enjoyed an atmosphere of ease and cordiality: 'The colonel with his mint juleps, the white-columned verandas peopled with belles in flouncing, ruffled gowns; the slim, aristocratic young swains proposing marriage on bended knee; the mammy, the faithful black retainer.'[1]

And so life might reasonably have been expected to continue, into a placid if not golden future. But the times were about to alter, shaking Southern society to its roots. In the Northern states, pressure for radical change was building. The tidal wave created by the release of that pressure was to surge over the happy Southern families, the society in which they lived, and Virginia itself, engulfing them in total ruin. As Winston Churchill put it: 'They had long dwelt comfortably upon the fertile slopes of a volcano. Now began the rumblings, tremors and exhalations which portended a frightful eruption.'[2]

It was during the 1850s that a volatile mix of political and economic issues began to polarise the Northern and Southern states, and to lead them towards a confrontation that would be resolved only by war. The crucible of conflict was the vast, undeveloped area of the Midwest, at first particularly in the regions that became known as Kansas and Nebraska – new territories with huge economic potential. Both North and South wanted their share of what they believed would be an economic treasure house, and, not least in order to maintain their political weight in the development of the Union, were equally anxious to harness the support of the people moving west, to settle and develop new lands.

The temperature rose sharply as Northern opinion coalesced in opposition to slavery – endemic in the political and economic life of much of the South. The voice of opposition grew all the more shrill with the astonishing success of the anti-slavery novel *Uncle Tom's Cabin*, published in 1852, and was refined and magnified by a lawyer from Springfield, Illinois: Abraham Lincoln.

In parallel with the political gulf that the slavery issue opened up between the two sides, there developed a stand-off over the sovereign right of states to secede from the Union. In December 1860, South Carolina broke its link with the Union, its example being soon followed by six other states, leading in February 1861 to the formation of a Confederacy of Southern states. For them, the question was one of jurisprudence: that their sovereignty was inalienable, a matter for themselves and not for the Federal Union; any state freely joining a union retained the right to leave it.

The leaders of the Northern states believed that a crisis was upon them: they would not countenance the right of secession, with its consequent weakening of the Union. They stiffened their resolve with moral indignation at the thought of the entrenchment of slave states, and even of an increase in their numbers.

At length the verbal confrontation between North and South led to physical violence. In April 1861, forces of the newly formed Confederacy bombarded Union troops occupying Fort Sumter, a coastal fortification at Charleston, South Carolina. It was the attack that effectively started the Civil War.

In the four-year conflict that followed, the Confederate forces began with a number of military successes. The first, in July 1861, was an action by the Bull Run stream at Manassas, which was close enough to Washington for many Union politicians to ride out from the capital, accompanied by food, drink and their ladies, to observe the promised excitement of a battle. On the day, however, their expectations of an enjoyable programme turned to consternation, for, standing 'like a stone wall' on a hillside in their path, the Confederate General Jackson halted the Federal advance in its tracks, turning the blue-coated Northerners to flight. In a short time the well-dressed spectators and their carriages found themselves dragged among a tangled rout of soldiers fleeing headlong back to the outskirts of their capital.

The following year the tables turned, and for the so-called rebels the bright start faded into the dark hardship of withdrawal. Thereafter, the Army of Northern Virginia fought seven great battles, but for the troops, despite the inspiring leadership of their great general, Robert E. Lee, each was a bleak station on the road to defeat.

For the families of Virginia, memories of the conflict were hallowed by the initial victories of the Confederate armies and their gentlemanly leaders, especially General Lee. A glorious and gallant image of the Civil War became fixed in the soul of the South and was long to dominate its folklore. For many years, before new roots took hold and a fresh start was fostered, Virginian society drew its comfort from dreams of the antebellum age, looking back rather than ahead, living on 'peanuts and past memories'. It was easier to recall a lost world with an image built on an illusion, 'a fabled country, a feudal order of gallantry, chivalry and slaves'.

> 'Oh, the lazy days, the warm, still, country twilight; the high, soft
> Negro laughter from the quarters, the golden warmth and *security*.'
> 'Don't look back, Ashley, don't look back.'[3]

The Langhornes and the Keens, like all such families, were drawn deep into the general ruin of the South. When war broke out, John Langhorne's plans for the James River had already taken shape: the deal was made, the contracts were signed, and the great project ready to be launched, opening the gates to a strong and steady flow of riches. But the approach of Union troops put paid to it all. Defeat and economic ruin snuffed out the millers' dreams before a stone was laid.

John Langhorne lost almost everything. He was rather a weak man, and, like his son, his temper was often uncontrolled. He was apt to speak without thinking – a trait inherited abundantly by his granddaughter Nancy – in consequence of which, when war came, he did not have a successful time in uniform, and had to resign from the army after an argument with a superior officer. Later he lost a great sum in a wheat speculation, and after disastrous floods in 1877, by which time he had been declared bankrupt, the family mills ceased to grind.

Personal records of the Confederate army are scant, and little firm evidence remains of the actual war service of the Keen or Langhorne families. On the other hand, there is plenty of family lore suggesting that Chillie 'saw the elephant', as front-line action was called, trudging with the Army of Northern Virginia around the Shenandoah Valley, surviving Bull Run, the Peninsula Campaign and – which still ranks as the bloodiest day in American history – the battle of Sharpsburg.

Chillie himself never embroidered the facts of his career, and he deprecated being addressed as 'Colonel', as were many Civil War veterans of a certain standing, whether they had held the rank or not. What is clear is that he joined Captain Otey's company of the 11th Regiment, Virginia Volunteers, a light artillery unit detailed for local defence, part of the Home Guard that had been formed in Virginia after John Brown's famous raid.

In April 1861, described as a student, five foot ten, with grey eyes and a rosy complexion, he enrolled for active service with a twelve-month contract. He mustered as a private in Richmond, but before seeing action he developed problems with his feet, and in October 1861 he was discharged for medical reasons. Although he later rejoined the Home Guard and became a second lieutenant, he did not see major action, and the recollections of his older grandchildren, whom he liked to take to the Gettysburg battlefield, suggest that missing the great fight, in which the 11th Virginia Regiment took part, left him with a lasting regret bordering on fixation.

However, near the end of the war he was able to compensate for his enforced exclusion from his regiment's heroic battles, as proudly described by Nancy in a memoir she wrote many years later:

Father took part in Wilson's defeat at Staunton River bridge in 1863, in the battle that saved Lee's army. In my mother's old scrap book there is a carefully pasted-up cutting about it. Two hundred and fifty hastily organised Confederates whipped twenty-five hundred Federals. 'A valuable contribution', says the headline, in masterly understatement. In her pretty, old-fashioned writing my mother has noted on top of the page, with pride, 'Your father, Mr C.D. Langhorne, was in this battle.'[4]

The 'valuable contribution', actually on 25 June 1864, took place as General Lee's soldiers were fighting their last defensive battles in Virginia and resisting the siege of Petersburg. At first fewer than 300 Confederates were caught up in the action at Staunton River Bridge, but they were hurriedly reinforced by 500 'old men and young boys', prison-camp guards and convalescent soldiers from Danville: 'With the river at their backs and a strong enemy crowding their front, failure meant capture or certain death and the loss of the bridge that General Lee had entrusted to their keeping.'[5] But hopes of wider deliverance were forlorn. Danville, swept by arson and looting before being occupied by Federal troops, was placed under martial law. Yet Chillie had briefly been in the thick of it, and for Nancy, the picture of her father as a gallant soldier formed part of the fiercely loyal and sentimental image of the South that she would sustain throughout her life.

Meanwhile, amid the chaos, Chillie had met Nanaire Keen, a ministering angel in a Danville hospital. It was love at first sight – he was the handsomest young man she ever had seen, his hair chestnut and curly – and not long after the return of the defiant band from Staunton River, she accepted the proposal of her soldier boy. The two were married on 20 December 1864, giving their ages to the parson as seventeen and twenty, although, considering the relevant dates, it would seem that Nanaire was not much over sixteen. Wedding parties lasting several days were held for them at Cottage Hill. Friends packed into a small brick house in the yard, and the day before the ceremony some of them went out shooting, after which a long line of dead partridges was laid out on the grass between the trees.

A few months later the war was over, its end sealed when the Confederate army, outnumbered by twelve to one, was finally vanquished at the battle of Appomattox Court House, the grass between the trees on this occasion being lined with dead soldiers. The grey-clad troops of the South abandoned the fight, and, on the afternoon of 9 April, bowed to the victorious Yankees. At General Lee's request they were allowed to retain their rifles, and to keep their mules and horses, to take them home and there eke out a living. 'Let them have their horses to plow with,' Lincoln had said, 'and, if you like, their guns to shoot crows with . . .'

The deep and lasting effect that the war had on the circumstances and attitudes of her family and friends was among the earliest significant influences on the formation of Nancy's character and opinions. The consequences of the conflict for her parents, and for the way that they raised their children, pervaded her soul as she grew from child to woman. 'My whole background,' she would often later say, 'was concerned with the Civil War', which for her was 'The War of Northern Aggression'. Throughout her life she was to retain the deep conviction that the Southern cause was right, a notion that fed into her own independent and sometimes rebellious spirit.

Besides the war's unhappy legacy, another significant influence on her character and upbringing was the great and repeated variations in her parents' standard of living throughout her childhood and youth. Although in those years she was too young to appreciate the seriousness of the family's plight, or to suffer from the dreadful feeling that it might not improve, her parents' confidence and security were frequently undermined by uncertainty and anxiety, and it deeply affected their relations both with each other and with their children.

The cost of the war to the South was certainly devastating. Eighteen per cent of young Southern white males lost their lives; several cities were reduced to rubble; 9,000 miles of railroad was destroyed; a third of all hogs were killed, and land values collapsed to half their pre-war levels. Alongside the emotional upheaval it brought, the abolition of slavery had a sudden and stark financial cost, with between two and three billion dollars of capital invested in slaves disappearing at the moment of emancipation. The war had swallowed all the gold and silver in circulation, and the Confederate paper money that replaced it depreciated rapidly, so that before long, what had been a planter's income for a year scarcely bought a suit of clothes.

Large numbers of Virginians were unable to cope with the wreckage and the prospect of impoverishment, or of seeing their former slaves and workers freed from their duties – a rankling reminder both of the failure of the old order and of the experience of losing in battle. Some abandoned their homeland and set off for a new life in South America. Many more fell into degeneration and slipped forever from the record.

Others, however, had enough of the Virginian character to hold fast at all costs, and defy whatever might follow the near annihilation of the South and the collapse of its economy. Chillie Langhorne was of that mould. He took his wife to the Keens' house at Cottage Hill, where, as Nancy later related, had once come word of the Yankees' approach, when the young Nanaire had helped her mother hurriedly bury silver and valuables in the garden. There she was now to remain, while her husband cast around for means to support her, a need that increased with the arrival of children.

In 1867, two years after the war's end, their first child, a daughter, was born, and named Lizzie. Two years later came a son. He was christened Keen – although somewhere along the line the Keen family seems to have acquired an extra 'e', which was subsequently added to the name of the Langhornes' eldest son. Nanaire later claimed not to have wanted any children at all – which was rather hard for a woman who eventually had eleven – but she then gave birth to three more in close succession, a girl and two boys. Sadly, however, the hardship, the lack of food and basic comforts, took the ultimate toll, and the three infants were buried near the family home. In June 1873, again overcoming apparent reluctance, Nanaire had another child, a daughter, christened Irene – meaning 'peace'; in time, her nature and looks reflected just that, and she would become so beautiful and widely admired that her fame spread throughout North America as the legendary Gibson Girl.

With his wife and three children based at Cottage Hill, Chillie went out in search of work – any work; or, as he put it, to 'root, hog or die'. He had been born to established forebears – son of a well-known businessman; grandson of a leading lawyer and landowner – but now he had to set his face to the future. First, however, he had to overcome his pride, and, acquiescing in the occupying army's requirement that anyone undertaking business, or even marriage, swear an oath of allegiance to the United States.

While the family lived frugally at Cottage Hill, Chillie took what work he could in Danville, ten miles distant: a small pocket of resilience in a country stunned and for the most part barely stirring, as the carpetbaggers arrived and the Yankee victors imposed their reconstruction upon the Confederacy. It was a hated political cleansing, in which the emancipation of slaves was followed by their gradual enfranchisement, amid the comprehensive usurping of Southern power. 'Homes and estates ruined,' Nancy later wrote, 'property split up, slaves all gone. An old order had passed. The new one had not begun. The smashers–up and pullers–down were busy, and the builders–up had not yet come on the scene.' [6]

Chillie was initially offered work auctioning horses; then – rather different, but he had to accept whatever was on offer – he became a clerk in a clothing store, staunchly holding his own until offered a commission peddling pianos. Doggedly he dragged them around on a mule cart, but, unable to play a note, he derived pleasure from neither the task nor the instruments. For a time he sold paintings, loading his cart with so-called masterpieces in colourful oils: still lifes of fruit and fish; *Romeo and Juliet*, *Stonewall Jackson Dying in his Tent* and other scenes of drama, love and war, at seven dollars each; and, a bargain at nine dollars, a portrait of Robert E. Lee.

He also looked for quicker ways to turn a dollar, and began to take part in long sessions of poker. He soon evidenced a natural skill at the game, sometimes winning large amounts, returning home tired and stained with tobacco spit, but ebullient and with cash in hand. Yet there were many other occasions when all his stakes vanished into smoke. For his young wife it must have been deeply unnerving. In the meantime, she sold her solitaire engagement ring to buy a sewing machine with which to apply much-needed patches to her husband's trousers. But wit and charm, as well as skill at cards, were part of Chillie's strength and vibrancy, and he soon turned them to more durable effect.

Danville was the centre of what had been the finest tobacco region in America, and not long after the end of the fighting, a market began to thrive once more. The 'Danville System' of selling tobacco in open piles on a warehouse floor gave Chillie a chance to make a name. Having previously tried his hand at selling horses, he was now given a trial as a tobacco auctioneer, and almost at once he disclosed exceptional natural ability. He began to perfect a peculiar rapid chant of his own, to stimulate sales; crowds, so it is said, began to gather, many admittedly keeping their hands in their pockets, but delighted to listen to Chillie in action. It did not earn him much money, but it kept alive the hopes of a family still seared by the pain of lost certainty, and gnawed by the fear of penury.

In 1873, Chillie decided that he should chance some of his small and hard-won savings in establishing a proper home for his family, so he bought a plot on Danville's Main Street. The plan for the house he built on it the following year was a faithful reflection of Cottage Hill, expressing Nanaire's affection for her family home. The total outlay was $2,000, but, perhaps because her husband's career was so volatile in those uncertain times, the deeds were drawn up in Nanaire's name 'free and clear from all liability' for her husband's debts. Completed in 1874, the new house would be the birthplace of three more children: a boy and then two girls.

With his new-found skills as salesman and auctioneer, Chillie found a partner who put up $1,600 for the two of them to go into business as 'C.D. Langhorne, Auctioneer'. They also, it seems, planned to speculate in property, in both Danville and its surroundings, and Chillie published a booklet about the town and 'its rapid growth, business and population', spicing it with what he termed 'amusing and suggestive dialogues', and using it in July 1875 to advertise the sale of lots 'in the best part of the city for family residences'.

Before long there was another development: a young man called Liggett, later to found a famous tobacco company, noticed Chillie's extrovert success as a salesman and invited him to join forces in a new venture. Raising their sights even beyond the reviving tobacco market, the two men turned to something that seemed to hold altogether more adventurous potential: railways.

The collapse of the South had left it wide open to agricultural and industrial development by rich entrepreneurs from New York, Boston and other northern cities. Eager to expand their fortunes, they had spotted opportunities in a defeated and occupied land. Their paths to the South were smoothed by Federal control of the political levers, abetted by local politicians who, while still bridling at the curtailment of their former prestige and purchasing power, now sniffed the aroma of a gravy train. As Yankee money began to pour into the cotton and tobacco markets, and also into iron and coal extraction, railway construction was perceived to be a paramount requirement. It was the key to linking plantations and mineheads to the ports from which the South's commodities could be shipped to buyers both in other parts of America and in the wider world.

Before the war, Richmond had been the meeting point of four railroads, all of which had been largely destroyed in the fighting. Ideas had begun to form, and plans to be made, even as the dust of war began to settle, and by the late 1870s the building of a new network had started; by the 1880s its construction was in full swing, and Virginia was in the midst of a boom.

Managers of the new projects, with Northern shareholders behind them, needed to involve people with local knowledge and expertise. Many men who had been engineers in the Confederate armies were now among those offered lucrative subcontracts. For their part, and to deliver on their engagements in a labour-intensive business, the subcontractors had to find efficient workforces which they could harness to their technical skill. Here was Chillie Langhorne's chance: he had no experience of railway construction or any form of civil engineering, but, perhaps even more than he initially realised, he was a born manager of men.

He now came up with an exceptionally good idea. He reckoned he might know people in this new and already thriving business, or at least where to find them. If he could win their support, he could bid for railway contracts himself. With charm and self-confidence, and particularly because he had been a loyal Confederate soldier, he was able to put out feelers to former army engineers with the right knowledge. At the same time, he and Liggett laid plans to bid for railway construction projects to subcontract to these experts.

It was a long shot for a man with no capital, but Chillie was, at least at that stage of his life, a ready gambler. There was also a factor which seemed not to have been of financial use to him before, but which, with a credible business plan, he was now able to capitalise on: his father-in-law was a state senator. Consequently, 'through the efforts of Col. E.F. Keen', a company was incorporated to build a railroad from Lynchburg to Danville. For a time all went well: Chillie managed to win a contract, and within a short time had turned a net profit of $8,000, at that time a huge sum of money. He bid for other contracts, sometimes with some success, sometimes with none whatsoever; there was no certainty in the process. It soon became apparent that the competition was strong and that success in such a business was both elusive and liable to be short-lived.

His expenditure was growing along with his family. Nevertheless, he had taken a small step forward, and he used some of the money he was able to put aside to invest in equipment to improve his chances of winning further work.

It was at street level in the newly built house at Danville, in a room with dull green walls and a bare wooden floor, that Nancy was born on 30 January 1879 – although subsequently, and throughout her adult life, her birthday was, for no clearly stated reason, given as 19 May.

Sharing the family's small pleasures, affections, fears and anxieties was Chillie's old black mammy, Harriet, 'a wonderful old lady, with lovely silver hair, no kinks', who was squeezed into a small room in the basement. Space had also to be found for Chillie and Nanaire, Keene, Lizzie, Irene, and Harry, who had been born in 1874, almost as soon as the family moved into the Danville house; now there was Nancy too, after whom was to come Phyllis, born eighteen months later, William, in 1882, and finally, in 1889, Nora. Irene later remembered her two youngest sisters always 'tied up in mosquito netting, kicking, laughing, crying'. The house was not large, and in an unkempt town reeking of distress and exposed to cholera, typhoid and other lethal diseases, eight people had to make do with two small bedrooms, a largely unused parlour, and two closet-like rooms under the sloping roof, for the youngest children. There was also a kitchen and dining room in the basement. The family lived cheek by jowl in crowded, noisy and stuffy conditions, with the children playing in the street or the backyard, which sloped down to a privy.

Yet within that close confinement, and despite the harsh life outside, it was fundamentally a happy household. The parents, although restricted to 'make-do-and-mend', cared for their offspring and did their best to provide them with childish delights. Irene remembered Nanaire, still in her twenties, with four lively children and three others dead, distributing at Christmas all kinds of dolls and toys that she had secretly made.

The impressions Nancy received as a small child were never to leave her, and gradually nurtured within her the determination that women, not excluding herself, should not unwillingly accept the imposition of a subordinate role to men. Her earliest days were spent with a strong but loving mother, and a charismatic father full of sound and fury, whose presence could not be missed, enlivening the atmosphere and begetting in equal parts argument, tears and laughter. Fortunately, at heart he was thoroughly good-natured. As Nancy later wrote, 'Mercifully Mother had a great sense of humour; she must have needed it . . .'[7]

Behind Nanaire's gentle demeanour, however, lay a strong resolve, and it would ultimately be she, rather than her loud and lively husband, who most influenced their children and quietly directed the ways of the family:

> In his prime Chillie was a short, muscular man who held himself sharply erect. He was loud and demanding, stubborn and overbearing. He was a martinet who bullied his way through life, all smiles when he was getting his way, but raising hell when he didn't. Nanaire knew how to handle him. Soft-spoken and gentle, she was a petite, fair-haired woman with huge blue-sky eyes and a trim figure which amazingly regained its shape after each pregnancy. She stood by unruffled while his temper flashed and his moods turned rapidly from utter charm to blustering rage and back again.[8]

Even when very young, Nancy could perceive where power ultimately lay:

> I cannot remember the time when I did not realise that my mother was stronger and more important from the family point of view than my father. Although he was a good father and splendid in many ways, it was my mother who had the spiritual vision, unselfish love and complete selflessness which made the family a unit.[9]

Tellingly, in view of her later career, Nancy added that it was those memories of her mother that made her feel that the qualities of women should be freed to give better service to society. Her older sister Irene put her parents' relationship more succinctly, saying that her mother had Chillie wrapped around her little finger. Nevertheless, Nanaire in general accepted her position in household affairs as ultimately subordinate to her husband.

By the end of the 1870s, Chillie was involved variously in railroad plans, property dealing, tobacco sales and sharecropping, but the family's circumstances remained precarious, if slightly less straitened than a year or two earlier. So it was not long before Chillie, and no doubt also Nanaire, began to feel that their uncertain way of life, with little security and no sure source of income, was not only disagreeable but also unfair to their growing family. Although Danville's tobacco sales more than doubled during the 1870s, the trade began to suffer from the inevitable overproduction and commensurate fall in prices. Chillie had salted away some money – not much, but enough to risk a new departure – and he now turned his gaze to the state capital, Richmond, to see what fortune might hold for him there.

During the last stages of the war, much of Richmond had been blasted into rubble by a retreating Confederate army determined that their former jewel should not fall intact into enemy hands. Fifteen years on from the end of the fighting, Virginia's social and political capital was emerging from its post-war desolation. Life there was beginning to re-establish itself, even within the parameters of the political reconstruction imposed by the winning side. Opportunities were greatly enhanced by cheap assets and plentiful labour, as the redevelopment of the former Confederate states attracted rich men from the North.

At first Chillie's luck seemed to hold. He was invited into business by William Henry, a successful tobacco entrepreneur with a thriving trade in Richmond. The family moved to the city in 1881, settling first into quarters in Main Street. Yet their insecurity remained: they still lacked a house that actually belonged to them, and it was not long before the going became tough. The Richmond tobacco market was keenly competitive, and since the competition related almost entirely to price, there was little that Chillie could add by charm or personality. The market was seasonal too, forcing him to look for other work to supplement his tobacco earnings. In their new surroundings the family's expenses soon outstripped their income, and they had to uproot themselves once more and move to a poor part of Third Street.

Now 'just a few dollars of income separated the Langhornes from the rude existence of the hordes of immigrants – Irish, Germans and Italians – who had recently swarmed into Richmond, settling in crowded tenements in the hollows and on the edges of ravines below the city's hills'. The burden of holding the household together fell mostly on Nanaire, who had to cope with barely enough money for subsistence. 'She was always the anchor, the homemaker, the seamstress, the housekeeper with the key chain hanging from her tiny waist, more than likely sometimes shedding a silent tear of utter exhaustion of an evening when "Dab" was away on a trip and the children in their beds.'[10]

Nevertheless, a year later, in November 1882, yet another child was born: a son whose life for a few days hung by a thread before he began to gather strength, so avoiding the imminent death confidently predicted for him by the onlookers around his cot. He was christened William Henry, in honour of his father's business associate, but he soon became known as Buck.

The city in which the infant Nancy was to spend her next few years was a hazardous place: with only primitive medical help, typhoid, diphtheria, smallpox and scarlet fever were real fears; exposed sewers, frequently containing supine drunkards, ran along many of the streets, while mosquitoes, flies and rats swarmed around carcasses in open abattoirs. Yet social life had begun to return: children played, at least in the cleaner streets, parties were held once more, and previously prosperous citizens were edging towards building a framework within which to replicate their former lives.

For the next few years life continued to be uncertain and difficult for Nancy's parents: weary but determined, they weathered fresh starts, and moves between rented houses of uneven appeal according to the degree of success or failure that attended Chillie's endeavours. His cavalier demeanour and carefree salesmanship cut less ice in the new Richmond than in war-torn Danville, but as long as he worked as a dealer in William Henry's tobacco business, he could at least retain hopes of regaining some of the stability that he had known before the Civil War. Optimism prevailed in the family – on the whole.

Indeed, by the time Nancy was five, Chillie's business schemes were steadily proving profitable, and apparent success enabled the family to move to a more attractive house. The younger children were given a pair of billy goats to take them around in a cart; they made friends with neighbouring children, played in their houses and along tree-lined paths, enjoyed each other's treats – spun candy in pyramids of nougat was a favourite – and shared simple parties. Ann and Ben Johnson, a Negro cook and butler, ministered to their needs, especially to Chillie's pleasure in food, though not always with success: only Nanaire's firm command 'Don't kill him, Dab' saved Ben from violence at his master's hands when he tripped and fell while carrying a keenly awaited tureen of oyster stew.

Their father's volatility must have disconcerted the children: Nancy recalled him solemnly looking his children over before each meal to make sure that they were properly dressed, then formally intoning grace, but apt immediately thereafter to yell, 'Dammit, shut that door!' or some similar command. 'Father was very strict. His word was law. He would have complete obedience. There was no talking back to your elders in those days. Though we were fond of Father we were always delighted when he went away and we had Mother to ourselves.'[11]

There was another factor that had affected Nancy's life: at about the age of four or five she was laid low by typhoid. Although she recovered from the disease, she was for some time left in delicate health, and thereafter was to remain small and slight for her years. She also began to suffer from bouts of what could only be described generally as neuralgia. Their cure, or even explanation, appeared to be beyond the wit of any available doctors, and they were to recur intermittently throughout her youth and young adult-hood, black intervals that contrasted with the predominant bright vitality of her character.

Meanwhile, the family's hopes and pleasures were enhanced by the ease with which Chillie and Nanaire made friends. As Irene recalled, 'parties were in the air. How young and gay mother and father were!' Nanaire would sing and play the piano – and the organ in church – while her husband would press uplifting refreshment on all who called.

Yet overall, for their first five years in Richmond the family's livelihood remained in doubt. Although, with brief exceptions, Nancy's childhood was not spent in the poverty and hardship that she would sometimes later claim, the atmosphere around her was often charged with tension. Her parents could not entirely shed the fear that the destitution that had extinguished their forebears' prosperity might return. They were determined at all costs to avoid that, and even during the bright periods when Chillie seemed to have found his feet and was bringing home money, anxiety haunted the background.

Nancy was of course too young to comprehend the meaning or implications of such matters, but their outward effects played their part in forming her character. In her early years there was no comforting atmosphere of permanence in her surroundings, although she seemed to meet that lack with a light heart coupled with resilience. Having four older siblings at close quarters also forced her to learn to stand her ground; she was enabled to do so partly by a keen sense of humour and an exceptional capacity for wit – probably innate, but sharpened by the frequent flashes of humour displayed by her parents.

At the same time, the surroundings and influences in her early years in Danville and Richmond, particularly the relationship between an outwardly loud and dominant father and a strong and loving mother, nourished the seed of a dogged self-will. Her incipient determination may have played a part in her recovery from typhoid. Thereafter it helped her through early attacks of neuralgia, and led to her gaining the carefree self-confidence that was to desert her only during the periods of apparent depression she was to continue to suffer throughout the first part of her life.

When Nancy was six years old, her father's business affairs took a sharp and sudden turn for the worse. In 1885, several of his transactions crumbled simultaneously to dust, and it became clear that the family had not attained any fundamental security after all. This time they were faced not with moving once again to a smaller, cheaper house, but with having insufficient money to remain in Richmond at all.

Yet another uprooting seemed imminent. It was quickly arranged that Nanaire and the children would go and live with a country cousin, while Chillie stayed behind in lodgings, in the anxious hope that things might again improve. While the young Nancy would have understood simply that the daily pattern of her life was again to change, and that she would have to abandon her familiar surroundings, she must also have realised more unhappily that her parents were in dismay.

However, instead of an upheaval and dispersal of the family, something very different was about to happen. Although time might have coloured their memories, Nancy and her sisters were always to retain a clear image: on the fateful and gloomy day of departure, they had everything packed and ready – even the goats were crated on a cart – and were standing outside their house consoling each other in their distress, when suddenly Chillie rushed back to the house in a state of high excitement, roaring, 'Hold everything, dammit, I've got a job.'

Once again he had met with opportunity, but this time it was one far greater and more hopeful than before. Chillie was about to make a breakthrough that would change the fortunes of them all.

TWO

Silver and Lead

Colonel Henry Douglas was a former engineer in the Confederate army, with Yankee contacts and the skills and knowledge that exactly met the needs of the hour. Now he was prospering in the railway boom, as reconstruction in Virginia began to erase the devastation of war.

Numerous Chinese whispers have distorted the record of how Douglas came to offer Chillie the railway building contracts that within a very short time transformed his family's fortunes. Somewhere in his colourful but chequered career Chillie had caught the eye of the colonel, and now, at one of the bleakest moments in his life, on the point of sending his family away and searching alone for work, their paths crossed again.

Quite what blend of charm, guile and display of apparent knowledge Chillie proffered can only be surmised, but if he said that he could provide labour and horses, teach them to work with equipment, and manage them well, it would surely have appealed to Douglas. The colonel needed labour, for the clearing of land and the delivery and laying of stone, gravel, wood and other materials on which could be placed rails to carry heavy trains. For that, slaves were no longer an option, nor did the mood of newly freed men readily dispose them to grinding hard work or to being bossed around even by the supposed champions of abolition who were now in the ascendancy. Yet there were plenty of Negroes and distressed whites who badly needed money, and Chillie claimed that he could set them to work. One way or another he managed to convince Douglas that he could make a valuable contribution: 'I am the man you want,' he said, 'for I can manage men and horses. Give me a chance.'

In whatever manner it occurred, a deal was struck, and for the Langhorne family it proved a bonanza. Their feelings might not have exactly matched those of a modern family in dire financial straits on being suddenly told that they had won a fortune on a lottery, because time had to pass for Chillie to perform the work for which he had contracted; yet the comparison is close, and in fact the money began to flow in almost at once. It was the first of two momentous financial events in Nancy's life, and was to have an enormous impact upon the development of her personality.

Chillie's first partner was a cousin who was a civil engineer, which brought at least some know-how to the operation; later he joined forces with another former soldier, and together the two of them prospered: the Langhorne name began to feature in newspaper reports on the burgeoning railway networks:

> *Buckingham* . . . C.D. Langhorne, of Richmond, Va., has the contract to build this road for the Rosney Iron Co. The line is to extend from Arvon, on a short branch of the Chesapeake & Ohio, south of the James River, through Buckingham County to Rosney, a distance of about 16 miles . . .

> . . . Huntington and other divisions of this system: Last year about 23 miles of double track was built, 14 miles in West Virginia and 9 miles in Virginia, and additional second track will probably be built this year. The company also built several branches last year from various points on its system, principally to reach coal or iron mines. The grading on the Buckingham branch, for which C.D. Langhorne, of Richmond, Va., has the contract, has been about completed and track has been laid for more than half the distance . . .'[1]

Within a year of meeting Colonel Douglas, Chillie had at last found security, and he expressed it in buying what Irene called 'a lovely big house at 101 W. Grace Street, with a beautiful garden on one side and five enormous oak trees'.[2] It was a large grey colonial building, flanked by magnolias. It had indoor plumbing and an upstairs bathroom, and was heated by a basement furnace sending up warm air through numerous ducts, like a villa in ancient Rome. The luxury that had come their way was indicated by the price of $22,000.[3] Chillie also bought the adjoining three vacant lots – one of which he sold three years later for $7,600. A fine new house, as much as anything else, can raise the spirits of a family, and for both parents and children it was a tremendous change.

Nancy was still a small child in a large family when this transformation took place, and not yet ready, as she soon would be, to question, challenge and force her own way. She was only seven, but even at that tender age she must have been imbued with the relief of her parents, and warmed by the sunbeams so unexpectedly touching her family.

She made friends with the neighbouring children, among whom before long a current of excitement would spread at the word that 'Nannie's coming out to play.' She soon became their leader, a little Pied Piper drawing them into all sorts of fun and mischief. They would gather at a confectionery shop run by a German family, and, sitting at a marble-topped table, Nancy would talk earnestly to the owner about her children – Adolf, Rudolf, Fritz and Heinie – asking in detail how they were and commenting: 'I am *so* pleased, Mrs Marks.'

Soon her horizons were widened by the beginnings of an education. Chillie and Nanaire enrolled their various children in a number of what were regarded as the best schools. Nancy's first was a day school run by Julia Lee, a cousin of the great general, where she began learning to read and write; when she was nine, she graduated to a larger private school, owned and run by Virginia Ellett, known to all as Miss Jennie. It seems possible that there may have been other schools along the way, as Chillie reportedly acceded to occasional impulsive requests from his daughter, on taking a dislike to a school, that she be allowed to move. Such spoiling may have been a contributory factor in her incipient self-centredness.

It was at Miss Jennie's, however, that Nancy began to learn about the wider world. Her teacher had the rare knack of capturing and retaining the interest of young children. She was fascinated by art, history and literature, with which she thrilled her charges:

> She began with philosophy, and on to Greece, then took us through Greek history and so to Italy, France and England As she taught, she took the history and geography along with it, so that what we got was a length of close woven tweed, rather than the untidy patchwork so many young minds are left with at the end of an education. She gave me a thirst for knowledge and a real liking for learning.[4]

It was certainly an eclectic syllabus to set before a nine-year-old.

The extent of Nancy's thirst for knowledge of philosophy, Greek history, Greece, Italy or France, is not wholly clear – it did not prevent her from later developing a stubborn aversion to Latins, and to the French in particular. Equally, the degree to which her mind was left with close-woven tweed rather than untidy patchwork is uncertain, as despite her response to Miss Jennie's teaching, at no time in her childhood or youth was her intellect successfully trained or disciplined.

Miss Jennie also stirred her pupils' imagination with well-told stories from history, albeit chosen deliberately: when her account of American history reached Lincoln's presidency, she would say, 'We'll skip that.' She also had the ability to instil in her charges an interest in words, an essential preliminary to their making the most of the books she set before them.

According to a school friend, Nancy dutifully responded by learning two new words a day from her dictionary. Miss Jennie's fervent religious approach also made a deep impression on Nancy, who began to pore over *Foxe's Book of Martyrs* and to absorb stories of the saints and apostles as though she were studying portraits of real people, believing every detail to be accurate.

Certainly she benefited from having to learn by heart dates and notes and literary passages; together with Miss Jennie's stories, they implanted in her the sense of history that contributed to her stature during her later years as a member of Parliament and a political hostess. But she struggled and stumbled with multiplication tables, and the effectiveness of her brain was hampered in both formal and informal circumstances by her chronic tendency to jump like a grasshopper between ideas that had no particular link or connection. This characteristic reflected her restless energy and her increasing lack of inhibition: years later, a school friend remembered Nancy as being easily the wildest pupil in the school, in part mitigated by her being a compulsive giggler.

Yet at this stage of her life she was small, slight and delicate, perhaps as a result of the earlier typhoid attack, compounded by chronic neuralgia. Her strength sometimes evaporated, as it was to do even when she grew up: 'I was always overworking,' she recalled, 'and overplaying and breaking down; but I liked that as it meant I slept in Mother's room and was made a lot of . . .'[5]

Despite her strength sometimes failing, it became apparent that Nancy would be an athletic girl: she loved rushing about and proved to be a fast runner. She also took to boys' games – baseball and prisoners' base, played in the yards of their friends – and it was noticeable that her excitable liveliness could veer into wildness. On the other hand, she tenderly loved the pets that the family accumulated, although at some point she developed a lasting aversion to cats. She was particularly pleased, at first, to be given a parrot; as she recalled, 'I think I had pictured the parrot and I having long, interesting conversations, in which I would learn as much from the parrot as he or she from me.' The bird, however, proved of limited intellect, and virtually monosyllabic.

Her physical enthusiasm was matched by imagination and a love of reading. Building on her grounding from Miss Jennie, she was drawn to Shakespeare, Scott and other elements of English literature, so that when, a few years later, she first travelled to England, she discovered – as many Virginians say they do – a feeling of recognition and affinity with the country. 'These writers,' she said, 'provided me with signposts. They stamped in my mind descriptions of Britain and also the characteristics of British people.'

Her father, however, did not approve of bookworms; he believed that education was not for women, and that 'all they needed was a few polite accomplishments and to be a good horsewoman'. Nancy was therefore unable to further her education by much reading at home. Years later she said: 'When I was a girl I wanted to study so much; my father wouldn't let me, I was punished for it . . . I've missed it all my life.' She proved to be less impressed by her father's bluff sentiments than by her aunt Liz Lewis. 'Father's clever sister', as Nancy called her, was an educated lady, an early champion of suffragettes in Virginia and of women's political rights. She was also an ardent educationist who founded some of the first schools for coloured people, and taught in them herself.[6] Her ideas took root in Nancy's mind.

Besides being enthralled by literature, Nancy began to respond to the first faint pull of religion. Like many families in their circle, the Langhornes had a strict, rather Low Church respect for observance. Meals began with grace, or at least with Chillie saying 'God bless us' wherever he happened to be when a meal was announced. On Sundays he would take the family out for walks, talking to the children as though they were grown-up, while they in return made efforts to shine and to please him. Despite that attraction, Nancy recalled Sundays as being dreary, with the gaslight dim. Nevertheless, she attended Sunday school and imbibed the sober Sabbath atmosphere with more enthusiasm than did most children. By the time she was fourteen she had read the Bible from end to end, although skipping what she called the 'Begats'. As with what Miss Jennie taught her, much of what she read there she believed to be literally true. The seeds were being sown of what became a lifelong attachment to the Bible and similar holy tracts, and of her advocacy of the conduct they demanded.

Chillie's new-found wealth now brought more earthly forms of satisfaction. Although in the past, in order to escape the stifling heat of Richmond in high summer, the children had occasionally been sent off to country relatives, now for the first time the family began to take holidays together.

Lizzie, the eldest daughter, had already married – unfortunately, for her, in 1884, before money changed the family's circumstances; it was a mishap to which she never became wholly reconciled, as she embarked on life with her husband, Moncure Perkins, from an old but impecunious Virginian family. However, with their new confidence fostering ambition for their unmarried children, Chillie, and more particularly Nanaire, determined that the rest of the family should assume a place in Richmond society, and that their younger daughters should ascend to even higher planes, perhaps each in their turn becoming a 'Southern belle'. Irene in particular, as Chillie and Nanaire had noted, was blossoming into a girl of outstanding beauty. The right sort of holidays might therefore offer benefits beyond satisfying a desire for health and pleasure.

Society in Richmond at that time was bound more by pedigree than money, of which there was still little in evidence – those few who had acquired it quickly were known as 'bouncers' and were usually not popular. There was a widespread desire among Virginians to restore a framework in which ancestry could retain its importance, so 'almost in inverse relationship to their threadbare circumstances, they revitalised elaborate social rituals and public rhetoric, which they adorned with carefully polished silver and phrases'. Chillie and Nanaire made their way to the heart of this courtly charade by choosing for their first family holiday White Sulphur Springs, a celebrated resort in the Allegheny Mountains. There, among the mountain springs of West Virginia, which had regained their fashionable antebellum role, were performed with the greatest dedication and purpose rituals that helped the South to forget its recent past. Each summer, the best of society would crowd the ballrooms and dining rooms of the spa hotels, greeting each other in a quaintly courteous vernacular ('Oh my! I ain't seen yew since the Age of Pericles'), parading on long, balconied piazzas, and enacting customs that were studied images of the 'Old South'.

It was in the summer of 1888, when Nancy was nine, that the family made its initial excursion to 'the White', a celebrated hotel at the top of a grassy, tree-studded valley in the Blue Ridge. By that time it had become the most famous watering hole in the South: 'a vast white caravansary' above the original spring, surmounted by a canopy on white columns, beyond which was a racetrack. By the time the Langhorne family first arrived at the Springs, the original health benefits had been, if not forgotten, supplanted by the pleasures and motives of social gratification, and, even if not openly alluded to, by a marriage market. It was a stately pleasure dome beginning to draw fashionable young blades even from such renowned playgrounds as Bar Harbor, Newport and Saratoga Springs, 'a place of wide galleries and big pillars, a rendezvous for important people attended by troops of servants, the meeting-place of politicians, the haunt of the belles, an arena of gaiety, romantic intrigue and fashion, where fortunes nightly were won and lost'.[7] With or without the nightly gambling, the cost excluded all but the well heeled, but twenty years on from the war it seemed that enough money was being made to sustain the rebirth of an expensive social life. For taking his family and servants to the White, Chillie's first holiday tariff was $800 – about $20,000 in modern money.

Nanaire rapidly took to the hectic social round and to the delights of playing the fashionable hostess: the *Richmond Dispatch* featured her as a member of the committee of the Colonial Ball, the season's grandest event, and described a memorable lunch party that she gave in which everything was violet, from the cake to the candle-shades – violets seem to have been greatly in vogue at that time in the South. Chillie was less enamoured of spa life – apart from its poker tables – but he was convinced that it was the place in which his daughters would meet rich young men from the wider world.

As Lizzie was now living her own life, she did not share the family's excursions; for Nancy, that was as well, for her eldest sister had always been rather abrupt with her and Phyllis, treating them more as though she were their mother. The rest of the family crammed noisily into Bruce Cottage, in 'Virginia Row', part of the hotel's accommodation: Keene, now nearly twenty, Irene, Harry, Buck, and Nora, the baby, with her nursemaid; also Nancy and Phyllis, by then very much a chattering, inseparable pair, though Phyllis, an attractive girl with dark brown hair and grey eyes, was quieter, and really preferred the peace of solitude. Nancy was the leader of the two, beginning to want her own way and occasionally displaying a rather harsh side – as when one night she solemnly informed Phyllis that she was not really one of the family at all, but had been found in a ditch and taken under her parents' wing. Nancy thought this idea funny and imaginative, while ignoring the muffled sobs coming from under Phyllis's bedclothes. Luckily she was also finding that a natural charm and wit enabled her to soften the edges of her childish humour.

Although the atmosphere at the Springs was distinctly Southern, in the high season rich and fashionable Northerners were also welcomed, guardedly, and the spa was able to play some part in healing the wounds of war. Gallant, grey-whiskered soldiers attended matriarchs maintaining an imposing presence on sofas along the walls, on the great 'fautcuil' or in the celebrated Treadmill parade. But it was the debutantes who took centre stage, and the belles the pride of place:

> . . . belledom was the beau ideal of life, and every Southern girl stretched every means to get herself to the Springs where she proceeded to throw herself into the race with a zeal and abandon later to be associated with having a career. If straightened circumstances kept their parents at home, young ladies grouped themselves under a chaperone, three to half a dozen at a time . . .[8]

For the debs, each day was packed: early morning rides with their beaux; walking along the paths and avenues; morning 'Germans' – parades around the ballrooms – in full evening dress; champagne and fruit parties on the lawns; photography sessions, for the benefit of posterity; a little gentle tennis;

cotillions and dancing until the small hours. The belles' appearance, activities and flirtations were spread across the pages of newspapers, in New York as much as in the South:

> They are such girls as you read about in novels . . . they were 'born in idleness' and the one compulsion of their lives was to have a 'real good time'. It was a half truth only. There was another compulsion in their lives and that was to get a real good husband, in a post-war world of stringencies and stratagems.[9]

At her age, Nancy could only look on, probably not greatly interested in the business of preening and courtship taking its carefully charted course. During the family's second summer at the Springs, however, her sister Irene made a spectacular debut. Even the previous year she had been noticed for her exceptional beauty; now she was fully formed, with golden hair, a twenty-inch waist, and eyes described as 'glowing with liquid fire'. One evening, sitting on the window seat of the ballroom, where the 'sub-belles' were permitted to look on for the first half-hour of each evening's dancing, she had caught the eye of a fashionable beau from Philadelphia:

> 'How old are you, Irene?'
> 'Sixteen.'
> 'Then it's time you were out', and he pulled her from her perch and whirled her into the dance.[10]

Even before her first spectacular season at the Springs, Irene's beauty had begun to bring her invitations to houses and resorts in other, more distant parts of the country, and to encourage suitors and love affairs, albeit innocent in that strictly chaperoned world. Consequently, at the time of her debut she was already in love, with Nicholas Longworth, from an old family and heir to a fortune; but this did not prevent her thoroughly enjoying the glamour and the attention that she received at the Springs.[11]

'I loved it, loved it, loved it,' Irene remembered. 'I never wore a speck of make-up of any kind, not even powder, and I ate everything.' If this was the case, it is remarkable that she retained a twenty-inch waist and eyes of liquid fire: guests were expected regularly to demolish 'soup, fish, removes, cold, entrées, vegetables, pastry and dessert'. A typical dinner at the health spa included 'Consommé with marrow; Broiled Rock; Baked Beans and pork, Boston style; Boiled Fresh Beef, mustard sauce; Virginia Ham glacé, champagne sauce; Loin of veal, demi glacé; Shrimps à la Tartare; Braised Sweetbreads with peas; Baked Sweet Potatoes; Plum Pudding with rum sauce, or Charlotte Russe.' No doubt the long night's cavorting called for such sustenance, together with Cliquot or Roederer Grand Vin Brut, at $4 a quart. In case of later need, Thompson's Bromine Arsenic was readily to hand, at 75 cents the half-gallon.

Even if too young to play much part in this social arabesque, Nancy was involved in all the activities laid on for her contemporaries, such as the Children's Ball, an after-dinner event requiring among other things the ability to dance in elaborate period dress. Altogether her summers began to open up her hitherto rather enclosed world, filling body and soul with the brightness and fun of the hotel:

> It had a swimming pool, and there was fishing and riding. It was at The Springs we first learned to ride, before we got ponies of our own. Every week Father gave us a certain sum of money and we could spend it as we liked, on fishing or swimming or riding. I never could make up my mind which to do most.[12]

There were other new delights too:

> I fell in love at the White Sulphur for the first time. A boy came to the same hotel, I was eleven. He came with his father, and his mother had just died. The chief thing I remember about him was his shoes. He wore the most beautiful shoes, and they were always spotlessly clean. I think this was my first love affair, and it is sad that I remember nothing whatever about him – only his shoes.[13]

In each of the next few years, and into a new decade, Nancy spent happy weeks at the White, increasingly receptive to the delights and influences of this playground of the rich, as she slowly emerged from childhood. Never before had she spent time at close quarters with other families, heard orchestras playing, watched courtly dancing to sophisticated music, seen enormous dining rooms filled with people, or fished or swum or ridden through hills.

These new pleasures, shared with those around her, enabled her innate characteristics to blossom. Her boyish outdoor skills, particularly at riding, at which she soon proved adept, her seemingly carefree nature, and a liveliness made the more noticeable by an increasingly fast wit – inherited and absorbed from her father, a past master at repartee – encouraged her confidence and zest. That had its counterpart, however, and although she was as yet too young to be bossy, she was at times becoming insistent. From her earliest childhood it had been obvious that she had a tender core, but she also evidenced a faint streak of resentment, which, as she grew older, was to evolve into, if not an actual desire to bully, then a tendency to self-assertion that sometimes made her seem heedless of the feelings of others. Her voluble chatter could annoy her family and companions, but she mitigated the dangers of being too direct with an inherited skill at repartee, which, then and later, usually caused irritation to dissolve in amusement.

The outside world did not yet concern her. Life's horizons still did not stretch much beyond the family's large and agreeable new home on Grace Street and summers at the Springs, and she was able to absorb the strange new influences of adolescence in an atmosphere of stability that contrasted with her earliest years.

Her father was now approaching fifty. Behind him lay the toil and the search for security that had dogged his daily life for most of the quarter-century since the war's end. He could begin to think of retirement, holding, as he did, the view that work was only 'fer niggers and damyankees'; it was a phrase often on his lips – in fact Nancy claimed to have been nearly grown-up before she realised that 'damn Yankee' was more than one word. Langhorne & Langhorne, as his company became after Keene joined the business, was now making a great deal of money, and its work was taking Chillie to many parts of the state. The hills, the valleys, the farms and orchards of the countryside rekindled in him thoughts of a more gracious age, and a finer living than urban Richmond offered. And at long last he could afford it; so in the summer of 1892 he realised the dream, paying $9,000 for Mirador, an estate near Greenwood, in western Albemarle County, at the foot of the Blue Ridge Mountains, countryside that he had loved as a child.

For Nancy and her brothers and sisters, summers by the mountain springs had been the first taste of an affluent lifestyle. Mirador was a further, and significant, upward step. The spacious square two-storey building, close to a lawn surrounded by old Virginia cedar trees, lay on a bluff just north of Stockton Creek, a tributary of the James River. Beyond it unfolded woods and meadows stretching to the distance and blending at length with the Blue Ridge, whose heights trended to the Shenandoah Valley far beyond.

In appearance the house was eighteenth century, fronted by broad steps leading to a colonial porch on Tuscan columns sheltering a wide front door beneath an imposing fanlight. At a convenient distance were old slave cabins, an icehouse, dairy, smokehouse, stables and barn, and a summerhouse like a miniature bandstand. Beyond a garden blowing with flowers reposed a family graveyard in a ring of cedar trees, near to an old brick church with a small cloister. In its quiet valley, Mirador was a small patch of order in the vast, tree-covered wilderness of western Virginia.

For Nancy, the romantic country house, set in gardens where every prospect pleased, was to leave an impression on her that would never fade. Its history stretched back to the aftermath of the American Revolution, when a certain William Ramsey established his family on the land, tilling it, grazing herds and operating a mill and distillery on the nearby creek. On Ramsey's death the estate passed to James Bowen, a prosperous merchant who continued his own trade as well as his predecessor's milling operations. In 1842 Bowen built the main house, a large, Flemish-bond brick building, with Federal and Greek revival details. He christened it El Mirador, a Spanish term suggesting 'marvellous prospect'. At his death in 1880 it passed to his widow, Frances, whose ghost has occasionally been sighted in the house's library.

A few years later a railway was laid through the mountains, for which a tunnel, the first in America, was dug above the farm by a Frenchman who had built roads for Napoleon. Along that line Stonewall Jackson had once sped his troops to Staunton, later marching them down the county road past the gates of Mirador, hastening to the relief of Richmond. When Chillie bought the estate, seventy-five miles west of Richmond, it was still in remote country; its point of contact with the world beyond was a halt on the railway line, from which, to serve the mill at Mirador, a rough track wound uphill towards the creek.

At first the family stayed mainly in Richmond, with Nancy and Phyllis continuing at Miss Jennie's school, going up to Mirador only in high summer when the city became grimy and oppressive. Then, with relief, they would shake off the urban dust and breathe instead the fresh air of the hillsides, which in parts were covered by the Scotch broom that long ago had arrived on ships with the fodder for the animals of the Hessian troops used by the English in the Revolution. The paths to Mirador wound between red clay banks leading deep into a countryside scented by honeysuckle and the dry aroma of boxwood, the home of scarlet cardinals, yellow orioles, mockingbirds, and hummingbirds hovering with their beaks deep in trumpet vines.

In the long summer days there would be picnics in the fields, beneath purple-blue hills sometimes hardly visible as they shimmered in the haze. At night, thunderstorms would rumble around the mountains. Family and guests would meet on the veranda for songs or quiet talk, as fireflies flickered in the dusk and bullfrogs croaked in the pond below.

Yet Mirador itself was still rather spartan, with no electricity, little indoor water, and the floors often covered in red dust. Two parents, three sons, four daughters and numerous servants filled the house to bursting point. At first meals were simple, the staples being eggs and corn bread, tomatoes,

27

beaten biscuits and molasses, with the occasional luxury of a barrel of roasted peanuts, for all to dig into at will.

However, Chillie's pocket was now deep, and with a will he began to refurbish the house and enlarge his manor, gradually adding to it adjoining farms, hillside timberland, and pastures for high summer grazing. To mark the entrance to the house, an imposing arch, soon ivy-grown, was built with concrete left over from a railway contract, the Langhorne arms emblazoned on its keystone. A wing was joined to each side of the house, fronted by bay windows, to accommodate a panelled library and dining room, as well as additional rooms for guests and family. The front entrance led into a central round hall with a black-and-white marble floor, then on to a rear veranda with views to the distant Blue Ridge, a cool respite from the heat of summer.

In these imposing surroundings Chillie began to lead the life of a 'gentleman of the old Virginia school', as he came to be described, and to envelop his children in its atmosphere. At heart he was a gourmet, and the Mirador table soon groaned with delicacies: terrapin from Baltimore; Spanish mackerel; joel and turnip salad; pickled watermelon rinds; black bean soup; cinnamon tea cakes; oysters and, inside them, tiny oyster crabs, crisped or cooked in cream and sherry, and poured over waffles. With juleps and wine from a well-stocked cellar, these offerings would be placed before an unceasing stream of friends. Chillie presided over all with pleasure, looking benign. 'Oh, Mrs Langhorne,' a friend said to Nanaire, 'your husband has such lovely eyes.' 'Don't be fooled by that,' came the soft reply, 'he looks just the same way at a batter cake.'

The family had come far since the war's end, and its long and bitter aftermath. As Chillie would tell his guests:

> There was nothing left of the old life . . . the country was decimated; there was practically no stock of any kind on the farms, neither horses, mules, cattle or sheep; they were using parched corn for coffee, if they could get it . . . I had nothing but a wife, two children, a ragged seat to my pants, and a barrel of whiskey.[14]

In high-crowned hat, keys and chain across his waistcoat, chewing and spitting tobacco or with cigar in gloved hand, the lord of Mirador would survey his domain: shouting orders to sundry servants; calling through a megaphone for traps or horses to be brought round the 'bullring' to the steps in front of the house; ringing down a makeshift line across the orchards to halt the 'No. 4 Express' at nearby Greenwood station; inspecting the farms and riding over his land, often with a child up behind him on his horse, as family and friends accompanied him with ponies or carts. Later, slowly rocking in a chair by the porch, fanning himself with a palm leaf, he would talk idly to family and guests; or, after a formal, many-coursed lunch, and cooled by the summer breeze, rest silently on a horsehair sofa in the hall, where the tables were laden with bowls of rosy winesaps and small lady apples.[15]

Nancy took her cue from her father, always keen for his approval, and conscious that in seeking his attention she must contend with the claims of the rest of the family, in particular Irene, who in her father's eyes could do little wrong. She often succeeded in melting his mood, and found herself growing in confidence. On one occasion, when he shouted at her for letting his terrapins escape from the cellar, she looked up sweetly and said, 'Don't talk to me like that: you know I am your trump card.' She remained at heart loving and obedient to her father, but she was restless, becoming wilful and often pugnacious, traits she had clearly inherited from him. At the same time she seemed to be carefree, chattering and readily laughing, partly due to the increasingly sharp sense of the ridiculous that was to characterise her throughout her life. With her fair hair and striking blue-grey eyes, her slightly aquiline features expressed vitality and strength. In the custom of the time, she was usually clothed from wrist to ankle, although she was occasionally smartly turned out in a favourite sailor suit.[16]

She loved running or riding through the fields and woods, or down to the creek, where she once dismounted and killed a moccasin snake with her riding crop – a brave and insouciant performance more characteristic perhaps than her lifelong fear of spiders and cats. At first there was only one horse, Duchess, for all to ride, but later Nancy was given one of her own, christened Tam O' Shanter. She and Phyllis, their faces veiled against the sun, always riding side saddle, would canter off together, leaping the high cedar snake-fences and clattering up the steep tracks of Humpback Mountain, squat and violet-blue at the end of the valley.

Nancy's natural athleticism was easily harnessed to her skill on a horse, and she spent long hours schooling hunters in the ring near the house, and roaming at will over the countryside in a rather battered riding habit. Her father put her on green four-year-olds, and she set about learning how to break them in. Before long she became almost fearless in the saddle, and was clearly on her way to becoming an accomplished horsewoman. While still living in Richmond she had begun hunting with the newly established Deep Run Hunt, and now she began to enter local horse shows, attracting notice for her proficiency. Chillie's encouragement was a great help: he was an excellent horseman himself, and spent hours teaching his daughters.

Besides a tennis court, Chillie built a squash court, where Nancy began her lifelong love of the game. It was a busy, active existence, but with its share of indoor pastimes too. 'We didn't have many toys,' Nancy recalled. 'My chief delight was to cut paper figures out of the illustrated papers and catalogues and magazines, and fashion plates. We made whole families of them, and cut out houses for them to live in.'[17] Running free at Mirador, rather the tomboy, she drank of a freedom denied to girls of her age in the society she was soon to enter in England, who, however rich their families, were kept in the schoolroom with a governess, and raised in an atmosphere of strictness, if not subjugation. Nancy's was a very different upbringing, and it left her considerably more opinionated and independent-minded than them – or even than most of her Virginian contemporaries.

In contrast to Phyllis, with her quiet and wistful nature, 'made in a minor key', the freedom of their new life at Mirador encouraged the wild element in Nancy. She was at an impressionable age, and much as he loved her, Chillie's influence was not in every respect good: his colourful characteristics, his swagger and self-confidence, and his lack of concern about the effect on others of his words or deeds, left their mark. Nancy was dismayed and sometimes frightened by her father's unpredictability and occasional rages, which left her with a loathing of hot temper. But she was becoming a defiant girl: she had absorbed, subconsciously at least, the ability of her eldest sister to stand up to her father. She found also that she had an invaluable shield – ready wit, which would often dissolve his anger or irritation.

But her fitness and energy affected her more general behaviour. Whether or not she copied Chillie consciously, she did not conceal an almost aggressive air, marked by her frequently saying whatever entered her head, regardless of effect, a trait made more noticeable by a growing impetuosity and sudden changes of mind. These habits were not suppressed when she reached adulthood, and lasted for the rest of her life.

For all the freedoms she herself enjoyed at Mirador, Nancy soon began to notice the burdens that life there had put on her beloved mother, who had now to manage the running of a large and busy household that revolved around her capricious husband, with his determination to entertain freely and copiously in the time-honoured Southern fashion. For Nanaire, the day started early:

She bustled through the house, consulted the butler, instructing the cleaning women, making sure the laundry was in full operation, and unlocking storerooms with keys from a curved wicker basket she carried in the crook of her arm. Chillie, loud and imperious, roared and bellowed, forever interfering with her routine with his demands. She was relieved when he finally closeted himself in his office with his male secretary and business associates who came to spend an hour or the week; or when he left the house, more than likely gone to the riding ring to instruct Nannie or Phyllis, or to the barn or into the fields to oversee whatever work was in progress.[18]

However, while she bridled when she saw her mother in the subordinate role thrust upon her, there was much in Nanaire that Nancy unreservedly admired, notably her example in consistently befriending the poor, often being unwilling to turn tramps away without food or other comforts.

Nancy's inherited goodness, encouraged by her study of the Bible and the stories of the saints, found practical expression after she made friends with the parish priest, Frederick Neve. This relationship was to demonstrate how her disapproval of some of her father's ways left her open to the influence of alternative figures of authority, particularly in relation to the charitable aspect of her character, which contrasted with the sharpness that she had inherited from Chillie.

Born in 1855 and educated at Oxford, where he had been moved by the sermons of the celebrated Dr Pusey, Neve had fallen prey to the Victorian zeal for civilising missions and for taking Christianity to the 'poor benighted heathen' in far corners of the world. He had gone first to Africa, but his health suffered in the Dark Continent, so, in his early thirties, he travelled to Virginia. He had heard rumours that in its hills were remote communities eking out an existence, speaking an archaic language derived from Elizabethan times, starved of life's comforts and lacking divine guidance. The eager young minister set out to make good their deficiencies, and was installed as incumbent archdeacon at St Paul's church at Ivy, a village not far from Charlottesville.

Paying a first pastoral visit to Mirador, he received a mixed reception from its owner, who regarded missionaries as wrong-headed zealots who spent too much time on other people's business. Nancy, characteristically blunt, called him the ugliest man ever, with eyes that looked 'one each way'. Yet his energetic enthusiasm made a deep impression:

He was six foot three and he had very large feet. He used to preach to us on Sundays and he was the worst preacher I ever heard. But he was a man of God. He went off with his Bible and a bottle of whisky and started the French Mountain Mission. From the first I loved and respected him. Father used to say of me that I didn't respect anything but goodness, and that is true. I have always liked and admired brilliance, but I loved goodness . . .

About this time I got to know about the Sheltering Arms, a home in Virginia where old people and cripples were taken care of; I began to take an interest in it and to visit people there. I don't think I had realised before how many poor and unwanted people there are in the world.[19]

The Sheltering Arms had been established, by a woman, some years earlier in Richmond, and soon after Nancy met Neve, he encouraged her to visit the home, and to comfort the old, poor and sick inmates. She soon realised that she had exceptional powers of communication and an ability to captivate an audience, not least with quips and laughter that gave enjoyment and satisfaction to Nancy as well as to her listeners.

She also endeavoured to join Neve on his missionary journeys into the hills, when he would set out in an ancient trap or mounted on his cob, Old Harry, to conduct baptisms or other services, and to offer solace and guidance. However, while Neve allowed Nancy to help out at the Sheltering Arms, or at the St John the Baptist mission house, in the Ragged Mountains near Charlottesville, he drew the line at taking her into the wildest parts of his new parish, such as the remote and dangerous Shiflett's Hollow. Some of the hillbillies in these places were the descendants of early settlers and adventurers whose families had long ago succumbed to their unforgiving surroundings; others were the descendants of Hessian mercenaries, cut off for generations beyond impassable tracks. They were largely inbred communities of a rough stamp, without medicine, hospitals, schools or churches, who clung to strange, primitive beliefs: when a woman had a baby, for example, she was forbidden to comb her hair or sweep under the bed for nine days, so as not to attract the Devil.

Despite the desire of the Reverend Neve, and also now of Nancy, to guide these hill dwellers into the ways of righteousness, their hostility to outsiders was too fierce to risk bringing into their midst an attractive teenage girl, whether or not accompanied by a priest. 'Those people,' Nancy recalled, 'would stick a knife in you – in the back, mostly.' Even Archdeacon Neve, although gradually gaining the confidence of his strange flock, was believed by many of them to be a disguised revenue official, after their few possessions.

As it happened, in contrast to the happy life at Mirador, not far away there were large numbers of people, especially children, living in sore need of the benevolence of their fellow man, and their plight would have greatly excited Nancy's Christian feelings, had she or any of her family or friends been aware of it. In the South, industrial revival from post-war stagnation, with the value of production increasing exponentially from about 1880, had been attended by the growth of a system of child slavery almost as dire as that which developed during the Industrial Revolution in England. In the Southern states, the process drew some 60,000 children under the age of fourteen, including a large number considerably younger than that, into work in the cotton mills, while in the bitumen mines of West Virginia, boys of nine or ten were commonly used. Although that was illegal, the law did permit twelve-year-olds to work – in practice for as long as it suited their employers; in reality for as long as their bodies stood the strain.

Many, often as young as ten years old, worked as trap boys, on shifts of up to fourteen hours a day, sitting alone in dark mine passages, their only company rats seeking to share their rations, or the occasional mule passing with its load. Ankle-deep in mud or water, chilled to the marrow, they would sit or stand exposed to the icy draughts that rushed in as they opened the traps for the mules to pass.

Children would also work in the mines as breaker boys, stooping over chutes to pick out slate or other impurities from the coal passing along to the washers. In air black with dust, deafened by the noise of crushers, screens and the rushing race of coal, a child would sometimes slip and be torn and mangled in the machinery, or disappear into the chute, to be picked out later, smothered and still. Those who survived death or violent injury might develop asthma or consumption from breathing in the clouds of coal dust all day.

Conditions in the homes of these children were not much better: a report described, as a typical occurrence, a four-year-old working late at night with her mother in a squalid tenement building, making artificial flowers for a few cents:

> the frail little thing was winding green paper around wires to make stems for artificial flowers to decorate ladies' hats. Every few minutes her head would droop, and her weary eyelids close, but her little fingers still kept moving – uselessly, helplessly, mechanically moving. Then the mother would shake her gently, saying, 'Sleep not, Anetta, only a few more, only a few more.' And the little eyes would open slowly and the tired fingers would once more move with intelligent direction and purpose.

Such child labour 'saps the constitution of the child, robs it of hope, and unfits it for life's struggle'[20] – which all too often it soon lost.

Many years later, Nancy worked hard to bring such situations to public notice, and to champion measures for their relief. As a teenager, however, she remained happily ignorant of life beyond her valley.

Meanwhile, it was among the servants at Mirador that she could continue to satisfy her desire to do good. The oldest of these, addressed respectfully by the children as 'Aunt' or 'Uncle', had once been slaves, staying on at Mirador after their emancipation. Set in their ways and beliefs, they were treated as part of the family. One aged friend was 'Fountain' Wilson, with whom Nancy and Phyllis spent long and happy hours – he spent most of his time in his log cabin, dressed in formal clothes and a top hat. Another, Aunt Liza Pratt, was the children's nurse, although only Buck, born in 1882, and Nora, seven years younger, still needed one.

Aunt Liza smoked a corncob pipe and, like many poor women of the time, kept her money in the knees of her stockings – Nancy and Phyllis would tease her and try to pull them down. She was a devout believer in 'Mr Jesus', with whom she apparently had frequent communion, as a result of which she often felt obliged to abstain from her domestic duties, explaining that God had come to her: 'Mr Jesus, he said to me, "don't you go for to do any washing this day – you go right to your prayers".' Nancy's faith was strengthened by listening to Aunt Liza and the other servants, despite their sketchy grasp of detail. She particularly liked the story of a Negro who had heard the call to God's ministry. On being questioned by the padre as to which part of the Bible he liked best, he had replied that it was the parables:

'Well, tell me the parable of the Good Samaritan.'

'Sure, suh, it goes dis way: once 'pon a time a man went down from Jerusalem to Jericho and he fell among thieves, an' the thorns grew an' choke dat man, and he went on and he didn't have any money, an' he met the Queen of Sheba, an' she gave him ten thousand – yes, suh – talents of gold, an' a hundred changes of raiment, an' he got in a chariot an' he rode furiously. And under a big tree his hair got caught in a lim' and left him hangin' many days an' many nights, an' the ravens brought him food to eat and watah to drink. An' one night his wife Delilah came along an' cut off his hair, an' he dropt an' fell on stony ground, an' it began to rain, on and off for forty days and forty nights. Den when he come to Jerusalem he seen Queen Jezebel sittin' high in a windah, and when she saw him she does laf an' laf at him, and he say "Throw her down out ob' dere", and dey throwed her down seventy times seven, and ob' de fragments dey picked up twelve basketfuls.'[21]

However, while Nancy and Phyllis continued to entertain themselves at Mirador, life there did not suit some of the other children quite as well.

The older boys had become restless under their father's jurisdiction, perhaps unsurprisingly, as Keene was twenty-seven when the family moved to Mirador, and Harry almost through his teens; both were ready for some independence, but Chillie remained the authoritarian father. His apparent determination to repress and dominate was never far below the surface, and he tried to keep his sons on a tight rein. Keene had not done well at secondary school, so his father had declined to extend his education thereafter and instead set him to work in his own business, sending him to supervise construction at remote railway junctions. Harry, meanwhile, was a frequent target for his younger sisters.

Harry also had the misfortune to share at least some of the nursery years with Nancy and Phyllis, who teased him mercilessly. He was the cleverest boy but also the least popular. He was humourless, compared to the others, with a streak of violence. He was also shy and excessively prudish, and it was this that Nancy and Phyllis found irresistible. They would kick up their heels and show him their knees, at a time when even ankles were hidden from view. It would drive him to paroxysms of rage. 'I have a real knack of infuriating people,' Nancy wrote to Phyllis much later, almost in surprise . . .[22]

Irene, for different reasons, at first declined to spend much time at Mirador, although she later came to love it. Her successes at White Sulphur had reduced for her the attractions of a hayseed existence far from the city lights, and she would have been only too aware that she had become the subject of comment in the newspapers and magazines of many states, often expressed in terms of admiration. 'Miss Langhorne,' gushed the *Richmond Dispatch*, 'is one of the greatest beauties in the South and, excepting Miss May Handy, it may be said that she stands unequalled and unrivalled in her regal beauty.'

By 1891, over a quarter of a century had passed since the war's end, and Northerners had become attracted to the idea of the former glamour of the South. That summer was Irene's last full season at the White, after which she was considered old enough to enter fully into Richmond society, although at that time the South, mainly because there were not enough rich Southern families, did not have the formal debutante customs of New York. However, it was not long before she began to find her beauty appreciated by eligible men far beyond Richmond, and by October of that year she had begun going to parties in cities further afield.

Others in the family were also widening their horizons: Irene's parents began to enjoy accompanying her, their travels leading, among other things, to valuable contracts for the railroad business. In the spring of 1893, Chillie hired a private railway carriage to take Nanaire, Irene, Nancy and their friends to a party at Hampton Roads, on the coast near Norfolk, where the fleets of many nations had anchored as part of the arrangements for the Chicago World's Fair. Afterwards, Nanaire took Nancy on to the World's Fair; there she caused a mild sensation in a huge auditorium when the band struck up the Yankee song 'Marching Through Georgia', and Nancy, a mere fourteen years old, jumped on to her chair in a sudden fury and cried out, 'Three cheers for General Lee.'

Irene was now 'leaping the Mason-Dixon Line' with increasing frequency, going to fashionable events and making friends well beyond Virginia, and it was not long before she was noticed by the leaders of New York society, the epicentre of high life in America's Gilded Age. Accordingly, in the autumn of 1893, Nanaire received a remarkable letter asking if she would permit her daughter to lead the Grand March at the New York Patriarchs' Ball. The invitation came from Mr Ward McAllister, at the time the organ-grinder and guide for those who lived in hope of re-creating the 'First Circle' of antebellum New York society – though he was to die, cast out and reviled, a year or so later.

He performed his role at the right hand of the lady he called 'The Mystic Rose', Mrs Caroline Webster Schermerhorn Astor. Her immense wealth and steely determination had established her at the pinnacle of society and made her 'the fount of fashion, the arbiter of taste, the high priestess of manners and etiquette, the chief justice of the supreme court of social acceptability'.[23] She was known to the press, to the 'Four Hundred' who constituted New York's high society, and to herself, as '*the* Mrs Astor'. The Patriarchs, to whose ball Irene was invited, included some of the richest and most venerable names of the day, such as John Jacob Astor, Frank Roosevelt, Buchanan Winthrop and Pierpont Morgan.

It was a remarkable coup: only once before had an unmarried girl been so honoured, and never a Southerner. For Chillie and Nanaire it was the crowning glory of their social ambitions for Irene, pushing aside Civil War memories and anti-Northern sentiment, and reinforcing their determination that she and their younger daughters should marry well. So on 13 December 1893, Chillie, the fifty-year-old Confederate veteran, proudly escorted his glamorous daughter, resplendent in white satin, into a ballroom filled with Yankee millionaires.

The party was held, by custom, at Delmonico's, the fashionable restaurant-cum-ballroom on Fifth Avenue. A few privileged journalists had been permitted to attend the rigidly exclusive event. During the one-and-a-half-hour cotillion, Irene was 'admirably led' by Mr Franklin Bartlett and by

Ward McAllister himself, 'renowned for his regal choice of partners'. Polkas, lancers and waltzes were danced by the cream of New York and a sprinkling of foreign socialites: 'The big ballroom at Delmonico's was a whirlpool, the waves of which were costly and beautiful costumes, and the foam sparkling jewels and fair faces . . . in point of brilliance, beauty, and brains, the ball last night has seldom, if ever, been equaled.'[24]

Irene's triumphal progress continued through the following eighteen months. In the spring of 1894 she opened the ball at the highly distinguished Philadelphia Assembly, and the following February she was offered the great privilege of being a queen of one of the courts at the Mardi Gras celebrations in New Orleans. Remarkably, such plaudits appeared to have had no effect on her character, which, radiating great sweetness, continued to reflect her friendly temperament.

Towards the end of that year, however, Irene's attention was drawn to one in particular of the large numbers of eligible young men who sought her company. Before finally entering society, in 1891, she had attended Mrs Reed's, a finishing school in New York, where one of the girls had posed for an already well-known young artist called Charles Dana Gibson. Irene's companions would 'rapturously and romantically' scan magazines featuring his pictures. Dana Gibson, descended from a family of early settlers in New England, had been a struggling nineteen-year-old artist, but his life had changed early in 1886, when his potential was recognised by the editor of the popular magazine *Life*. His work was soon also taken by other magazines, such as *Collier's*. He achieved almost instant fame, and was soon astonished to hear that a large portion of the population was doing its utmost to make itself into the 'American Girl', as portrayed in his drawings.

Some of his models were young New York socialites, among them friends Irene had made at Mrs Reed's. Irene herself had been attracted by Northern society, and had returned to New York towards the end of 1894. One evening she was introduced to the now famous Gibson at a dinner given for her at Delmonico's. They met again the next day at the New York Horse Show, in Madison Square Garden, where the artist had gone to make sketches. Within a very short time they had fallen in love.

None of this was lost on Nancy. Although by nature competitive, however, she found for a time that there was little she could offer by way of competition. Later, she reminisced with a few tart and colourful details about Irene:

We began to spend a lot of time speculating who, of her many beaux, Irene would finally marry. The house was always full of suitors. Young men, old men, foreigners of every kind, literary men, rich bankers – all came along to ask for Irene's hand. She had sixty-two proposals. I certainly did enjoy Irene's beaux. Many of them were literary men and as Irene had no literary talent whatever they often recited to me the poetry they had prepared for her. I could appreciate it . . . The funniest of Irene's beaux was a rich banker. He was quite twenty years older than she was when he appeared to pay his addresses . . . He sent her a diamond watch and a letter in which he said, 'If you don't like it, take it to the mill pond and throw it into the deepest part.' . . . We were all thrilled and had our swim suits ready, for it looked as though this might turn out to be a good thing . . . Then Dana Gibson came on the scene. Looking back over the years, it seems to me that with his coming the great cloud of suitors just melted in silent summer heaven.[25]

Taken up by society in New York and in fashionable resorts such as Newport and Bar Harbor, where 'people are rich together', Irene did receive a very large number of proposals. In time, Nora, it was said, had fifty, while Nancy received sixteen. The picture is sketchy, but it seems from her memoirs that Nancy's suitors courted her both before and during the time, in 1894 and 1895, when Irene also was being wooed:

I had the usual early love affairs. At fourteen I was in love with St George Bryan. He was eighteen and very good looking and I adored him, but as far as I can remember our romance consisted mainly in our going for rides together. He whistled beautifully and would whistle me the latest tunes. That friendship lasted quite a few years, but then it just faded out.[26]

The whistling St George was also a keen steeplechaser, which for Nancy, who was tone deaf, was perhaps more of an attraction than the tunes. But even a dramatic fall from his horse at a Charlottesville race meeting, which Nancy witnessed, was insufficient to melt her heart. Two years later another suitor appeared, and pursued his cause with poems and love letters, but to no avail. Nancy prosaically described her feeling on reading them as 'nausea'; nor was Nanaire greatly impressed, telling her daughter that she had no business to be 'getting letters like that' at her age. She also attracted the love of a Frederick Kemochan, whom she met at the Yale Proms – presumably a little later, as she did not spend time in New England until she was at least seventeen. To her annoyance, he failed to propose, though he was, Nancy said, part of her life for some time. 'It is difficult to recall these early love affairs,' she wrote, 'though no doubt they meant a lot at the time.'

In June 1895, Dana Gibson, tall, distinguished and urbane, finally arrived at Mirador. He was met at the gate by Irene's father, in forbidding mood. Chillie was apt later to grumble that his eldest daughter had married 'a meat packer who could barely support his family', and he did not want the beautiful and eligible Irene to settle for someone he described as 'a damn sign painter from the North'. He advised the hopeful suitor not to pay off the station wagon, as he would not be staying long. On Gibson's good-naturedly querying such Southern hospitality, however, Chillie relented: 'Pay him off, young man,' he said, 'and come in.' In due course, despite the occasional irascible reference to 'that damyankee charcoal artist', Dana finally won over Irene's parents, and received their permission to marry her.

The wedding took place on 7 November 1895 at St Paul's, Richmond, the church in which the Confederate leaders had often gathered at dark times during the war. Nancy and Phyllis were among the bridesmaids at what was clearly a most impressive spectacle, as crowds thronged around the church and the railway sidings were filled with private carriages that had brought Dana's fashionable friends down from the North. The news-paper columns suggested, with colourful hyperbole, that 'it will be one of the most brilliant social functions witnessed in Richmond for years, and will draw within the walls of that historic structure an audience representing the fashion and culture of many states . . .'[27]

Following an extensive honeymoon around the Mediterranean and through Italy, the couple spent the winter in London, where the American ambassador arranged for them to be invited to one of Queen Victoria's Drawing Rooms, held for the presentation of young ladies – although on that occasion the Queen was ill and was represented by her daughter, Princess Helena. Dana was commissioned by a London newspaper to sketch the proceedings, the results receiving considerable popular acclaim.

On their return home, Irene became the central figure in her husband's hugely popular illustrations, and he soon produced a book of drawings featuring his bride:

The New York *Journal* dedicated an entire page reviewing *Pictures of People*, and its headline blared, '*Mr Gibson Selects His Wife As His New Type Of American Girl*'. . .

. . . Within weeks after his first drawings of Irene appeared the term 'American Girl' gave way entirely to 'The Gibson Girl'. . .' [28]

With Irene safely married into high society, the prospects for Nancy, in her parents' minds at least, took a new turn. Now seventeen, she was sent off to New York's finishing school of choice, Miss Brown's Academy for

Young Ladies. While Irene appeared to have found her finishing school worthwhile and enjoyable, however, matters went differently with her younger sister. The available evidence of what occurred comes only from Nancy, so it may not be quite the full story. At all events, it seems that sparks flew. Like other such schools, the prime purpose of Miss Brown's Academy was to apply the final touches to its charges' social graces, and to prepare them for their entry into society. That, it seems, did not accord with the expectations of the clean-limbed girl from Virginia. 'We had all been brought up,' she wrote, 'in a forthright and natural atmosphere, where nobody talked of money or thought a great deal about clothes, and our approach to boys and young men was healthy and unsentimental.' The other girls had a different attitude, perhaps one more usual in seventeen-year-olds, and thought mainly of their wardrobes, which were far larger than Nancy's, and of how much money their fathers made, and of boys: 'there was always a selection of odd and, to me, quite revolting affairs going on between them and young men' – a comment that may throw light on Nancy's apparently casual tone in referring to her own early love affairs.

At Miss Brown's she learned little that appealed to her or that she considered useful. She was too individualistic by nature to be able to absorb the school's communal ethos, and she did not like being required to fit a mould. As a result, she found herself looked down upon and rather disliked. It was a new experience for her, and she did not rise above it. Instead, her combative instincts led her to respond by exaggerating the faults she was thought to possess, portraying her family as one where her mother took in washing and her father was a drunk – not the thing at all for young ladies. It apparently made her exciting, if undesirable, to the others, but their thrill turned to disbelief when Irene arrived at the Academy explaining that she had come to take her sister out. That the famous Gibson Girl herself should be Nancy's sister caused astonishment.

At length Chillie and Nanaire came up to New York to see how their daughter was progressing, no doubt hoping to find her being polished into a young lady at ease in society. Even if they were disappointed by the rather different outcome, they accepted that the Academy was not having the desired effect, and told a grateful Nancy that she need stay no longer.

Delighted to be back again at Mirador, after what she called 'that ghastly finishing school', she resumed her accustomed life there in the summer of 1896. But she did not stay for long. Perhaps in her time at the Academy in New York she had after all felt the pull of the 'great monetary, scientific, artistic and intellectual centre of the western world'. Or it may have been that the novelty and excitement of Dana's friends and Irene's beaux had aroused her curiosity about life beyond Virginia. She had made some new friends in New York, despite her reaction to most of the young ladies at the Academy, and so, in the spring of 1897, an invitation from Irene and Dana to stay with them tempted her to go north once more. Her parents put up no opposition: the matrimonial prospects for a vivacious eighteen-year-old from a rich family were considerably better in New York than in Richmond, let alone in rural Greenwood.

When Nancy reached New York, the gossip columns took up the new arrival – 'petite, freshly turned out, sparkling with life' – describing her also, not wholly accurately, as 'a pretty, dashing and sweet schoolgirl', but frequently, to her slight resentment, as the 'Gibson Girl's younger sister'. Forgotten now was her distaste for the girls of Miss Brown's, instead she joined with zest in their type of life, and was soon accompanying the Gibsons around much of their social circuit. In the process she made plenty of friends, to whom she seemed attractive and fascinating – small and slight, but highly animated. Those two factors were closely related, however, because it was when Nancy began to go to parties and dances in the North that she became fully conscious that, at five feet two in height, she was not only a good eight inches shorter than Irene, but also smaller than most of her female contemporaries. Her way of dealing with what was to her a disagreeable fact of life was to inflate and strengthen her animus, both as a form of defence and compensation, and as a means of attracting the interest and admiration of those she met. This became an ingrained characteristic, and was to inform her behaviour for the rest of her life, and give her body, although small, an impression of strength, thrusting itself forward.

Thanks to her energy and enthusiasm, within a few months Nancy was recognised as a belle of Newport, where polo and hunting bloods, Astors, Whitneys and other scions of the rich would escort beautiful girls in picture hats and organdies along Bellevue Avenue, take part in the casino tennis week, and trot around the paths in curricles and sociables, while the Vanderbilt yacht *Valiant* rested at anchor in the harbour.

In the summer of 1897, while staying with Pem Shaw, a friend from Boston, Nancy was introduced to Pem's brother-in-law, Robert Gould Shaw II, known to his family as Robbie, and more generally as Bob. Their first meeting took place at a polo match in which Bob was playing, and although Nancy recalled that when she first saw him it was on a one-eyed pony from which he frequently fell, he was a very experienced player, having represented Harvard in 1890, and five years later played for the celebrated Myopia Chase team, winners of the much-prized Astor Cup. She was immediately struck by his good looks and confident air. In fact, as her friends could see, she was bowled over. Seven years older than her, handsome and easy-going, Bob took equally to this slender, graceful girl, with her fine eyes and slightly saucy demeanour.

Bob Shaw seemed charming and sophisticated, and Nancy was flattered by the attentions of someone so glamorous and prominent on the social scene. She had been impressed by the example of young love presented by Irene and Dana, who no doubt made marriage look fun and exciting. At all events, an engagement was soon announced. Even allowing for the speed with which in those days first meetings seemed to lead on to proposals, the news caused surprise. Nancy was only eighteen, and as she recalled, 'I was so young that when rumours began to go round everyone said there must be some mistake. I wasn't officially "out".' She added:

> I suppose I was flattered and pleased to have made this spectacular conquest. I liked him, and it was pleasant to be the centre of the picture all of a sudden. But in my own heart I was never sure. The still, small voice that is in most girls' hearts warned me I was not really in love with him, but I did not listen or, if I did, I could not understand the message. The entire family were in favour of the marriage and threw in their weight against me. Everyone had a piece of well-meant advice. Mother was amongst them.[29]

It would seem that her competitive spirit had got the better of her in a matter of major importance: she later said that she married Bob because she didn't want anyone else to marry him. Among the family, recorded opinions of Bob Shaw are varied and inconclusive. Nancy would certainly have been justified in having doubts, as along with Shaw's glamour came a reputation: he was wild, he was a heavy drinker, and he had a mistress. Even if such attributes were common among rich young men at the time, there were eventually enough questions about him, particularly about his drinking, to lead Chillie to journey to Boston to discuss Nancy's fiancé with his parents, who, it might have been thought, would be able to exert some influence on the young man. However, Bob's father was nearly fifty years older than his son, and with the wisdom of age he appears to have been unusually frank: 'I would not like my daughter to marry him,' he told Chillie, 'although he is my son; he is wild, dissipated and always had his way.'

While accounts of the engagement tend to contradict each other, they leave the impression that Nanaire's enthusiasm for the match was not shared by her husband. Nancy herself suggested that after a few months she found her fiancé too hot to handle and broke off the engagement, only to resume it under pressure from Bob's mother, who was sure that Nancy's moral outlook would influence her son and that marriage would make him settle down.

According to Nancy's niece, daughter of her eldest sister Lizzie, the recollection of three of Nancy's sisters and her eldest brother runs contrary to Nancy's version, and bears the ring of truth: 'Nothing would stop Nannie – she was as headstrong as she always was. Grandfather did everything he could to dissuade her: this I had from my mother, Keene, Aunt Irene and Phyllis . . .'[30]

The Shaws were a well-known Boston Brahmin family, at one time large landowners. One of Bob's cousins, Robert Gould Shaw I, had been a noted abolitionist, and was famous for his role in the Civil War, raising a Negro regiment and dying at its head in an attack on Fort Wagner. Bob's Swiss-born mother, Pauline Agassiz, daughter of an eminent botanist, was the second wife of his father, Quincy Adams Shaw, who was very rich, both by inheritance and in his own right as a successful copper magnate. He had built up an exceptional art collection, including works by Jean-François Millet, from whom he had commissioned pictures in France many years earlier.

After a three-month engagement, the marriage took place on 27 October 1897. It had been postponed for a fortnight when Nancy fell ill with a 'nervous attack'. She was almost nineteen; Bob was twenty-five. Initial plans for a grand wedding in Richmond had been abandoned. There were no widespread celebrations as there had been in Irene's case, and the occasion was quiet, with only Nancy's immediate family and a few of the bridegroom's friends present. The marriage was celebrated before an altar decorated with flowers and silver candlesticks at one end of Mirador's drawing room, conducted by Rev. Hartley Carmichael, a Richmond vicar, assisted by Nancy's old friend, Archdeacon Neve. Phyllis, the maid of honour, later described the event as one of 'deep gloom'; the spirits of the bride may have been lowered by the effects of her having touched some poison ivy.

Afterwards, the couple set off for the Homestead Hotel, at Hot Springs, a resort in the Appalachian Mountains. The private aspects of such matters are usually known only to the participants, but in this case it is clear that the honeymoon was a disaster. Nancy had already witnessed the effects of alcohol on her high-spirited husband, but until she reached Hot Springs she had probably not understood in detail what else she might expect, and bold and animated as she might be, she was also prudish. Her husband naturally wanted to exercise his conjugal rights, and, notwithstanding his experience, he may have rather roughly set about a matter that by its nature might have involved pain as well as pleasure. Even so, it is unlikely that he would have anticipated Nancy's reaction.

She had not, it would seem, comprehended the facts of life, and with the Puritan strain in her character, she seems to have met them with the revulsion that John Ruskin reputedly felt on discovering on his wedding night that women did not look like marble statues, as he had fondly imagined, but instead possessed pubic hair and other animal attributes. For Nancy, one night of Bob's ways and means was sufficient, and after some brief, unproductive tumult she climbed out of the marriage bed, feeling, as she later described it, like a child marooned, and leaving a baffled husband to ponder his next move.

She fled home almost immediately. Her parents, however, rejected the idea of her giving up so soon, and pressed her firmly to return to her husband and try and make the marriage work. After a few days she did so; in due course the couple took on an attractive house near Mirador, and then arranged a tour in Europe.

They set off from Richmond on 20 January 1898. 'Last goodbyes to dear ones,' Nancy wrote, 'with heavy heart.' Before they could experience the delights of Europe, however, they had to cross the sea, a new and trying experience for Nancy, as she confided, somewhat briefly, to her diary:

23 January: Nice looking passengers.
24 January: Desperate.
25 January: All of us have been desperately ill. I hate the beautiful sea. Oh my.

As they drew near the Italian coast, her spirits revived a little: 'We have made such nice friends,' she wrote. 'Funny time learning the currency. It is fine on the steamer now, rather monotonous . . . these last days on the water are as beautiful as a dream.'[31]

After visiting Pompeii, by 7 February the couple were in Rome, where they met Pope Leo XIII, and a week later they were in Florence. But no miracles had been worked, and Nancy was no longer exhilarated, writing in her diary on St Valentine's Day that she was 'really homesick'. Despite the novelty of travelling, the search for happiness was in vain: it seemed that the two were incompatible, or perhaps not even that. An alternative that would appear equally possible might be that once their initial infatuation had faded, they realised that they simply did not love each other.

Nevertheless, when they returned from Europe they continued to try to live amicably together. They bought a house at Pride's Crossing, near Boston, where for a short while they were prominent at the Boston Country Club, the Myopia Chase and other fashionable gatherings. Some of Bob's letters to his bride, when his social life took him away from her, indicate that he missed her even during short periods of absence:

My own precious Nancy,

. . . I do hate to leave you darling but it can't be helped, and how glad I shall be when Friday comes and I am with you again . . . I shall be so lonely tonight again. Do write me lots and love me always, for I love my sweet wife better than anyone in the whole world.

'. . . How I wish I were back with you,' he wrote on another occasion. 'I love you so much and will try never to be disagreeable again. With all the love of your Robs.'[32]

Whatever the true nature of their feelings towards each other, a further complication arose to compound the difficulties: Nancy became pregnant. Considering her initial reaction to the notion of sex with her husband, this might seem surprising, yet the marriage was clearly consummated at some point, though perhaps not very romantically. One night, for example, Nancy claimed to have woken up to find her husband in the bedroom with a chloroformed sponge; extreme as this would have been, to Bob, with such an obdurate wife, it might have seemed the only way to get his due.[33]

Disagreeable occasions persisted, and it became clear that the marriage was doomed. Nancy's distaste for physical relations with Bob was now compounded by the galling mental hurt of his infidelity. 'I won't bed with him when he wants,' she admitted to Phyllis, and Bob, denied willing sex by his wife, had resorted to someone more obliging, a Mary Converse, by reputation formerly an English actress but now a widow from Newport, Rhode Island. Nancy did not know how long it had been going on, but her husband had obviously been having an affair while she – together, as she thought, with him – had been attempting to make the marriage work. The discovery of the truth, she recorded, filled her with horror.

Several times during the ensuing months, despite her pregnancy, Nancy ran away from their new home, or perhaps was ordered out of it by a husband whose patience was exhausted. On one occasion she was recognised and rescued by Nicholas Longworth, Irene's old friend, who found her downcast on a bench at a railway station in Washington, having fled without enough money to get back to Mirador. Bob's propensity to drink was aggravated by his bride's wilfulness, and it also sometimes led to the threat, or worse, of violence, to which, because of her small size and her condition, she was particularly vulnerable.

Nancy's aversion to drink had been formed long before she met Bob Shaw, and had its roots in the behaviour of members of her own family. Her father drank regularly and sometimes heavily, when he would become tempestuous as a result. He prided himself on his wine cellar, his juleps and eggnogs, and, conscious of Virginia's customary hospitality, pressed liberal amounts of drink upon his guests. However, his generosity did not in this respect extend to his sons, and despite exposing them to temptation, he forbade them to drink at all; in fact he offered them a large sum of money should they abstain until they were twenty-one. Even then he restricted and fiercely controlled the amount of refreshment they were allowed. Unfortunately, it proved a futile idea: excluding them from an appealing form of relaxation while liberally indulging his friends – and himself – must have irritated his sons and made them determined to rebel.

As a result, Keene in particular, but on many occasions also Harry, and sometimes even Buck, drank heavily, something that Nancy found distressing. Alcohol frequently led her brothers into scrapes, even when they grew up. Nancy was long remembered by the family for calmly removing a loaded pistol from a drunken Harry's hand when he was threatening his future wife, Genevieve, with it. Meanwhile Keene, 'intelligent, versatile, idle and wild', would excuse himself from his father's office and disappear on drink-fuelled sprees. Handsome, amusing and his father's favourite son, he was eventually banished to a remote farm that Chillie bought for him. However, he was unable to kick the habit of alcohol or flourish in his work, goals made more difficult by recurrent tuberculosis, which in time was to kill both of his brothers as well.

Having to witness these excesses as a child and as she grew up left a painful and indelible mark on Nancy, and when, very soon after her wedding, she realised that her husband had the same problem, she was distraught. Alcohol had become associated for her not only with loud and gross behaviour, but with violence too; it also consolidated within her a distaste for sex. In later years these perceived connections were to orientate much of her political career towards promoting measures for the protection of women and children, and for the restriction of drink.

After nearly ten months of marriage, on 18 August 1898, Nancy's child was born, in Beverly, Massachusetts, and named Robert Gould Shaw III. Her love for her son later became almost overwhelming in its possessiveness, and was to cause tension in a relationship that was often tempestuous but always essential for both mother and son. But from the very first, she showed her child passionate devotion, finding in Bobbie, as he became known, a refuge from her volatile relations with his father.

The fact that Nancy's marital difficulties were partially self-inflicted did nothing to lessen their pain. She needed to escape and find respite, at least, as she thought, for a time. Eventually, having exhausted all attempts to tolerate her husband, she went to his father, whom she liked and admired:

. . . I told him I could not go on. Mr Shaw was very kind and much distressed by the whole affair. I think they had hoped marriage was to put an end to all Bob's difficulties, but it had not done so.

'Go back home for six months', he said. 'I'll get him right.'[34]

Respite at Mirador proved ineffectual. Bob remained set in his ways, and, like many vain men, he greatly disliked ridicule, which was often Nancy's reaction to his behaviour. Nor had she herself changed: she still hated drink, and was repelled by the belief that her husband was being unfaithful. It was a disastrous combination, and although Nancy struggled on for the next few years, she eventually found the situation intolerable. Emotionally exhausted, she returned once more to Mirador. Her niece later recorded:

Grandfather often said any other daughter he had might have made a success of it but they were both unbridled and too much alike in getting their way. Sex & Drink – the vices he had – Nannie could not abide. In fact she slept on her face most of the honeymoon and nobody knows how Bobby got there. It was enough to drive him to other ladies more willing – but it is wrong to say anyone influenced her: nobody ever could.[35]

Any affection that Nancy might once have had for Bob had been battered out of her by his habits. She had had enough, and decided to say so to his father.

I hadn't been married a month before I found out that he drank. I've always had a perfect horror of that . . . and when I knew I was going to have a child I was in deep despair. It was dreadful to have a child to a drunkard. I tried to get rid of it. I went to doctors. Then when Bobbie was four I went to Mr Shaw and told him I could never live with Bob again.

She received plentiful advice, from several quarters, that she should petition for divorce. The Shaws, however, did not want the disgrace of a divorce, and in Nancy's mind, despite the obvious good sense in such a course from the secular point of view, there was an immovable religious obstacle: she was convinced that it would be a sin. Even Archdeacon Neve tried to persuade her that the Bible condoned divorce for adultery, but she was unmoved. She proposed the alternative of a judicial separation, even though it would deny her the chance of marrying again and starting a new life. Her religious stance was reinforced by the admittedly valid belief that a divorce would bring disgrace upon her own family, such an event, in those days and in the circles in which her family moved, being both rare and usually tainted with scandal. 'I was so horrified by the whole thing,' she wrote, 'that I did not listen to anyone's advice. To me, to be divorced seemed the last degradation for that was how I had always been brought up to regard it. It was something that decent people had nothing whatever to do with . . .'[36]

The matter lay unresolved, and Nancy remained at Mirador, cherishing her son, happy to be back with her parents, but in exile nevertheless. She could draw some solace from the letters she received from Bob's family, which expressed sorrow rather than anger, however upset they must have been. 'I had hoped,' wrote Bob's sister, Mary, 'that this winter's long separation would help you to be more patient with one another and that this summer you would be with us again . . . Goodbye, dear child, I hope we shall hear from you sometimes, and that your future may be happy.'[37] Bob's mother was equally sorry, and bemused:

> . . . Of course I shall miss you and Baboo – no-one can go out of a family as you are going and not be missed. And it does seem such a pity, the whole thing so unnecessary – if either you or Bob had really taken hold of yourselves and from the start tried to make the best of things, and with so much to do it with, it seems extraordinary that you have both failed . . .[38]

Nancy could try and make the best of things only after fleeing her husband. Gradually she resumed her accustomed life at Mirador, riding a great deal, hunting with the local packs, and trying to put the recent past behind her. In doing so, she made friends with some young Englishmen who had come out to seek their fortune, or at least to occupy some time in an enjoyable manner in Virginia, where people 'shared an idea of caste, of paternalism, of the horse-centred, mildly dilapidated pastoral life'.[39] Two brothers, Ned and Algie Craven, whose father was a master of foxhounds in England, were working near Mirador. Nancy believed that Algie was in love with her, and she learned much from him about riding, while Ned inspired her with tales of fox hunting in Leicestershire, its spiritual home.

Another new friend to appear at Mirador was Angus McDonnell, the younger son of an Irish earl, who had taken a job on the railways and was working at Manassas. News of his imminent arrival put 'the girls', at this point consisting of Nora, Nancy and Phyllis, into a flurry. Here was a real live English aristocrat – or, more exotic, an Irishman – coming to see them. They were about to meet face to face what they had read about in books; what dandified presence would manifest itself? They went up to prepare themselves in their best Southern finery. Meanwhile, with an introduction to the Langhornes, McDonnell had set off for Mirador. Many years later a nephew recalled his uncle's account of his reception when he first arrived:

> Uncle Angus journeyed for days, by mule, train and on foot in order to visit Nancy's family, finally arriving at the front door, in a very unfresh state, rather battered and with the dust of the road adhering to the grease spots on his suit. He knocked several times, heard nothing, so thought 'well maybe this is like Ireland', and went round to the kitchen door at the back; opening it, he started wandering through the house, only to hear Nancy's mother disappearing up the stairs, shouting 'Girls! Girls! I've seen him! Come on down, you needn't change after all!'[40]

McDonnell soon fell in love with Nancy, but although she was flattered, flirting with him and enjoying his company, she never came near to requiting his love. Good-natured though he was, her basic reaction to his rather abject demeanour and open devotion was one of disdain, a rather harsh attitude that she was to display in other and similar circumstances.

In October 1902, holding fast to her position, Nancy duly signed a deed of separation from Bob Shaw, satisfying her conscience but rendering herself, as she put it, 'unwanted, unsought and part widowed for life', or at least for the foreseeable future. Further, it removed her ability to keep in good repair many of the friendships that she had made in the North.

However, the deed of separation was to prove only a temporary measure. To everybody's surprise, it was discovered that Bob Shaw and his mistress had gone through a marriage ceremony. Alerted and alarmed, 'Old Mr Shaw', as Nancy called her father-in-law, arrived at Mirador with his wife, and explained what had happened. To what extent, if any, Bob Shaw's mistress knew of Nancy's situation, or more importantly what Shaw himself believed was the legal position, was immaterial. In the eyes of the law he would be considered to have committed bigamy; if the charge were brought against him he risked being sent to prison, even if he claimed to believe that he was no longer married to Nancy, and therefore had no guilty intent.

The idea of a convict in the family appalled the Shaws. They urged Nancy to agree to a divorce, presumably believing that if Bob and his mistress then went through another ceremony, the previous marriage would be retrospectively validated, so that their son would no longer risk a criminal charge. Whether or not that was theoretically correct in law, in practice it might persuade the authorities, should they look into the matter, not to prosecute. Bob's parents proposed petitioning on grounds of 'incompatibility of temperament', about which there could be little question. Chillie also pressed Nancy to divorce. Shocked by the threat to Bob, she accepted that he needed protection from the law, but she demurred at proposing incompatibility and turned again to the Bible, finally accepting that in the case of a man's adultery it allowed divorce. After a certain amount of acrimony, agreement was reached.

On 3 February 1903, in Charlottesville, with neither party present and with minimal publicity, a divorce was decreed. Nancy was awarded a handsome settlement and custody of her son, whose father was awarded the right of access at 'regular intervals'; the arrangements were to be reviewed when Bobbie reached the age of eight. Forty-eight hours later, Bob went through another ceremony with Mrs Charles H. Converse; Boston society circles were dumbfounded, and Bob's remarriage, so soon after his divorce, 'caused no end of talk'.[41]

Meanwhile, Nancy seems to have been reluctant to shun society entirely. There were many contrasts in her nature, and she could not long remain happy without the company of friends; so much so that it was only a short time after her divorce that the newspapers picked up on talk of a new affair:

Society is looking forward to the formal announcement of Robert Walton Goelet, the richest single young man in New York, and Mrs Nannie Langhorne Shaw, which betrothal has been rumoured frequently since Mrs Shaw obtained her divorce a few weeks ago. Mrs Shaw is in Paris, and Mrs Goelet and her son will shortly start for the other side in the former's yacht *Nahma*. It is thought that the engagement will be announced in Paris.[42]

Whatever caused such talk, Nancy's family had suggested that she might benefit from a complete change of scene. So, although her previous experience might have left her with only a tepid desire for European travel, she set sail across the Atlantic once more. On this trip she was accompanied by Bobbie and Nanaire, and also by Alice Babcock, one of her very few friends from Miss Brown's Academy, who it was hoped would prove cheerful company, despite herself suffering from the pangs of lost love.

Having spent some time in France, they crossed the Channel with letters of introduction from Dana and Irene, who by then had many friends in England. Now calling herself Mrs Nannie Langhorne Shaw, Nancy's entrée into London society was also helped by her meeting Ava Astor, the estranged wife of John Jacob Astor.[43] Mrs Astor was a glamorous, amusing and influential woman, a former belle of Philadelphia; happy to befriend the two young women, she asked Nancy and Alice to stay on for a month while Nanaire returned to America with Bobbie.

By the late summer of 1903 Nancy was back again at Mirador, pleased by her adventure – and by some of its trappings, such as a complete set of Louis Vuitton luggage – but happy to be reunited with her child in familiar, well-loved surroundings. Yet a shattering blow was about to fall, and in a way that she maintained she did not overcome for the rest of her life. 'The memory of those days,' she wrote many years later, 'is like a shadow on the heart still.' She had entered her prized horse Queen Bee in a Lynchburg horse show to be held in October. When the day arrived, she and Keene set off in time for the opening of the event, leaving their parents to follow on shortly. 'But,' as Nancy recorded, 'they did not come. Suddenly I, who was so seldom nervous or given to any sort of foreboding, was full of them and could not say why. I left the show and went home. I found the house in darkness and Mother dead.' Nanaire had suffered a stroke at the entrance to the horse show, and had died very soon afterwards. She was only in her early fifties and her death came as a complete surprise and shock to her family.

Devastated, Nancy for a time tried to fill Nanaire's role, to look after her father and fourteen-year-old Nora, and to manage the household in the way her mother would have done. She was almost inconsolable:

I even took to gardening, a thing I thoroughly disliked and had never turned a hand to before. I remember kneeling one day, weeding one of her flower beds, trying to keep it the way she would have liked it, trying not to think about the days that were no more. William the coloured gardener was working nearby, but he left that job and knelt on the opposite side of the flower bed and worked with me. He knew how I was feeling. I was ill with misery and I remember what a comfort it was when I looked up through the tears I could not control, to see his kindly black face smiling at me.[44]

Although Nancy proved in later years in England to be a spectacular hostess, the short time she now spent running the affairs of her father's house was not a great success. Her temperament was not then suited to the close management of practical detail, especially while she yearned so deeply for her mother. She may also have set her sights beyond Mirador's horizons. Being a divorcée, she was now barred from New England society, and Bostonians anyway took the Shaws' side in the matter, but there was no reason why her thoughts might not stray to England. She had loved the brief time she had spent there after her divorce, and according to Angus

McDonnell, who saw much of her at Mirador after Nanaire's death, and who in his infatuation paid close attention to her moods, she made no secret of her intention to seek 'pastures new' again.

In fact the idea was first put up by Archdeacon Neve. He looked with sorrow upon Nancy's plight and proposed that she go to England and stay for a time with his own family. Chillie also seems to have thought that she should leave Mirador and have a break from the recent past, and it was his intervention that proved crucial. He had reason enough of his own: he and Nancy were rather too similar in temperament to feel easy, in the circumstances, at close quarters, not least as Nancy was sunk in gloom and believing her life to be over and done with. 'I had no plans,' she wrote, 'no dreams, no hopes save that my little son, then at his most enchanting, would grow up sober.' When, therefore, Chillie suggested that Nancy might like a season's hunting in England, he struck on perhaps the only solution that his unhappy daughter could have contemplated with pleasure. As an added incentive he said that he himself would go over in time for Christmas, and also that Nancy should be accompanied by Phyllis, whose own marriage, to Reggie Brooks, was becoming unsettled.

So in late 1904, the two sisters, with their respective children, Bobbie, and Phyllis's son Peter, now aged two, and their servants, left for England. For Nancy, the coming winter would be spent in making new friends, and enjoying the best fox hunting the world could offer. It was also the prelude to a momentous new development in her life.

THREE

The Chase

Having arrived in London, Nancy and Phyllis settled with their entourage in a private hotel in Half Moon Street, just north of Piccadilly. Fleming's Hotel was fashionable and respectable – it was on the Brigade of Guards' list of acceptable hotels – and within sight of Green Park, where Bobbie and his infant cousin could be taken to play. They were quickly in touch with friends of Dana and Irene, and with others whom Nancy herself had met on her previous visit. Taken under the wing of Mrs John Jacob Astor, they soon began to have a busy time with people like Mrs Cornelius Vanderbilt and the Duchess of Marlborough, and a number of other Gilded Age Americans immersed in London's social life. Nancy, who had now abandoned the name Nannie, was also introduced to Pauline Astor, who was in London buying a trousseau before her marriage to an English cavalry officer, and whose father had been the richest man in America when he emigrated to England a decade or so earlier.

Such ideas were not for Nancy. 'I came in 1904,' she said, 'not to catch a husband but to catch a fox', so after a short time she set off for Leicestershire, to forget her troubles in the excitement of hunting. With introductions to people who might help her get established, she arranged to rent Highfield House in Market Harborough, a small town deep in hunting country; there, to see to her needs, she engaged 'one butler, a dreadful cook and a faint-hearted housemaid'.

Of the two main bases for hunting in Leicestershire, Market Harborough was the more staid, the 'high jinks' being centred in Melton Mowbray, in the country of the celebrated Quorn hunt. Nearby lived the exiled Grand Duke Michael of Russia, later a friend of Nancy, and the Cunard family, well known in both shipping and hunting circles, and she found herself among a large number of vigorous, rich and fashionable people all set on spending the winter riding to hounds and having a thoroughly good time. Small, fit and lively, and just beginning to sparkle once more, Nancy was ready to join in the fun. She took to it at once: 'It was what I wanted,' she later recalled, 'like getting on a stretch of good ice when you are skating.'

To some it may have seemed excessive to travel all the way from Virginia to England for the purpose of hunting foxes, but for those who loved the sport – and for many it was an addiction – almost any journey was worth the trouble. Not that there was a lack of good hunting back home in America: in Virginia Nancy had hunted with the Deep Run Hunt and the Albemarle County Hounds, and later, when she was living with Bob Shaw, with the Meadowbrook Hounds and the Myopia Chase. The Piedmont country around Mirador also provided good hunting, to fly with the wind and soar over rails in long, hard runs, free of fence, ditch or wire. But hunting in the best English country was a thing apart, and many people ensured they were out for six days of the seven. From an early age children of the 'county' were bred to it: 'We're not allowed to hunt more than three times a week until we are five,' said the scion of a well-known family, while the young Marquess of Worcester, heir to the Duke of Beaufort, was given a pack of hounds for his ninth birthday – and was known as 'Master' ever after.

By the time Nancy arrived for her first English season, the countryside had reached a near-perfect condition for fox hunting. The competition from many years of cheap food imports had led to a deep depression in British agriculture. Although in the mid-1890s a slow recovery had begun, farmers and landowners, for years submerged by imports of corn, had turned to beef and dairy, returning arable land to pasture and in the process transforming the rolling landscape of the English shires. Now on all sides unfolded verdant fields of fifty or a hundred acres, enclosed by stout ox fences grown to hold fattening cattle in their pasture. Across the chequered miles of gently undulating turf, horse and hound would race, flying from fence to ditch, shaking the ground with pounding hooves, the air singing with the sound of the horn and the hounds.

In her first Leicestershire season Nancy rode with the Pytchley Hunt, whose country had once been the scene of battle between Cavalier and Roundhead in England's murderous Civil War. It was a grand and exclusive fraternity, and still a man's world. Women who rode to hounds were a small minority, and frequently criticised. They were also, in principle, suspected of being 'fast', an image inspired by the legendary Victorian courtesan 'Skittles', whose lovers had included Napoleon III and the Prince of Wales. She too had hunted in Leicestershire, where she had long been remembered for her beauty and boldness both on and off a horse.

In the first years of the new century, while English magazines ran regular columns about the parties, travels, clothes and other excitements of Americans in London, it was rather a different matter in the shires, where such beings were more rarely glimpsed. There, the initial reaction of many Englishmen – and of their readily jealous wives – was suspicion of the seemingly crisp ways and well-laundered appearance of American women, in stark contrast with the languid, willowy demeanour of English girls. It was increased not only by the latent resentment of landowners whose livelihood had been jeopardised by low-priced American imports, but also by ignorance: Nancy often recalled that some of her early English acquaintances thought that America was peopled mainly by redskins, while others were sure that the Civil War had been fought between North and South America.

Nevertheless, into the exclusive and largely xenophobic atmosphere of Leicestershire hunting there now trotted Nancy. As a woman and also an American, she was a ready target for the haughty looks, the turning of backs and the closing of ranks of which the English were past masters. But she was game for all that, partly through her cavalier nature but also because she had the advantage of being an extremely good horsewoman, a skill that was to provide a short cut into the tightly knit upper-class hunting set, and from there to fashionable London society. The Americans who had preceded her out hunting in England had mostly been unused to the deep ditches and high hedges of the shires, but Nancy was a hard rider and for her the terrain presented few problems. Her appearance was also in her favour: dressed to kill in top hat, flared Wolmerhausen Melton jacket, white cambric tie and coral pin, she presented to the cocksure, forbidding, weather-beaten habitués around her a charming, decorative picture.

In the hunting field she admitted to difficulty in finding her way across country, but despite initial doubts and distaste, people soon began to note her grace and courage in the saddle. It was also not long before they saw that here was no shrinking violet, ready to accept the role of newcomer on sufferance. In fact her whiplash repartee escaped on her first day out. She was determined to impress the field, and so arrived on the largest hireling she could find, a proper, go-where-you-please hunter. She was soon unseated by a low-hanging branch, and as she got to her feet, a soldierly man rode up and asked if he could hold her horse and help her to mount. It was a reasonable offer, as it was unusual for women to mount without help, but Nancy treated it as a bruise to add to those on her body, and flashed back, 'You don't suppose, do you, that I'd be such an ass as to come out huntin' if I couldn't mount from the ground?' This startling reply was soon travelling around the hunting field.

A little later, while waiting for hounds to appear from a wood, a matronly lady observed archly to Nancy, 'I suppose you've come over here to capture one of our husbands.' 'If,' Nancy retorted, 'you knew what trouble I had in gettin' rid of my own, you'd know I don't want any of yours.' After a moment's gasping silence, laughter broke out: the ice was broken, and Nancy had made a new friend.[1]

Impish and outspoken, with a mixture of effrontery and charm, she spurned English self-restraint, and soon attracted a reputation for wit; that can be a mixed blessing, however, if its owner feels it has at all times to be maintained. That might have been the case with Nancy. A friend who had met her in America told how she heard her making fun of the garish colours worn by those who rode to hounds through the winter and in summer played cricket for a fashionable club called I Zingari:

> I remember her on one occasion asking a man who wore the red, black and orange Zingaree ribbon why he wore such bright colours. He told her what it was. 'What's that?' she said. 'Some kind of marmalade?' Within half an hour she repeated the same remark, having led up to it with the same question to someone else . . .[2]

Despite the occasional barb, Nancy usually meant well. Gradually regaining her sense of fun as the harsh memories of her experiment with marriage began to fade, she became a sought-after guest at dances and dinner parties. On the other hand, it was soon suspected that she was sexually unavailable, a virtue lacking in many others of the hunting set. Her habits were sober, contrasting with her vivacity: she attended church regularly and avoided cards and gambling. Although at that time it was acceptable for women to drink sparingly, Nancy stuck to tea and barley water, abjuring alcohol altogether – memories of its effect on her brothers and father, and most of all on her husband, having firmly convinced her that drink had no merits.

Except in a few cases Nancy avoided Christian names, but in other respects she adopted a casual American attitude to many conventions, and her presence often proved a welcome leavening at many Leicestershire parties, which were often heavy going despite the hedonistic nature of the guests. She also recalled that despite her alluring looks, she was treated with propriety and unfailing courtesy. She might not at first have expected it from some of the leading figures in the social landscape, such as Lady de Trafford, 'a sleek jackdaw', and her husband, Sir Humphrey, known as the 'Wicked Squire'. Yet of the things that struck her during her first year in England, she particularly remembered 'how chivalrous most Englishmen were, and how correct their attitude was towards women', adding, 'I was tremendously looked after and taken care of. At that time women were treated with a respect and courtesy they probably forfeited when they cut off their hair and their skirts. I began to live again.'

Despite her skill in the saddle, and perhaps because of some pique at her swift success, she was not universally liked. Her wit could disarm animosity, but its mixture of timing, gaiety and impertinence was often in unwelcome proportions. 'I had a sharp tongue,' she wrote, 'and I was quick off the trigger. Things just popped out.' Among the many things that Miss Brown's Academy had failed to teach her was the custom in society that good-natured wit was well received but the caustic variety was not.

She also acquired a reputation for following too closely in the hunting field, a dangerous habit that on one occasion led to an exchange in which for once she did not have the last word. Waiting by a covert one afternoon, she found herself next to a well-known member of the Pytchley, who remarked that he intended selling his horses at the end of the season. 'They're no use to me,' said Nancy. 'I've given up keepin' carriages.' 'Never mind that,' returned the man, somewhat nettled. 'One might serve to draw the hearse for the next man you jump on.'

On the surface it seemed that as the months passed Nancy was recovering the liveliness that had faded with the strain of her marriage, and retrieving her effervescent blend of courage, frankness, simplicity and wit. Unhappy memories of her married life appeared to recede, and she was also cheered to see Bobbie thriving in his new surroundings. With her natural self-confidence she began to make many friends in Leicestershire, and although neuralgia and its accompanying malaise still laid her low from time to time, her energy in the hunting field seemed to add to her resilience.

Her natural gregariousness soon began to draw her more frequently to London. This two-way pull was noted by the press, which drew attention to her connection with Dana and Irene, who had been feted by the newspapers during their time in London. Early in 1905, a society magazine published a photograph of Nancy beautifully decked out in lace and jewels, the authoritative tone of its accompanying comments disguising its guesswork:

> We publish this week a very charming photograph of Mrs Langhorne Shaw, who is spending the winter at Market Harborough, where she has taken a house for the hunting season. There was a great idea amongst those who know her that she had made up her mind to live over here altogether; but this she never intended. She does not mean to go in for general society in England at all. On the contrary, she has arranged to return to Virginia so soon as the hunting season is over. Her young son, who is quite a child, and one of her sisters are with her.[3]

Reports of her intention not to 'go in for general society' were proving wide of the mark. She would spend much of the winter deep in the country, trying to iron the sorrows out of her soul, seeking consolation in the company of her son, but she also began to respond to the call of London society as well as of the hunting elite.

On 17 February 1905, at the first court of the year, Nancy was presented to the King and Queen. It was a privilege that required a certain amount of finesse. At that time the court was barred to a woman who had been divorced by her husband. However, a lady who had herself been the petitioner for divorce was permitted to explain the details to the Lord Chamberlain, who might sometimes be persuaded that presentation at court would after all be acceptable. Nancy's case was put forward by the wife of the American ambassador, Joseph Choate, and permission was duly granted. Dressed in lace and silver cloth, the customary three white feathers entwined in her hair, and wearing what the press described as magnificent diamonds, she made her curtsey to King Edward VII and Queen Alexandra.

Observing a number of such presentations, the gossip columns had noted that 'the American girl entirely lacks the shyness which so often spoils the ceremony for her English sister, but regards it merely as an amusing, very pleasurable and unique incident not to be missed on any account'. Nancy appeared to agree, at least in part:

> . . . for perhaps the first time in my life I felt desperately shy when my name was called out and I had to walk alone past the experienced eye of King Edward. The fantastic splendour of it all, the gold plate, the flunkeys in their scarlet uniforms and powdered hair, I found magnificent but just a little amusing. I had never seen anything like it before. But I was never much impressed by ceremonial show.[4]

Impressed or not, it was not to be long before flunkeys and powdered hair would be fully in evidence in her own household.

Despite her apparent cheerfulness, however, Nancy was often tense and unsettled. She had no permanent home in England, only hotel rooms and rented hunting boxes of limited comfort. Her intense love for Bobbie kept her continually anxious for his happiness, while driving herself at full pace both to forget her marriage and to keep ill health at bay.

Although most of her new friends among the hunting men impressed her with their propriety and courtesy, some of them expressed more natural feelings. She deflected them with a cheerful but apparently firm lack of interest: at one dance a man who had been assiduously paying her attention finally said, 'I would like to ask you to kiss me, Mrs Shaw, but I am afraid you would tell my wife.'

> 'I would not tell your wife,' I assured him.
> 'You wouldn't?' he said, brightening.
> I said, 'No, I would tell the whole hunting field' . . .

There were other similar instances. As Nancy recalled:

> I made a rule never to let anyone see me home. There was a certain society Gallant, who was later co-respondent in several divorce cases. He saw me to my cab and said: 'Poor Mrs Shaw. Not much fun, a maid to see you home!' I said, 'If I'd known who I was going to meet, I would have had a policeman.'[5]

She regarded herself as lucky that vice held no allure for her: when a friend said to her, 'I don't understand you. You are so proper and prudish, and you don't have any affairs. What is the matter with you?' Nancy replied, 'I have looked at the faces of the women who have had that kind of life and – no, thank you, I prefer to go my own way.'[6]

Nevertheless, she recalled, she had suitors and to spare, 'but with wisdom beyond my years I kept them all at bay'. Her claim was quite justified: only a short time after her arrival in England, a number of drones had begun to buzz around her hive. The speed with which some of them reacted to her presence is partly explained by the traditionally short interval between the ritual of 'coming out' in English society and receiving a proposal of marriage. At seventeen, a girl of good family would leave the schoolroom and for the first time put her hair up, in effect a sign that she had entered the marriage market, there to remain, she, or at least her parents, might hope, for a short time only. Consequently, as in America, it was quite usual for proposals to be made on comparatively short acquaintance.

Accordingly, Nancy was soon an object of desire, and she began to attract and reciprocate the sentiments of two men in particular. The first was John Baring, who had become Lord Revelstoke on his father's death in 1897. An exceptionally capable banker, he headed the family firm, Baring Brothers, which was by then one of the world's foremost finance houses, although not many years earlier it had tottered on the edge of a collapse caused by ill-starred speculation.

Revelstoke had won his spurs by returning Barings from its brush with bankruptcy to health and prosperity, and a decade or so later the firm was back in clover, with the family restored to the life to which it had been accustomed. Revelstoke himself was able to hunt in Leicestershire, patronise top craftsmen like Fabergé, and indulge his guests in the finest wine and food – his cook, the celebrated Rosa Lewis, was probably the best in England. He now drove beautiful carriages – and motor cars, the new luxury – and bought a splendid 150-ton yacht, *Water Witch*. King Edward, an expert in such matters, dubbed him the 'Prince of Bon Viveurs'. Baring was a good-looking man who delighted in the company of pretty women, but, aged forty-one, he was still unmarried. Now his eye lighted upon Nancy, fifteen years his junior, and soon after his first sight of the sparkling young Virginian he fell in love.[7]

They were introduced in October 1904, and their friendship soon became close. Revelstoke proved a gushing source of letters and telegrams, besides assiduously paying Nancy the small attentions of a suitor – such as arranging for her train to be met by a servant bearing a pot of caviar, to nourish her after she had journeyed through the snow to dine with him in London early in the new year. Although such gestures contrasted with other, more solemn, aspects of his character, he was generous with presents, especially of pearls – highly prized in the days before cultured pearls.

Unfortunately Nancy's letters to Revelstoke seem to have been lost, but his to her have survived. She appears to have responded warmly to his advances, sending him her photograph, and their correspondence portrays a friendship that before long began to verge on love. Yet Revelstoke worried about Nancy's mercurial changes between affection and coldness, writing at the end of March:

> . . . I really can't bear that kind of letter from you. It makes me deeply unhappy. But don't you think that it is a bad attack of nerves on both sides? Because, just think, nothing has changed since last Saturday evening, has it? Or have you forgotten our conversation and the 'Knees of the Gods' – and everything? I thought it was a happy talk? Yet everything has gone impossibly wrong since . . .[8]

For all his importance, the infatuated Revelstoke was reduced to meek docility in the face of Nancy's capricious outbursts. Yet her liking for her Apollo, as she described him, increased to the point where she was 'deliriously happy', the more so as her happiness was spiced with physical desire, a feeling that seemed hardly to stir her at other times in her life. Much as both might secretly have wanted it, however, her rigid moral principles, and his sense of propriety, precluded sex from sealing their affair. But they had become so close in other respects that Revelstoke believed that Nancy had got to know him 'as well as any one human being can know another'. They began to discuss their future together, although without becoming officially engaged.

Plenty of hunting and the fresh air of an English winter proved a tonic for Nancy's looks, which were enhanced further by the smartness of hunting clothes and a naturally good dress sense. These, together with her invigorating character, strongly attracted a number of other admirers, the most assiduous of whom was Sidney, 16th Baron Elphinstone, who began to pay court to her soon after meeting her during the early months of 1905. He was a good-natured and dashing scion of a landowning family from the Scottish borders, and he opened his heart to Nancy with an infectious enthusiasm. His chief pleasure was the pursuit of prey of many varieties, and although he did not bother with hunting, he began repeatedly going to Leicestershire in order to be in Nancy's company.

Originally, Nancy had planned to return to Virginia as soon as the hunting season ended in April. Instead, she and Phyllis went on a motoring tour in France, despite Nancy having formed a dislike of the French, even if from intuition rather than experience:

> We went to Paris, where we saw some French plays, but I was no fonder then of the French theatre than I am now. They always seem to be about one thing only – going to bed with the wrong woman . . . The only people I have always found it difficult to understand are the Latins. They look at life from an entirely different angle. They have a different approach and an entirely different set of moral values – which permits them to be proud about, and boast of, things no other man would be anything but heartily ashamed of.[9]

Her rather prudish views were not widely shared among the circle she was soon to join in Edwardian England.

Meanwhile, turning from the beds of Paris, Nancy and Phyllis were chauffeured around the French countryside, swathed in the veils and other protective clothes essential at that time, as the open cars struggled and bumped along the unpaved roads, with ankle-deep dust rising like steam around them. They had arranged to meet Lord Revelstoke in Monte Carlo, but whether from impatience to get home, or in one of her sudden changes of heart, Nancy cancelled the rendezvous before they reached it.

Back in England, taken up with Revelstoke, and with the infectiously attractive Elphinstone also pressing his attentions upon her, Nancy abandoned her plans for returning to America and instead arranged to stay, together with Bobbie and his nurse, with Mrs Astor, who had taken a house near London's Regent's Park.

By May, the London Season was in full swing, and Nancy was ready to play her part. She had enough money to buy fine clothes, and to spend her time entirely as she wished. Pretty, single and high-spirited, she seemed to add a little lustre even to the glittering social round into which she was now invited. Her entrée into society had been formalised by her presentation at court, and her acquaintance quickly widened as she was swept up in a whirl of courts, levées, banquets, promenades, lunches, tea parties, bazaars, dinners, theatre, opera, concerts, dances, balls, house parties, horse shows, polo, racing and regattas.

In July, after two energetic months, the Season drew near its close. Although by custom it was followed by Cowes, cricket, and the shooting of grouse, partridge and pheasant, before another five months' hunting, Nancy and Phyllis decided to return to America on 5 July. Revelstoke was downcast:

> I hate to think of you going away; you have been so *very* wonderful and perfect that it is impossible to write about it. But you understand all is well and have been very, *very* golden . . . It's quite impossible to write today, Nancy dear, I simply can't. My heart is so full.[10]

Nancy's heart was not so full: deep down, she still felt the scars of marriage, although, far from the scene of its unhappiness, the wounds were healing. In fact, there was now a very real possibility that she might actually marry again. Just as she was setting off for the liner that would take her home, she received a rather dramatic proposal from the irrepressible Lord Elphinstone, who had boarded her train as it was leaving London, entered her compartment, and asked her to be his wife. She declined the offer, but not so emphatically or finally as to put him off, and during the following months he matched Lord Revelstoke by sending her a series of letters to which she seemed happy to respond.

Whether to settle for an English husband, and if so, whom, was a question that, perhaps not too seriously, she had put to a new friend, Henry Asquith, a leading barrister and deputy leader of the Liberal opposition in Parliament. Nancy had been introduced to Asquith and his wife Margot in London, and in due course they were to become good friends. Asquith failed to come up with an answer, and after she had been back in America for some time, Nancy wrote to remind him of her quest. This time, he did reply:

> You must not reproach me, my dear Mrs Shaw;
> It's not like a Redskin selecting a squaw;
> For there's no tougher problem, in logic or law
> Than to find a fit mate for the lady called Shaw.

'You would have adopted a gentler and more patient tone,' he continued, 'if you had known or guessed – as you ought to have done, for what is a woman worth who is without these finer & subtler intuitions? – what hours of hard but futile thinking, of eager but baffled searching, I have given to the fulfilment of my promise . . .'[11]

Back at Mirador with Bobbie, and happy to be with her father again, the pleasures and emotions of her time in England receded a little into the distance. But she did not withdraw entirely, taking up once more with her friends in America, and seeing some of those she had met in England who were now on their own journeys abroad, including Prince Louis of Battenberg, whom Nancy entertained in New York. At the end of October she went up to Roslyn to support her old friend Alice Babcock at her marriage – where, as had occurred in England, she was sighted by society columnists:

> Mrs John Jacob Astor, who has always been a great friend of Miss Babcock's, was one of the handsomest women present, and of course Mrs Langhorne Shaw came in for much admiration. She was the matron of honour, and was beautifully dressed as usual, and looked very graceful and charming, besides being the life of the party.[12]

Whether, as the winter of 1905 drew near, Nancy was still thinking of her recent English amours is no longer clear, but she had not forgotten the exhilaration of her season's hunting, and she now asked her father to send her back for more. So it was arranged that she would return to England in time for Christmas, together with Chillie and Nora, as well as Bobbie and the customary retinue of servants.

In December 1905, they journeyed to New York to board the White Star Line's SS *Cedric*. The ship was the last word in transatlantic luxury. Lying sleek and smart alongside its berth in New York harbour, and towering above the quay, it seemed strong enough to surmount even the fiercest storm at sea. At the dockside, the crowd of passengers travelling steerage, herded and hurried by brisk officials, filed down the gangways to quarters far below; in the quiet and spacious part of the ship, smiling white-coated stewards stood waiting to greet those in first class. On the quay, Nancy was talking to a group of friends including Ava Astor, who had come down to see off a young cousin of hers, called Waldorf. He was 'very good looking', Nancy recalled, as she was introduced to him. Tall, dark and in his mid-twenties, he seemed slightly reserved as he stood talking quietly in a low-pitched voice.

As the *Cedric* ploughed through the giant waves of the North Atlantic, even the first-class cabins shuddered and heaved and plunged. Nancy, a poor sailor, remained below. Waldorf, it seems, had been entranced by his first, brief meeting with her; she later discovered that within a very short time 'he had made up his mind that he was going to marry me'.[13] For the time being, however, deprived of the chance of seeing her, he turned his attention to her father.

Meanwhile, another, and more emotional, suitor was ready to renew his advances. Word had reached England of Nancy's imminent return, and at the end of November Lord Elphinstone had dispatched an excited letter:

Dear Mrs Shaw,
    . . . Hooray . . . It is ripping to think you'll be here before Xmas but there are such a lot of things I want to know. Are you coming alone, and where are you going to first? It's no good trying to write a letter because I can only think of one thing and that is that you're coming and will be here soon, and I shall really see you again before long . . .[14]

The *Cedric* was due on 14 December, and Elphinstone could hardly wait. As the ship drew near, he hurried to Liverpool and booked into the station hotel, ready for the liner's arrival, telegraphing to Nancy on board:

I was the last to say goodbye to you when you left and I want to be the first to welcome you to England again. I've told them to reserve a carriage for you on the special train . . . May I go back with you? I'll come to the landing place in the morning and see if I can do anything for you.[15]

Whether he did go back with her is not recorded, but Nancy clearly again left him with hope. He was soon back in Scotland, promising to send violets from his gardens and to book a box for a pantomime after Christmas, presumably with Bobbie in mind. 'The violets are going off today,' he wrote, 'and I told the gardener to send rather a nice orchid which is out. I do wish I could do something – anything – to help you . . .'

'. . . How I wish,' he added, varying his theme, 'we were peacefully going to get onto a boat and go to Ceylon!'

The Langhorne family spent Christmas 1905 at Fleming's Hotel, Chillie busy with juleps and eggnogs: in whatever country he was, as his relations used to say, he was always himself. It was perhaps unfortunate, therefore, that one of the friends that Nancy introduced to him in London was Lord Revelstoke. It was not a successful meeting. Revelstoke may not have concealed his self-importance, which, alongside his oppressive gravity, would have tested the patience of a man like Chillie; at all events he made a poor impression.

In due course Nancy found a house in Leicestershire from which to resume hunting, taking High Crest from a Mrs Peabody, in Market Harborough. She began to go out with a number of different hunts, first with the Fernie, then the Warwickshire, and the press also noted her out hunting with the Duke of Beaufort's hounds in Gloucestershire, looking 'as charming as ever, and everyone in that country is delighted to have her amongst them. She is very much captivated by English life . . .'16

She was becoming less captivated, however, with the men who wanted to marry her. But Elphinstone persisted, believing that the time he had spent with her since her return had improved his chances of winning her. He admitted to her on 8 February that he had been mad to propose in the train as she was going back to America the previous summer . . .

. . . and still madder to have hoped you might have said yes on what was after all a very short acquaintance and really you knew as little of me or my past as I did of yours. Now we know each other very well – my love for you has grown and grown till it has swallowed up everything else and becomes the whole world to me and I hope and pray I may some day win your love . . .17

Three other men, Nancy later wrote, proposed to her that season, while Revelstoke also continued to press his case. Five proposals of marriage, from men in fashionable society, to an American who was not thought to be a great heiress and who had only lately appeared in England, was testimony to both her physical attraction and her captivating vitality. But she remained wary of letting her heart rule her head for a second time, and her devotion to Bobbie and the unsettled nature of her life ensured that she remained cautious. In fact her mood now changed, and, no longer responsive towards the men who had been courting her in England, she became deaf to persuasion. Revelstoke was the first casualty.

The great banker was convinced that he and Nancy had been brought together by fate. Obedient to its decree, he embarked on his plan, an important part of which was to examine Nancy on whether she would enjoy being the wife of a leading international financier, the career to which he was committed. He could leave her in no doubt of her duty, and of what would be required of her, but he did not help his case by the portentous manner in which he made his points – asking her whether she would be able to mix with 'Kings and Queens and Ambassadors' as his banking career would demand of both him and his wife.

But there may have been doubts in his own mind. In the summer, a friend had written to him in rather blunt terms: 'The only thing I ask myself about you [and Nancy] is that (I have not seen her very often) the thing that has principally struck me about her is her enormous vitality and quickness, and I ask myself whether she could stand you and your many business preoccupations for the term of your natural life.'

Revelstoke was far from pleased to be given such frank advice, but he had disclosed it to Nancy in one of his letters to her after she had returned to America. 'It went like a knife into me,' he told her, 'as it was a friend, and not meant spitefully to me.'[18]

Confronted with all this questioning, Nancy reacted hotly, accusing him of thinking her empty-headed. But then she too began to reconsider: perhaps she was after all rather lively, and too self-centred, for a supporting role on such a formal stage – although as things were to turn out, that would prove not to be the case; she would in due course become famous for entertaining Kings and Queens and Ambassadors, and countless others as well.

She now began to regain her balance and to see things differently, unmoved by the notes and telegrams that continued to arrive from Revelstoke.

I came to my senses and discovered that he was an appalling snob. Other things also came to light. I had taken it for granted he was an unattached bachelor, but he wasn't. He had been having an affair that had gone on for years, with a married woman years older than I was . . .[19]

For Nancy had now convinced herself that Revelstoke was in love with another woman: Lady Desborough, a fashionable hostess, particularly to the group of well-born intellectual friends known as the Souls. Some of Revelstoke's letters, written to Lady Desborough long before he had taken up with Nancy, clearly implied some form of passion, but it seems probable that after Nancy arrived on the scene he had switched his affections to her. The fact that she was able to do no more than guess at the truth made no difference to Nancy, however: she was very possessive and now felt scorned.

Years later, she recalled her feelings:

Then I fell in love, but not with the right man. How difficult it is to remember old love stories. It is like trying to remember what daffodils looked like, when snow is on the ground. For a time I was deliriously happy, the way young people in love are happy – so that when I look back on those days, the sun seems always to have been shining. Falling in love is a sort of disease. If you are balanced there must come a time when you stand back, and wonder dispassionately what it is you love. He had wit and charm and an amusing mind, but he had not the right values . . .

   . . . Father disapproved of him on sight. He saw through him. But I thought him Apollo (although he was bald). . .[20]

Revelstoke was rejected.

Meanwhile, despite her underlying wariness, Nancy continued to write to Elphinstone. Near the end of February he had again poured his heart out, saying how he had built up 'a happy, such a happy picture, these last weeks, of a happy, such a happy future'. But romance, it is said, is a bird that will not sing in every bush, and the happy baron, like the solemn Revelstoke, was soon to be overtaken by a new turn of events.

For now, after a brief interval, into the jousts with these champions of the English and Scottish peerage rode a third man determined to capture Nancy's heart: Waldorf Astor, the quiet American who had been entranced by his first sight of her laughing with her friends on the quay as they waited to board the *Cedric*.

He had found that the feelings sparked when he first set eyes on Nancy were kindled by meeting her with her family at Christmas in London. Even on Christmas Day he had written to her asking her to come and stay at Cliveden, his father's magnificent country house, and he soon reached the point at which he could not get her out of his mind. Now he resolved to win her.

Waldorf seemed to have much to envy: clever, handsome and good-natured, he was also immensely rich, heir to the wealth that his father, William Waldorf Astor, had himself inherited when Waldorf was a child, and which at that time amounted to the largest personal fortune in America.

The Astors were a remarkable family whose assets had grown in barely three generations from nothing to a dimension unrivalled almost anywhere in the world. A simple account of their rise was written by Waldorf's father in a magazine that he founded while building a press empire to accompany his other, more tangible assets. He described how his great-grandfather, John Jacob, a poor butcher's son, had left his native Germany and set out to find his fortune:

My great-grandfather was born in a peasant's cottage in the village of Waldorf, 'the village in a wood', near Heidelberg, on July 17, 1763. He received the usual parish school education and at the age of sixteen left home to escape a stepmother's ill usage. He set out on foot for the Rhine, and pausing for a last look at the familiar scenes he was to behold no more for many years, made three valuable resolves to which he adhered through life – to be honest, to be industrious, and never to gamble . . .[21]

Having reached New York, John Jacob found his way into the already profitable fur trade, where he set about mastering its intricacies until, gradually but with 'unremitting vigour', he won an unrivalled position. He would travel deep into unexplored territory, displaying great courage in facing hostile men and animals, bargaining with the Indians he met in faraway places and buying their furs in return for alcohol. Then he would make his way back from the wild interior to direct, from a counting-house in New York, all the ensuing commercial details.

Eventually his endeavours paid off handsomely, and by the end of the eighteenth century he had acquired a fleet of a dozen ships – 'a million dollars afloat', as he described it. Circumnavigating the globe, they would sail to England laden with furs to sell in exchange for British goods; then on to China, before returning finally to America, the holds stacked with tea. Making and executing plans of great complexity, overcoming political upheavals and severe reverses, John Jacob Astor finally found his fortune.

At sixty-four he retired from active trading, enormous riches safely banked. By then, he had presciently ensured that the family's assets were, quite literally, set in stone. Realising that New York, a commercial hub even when he first reached America, was set to grow far beyond the scale and ideas of his day, he channelled the increasingly fast-flowing profits of his trading empire into real estate on New York Island.

These purchases were made with such judgment in the line of approaching expansion as frequently to be sold again after a few years for double or treble what he had paid for them. With enlarged means these acquisitions of real estate assumed larger proportions, and took in whole farms, which gradually became covered with houses . . .[22]

By the time John Jacob's great-grandson, William Waldorf, was thirty, there was no longer much need to make money, merely to keep an iron resolve and to count it.

William Waldorf Astor was himself a remarkable man. Born in 1848, the year John Jacob died, he was the only child of parents with fixed conceptions of right and wrong. He grew up tall and good-looking, his piercing blue eyes contributing to a slightly forbidding aspect, and he kept healthy, becoming adept at boxing and fencing. But his nature was romantic, and he was deeply affected when he and the love of his youth were separated at the insistence of his parents, who had discovered that there was tuber-culosis in the girl's family, a disease then deadly and believed to be hereditary. 'At twenty-one,' he recorded in a memoir, 'a love affair with a young lady of rare charm touched me . . . it was a strange and delicious emotion, an intense dreaming and anguish . . . the remembrance of my first love keeps its lifelong charm. She has always been the Princess of my fairy tale . . . Had we been allowed to marry,' he added, 'would life have been happier for us both?'[23]

By 1877, William had been handed complete control of his father's busi-ness affairs. He then decided to try for politics. 'It was a fine roll in the mire,' he recalled, and although by hard work as well as well-directed dona-tions he was elected both to the New York State Assembly and then to its Senate, the commentaries on his campaign were unflattering. At the same time, the newly emergent 'Yellow Press' sustained a series of attacks on his family in general and on him in particular. It left him with a lasting contempt for the American press – 'that atrocity', as he called it – and, at a deeper level, with an incipient dislike of America itself.[24]

Meanwhile, in 1878, he had married Mary Dahlgren Paul. Dark and beautiful, a former belle of Philadelphia, 'Mamie' was to prove a loving mother to Waldorf, born a year later; to his sister Pauline; to their younger brother John Jacob; and to Gwendolyn, who was to die young. Another child, Rudolph, had died in infancy.

William Astor's disaffection with the United States became sharper when he received kidnap threats to his children – he was later to sleep with two loaded revolvers by his bed in fear of his own life. He therefore resolved finally to activate a plan that had long been in his mind: to leave America for good. Determined to bring his children up in what he saw as a safer and more civilised country, in 1891 he emigrated to England.

Once there, he began to live on a stupendous scale. He leased Taplow Court, overlooking the Thames near Maidenhead, and rented Lansdowne House, an enormous property off London's Berkeley Square, before buying a lease in Carlton House Terrace, thereby installing himself among the highest and richest in the land. In 1895, he built another house, largely to serve as an office to administer the Astor estate, the revenues of which exceeded those of many sovereign countries. Built in the 'Francois Premier' style, it stood on the newly reclaimed Victoria Embankment, next to the Temple Gardens, overlooking the river.

However, William's most inspired transaction, and the one that was deeply to colour the lives of Waldorf and Nancy, was the purchase of Cliveden from the Duke of Westminster. It was a country estate dominated by a majestic house conceived at the very end of the Palladian tradition, and was situated a mere twenty miles from London. Queen Victoria, who had stayed at the house eight times over the previous forty years, was not amused when she heard of its sale to the American newcomer, saying how *grievous* it was that it should fall into 'these hands'. In reality, however, it would have been hard to find hands more suitable than those of William Waldorf, who at once began to endow the estate with his sense of history, romantic imagination and money bags.

Set high above a beautiful reach of the Thames near Maidenhead, where woods of beech, yew and elm stretched to the river below, the imposing Italianate mansion commanded a wide prospect of the verdant Thames valley and of the sleek ribbon of water meandering towards Windsor Castle, a few miles distant. Cliveden's new owner was entranced by what he found, but soon developed grandiose plans for its refurbishment.

Waldorf had been twelve when his father decided to settle permanently in England, and had spent the ensuing years under his father's various roofs. In 1905, when he first met Nancy, he was still living mainly at Cliveden, but his father was away for much of the time and it was rather an isolated existence. Waldorf was then twenty-six, and his outlook and character reflected not just a complex mixture of American childhood and English youth, but also an upbringing at the hands of an extraordinary father, who within a decade was significantly to affect the direction of his son's life, and that of Nancy also.

Waldorf's mother had died suddenly just before Christmas 1894; it was very distressing for the fifteen-year-old boy and it also had a great effect on the character of his father, whose attitude to both friends and family seemed to change radically. His wife's death, added to his unhappiness at the loss of an infant son a few years earlier, cast a pall over William, and he gradually withdrew, increasingly vain and humourless, into his own private world.

As Waldorf's youth progressed, his father's shyness and lack of tact gradually hardened into a dictatorial manner, expressed not least in harassing his family and guests with an obsessive insistence on punctuality. Yet although remote and stern, William remained enormously generous to his children. 'He gave much thought to us,' remembered his younger son, 'and spoilt us beyond measure. No presents at Christmas or Birthday were too good for us; seldom was any wish not met, for example the covered tennis court, the riding-school which Waldorf asked for.' But while he wanted his children to be happy, and to have the very best, he did not seem to want to play a close part in their lives, and Waldorf felt deeply the distance between them.

Waldorf's formative years, their background of luxury marred by a strange mixture of coldness and kindliness, were stamped also by an education of the sort that his father hoped would make him a proper Englishman. He was sent to a typical preparatory school, and then to Eton. There he overcame the hurdle of being American, and having rather a strange home life, and excelled at both work and games. He rowed for the school, won several academic prizes, and was elected to Eton's most exclusive and influential society.[25] His father's hopes were amply realised.

Waldorf's education was completed by four years at Oxford. There, in contrast to the rather earnest approach to life that soon afterwards became his hallmark, his work came second to sport and his social life. He was awarded a fourth-class history degree, but to his peers if not the dons, his academic achievements were eclipsed by his being an excellent oarsman, master of the Oxford draghounds, captain of the university fencing and polo teams, and a skilled steeplechaser, the winner of several races.

He then had the great misfortune to overdo his involvement in these energetic activities and strain his heart, in which there had been a sign of weakness even at Eton; that, together with suggestions of tuberculosis, largely put an end to his rowing, riding and also to the winter sports that he loved. It did mean, though, that he was able to find the time for a first serious interest in politics, joining the Chatham Club, where he was a frequent debater – no doubt heedless of Ruskin's dictum that undergraduates had no more business with politics than with rat-catching.

The splendours of Oxford were followed by miseries, some of which were witnessed by Princess Marie of Roumania, a very close friend of Waldorf and his sister Pauline. She related how Waldorf was distressed by his father's seemingly cold and hard attitude, and by feeling that he had no encouragement or love, nor any real home; and how he was further upset when his sister Gwendolyn, who had struggled through childhood with a weak heart, died aged eight.

It all contributed to his having a breakdown, afterwards complicated by a difficult operation and a long convalescence. He was then made to join the Inner Temple and to spend a year in a lawyer's office, where he was allotted a sparse room with a window overlooking a brick wall. Each day he would travel to the office, if in slightly grander style than most commuters, but as relieved as any to go home in the evening, and, at Cliveden's park gates, as he told Nancy, to 'chuck hat and coat in the carriage, and walk up the Green Drive'. He greatly disliked his time there, and found only slight relief after moving to a desk job at his father's influential and highly regarded London evening newspaper, the *Pall Mall Gazette* – cradle of the careers of, among others, Hilaire Belloc, H.G. Wells, J.M. Barrie and Rudyard Kipling.

For Waldorf, rebellion as a response to his upbringing was ruled out by his nature, and more particularly by his father's strength of character and position as head of the family. Instead he grew into a patient, tolerant man, his fair share of the Astor willpower camouflaged by kindly good nature. Yet at the time he first met Nancy, he was discontented, partly by still having no home of his own, and continuing to live in a part of his father's house.

Waldorf's luxurious surroundings gave him no real satisfaction, even if he was wryly amused at their formality; alone in Cliveden's stately dining room, motionless servants awaiting his command, he would often dine in silence. Even when his father was at home there was not much conviviality, as there was little meeting of minds between parent and child. On 25 February Waldorf wrote:

> . . . Many a time have I returned tired but happy from a good day in the Vale of Aylesbury, gone through a tiresome, slow train journey, arrived home bubbling with youth just in time for dinner. And then – not a word; all attempts no good; bit by bit all the jolly recollections have faded away in front of lengthy dissertations upon Hever and the Boleyn family. No wonder that the next day I'd neglect the book which had been given to me to read and go and ostentatiously ride three ponies and two hunters one after the other . . .[26]

The obstacles that Waldorf felt had confronted him during a strange and rather lonely childhood had added a reserve of determination to his innately gentle character. Now, in early 1906, he drew upon it as the full swing of the hunting season gave him the opportunity to enter the chase for the lady for whom he had fallen.

He set about building upon his introduction by arranging to be at a number of the same events as Nancy, which his natural efficiency, family name and deep pocket made possible. And when there was no hunting, or when Nancy came up to London to shop or see friends, he would ensure that he too was there to meet her.

At some point near the beginning of the year there came an electric moment when a word or look or gesture from Nancy seemed to show him favour and filled him with hope. At once he began to send her letters expressing, at first tentatively, but soon explicitly, the thoughts that had begun to swirl through his mind. During January and into February he courted her with fervour, seeing her more and more often, writing to her and sending telegrams whenever he had to be away. Nancy received his attentions with increasing interest, even in the midst of her convivial hunting life. Yet her uneven state of mind – still disturbed by her recent past, by anxiety about Bobbie, and by bouts of neuralgia – was further unsettled by Waldorf's addresses. She answered them with the contrasting mix of qualities in her character, by turn capricious, charming, harsh, scornful, sweet and cruel.

In letters Waldorf wrote to Nancy in February and March 1906, he disclosed his increasing passion, explaining his background – why, as an American, he lived in England – and describing the emotions his upbringing there had engendered. 'I've fought prejudices before,' he said. 'In a way, all my life I've had to fight against difficulties – in England at school I was a foreigner; I was sent there too old, with no education. I fought it all – worked hard, and from having been last, came to be first. This was when I was quite a little boy, before going to Eton.'

Later he told her how, through success at Eton and then Oxford, he had overcome the difficulties his background had at first caused him with his English contemporaries; and he described how this success had come too late to share with his father, who, although well meaning, had lost the will or the ability to display more than token sympathy or interest. Yet Waldorf had hardly complained; the magnificence of his surroundings helped him maintain his outward spirits and mitigated a little his inner unhappiness. However, he had been deprived of his closest companion, his sister Pauline, when she had married in 1904, and that made him even more vulnerable to a lack of family warmth; it perhaps intensified the ardour for Nancy that had now begun to consume him.

Besides sending loving letters, Waldorf paid her constant small attentions, and took an interest in Bobbie, who, albeit with a nanny to look after him, was with Nancy all through the months of Waldorf's courtship. Although she often had the use of Lord Elphinstone's motor car to enable her to get to meets, Waldorf sent a pony and trap when she had need of one. When he did manage to meet her away from the hunting field, they talked over all manner of subjects besides hunting, and soon discovered with relief and pleasure that they shared many interests, likes and dislikes. He felt increasingly encouraged.

In a way it might seem strange that the quiet, diffident Waldorf had begun to enjoy so much the firebrand company of Nancy, but her character was an exciting contrast to the stiff formality of his childhood, from which he may have wished to escape. Perhaps it was the attraction of opposites: Nancy's impetuousness, lack of inhibition, combative intolerance and tendency to bully blending with Waldorf's reserve and deep well of sympathy.

Like Nancy, Waldorf was dogged by uncertain health. It would suddenly lay him low and force him to take to his bed, leaving her to the attentions of Lord Elphinstone and friends in the lively hunting crowd; and all the time the season drew nearer its close, after which their natural ways might part, making it hard for him to see her at all. Worse, her changes of mood temporarily sapped his confidence: just when he thought he was getting close to her, she would go cold, put him down and turn away to her other friends. She would reproach him for being cold himself, for not opening his heart, and would insist that he was too young to help Bobbie, and that his father would deplore him seeing her. Having been thrilled to believe at first that their feelings were mutual, he would be crushed by Nancy suddenly withdrawing, and would write to her in despair and misery:

You've so duly rubbed it into me, on any and every occasion, that I've none of the virtues of Elphinstone, that I'm merely a rotten sort of selfish, unhealthy, unlovable, untrustworthy sort of weakling, that I'm beginning to feel I've no right to ask you, or for the matter of that anyone else, to marry me. I've done my best, or at least I've always tried to. I've tried to face it all smiling, and bravely to bear up under all snubbing and abuse, but there comes a time when one feels one can do no more – when all the stuffing and kick has been knocked out of one, when there's nothing left but to turn one's face to the wall and to harden one's heart and to pray for strength, to put a smiling face on before the world. Nancy sometimes I hate you for all you make me suffer and yet all the time I love and adore you: you are all and everything to me; I would give anything in the world to win your love and trust and regard – to have the right of fighting your battles and protecting you from all the evils of the world, to have your confidence and sympathy. Nancy, dearest Nancy, I wish I felt as young as you are perpetually accusing me of looking. May God help and bless you, Nancy, may He grant my daily prayer.

Yet he could not be downhearted for long: he maintained his hopes, excused his faltering words, and kept up the quest.

Upset as she was by the recent past, uncertain of the present, anxious about the future, with the happiness of her child at the core of her well-being, Nancy, gregarious by temperament, was nevertheless intrigued by the rather solitary Waldorf. She was moved when he told her that he knew what she had endured, and that he understood the state she was in, and how he did not want to add to her worries in any way. She reverted to her charm and friendliness, and his hopes rose once more. He knew that he

could relieve her of the anxiety that she said hung over her, and it made
him realise how much he wanted to offer her a home:

> . . . Nancy, what is life without a home. Don't tell me that a big empty
> house is a home, that a few friends are satisfying . . . Nancy, home is
> the first thing, after that one can go forward. One can face the world
> from a substantial basis. One can try and help those that need help
> and care, dependent on one. One can take one's proper position in
> the world, for one has what is God's richest gift, a home. Yes, Nancy,
> that's at the bottom of all one's usefulness in this world. Nancy, all
> would I give up for a home, however small, with you. But there is no
> need of that. I can give you a home worthy of you, and you can give
> me one more than worthy of my deserts . . .

His resolve was quickened when he reflected that his father, of whom
he remained in awe, had told him that for his years he was older than
most, more settled in his ways, and that he should think of marriage. His
impatience became compelling, an urgency to win Nancy, to force her to
make up her mind, to make her choice. All his eager, jostling thoughts now
came together; consumed by desire, he sent her an impassioned appeal,
dressed in the most persuasive eloquence:

> Oh Nancy, dearest Nancy, you are all and everything to me. I worship
> and adore and love you. I have not the slightest hesitation or fear or
> misgiving. I have looked at it all calmly and impassionedly. I have
> studied it from your side, from your family's side, from your friends'
> and the world's side, and I know I'm right – I know it just as thor-
> oughly and absolutely as I know that I have prayed to God to give you
> to me and me to you – I know it just as certainly and surely as I know
> that you will agree with me, later on when you have cast hesitation
> and indecision aside, and when you have become strong, decided and
> trustful. I know it's hard dearest Nancy mine but I know also that
> peace perfect peace can only come when you say yes, and allow me to
> help you, and stand up by you – Oh Nancy I pray to God that He
> may show you this.

Nancy was finally convinced. The lingering doubts and anxieties in her
mind dissolved, in part dispelled by Bobbie's enthusiasm for her friendship
with Waldorf. Soon after sending his letter, Waldorf received her telegram
saying 'yes'.

Within a short time Nancy journeyed to see him at Cliveden, and for a moment their pleasure engulfed them. They wandered through the woods and magnificent grounds, sharing their ideas and making all manner of plans; and Nancy put her arms around his neck and told him how she liked getting close to him.

One obstacle now remained: William Waldorf Astor, spending the winter at his clifftop retreat at Sorrento, in the Bay of Naples. Perhaps he would object when he learned that his son had chosen not the daughter of a noble and ancient English dynasty but instead an American divorcée. Waldorf steeled himself to make the journey and address his father. Yet all anxiety proved unfounded, and William, consistent with the affection that at heart he felt for his children, obscured though it might be by aloof formality, responded warmly: 'I read with great interest your allusion to Mrs Shaw. You have my best sympathy and wishes in a matter which is of such vital importance to you . . . If she's good enough for you, Waldorf,' he said, 'she's good enough for me.'

He reacted not only with warmth but with astonishing generosity, giving as a wedding present the fabulous Sancy diamond,[27] one of the world's largest and most famous diamonds, which he had bought not long after his arrival in London, and also the Cliveden estate – conceding that it was 'the most magnificent wedding gift ever made, I should imagine'.[28] Even if it was the case that in handing over Cliveden he was in some degree influenced by sad memories of his dead wife and young daughter, it was a magnanimous decision.

Waldorf was overwhelmed. 'I feel a great deal and am kind of knocked flat as if a garden roller had passed over one,' he told Nancy. 'Great kindness and love and confidence like this absolutely knocks me silly . . . I feel quite crushed both by the responsibility which has been placed upon me and also by the prospect of great happiness which the future seems to present to me.'[29]

On 6 March, some three months after her first glimpse of Waldorf, Nancy told friends and family of his offer of marriage. The pleas and plaudits of the 16th Baron Elphinstone faded into the mist and snow of Leicestershire, as, on 7 March, she sent him a poignant letter of farewell, telling him finally that she could not reciprocate his love, that she had lost her heart to Waldorf Astor: 'When I think of your letters,' she wrote, 'and what they were to me, and though you wrote every day, what a long blank it seemed between them . . .' Elphinstone responded with despair: '. . . I had built up such a happy future, which half a dozen words from you yesterday crumbled into dust.' Three weeks later Revelstoke also accepted that he had lost the race: 'And you know, my dear,' he wrote, 'that nothing will ever be able to alter my friendship or my deep regard for you . . . may you ever have happiness.'

On 8 March, she told Chillie to announce the engagement: 'Dearest, dearest father,' she wrote. 'It's Waldorf . . . I am very much in love. More than I've ever been before in my life.' In the excitement of the moment, she might indeed have believed herself in love. Waldorf certainly was, yet it is hard to accept too readily that it was really so with Nancy; the correspondence between them does not indicate deep passion on her part, and it also seems that the care of Bobbie played a significant part in her decision. However, her father believed her and was delighted: he sent her a telegram expressing his feelings: 'I am very glad that you are in love for once in your life. It will do you good to feel the tender passion once.'[30]

On 11 March, William Astor wrote to Nancy, whom he had never met but who he realised was about to enter his family's life:

Dear Mrs Shaw,
   I have received a letter from Waldorf, written in terms of exuberant joy, in which he tells me that you have promised to marry him. I am writing these lines to assure you how earnestly I trust that this event may be a source of great happiness to you both . . .'[31]

Meanwhile, press references to Nancy began to multiply:

Everyone is much interested in the announcement of Mrs Langhorne Shaw's engagement to Mr Waldorf Astor. Mrs Shaw is one of the most charming Virginians who have ever come to England. She has made a very large number of friends since she first arrived last winter, when she hunted from Melton the whole season . . .'[32]

A week later, *The Queen*, fulsome if inaccurate, elaborated:

Everyone over here hopes very much that the wedding will take place in London, although I have been told it will be in Virginia. Mr Astor *père* is delighted at his son's choice, and everyone seems to think the engagement quite an ideal one. Mrs Shaw is a very clever woman; indeed, the fairy godmother seems to have endowed her with very many valuable gifts, and few people have such a power of attracting genuine friendship. She and Mr Astor met on board ship as they were crossing the Atlantic, and the latter never swerved from his allegiance from that moment . . .[33]

Tradesmen, even of the most distinguished variety, began to rub their hands: 'Fabergé,' Waldorf wrote on 18 April, 'calls me up twice a day on the 'phone', and Boucheron, a celebrated Paris jeweller, sent over a consignment for his inspection. American magazines also lapped up the story:

> Mrs Shaw is just the kind of woman to make a success in English Society. She has lots of esprit and without perhaps being a particularly pretty woman she is exceedingly attractive in appearance. She is svelte, chic and petite, with a girlish grace which is very fetching, and like her sister is fascinating in manner and conversation . . .[34]

Nancy's judgement was sound: over very many years, her feelings were to be more than reciprocated by Waldorf's steady love. The current between them flowed all the more easily with their shared desire to be kind to their fellow creatures and to do good wherever they saw a need. In any event, with his faithful heart and clear, determined mind, Waldorf was to prove the perfect complement for Nancy's mercurial qualities, providing her with a rock-solid base, and willing to tolerate her desire to be at the centre of any stage on which she walked.

Nancy now came up against a problem that she characteristically lost no time in meeting head-on. As part of her emancipation from the status of divorced single mother, and to satisfy the piety that mixed with her sometimes wild worldliness, she thought it of great importance to marry in church. However, the Anglican faith insisted that 'Those whom God hath joined together let no man put asunder', and did not allow divorcees to remarry in church. Nancy was not to be put off; she took Waldorf straight to the Bishop of London. They received a sympathetic hearing, and having listened to Nancy's claim that she had been in no way to blame for her divorce, the Bishop sanctioned a church service.

On 3 May, 1906, Waldorf and Nancy were married at All Souls, Langham Place, by Rev. Francis Scott Webster. The church authorities had imposed the condition that the service should not be publicly announced, but, although discreet, it was a formal service, with a full choir and the church filled with palms and white lilies. Nancy wore ivory chiffon and lace, and around her neck three rows of magnificent pearls that were her present from Waldorf. Because of the Bishop's stipulations, only immediate relatives and a few close friends attended, although neither parent was among them, as both fathers were laid up with gout. In fact, Chillie was only just abreast of the news: 'Are you married,' he had cabled Nancy, a mere week before the wedding, 'if so, when? I haven't heard a word & it's rather embarrassing not to know.' He had also been upset to hear, from Lizzie, that Nancy was in a 'run-down condition' in the weeks before her marriage; even so, he could not face travelling all the way to see her: '. . . It's a devil of a trip,' as he told her, 'for ten minutes work.' Also, he wanted to go to Hot Springs to 'boil out' his gout.

The press soon caught up with events, and cables were at once sent off to the American newspapers: 'The newly married couple received many handsome presents, including the beautiful Cliveden estate, which Mr Astor presented to his son, with all its contents, as a wedding gift. Mr Astor also gave the bride a tiara in which is set the famous Sancy diamond, weighing 53½ carats . . .'[35] The present of the Sancy diamond, and of Cliveden together with more than enough money to reside there in a manner of which even Queen Victoria might approve, was an act of true magnificence. Only twenty years earlier, Nancy had been standing with her sisters outside a house in Richmond, their few possessions stacked next to two goats in a crate. Now she was joined to a man of faultless character and great wealth, who adored her and who would look after her beloved son. Her cup seemed full.

FOUR

Gilded Youth

The honeymoon began at the Sussex estate of Waldorf's sister Pauline, from where Nancy lost no time in writing to her beloved father: 'Well the girls will tell you that everything went off well and I am married at last . . .' She went on to describe their plans and pleasures, including a remarkable present that her husband had received: '. . . His father gave him one hundred thousand dollars for his birthday but we have decided to put that aside, as Waldorf wants to buy a place adjoining Cliveden – for his farm.' Yet even amid the nuptial excitements Nancy thought of Mirador: 'I'm longing to get home,' she said, 'and I feel there's lots for me to do – in fact I had no right marrying and leaving you in the lurch.'

After a short time, they crossed the Channel for a few days in Paris, before setting off for Cortina, in the Italian Alps; even before the days of skiing it was a popular resort with the rich, and there was much to do in the crisp sunshine, including skating and curling, which had recently caught on in Switzerland. They had also been invited to stay in Roumania by the country's Crown Princess Marie. A granddaughter of Queen Victoria, when only seventeen she had entered into a dynastic marriage with the heir to the Roumanian throne, Prince Ferdinand, and had met Waldorf and his sister Pauline while attending King Edward VII's coronation in August 1902.

However, appealing as it was to be asked to stay in Roumania's royal palace, the princess's interest stirred in Nancy a certain resentment. When Marie had first heard of Waldorf's growing friendship with Nancy, she had sent her a series of expressive personal letters filled with advice that was unsolicited even if no doubt well meaning. 'You must never,' she wrote, a few weeks before the wedding, 'let Waldorf shut things up in his heart without talking them over. If you notice his becoming mute and reserved just shake him till it all comes out . . .'

The princess had lovely, animated features, the bluest of eyes and a luscious figure, but what was more unwelcome to Nancy was that such letters continued to arrive even on her honeymoon; her possessive instincts, never more than skin-deep, were naturally aroused and she decided that she could manage without advice from Roumania. Although vague rumours that Waldorf had had an affair with Marie were fanciful – there was no place in his character for such a notion – Nancy firmly suggested to her husband that the correspondence should cease. Thereafter, in her friendship with Marie there was always the taint of suspicion, as expressed in a letter to Phyllis two years later:

> The Crown Princess of Roumania is expecting in December. I hear she tells everyone that I am jealous of her – I am furious – I hear her hair is very yellow these days and her cheeks very pink. Pauline adores her still and I think Waldorf has a fondness . . .[1]

Besides enjoying the pleasures of Cortina, both Waldorf and Nancy were invigorated by the mountain air. Even so, it probably suited both of them that the doctors ruled it 'absolutely necessary' that after the first excitements of her honeymoon Nancy should have a long rest and a quiet summer. New England seemed to meet that need: it was cool and healthy, and although Nancy would have preferred a long stay at Mirador, the climate there was unsuitable for Waldorf: 'I am afraid,' she told her father, adding to the already crowded medical catalogue, 'that Virginia would be too hot for Waldorf this summer on account of his sunstroke, else I'd rather be home.'

One upsetting matter that now arose was a tug-of-war over Bobbie. The new developments in Nancy's life led her to cancel the arrangement for her son, now nearly eight, to make regular visits to his father's family. His grandmother, Pauline Shaw, was aghast:

> . . . It seems to us impossible that you should keep Robbie away from us this summer, or at any time give up these visits which are now a fixed fact in his life and in ours and which nothing should prevent for his sake and for ours as long as we all live. We therefore write to say that we expect him for his usual visit, for it is hard enough to have it so short, and to come only once a year.[2]

Nancy had originally warmed to Bob Shaw's parents, but relations had since become less cordial; she now thought the family was 'hard and cold', and gave thanks that Bobbie was '3000 miles away from them', describing Bob's mother, for good measure, as 'that old buzzard'.

Having spent the summer in America, briefly at Mirador so that Waldorf could meet the Langhorne family and friends, but mainly with Irene and

Dana in Maine, the newly-weds returned to England. Cliveden, basking in its autumn splendour, did not yet meet Nancy's requirements: 'Here we are with no servants,' she wrote to her father. 'They all went with Mr Astor except the butler, who went mad.' Once home, they began to plan great alterations to their wonderful wedding present, while celebrating their first Christmas at Cliveden with twenty-two guests, a large proportion being Langhornes. With her marriage bringing her enormous wealth and the security of a deeply loving husband, Nancy's confidence soared, the society success gradually tempering the youthful tomboy, even if the fun and laughter remained.

Early in the New Year, however, Nancy's happiness faded. Her diary shows that at the beginning of January her chronic but undiagnosed illness returned to smother her with lassitude and depression. As 1907 unfolded, she was forced to spend a great amount of time in bed, frequently at least all morning, often until the early evening, very tired and sometimes unable to get up at all. 'If all the days of the year are to be as this one,' she wrote on 1 January, 'may 1907 pass like lightning – bed all day.' 'Have done no good to anyone,' she wrote the next evening, 'a selfish, useless day.' Chillie, Buck and Nora stayed on after Christmas, but by the time they left for Paris, Nancy had been bedridden for a whole week.

It was disconcerting for her that the experts had little accurate idea of what was the matter. It seems possible that she had colitis, or perhaps glandular fever – a disease for which there was no very effective cure, and which for some opaque reason attacks people with a highly developed animus of the sort that for much of her life affected Nancy's behaviour. The paradox was that although small and delicate-looking, she was physically robust; she may have found it strange that despite her strength and vitality she was so often ill. At all events, it puzzled the doctors.

The glitter of a wonderful life in prospect was dimmed by this mist of unexplained illness, and by the thought that although she could rejoice in the company of her husband, and the security he offered to her son, all the wealth and possessions of the Astors would be of little use to an invalid.

As if that were not enough, Waldorf's health was also discouraging. He suffered occasionally from the angina that had forced him to give up rowing, hunting and other favourite sports, but he had also been diagnosed with tuberculosis when he was twenty-six. In their plans for the future, therefore, the newly-wed couple would have to allow for repeated interruptions for medical 'cures'. They were soon to be found at fashionable spas on the Continent, such as Homburg, Kissingen and Marienbad, where the famous Dr Dengler administered his electrical treatments, but sometimes closer to home, at Folkestone, which was rather bleaker, though Nancy, determined to join her husband whenever she was well enough to do so, seemed to thrive in its cold grey air and bracing wind.

Despite the mysterious setbacks, she strove to lead an active life. In mid-January she spent a week in Leicestershire, staying with her friends Gordon and Edith Cunard, and went out hunting on several occasions. She also seemed well enough to go to a number of parties in London.

Early in February, the work at Cliveden began in earnest, and Waldorf and Nancy moved out. On a number of occasions they stayed with Waldorf's sister Pauline in Sussex, and they established a temporary base in William Astor's 'marble palace' in Carlton House Terrace, an arrangement made more palatable by the fact that Waldorf's father was spending much of his time at his castle in Kent. There were plenty of shops to visit, which Nancy did mainly with Phyllis, and many invitations, although she often felt too tired to stay on when there was dancing. On 11 February, she had an early taste of political talk at a party at Lansdowne House, formerly rented by Waldorf's father, whose owner, the Marquess of Lansdowne, had been Foreign Secretary and was now the leader of the Conservatives in the House of Lords. 'I like political parties,' Nancy wrote, 'and am getting too old for balls.'

On Friday, 22 February, she attended the first presentation court of the year. As she had married since being presented two years earlier, protocol required a second appearance, so once again she entered the vast ballroom of Buckingham Palace – together with seven or eight hundred others, as the first court of the year customarily included officials and diplomats as well as those with blue blood. Determined that her appearance should again be fit for a queen as she was ceremoniously called forward to be presented to the Sovereign, she was arrayed with the Sancy diamond and the coronet given to Mme de Montespan by Louis XV, and resplendent in a 'Josephine robe with Brussels lace and ermine, and a star of diamonds . . .'[3] She was not eclipsed even by her fellow American standing next in the line: the opulent Grace Duggan, later Marchioness Curzon, for whom Jacques Doucet, the celebrated Paris couturier, had created an 'exquisite' dress of cream duchesse satin and diamanté train embroidered with silver roses and seed pearls. Emerging from the glitter and gold of the court of King Edward, Nancy was now without doubt a fully fledged member of society.

Meanwhile at Cliveden, the work was proceeding apace. They had decided to try to get the whole job done within two months, and had accordingly engaged a force of some 120 workmen. Such an order was easy to fulfil, not just because the Astors had plenty of ready money, but also because at that time there were great numbers of willing hands. England was in the grip of depression, and it was feared that the trade cycle was about to take a further sharp downturn. Profitable building work was scarce, and the Cliveden project would have been an exceptional bounty for local firms even if they had to share the job with skilled workers from further afield. Everywhere men were 'walking about', as unemployment was termed, and offers of jobs, even those involving long hours of hard and boring labour in return for seven, six or even five pence an hour, had instant takers, disagreeable as they found the work:

When the workers arrived in the morning they wished it was breakfast time. When they resumed work after breakfast they wished it was dinner-time. After dinner they wished it was one o'clock on Saturday. So they went on, day after day, year after year, wishing their time was over and, without realising it, really wishing they were dead . . .[4]

At least there could have been few building sites in a more interesting or attractive place than Cliveden.

When he had bought the estate, in 1893, William Astor had found the house and grounds in a state of dilapidation and neglect. He soon began to put all that right. By embellishment rather than rebuilding, he lovingly lifted the house from the condition in which he had bought it from the Duke of Westminster, and eradicated many of the traces of the interior that had been designed comparatively recently by Sir Charles Barry, architect of the Houses of Parliament. In order to refashion the house and gardens to accord with his taste and his sense of history, he had employed the architect John Loughborough Pearson. A prophet of the Gothic Revival, and famous for his work on Truro Cathedral, he was not much associated with country-house design. Yet he had taken easily to Renaissance motifs, which had suited William Astor's purpose, and between the two they had enriched Cliveden with imagination, history and technical skill.

Opposite the front entrance they had built an imposing staircase with an abundance of carved woodwork, its upward march marked at intervals by wooden statues of people associated with Cliveden. The rooms at its foot were run together to create a large reception hall, dominated by a huge sixteenth-century fireplace originally in a French castle. Just as he had ransacked the salerooms of Europe to furnish his mansion on New York's Fifth Avenue, William had searched far afield until he had found what he deemed to be exactly right for Cliveden: Louis Seize chairs with their original covering, South African wild tamarind wood panelling for the library – later dubbed 'the cigar box' by Nancy – and, to transform the dining room with particular splendour, Louis Quinze rococo panelling from the Chateau d'Asnières, the hunting lodge near Paris once lent by Louis XV to his mistress Madame de Pompadour. Some of the woodwork bore the marks of bullets fired during a fight in the room in the days of the Paris Commune in 1871. The painted ceilings and mosaic floors, with an abundance of *objets d'art*, created an imposing effect, but there were few openings for daylight, and overall the atmosphere was ponderous.

The garden was clothed in an antiquity unusual in the Thames Valley. Besides reassembling the world-famous balustrade from the gardens of the Villa Borghese in Rome, which he had bought and shipped to England amid much controversy, William filled the nooks of the yew hedges with Roman sarcophagi, also originally from the Villa Borghese; he reconstructed a pagoda that had stood in the Paris Exhibition of 1867, developing around it a skating pond; and at the head of the wide gravel approach to the house he installed a gigantic marble cockle shell surrounded by nymphs and cherubs, created by the Anglo-American sculptor Waldo Story, whom he had met in Rome; the ladies it depicted were supposedly experiencing the uplifting effects of a fountain of love.

Many of William's purchases and installations, including tapestries, and important pictures by Romney, Gainsborough and Reynolds, were either too large or of too high a quality to move; much else was too fundamental to alter. Nevertheless, for all the house's magnificence, now that it was theirs, Waldorf and Nancy were determined to make their own mark on it; they were perhaps reassured by the thought that their predecessor and benefactor had promised never to return, and so would not cast a jaundiced eye upon their alterations to his cherished creation.

Deciding to set aside many of the agglomerations from bygone ages, they instructed that the antiquities inside the hall be removed, and that the mosaics and Minton tiles be torn up and replaced by stone flags. Instead, they would import light, air and colour, and refresh the scene with Nancy's own particular choice of chic American ideas.

While the huge numbers of workmen were busy at Cliveden, Waldorf and Nancy made occasional visits to oversee matters of particular importance, and to arrange the furniture. 'The house in a great mess,' Nancy had noted on 7 February, 'but I think will be lovely.' One of the reasons for the mess was that the house was to be wired for electricity, making redundant the fifty-year-old gas yard with its concrete tree chimney installed by William Astor, and also providing for a 'telephone apparatus', as it was then known.

They were equally bent on transforming the gardens. Waldorf's vision was to replace the long avenues and vistas of its original classical landscaping with many smaller areas, diverse in shape and colour. Meanwhile Nancy set about denuding the garden of many of its Roman relics. They also ordered that the skating pond be redesigned as an oriental water garden, and that the octagonal temple, originally a gazebo used as a tea room, which William had converted into a chapel the previous year, be remodelled and reconsecrated.

By the end of February 1907, enough progress had been made for them to leave London and move back to Cliveden; there, installed in rooms on the third floor, Nancy could dart about and direct the continuing alterations. Yet their bouts of ill-health recurred. Waldorf was advised to go for a short cure, while Nancy's days were punctuated by spells of discomfort and deep lethargy. 'In a dark room all day, neuralgia ghastly,' she recorded on 16 March. To compound matters, Bobbie, who to Nancy's dismay was on the point of going off to boarding school, was taken in to hospital for a minor operation. Nancy had another problem: 'Find I have an abscess,' she wrote on 20 March. 'Bobbie going on well but can't come back yet. I can't go out either so we send each other messages.' Yet somehow the periods during which she could do nothing but stay in her room seemed to vanish as quickly and as unexpectedly as they arrived, leaving her ready to spring back to the delights of the rich and fashionable world.

A month after the Lansdowne party she had a further taste of political talk, sitting at a dinner party between two politicians of considerable significance: Winston Churchill and Arthur Balfour. Until a little over a year previously, Balfour, son of a Scottish MP and godson of the Duke of Wellington, victor of Waterloo, had been Prime Minister, an office he had taken over from his uncle, the Marquess of Salisbury; now he was leader of the Conservative Party, but in opposition. Churchill, who was at this time an undersecretary of state in the Liberal government, was to become a good friend of Nancy and, for some years, a frequent visitor to Cliveden. This was despite Nancy unwisely telling friends, when Churchill was engaged to Clementine Hozier, that the girl Winston was to marry was 'lovely but *very* stupid'. She was to be more diplomatic to Winston himself, writing:

> I am so glad you are marrying and I feel you will be v. happy. You are both fortunate, especially you as she's v. lovely – and especially her as you are v. domestic and ripe for a nice settled home. I shall have to send my present later – if you will marry in such a hurry.

Such pleasantries were to cease once Nancy had entered Parliament, when her friendship with Churchill would turn sour.

Nancy had entered a world that was peopled with politicians as well as the social elite, at a time when the path to Parliament was less crowded than it is today, and relatively easy for the rich and well connected to tread. The

Labour Party was in its infancy, posing little threat, and both the Conservative and Liberal parties selected a large proportion of their MPs on personal recommendation; peers meanwhile had the right, *ex officio*, to sit and vote in the House of Lords. Political and social leaders swam in the same pool, and affairs of state were often conducted at house parties and other social gatherings, as well as in Westminster.

At the beginning of April, William Astor paid a visit to Nancy and gave her a 'nice check' with which to buy furniture, for which there was plenty of room now that so much of his own had been cast out. Earlier that day she and Waldorf had lunched at the Ritz. Since opening the previous May, it had become a popular place with the rich, and certainly represented the sumptousness of the times. Waldorf and Nancy would often meet there when on separate errands in London, and saunter into the Louis XVI dining room, where gilt-bronze garlands hung from electroliers below a painted sky were designed to represent the flower decorations of Marie Antoinette's feasts. Quiet strains from the orchestra in the Winter Garden would reach the restaurant, its marble walls faced in soft shades of green, rose and cream, its tables set on an Aubusson carpet stretching the length of the room, over one end of which presided a gilt figure of Father Thames contemplating a bare-breasted beauty representing the ocean. Long arched windows facing Green Park opened on to a paved court where on warm evenings the quiet talk of diners might be sustained by Consommé Glacé Madrilène, Filet de Sole Romanoff, Poulet en Chaudfroid, Pêche Belle Dijonnaise, and other inspirations of the new hotel's chef and his celebrated mentor, Auguste Escoffier.

Back at Cliveden, Nancy, Waldorf and Bobbie would have breakfast every morning in the schoolroom on an upper floor, while the army of workers continued with the massive project below, now within sight of completion.

On 8 May, Waldorf, who seemed to have accumulated a number of ailments, went off for another cure. They had been married only a year, and Nancy was greatly upset whenever he had to leave. 'I wept as I so hate his going,' she wrote in her diary, '. . . we dine alone, very sadly.' He went first to Marienbad, before returning to England to stay in a spa in Folkestone. Nancy dreaded being left alone, 'helpless at Cliveden with a butler, groom of the chambers and three footmen to manage'. It was a far cry from the easy-going arrangements at Mirador, and even those had proved a considerable test for her.

Just after Waldorf had gone, Nancy received a letter from his father, also on a cure in Germany:

Dear Nancy,

It pleases me very much to read your praise of Cliveden for it assures me that the place has fallen into appreciative hands . . . You are quite right to give the house a severe pulling about, for to do so is one of the first pleasures of ownership. I did the same with the Newport villa my father gave me in 1888, and I fairly disembowelled Cliveden . . .

. . . At the same time I am frank enough – forgive me please – to say that I prefer not to see what you have done and to content myself with my modest and humble arrangements as I remember them . . .[5]

The letter must have bolstered her confidence, and would at least have relieved her of any doubts about the scale of the alterations they were making to the house. It was an example of how, then and for many years to come, Waldorf's father, for all his aloofness, showed Nancy and Waldorf a generous heart. A week later, he sent her a 'huge ruby' as a birthday present.

A few days afterwards, with the arrival of Nancy's sister Irene and her family, Nancy took the first tentative steps towards entertaining in the newly refurbished house. She and Waldorf had given some house parties the previous October and November, but they were small, and just for a few friends, although these included fashionable Americans such as the Countess of Essex and the Duchess of Manchester, spiced by royalty in the form of Prince Arthur of Connaught and his family.[6]

Now, although Waldorf was still away, Nancy felt that she and the house were ready for something larger. At the beginning of June, she invited nearly twenty people to a dinner party. It was a mix that, although later widened in line with Nancy's social and charitable interests, would form a pattern as she set a pace and standard of entertaining both at Cliveden and in London that was to rival the most prolific hostesses of the age. On this early occasion there were family, in the form of Irene, leading politicians, including Churchill, royalty – that evening it was the Duchess of Connaught – fashionable Americans, and friends, mostly Nancy's approximate contemporaries, from the old English aristocracy.

Being sole host, Nancy's energy was drained by the party, and coming to terms with the responsibility in Waldorf's frequent absences was probably a factor weighing upon her health. 'I am so awfully sorry and sad for you being shut up all alone,' the Duchess of Connaught wrote on 5 June, after the dinner party. 'I do hope it will do you good and that you will be quite well and strong after a good rest. Sir B. Dawson is so clever, he will put you quite right – he told me so.'[7] Sir Bertrand Dawson was one of the fashionable doctors of the day, but not, it seemed, possessed of a great understanding of neuralgia.

A few days after her dinner party, Nancy combined a remedy for her exhaustion with her longing to see Waldorf – 'my darling Wal', as she called him – by arranging to join him in Folkestone.

> I took the 3.18 train to Folkestone – was met by a fat man whom I hardly recognised. He tells me his name is Waldorf Astor – Hurrah, for his 10 lbs of Germany and health . . . Rest, rest, rest; I slept well and rested, rested, rested . . . Went to beach, luncheon, sleep, walk, dined in our room and so to bed – a restful place . . . only golf croquet – such a good game but Waldorf always wins – howling wind and coolish – how I hate the sea, except to look at . . .[8]

By the beginning of June, the works at Cliveden were finished. The house, a magnificent newly polished jewel set in surroundings of green splendour, was complemented that summer by a glittering array of guests – 'tall, cool, ornate people who hadn't packed their own things' – in what later came to be regarded as a brilliant season. 'Cliveden now became a fully occupied house,' wrote Nancy. 'Waldorf and I did a great deal of entertaining. We were young, and we had a great many friends.'

Word of the changes at Cliveden began to excite interest even among Englishmen set in their ways and prejudiced against Americans, as many of them were, without experience to justify it. In English eyes, many of the Americans who had come over to live in England, including those who had married Englishmen, did seem different at first, although most gradually became assimilated. Nancy, however, was always to remain different. She did not discuss her friends in much detail, but those of whom she did talk tended to be back at home: being a Virginian was, and would always remain, of paramount importance to her. As her friend Consuelo, Duchess of Marlborough, also an American, remembered:

> Looking back on the little circle I knew of American women married to Englishmen, there are, I realize, very few who remained definitely American. Nancy Astor was one of these. Her high spirits, her sense of humor, her self-assurance, her courage, her independence are all of the American variety; and also her beauty . . .[9]

Although the Astors had had until now comparatively few very close friends in England, the society they had entered was generous in its hospitality, and had they wished to, or felt up to it, they could have filled each day with invitations of one sort or another: Waldorf was widely regarded as good-natured, and the frosts caused by Nancy's darting tongue generally soon melted. For both Waldorf and Nancy, entertaining was very soon to become a compulsion. The gilded couple, still in their twenties, opened their doors to an almost unceasing flow of friends. The hallmark of their parties was variety, particularly of the guests, and it was to be an ongoing characteristic for many years to come. If people did have a common attribute, it was what today might be called 'celebrity'; and also simply the fact that Nancy or Waldorf liked them.

In their early days as hosts, the celebrity was mainly social, but gradually other elements entered the rationale of their hospitality, among them politics and good works. Almost as soon as Waldorf and Nancy had refashioned the house their parties began to be talked about, and at length their renown widened and spread through much of the world, although for a time, at an exceptionally dangerous period in Britain's history, they attracted noto-riety as well as fame. Their guests would include, besides their families, emperors, kings, princes and peers, English, European and American. Nancy was the first hostess regularly to introduce prominent Americans to the English, and the fact of her doing so resulted in friendship and understanding between men of influence in the two countries. In the years to come, it was to prove of great political benefit to each, although perhaps more so to England, and was to be one of the main contributions of Nancy's life.

The wider aim became evident within two or three years of the Astors' marriage: 'Purposeless and purely fashionable people are not asked to Astor parties. There is a splendid mix-up of welfare duchesses and flat-heeled democratic women workers' – or so it seemed to readers of American news-papers. Nancy was later to agree that there were usually 'special and particu-lar purposes' for her parties.

June 1907 also saw the inuguration of what was in due course to become the high point of the Cliveden calendar, the house party for the races at Ascot. For their first party, they had asked twenty-six people to stay. What had started as a trickle of guests was about to develop into a broad and fast flow, and it would be essential to ensure that management of the house and its estate was in order. For that purpose Nancy had assembled a largely new staff. A fine French chef, Monsieur Papillon, had five girls to work under him; he would stay until his death in 1914, to be succeeded by the equally skilled Monsieur Gilbert. Nancy also found a highly efficient housekeeper, a Mrs Addison. As in other large houses, the housekeeper and butler led a retinue of indoor servants. At Cliveden, their world lay beyond a green baize door at one end of the hall, and was largely invisible to the occupants of the main house. It included housemaids, scullery maids, an 'odd-man', a valet, a groom of the chambers and several footmen, who usually had to discard their own Christian names for acceptable traditional ones, as did the maids.

The steward, Parr, had stayed on after William Astor moved out, and his experience of Cliveden's ways was a boon for Nancy, although some years later it all became too much for him, and, succumbing to the butler's traditional enemy, he began to spend too much time in the wine cellar. In fact that was a fortunate development, as the old steward's enforced retirement led to the promotion of one of the footmen, Edwin Lee, who eventually became one of the world's best butlers. He later gave a vivid account of his first meeting with Nancy, when introduced to her by Parr:

When I saw her that evening I thought her perhaps the loveliest creature I had ever seen. There was a bloom about her, she had beautiful hair and skin, and lovely doe-like eyes, which I later found could change to a tiger's in a second . . .

'You're new,' she said, and then gunned me down with questions. 'What's your name? Where are you from? How old are you? How long have you been here? How do you like it? Have they made you comfortable?' Ending up with, 'Have you got a mother and father?'

I blushed to the roots and began stammering answers.

'Never mind, you can tell me later. I hope you stay. Look after him, Parr, he seems a nice boy.' Then she turned her attention to her guests and ignored me for the rest of the evening. It was as if I had ceased to exist.[10]

Lee was to bring to a job of great complexity – made more so by Nancy's idiosyncrasies – a mix of efficiency, good nature and natural authority that would enable him to cope with the regular and enormous scale of entertainment that was to characterise Cliveden. It was fortunate that he did so. Below stairs the pace was fast, in order to provide the smooth efficiency expected by the guests and demanded by the hosts. The lack of any labour-saving devices made for a long, hard day. It began at about 5.30 in the morning, with the housemaids creeping silently into the thirty or so guest bedrooms in order to clear out the previous night's fire, clean and black the grate, and lay a new fire so that the room would be warm for the slumbering occupants of the bed when they were woken with early morning tea and arrowroot or digestive biscuits. Before the days of central heating, houses were often icy cold both upstairs and down unless fires were kept burning, and even then the warmth did not penetrate far into a large room: women could warm their bare shoulders near the fire and risk their faces turning red in the heat, or they could move away and shiver.

Even at Cliveden, central heating was not introduced until the inter-war years, and until then, in order to try to keep the main house warm, a hundred tons of coal was burned each year, trundled from bunker to dispersal point by handcarts pushed along a light railway in the basement. It was mainly the odd-men who had to carry up scuttles of coal for each bedroom, as well as cans of water for the hip baths – two of hot, habitually smelling of paint, and one of cold. At least these enabled people to keep clean, if not warm. In the Edwardian age, most houses had been built without modern plumbing, and even in the best houses there was usually not enough of it, old or new. In Nancy's early days at Cliveden there were two bathrooms on each floor, an unusual abundance, and to use them the male guests might queue in the corridor, carrying their sponge bags; most though would choose to be doused by their valet in front of their bedroom fire. Almost all men had a valet and women a lady's maid; Nancy herself had engaged a new one in April. 'I have a new English maid,' she told Phyllis, 'a really nice girl, but what the French call "a naturelle"; she's so stupid but she's here for good as I haven't the slightest notion of how to get rid of her.'

Most employers had no such difficulty: in Edwardian England there was a profusion of domestic servants. They were mostly tied to their jobs, as over them hung what they regarded as the tyranny of the 'character': without a good reference it was hard to find a new position, and many employers withheld them, either to avoid losing a valued servant, or for simple convenience, or sometimes even out of spite. The lack of public transport throughout much of rural England also impeded servants' opportunity to change jobs: in much of the country travelling any distance to work was not an option, so the 'Big House' was the only employer, other than the tenant farmers. Yet the status quo – 'the rich man in his castle, the poor man at his gate' – was broadly accepted: servants knew their jobs and were prepared to carry them out, and Cliveden, below stairs as well as above, was a happy ship.

The guests at the first of Cliveden's Ascot parties included Winston Churchill; the Duke and Duchess of Connaught, and their daughter Princess Patricia; the Duchess of Somerset; the Ladies Lytton, Kenmare and Pembroke; Ava Astor and Waldorf's brother John; Count Constantin Breckendorf, the Russian ambassador's son – 'a great fat creature of twenty-four' – and American friends including Lady Essex and the rather older, half-Cuban Duchess of Manchester. There was also Sir Schomberg McDonnell, private secretary to Lord Salisbury when he was Prime Minister. They arrived at a magnificent house in all its glory; at its core was the concept of a traditional English country house, but it would have seemed to the guests rather different to their own homes and others in which they stayed, however grand, partly due to its opulence, albeit in an opulent age, partly for its Italianate design, and perhaps mostly because of the imprint of its American hostess.

As soon as they entered the great hall, the guests would have noticed the touch of the American who loved European ways. The main drawing room was of French Empire design, with a fireplace at each end, tall pillars supporting a stuccoed ceiling, and, on a wall, too large to have been removed, tapestries depicting the Battle of Blenheim, said to have been given by the Duke of Marlborough to the Earl of Orkney, one of his generals and at that time owner of Cliveden. Victorian clutter had been swept out by the new broom, and the hall made light and spacious, with a harp and grand piano in the background.

With its furniture made for Madame La Pompadour, whose bust surveyed the room, the dining room needed no improvement on William Astor's arrangements, but in her mission to lighten the house's atmosphere, Nancy had paid great attention to the bedrooms, the grander of which were on the first floor. One became a Chinese Room, with a fireplace topped by a canopy of old Siena marble with festoons of white and grey, reminiscent of Chippendale; a similar impression was created in another bedroom with eighteenth-century Chinese wallpaper of a type fashionable in its day. Just before Christmas, Waldorf had bought an entire room's worth of Elizabethan panelling, and the precious items were installed with the utmost care, while the ceiling was decorated with plasterwork 'proper to the period'. Contemporary fiction accurately describes what a guest might have found on retiring to change for dinner in a house such as Cliveden:

> The dressing-table, the washstand, the writing-table with its appointments, the vast four-poster on which some unseen hand had already laid out her clothes, the drawn curtains, the brightly burning fire, the muslin cushions, the couch with a chinchilla rug folded across it . . . Printed cards on the writing-table: 'Post arrives 8 a.m., 4 p.m.; leaves 5 p.m. Luncheon 1.30, Dinner 8.30.'[11]

The library and drawing rooms were on the ground floor, and, like most of the main bedrooms, overlooked the seven-acre parterre with superb views to the river beyond. On the horizon, over a mile distant, was plainly visible a tall cedar tree, below which were steeply hanging woods, in springtime whitened by banners of wild cherry, in summer beechen green. Waldorf's rooms faced north, while Nancy's adjoining bedroom, decorated with yellow-painted woodwork, had perhaps the finest position, the corner facing south over the gardens – 'a dream too good to be true', she wrote. There was also her own boudoir, with vanilla walls picked out in royal blue; in among the works of art was a bust of an old Negro, sculpted by Phyllis. On the floors above were more guest bedrooms and what in due course would become nurseries and children's rooms.

Nancy had received plenty of suggestions and advice from friends, some of which she allowed to permeate her own ideas, which were characteristically fixed despite her never acquiring much interest in fine arts. The redecoration of one of the drawing rooms, at least in terms of colour, was suggested by the Countess of Essex. Lord Curzon later magisterially described it:

> 'Not quite regal. Green a little too fierce. I dare say it will tone down. Orange curtains rather a violent contrast. Books in wall quite charming, but pictures not suited. Chintzes very effective and easy chairs most comfortable and well-arranged. Little new tables and mahogany chairs not quite good enough for such a house. With a little pulling together the whole thing can be made successful.

Nancy may not always have relished Curzon's comments, as he sometimes subordinated his great sense of humour to pleasure at his place in the social firmament: 'It is wonderful,' he once told her, 'to be a member of a family going back three or four hundred years; of course, Nancy dear, you cannot understand that, coming from Virginia.'[12]

Besides a Lely portrait in the hall, the famous pictures collected by Waldorf's father added attraction to the main rooms. There was also contemporary art: by May 1907, Nancy had caught the attention of John Singer Sargent, a cousin of Bob Shaw and, although American, the most celebrated portraitist of England's Edwardian Age. He did a preliminary sketch, describing her as looking like Ophelia – 'in other words, "bats"', as Nancy typically put it.

The following year, Sargent completed a full-length portrait of Nancy in a simple white dress with a primrose sash, half turning to the front and with her hands behind her back. The picture was exhibited at the Royal Academy in 1910, after which it was returned to Cliveden and given pride of place in the hall. Sargent also portrayed Waldorf, although Nancy did not much care for the result. To many people, Sargent was rather a prickly character who did not welcome criticism. But the Astors considered him a most attractive guest, happy to play duets with Nancy's friend Alice Mildmay, an accomplished pianist; though that may not really have appealed to Nancy, who disliked music. After a time, such interludes also ceased to give much pleasure to Sargent, who, tiring both of portraits and of society, firmly told Nancy, 'Cliveden is not for me'; it did not, however, stop her from vainly plying him with invitations.

Nancy wanted to expose the stuffier corners of English society to fresh American air. Waldorf seemed happy with that, and it soon became apparent that going to Cliveden, or to other parties where she was the driving force, was a distinctive and exciting variation of Edwardian pleasure, reflecting the effect of almost unlimited means on her vivid character.

With her stream of ideas for entertaining their friends now in full flow, Nancy took increasing pride and delight in the house. That applied to matters of form as well as substance. In her pioneering way, she brought light and sparkle to Victorian decoration; her ideas for flower arrangement, for example, soon became widely copied. However, she was not alone in her preferences, and in other fashionable houses too, the ottomans and anti-macassars of the old century were fast being set aside:

> Taste took a feminine, frivolous turn, expressing itself in little gilt papier maché chairs, in chaises-longue smothered with lace cushions, in 'Lady Teazle' screens covered with machine-made Beauvais, in masses of maddeningly midget tables. The colours became nebulous. As a transition between grey and blue, mauve predominated. The new sunshine was shut out at an early hour each day, and artificially replaced with light glowing softly through pink shades. The character (and cost) of flower decoration changed completely. Orchids replaced begonias; malmaisons replaced petunias.[13]

Nancy attached great importance to flowers, as a way of infusing rooms with colour and aroma. 'It was the era,' she recalled, 'of the sweet pea and gypsophila in the stiff silver vase, all muddled up with photograph frames.' She was having none of that. Camm, Cliveden's head gardener, one of the country's best, took readily to her ideas, and filled the greenhouses accordingly. At Mirador, Nancy had seen how attractive flowers were when loosely mixed up in large bowls, and she introduced her gardener to French flower pictures, teaching him to copy the arrangements they portrayed. Weaned off the orchids, malmaisons and lilies in their tall cut-glass vases that adorned so many Edwardian houses, Camm passed the lesson on to his juniors, and from then on a gardener came in each day to do the flowers in the house Nancy's way; camellias now floated in bowls on the tables, and in the hall were young apple trees in large tubs, and at Christmas poinsettias and six-foot orange trees.

Far as the arrangements were from the ways of Albemarle County, Nancy was a quick learner, and even quicker to decide how she wanted things done. Besides issuing detailed instructions for the flower arrangements, she took tight control of the organisation of the indoor staff, chose the menus, and planned where each guest would sleep. Although neither she nor Waldorf was interested in drink – except, in due course, as to ways of restricting its availability – the cellar was filled with the finest wine. The hothouses ensured that delicious fruit and vegetables would be available all year round, almost regardless of season, and the many courses required at each meal consisted of dishes that would have delighted even William Astor, by now in the foremost league of gourmets. Consequently, the guests who stayed for the first year's Ascot were entertained in a manner that would retain its luxury far into the future, and longer than would endure at almost any other private house in England.

Although she loved hunting and horses, Ascot was not for Nancy. She was bored by racing: it was generally agreed that she would enjoy it only if she were one of the jockeys. Nor did she take to the racing set, which had Newmarket for its headquarters and among whom the King found many of his friends. Nevertheless, the focal point of the young Astors' entertaining in their first full year at Cliveden, and thereafter, was the week of the royal meeting at Ascot.

At the end of each day at the races the party would return to Cliveden, where the women would put aside their large picture hats with osprey feathers – much in fashion in 1907 – and exchange their mauve or white chiffon or lace creations for dresses of linen or cotton. Their consorts would don flannels, coats, ties and white buckskin shoes for croquet or tennis – at Cliveden there were both open and covered courts – or they might simply rest in the shade of magnolia-covered walls, or indoors in the comfort of chairs newly covered in chintz, on soft carpets, in quiet rooms scented by flowers. When the weather was clear, the guests might descend through the woods to the riverside, where a boathouse, manned by a ferryman, was set in well-mown lawns beneath the chalk cliffs and leafy beech trees. There, sheltered by parasols to keep off the sun's rays, they could lie back on the cushions of the punts moored by the bank or, with the silent swans, lazily watch footmen loading wicker hampers on to a steam launch, its railings and brass funnel polished and gleaming in the sun. While gliding down the river, there would be tea and a spread of delicacies created by M. Papillon. After that, it would be time to change for dinner.

Most Edwardian weekend parties were from Saturday to Monday, but at Cliveden people often came for Sunday only, while weekend parties frequently began on Fridays. Carriages, and subsequently motor cars, would meet guests arriving at Taplow railway station, a mere twenty minutes by express from London. From Nancy's earliest days as a hostess, guests were left much to their own devices until about midday. In the late morning and at teatime, when the weather was fine, they would assemble on the long paved terrace overlooking the formal garden, the air fragrant with the scent of the geraniums that filled the stone vases outside the drawing room windows. In specially designed tea gowns – eau de Nil satin, spangled mousseline de soie, gold belt at the waist, fur at hem and neck – the fashionable ladies looked like a collection of life-sized dolls. The men would talk and murmur and laugh; the dolls would glide along the terrace, stirring with soft shoes the sweet-smelling herbs between the flagstones; swifts would swoop silently from the eaves, and from the trees below could be heard, in their season, cuckoos, pheasants and the occasional nightingale.

For dinner, the men would don starched shirts; tall, stiff collars; white waistcoats, and close-fitting tail coats with a gardenia in the buttonhole. With shoes glistening from the labours of a servant, their hair sleek with violet oil, their beards scented with a dab of Cèdre, pockets flat and containing only a silk handkerchief, a Cartier watch and perhaps a slim gold cigarette case with half a dozen Egyptian cigarettes, they would descend to dinner.

The party would congregate in the hall before entering the dining room in a line. Each man would escort a woman, her hair done in the halo style ubiquitous in Edwardian England, her neck encased in a diamond-and-pearl collar, her arms in tight white gloves buttoned to the elbow; rose pink and mauve were the fashion of the day, and jewelled dragonflies, daggers or bows would glitter on heavy brocade or satin dresses from the leading designers – Vionnet, Worth, Doucet and Paul Poiret. The profusion of valets and ladies' maids had the effect not just of their employers being well turned out, their clothes clean, brushed and pressed, but of their being turned out at all. Much of what was worn, especially women's dresses, with all their hooks and hindrances, would have been impossible to get in and out of single-handedly, a hopeless prospect when, at formal house parties such as those at Cliveden, several changes of dress were required each day – morning and afternoon; indoors and out; lunch, tea and dinner.

As the guests gathered for dinner, Nancy's neat figure would move ceaselessly among them, her face bright, her quips and comments directed generally to anyone within earshot. Although her talk was still lightly dusted with American idoms – she would dismiss, for example, a trivial matter by saying 'it don' amount to a hill o' beans', and would often prefix her remarks with 'See here' – she was beginning to lose a little of her languorous Southern accent, using instead the clipped inflection of the English; she had caught the habit of dropping her 'g's, referring to 'huntin', for example, and her voice moved to rather a high pitch when she expressed opinions, a frequent occurrence.

It would be an exaggeration to describe her as a chatterbox, but she did not let the conversation flag, and since she was never in awe of eminent persons – always excepting the King and Queen – she was careless of the controversial effect of some of her comments. For the novelty of her glamorous surroundings was now beginning slightly to fade, and as she became accustomed to living not only in a new country but in circumstances of wealth and the authority that accompanied it, her self-confidence and independent spirit began to assert themselves. They affected her behaviour in a way that her guests could not fail to notice, but her ability to wound and her determination to have the last word were usually tempered by the fact that she did not take herself very seriously, and the ease with which she was moved to laughter.

Dinner at Cliveden involved a considerable amount of food, and would usually take about an hour: two soups; choice of fish; entrée; game in season, usually rather high, or chicken or duck; joint; savoury; dessert. It was not considered proper for women to drink more than a token glass of wine; instead there were the delights of Apollinaris water. For the men, champagne was usual, but, in accordance with the Astors' ideas of restraint, not much of it – enough to satisfy ritual rather than thirst; however, as with the other wine on offer, it was always of the best. Nancy strongly disapproved of alcohol and would not touch it at all; Waldorf drank none for pleasure, but he would taste the champagne before it was poured, to satisfy himself that it was good enough for his guests. With the final courses there would be liqueurs – 'spirits to clear and oils to soothe' – and little silver dishes of pink otto of rose sweets to refresh the palate. The decanters were under the watchful eye of the butler, and footmen stood silent in their allotted places, ready to serve.

If, as was usually the case, there were more than eight at dinner, the footmen wore livery: powdered hair, brown coats, striped waistcoats, breeches, yellow silk stockings, white gloves, and black pumps with gold buckles. The butler, as his mark of distinction, wore a blue tail coat. After dinner the servants would remain on hand to supply all needs, or, yawning in a basement corridor, would await the ring of a bell summoning them to action. 'This is where,' said one old butler, 'that patent handle is required to wind servants up, to work on again for another fifteen hours.'

When, eventually, the ladies withdrew, they would be greeted by their maids, who would brush out their hair and prepare them for bed, before creeping off for a few hours' sleep of their own, too exhausted to worry much about the state of their accommodation. Even rich and great houses like Cliveden quickly became cold and damp unless constantly heated, and there was little comfort to be had late at night in the lower servants' quarters. With no one having the time or obligation to light a fire, the bedrooms the maids reached for their brief repose were hardly welcoming. Such things were accepted for the most part without much question, although indignation was occasionally aroused: in the servants' hall, always an efficient gossip exchange, the story was wryly repeated of the butler confronted by a master returning home after a short absence:

'Those boxes of new cartridges must have arrived by now, Gibson?' said the master to his butler. 'Where have you been keeping them?'

'Well, M'Lord,' replied the servant, 'I have them up in my bedroom, I thought that . . .'

'Oh no, no, that won't do,' said his master. 'It's far too damp up there. Take them down to the laundry-room passage for now, and find a dry space near the gun-room.'

'Yes, M'Lord,' said the butler, hiding his annoyance, but, as the story went, he remained in high dudgeon, which he later expressed: 'So I said to the housekeeper that evening, "It's all right for the servants, of course, Ho yes, but it's far too damp for the bloomin' cartridges."' [14]

Nancy was full of sparkle, but she was enough of a newcomer for her talk and outlook usually to remain within the rules and conduct of a formal society – unlike in later years, when her self-confidence was almost unshakeable and her idiosyncrasies such that when she entered a room no one could be sure quite what might happen. However, even at this early stage of their marriage, she sometimes behaved in a rather harsh way towards her patient husband, apparently heedless that her position and the circumstances in which she was already thriving stemmed almost wholly from his good nature.

But if there were moments when her vociferous strictures discomfited her guests, she would, as if by telepathy, perceive the ultimate boundaries that her husband thought proper, and hold back from crossing them. Despite the numbers of guests at Cliveden, its august surroundings and the formality of the Edwardian era excluded raised voices or loud dissent. Waldorf disliked dining room argument, thinking it in bad taste, and if a certain point was reached, his quiet personality would deflate the vigour. At one dinner party, when Nancy was giving tongue in a particularly dogmatic way, the lady on Waldorf's right turned to him and said, 'You're being very quiet, aren't you, Waldorf, through all this?' He slowly inclined his head and murmured, 'Wouldn't you?' He preferred to be thought serious, but he did in fact have a small mischievous side, although he did not really like showing it; and he also had the sense of humour without which it would have been difficult to live with Nancy.

At that time there were a number of popular musicians in London making or maintaining their reputations, including Melba, Paderewski and Caruso, and although Nancy disliked music, she felt it right that it should sometimes be included in the entertainment at Cliveden. If the party were sufficiently large, the best performers might be summoned – the Sicilian Players, or perhaps Casano and his eight-piece band, would be lured from their normal place at the Berkeley or the Hans Crescent Hotel. On arrival they would be assigned a discreet area to establish themselves and their instruments, and would get to work, heard but more or less unseen. Late in the evening on such occasions, after the immediate memories of dinner had faded, there would be supper: prawns, plovers' eggs, chaudfroid quails with truffle designs, cutlets in aspic, caviare from M. Benoist, and other delicacies in their season.

At Cliveden, the Astors were at first happy to adopt the conventional pattern of entertaining. Yet Nancy was not conventional, although she was strongly attracted to an atmosphere of pleasure and well-being. A part of her character was made restless if not rebellious by the comfortable circumstances, the fine houses and estates, and the general enjoyment of life that permeated the society she had entered – a society of easy confidence, of settled income, without yet much fear of change or upset.

Although she still had to fight the instinctive unwillingness of Englishmen to welcome outsiders – as she had found in the hunting field – gradually she and Waldorf began successfully to bring together friends and guests who had hardly a thought in common, and to invite not only the well born, as had always been accepted in Victorian and Edwardian society, and the opulent, who in the new century were usually welcome, but also those who were neither: who were simply entertaining, or who had achieved distinction in some field and were not boring about it. The Astors' guests began to find that going to Cliveden was a distinctive and exciting variation of the customary house party.

As much as anywhere, the new regime at Cliveden aroused interest on the neighbouring estates. One with a considerable reputation of its own was Taplow Court, the home of Lord and Lady Desborough,[15] whose grounds adjoined Cliveden. It was one of the houses in which the group known as the Souls still gathered, largely because of its chatelaine. The heyday of the Souls, for whom Lady Desborough, generally known as Ettie, played a centripetal role, had been fifteen to twenty years earlier, when they had been described by the press as

> . . . a select and a most private coterie of distinguished and brilliant men, and of beautiful and accomplished women, whose main object in association is mental and literary pleasure and improvement. Their union is purely spiritual. They read and write to each other and indulge in sweet converse generally.[16]

The coterie was still in evidence well into the new century, not least in the hothouse atmosphere of Taplow, where they amused each other with intellectual games such as Styles, Breaking the News, and Clumps – in which players had to act out phrases such as 'The Last Straw' or 'A Lost Cause'. But they were not wholly introvert, and their stature in the social and political worlds was such that by the end of the century they had by their initiative extinguished the convention that Tories and Liberals did not mix, or even dine together.

The bewitching Lady Desborough, widely read, stimulating, with an entrancing voice and an eighteen-inch waist, gathered the men of the Souls around her like a queen bee. Lord Revelstoke was a Soul, as were Lady Horner, Lord and Lady Ribblesdale and the Duke and Duchess of Sutherland. Lady Horner was the daughter of a patron of the Pre-Raphaelites, and was the subject of a celebrated portrait by Burne-Jones; Ribblesdale was also the subject of a famous portrait, by Sargent, depicting him in his official clothes as Master of the Buckhounds, and in later life he married the widow of John Jacob Astor, who had gone down with the *Titanic*; at Taplow the Duke of Sutherland was close to home, as his father had sold Cliveden to the Duke of Westminster, who in turn had sold it to William Astor.

Others included Margot Tennant, who, with her sister Laura, was a central figure in the 'Souls'. Margot was to marry Henry Asquith, later Prime Minister; in her opinion the diaphanous Ettie, with her lisp, her soft, low voice and her alluring downward glances, was in fact as strong as an ox, and would be 'turned into Bovril when she dies'. Margot and Nancy later developed a friendship, if not perhaps shared in equal parts: 'You and I have much in common,' Margot later told Nancy, 'joie de vivre & I think love of our fellow creatures' although in Margot's case, such love was often effectively disguised by her notorious frankness. Many people detected similarities between the two, and the wags would say that Margot was a kind Nancy Astor, while Nancy was a good-looking Margot. Certainly Nancy's accurate but unflattering mimicry of Margot was one of the acts with which she would amuse her guests at Cliveden. Margot's own direct and self-confident comments, especially in her earlier days in society, were not always well received by her older acquaintances: one impatient hostess, while entertaining the Prince of Wales to dinner, had to interrupt the young Soul's flow with 'There were *some* clever people in the world, you know, Miss Tennant, before *you* were born.'

Other Souls included Arthur Balfour – perhaps the core member of the group – and Lord Curzon, Viceroy of India and holder of a succession of other high offices of state. Both Balfour and Curzon were soon to prove influential in the political lives of Waldorf and, subsequently, Nancy.

It was to Ettie Grenfell, as she had been until 1905, when her MP husband was created Lord Desborough, that Nancy's erstwhile suitor John Revelstoke had written many florid letters, couched in language suggesting something less than the ethereal, but if they had in fact had a love affair it is likely that it was many years previously, and that Nancy's anger with Revelstoke had, on that account at least, been misplaced. Friendships among the Souls were often described by the term '*amitié amoureuse*', which was probably more accurate than magazine suggestions that they were 'purely spiritual', although in most cases they probably stopped short of being sexual – expressing instead 'romantic, but well-muzzled love'. However, the matter was suitably ambiguous: many of the Souls were talented writers, and they habitually sent each other notes and poems, many of which could have borne innuendo:

> *Now – & Then!*
> *Here is the Spring*
> *Late on the wing.*
> *& Where are you,*
> *Child of the Blue,*
> *And when?*

Nancy was emphatically not a member of the Souls, but she came to know many of them well, and for a period her own house parties took on a similar flavour, although only when a number of the guests actually were Souls. Nevertheless, during the early years of her marriage there remained between her and Ettie little love lost. Nancy was apt to disparage Ettie, saying that she 'never misses a trick', and her own brand of sharp-tongued humour was far from the type that appealed to Lady Desborough or her fastidious, if genial, friends, to whom conversation was such an important pleasure. An example of the clash of cultures was recorded by a young guest at a house party attended by Arthur Balfour and other Souls, when Ettie experimented with an invitation to the Astors:

After luncheon a 'shrieking' Nancy Astor seized Balfour's hand, and demanded if he knew the song 'May I hold this darling little hand?' Mr Balfour, laughing, looked rather embarrassed. She has a rough, harsh voice, and looks like a costermonger's girl. I looked at Ettie, a gracious Princess in her tight velvet gown, and wondered. Nancy Astor has said such vile things of her, saying one would get painter's colic from sitting near her, and that she was angry because she had taken a bald-headed coot [John Revelstoke] away from her, etc . . . but her high confident spirits are infectious. It is not surprising that she told Billy that she judged Nancy 'an excellent friend for her children, but avoided her as best she could'.[17]

One thing that the two women did have in common was a lack of interest in music, in Ettie's case once rather unfortunately expressed when, as a seventeen-year-old and at one of her first parties, she was placed next to the eminent composer Sir Hubert Parry, and opened the conversation by saying, 'I do so hate music, don't you?'

Despite tentative contacts between Ettie and Nancy, it was in general accepted by most guests at both Cliveden and Taplow that the frontier between the two rival fiefdoms was not to be crossed – certainly that was the preference of the hostesses themselves. Even so, a few people, such as Nancy's former suitors Revelstoke and Elphinstone, and her later admirer, Lord Curzon, slipped past the barrier, and before long the flow quickened, to include Maurice Baring, Revelstoke's brother and an archetypal man of letters, politicians such as Hugh Cecil, Lord Castlereagh and Lord Grey, and the famous soldier Herbert Kitchener.

. . Other of Ettie's best men became favoured visitors at Cliveden, and such adored women friends as Alice Salisbury, Mabell Airlie, Mary Elcho and Rachel Dudley succumbed to young Nancy Astor's bland-ishments and became her devotees. The overlap became so pronounced that one wonders if Nancy Astor mischievously set out to net Ettie's dearest friends . . .[18]

Occasionally higher authority also intervened to have the barriers lowered, as in the following summer, of 1908, when the King himself decided to sample the delights of Cliveden, about which he had heard much:

Lady Desborough telephoned Waldorf that the King wished to come over so he came followed by 16 courtiers for tea & stopped for two hours & went over the house and garden & seemed v. pleased with it all. Of course Mrs Keppel came & John Revelstoke who went back and wrote me how wonderfully well I had received His Majesty. The 'nephews and nieces' were furious at his coming as it broke up their tennis. He was v. pleasant and thought Cliveden the prettiest place in England. I don't think the Desboroughs enjoyed the visit but behaved 'nicely' – though I think it slightly strong to bring 16 people. It made us 40 for tea . . .[19]

The fact that Nancy managed to offer hospitality of great comfort, luxury and interest despite her recurrent bouts of ill-health was a testament to her character. It says still more for her that during this first summer she was also pregnant. In such an important family matter she had put her own preferences to one side. However much she may have disliked certain aspects of married life, in general she fulfilled the promises that she had made before the altar: her sense of a woman's obligations was fixed, partly perhaps as a result of growing up with a dominant father.

Although Nancy was to have six children, her distaste for sex, made very evident on her first honeymoon, endured in her life with Waldorf. She considered lust a mortal sin; she was willing to do her conjugal duty but without enthusiasm: 'conceived without pleasure, born without pain' was how she described the brushes with procreation that resulted in her offspring. There would even be occasions on which she would distract herself by eating an apple during the performance – not an appropriate choice of fruit. Nancy admired Waldorf's 'will' but confessed that she could not get used to sharing her bed with anyone – 'Some day,' she told her sister Phyllis, 'I shall be firm about that.' But it did not seem to matter much: between them Waldorf and Nancy were to find other forms of satisfaction that enabled them to stay together in a long-lasting marriage.

Nancy's first child with Waldorf was due in August 1907. She seemed to make light of the matter, but in those days death in childbirth was common, and it was certainly in her thoughts, expressed to Phyllis in a letter of 4 August – having first described the five large pearls that Waldorf had just given her, 'really lovely ones', for a necklace:

. . . I have such pains in my head & oh such indigestion . . . I am very well otherwise and have little to complain of. My room is beautiful and cool and the view glorious. In fact I feel death must be near as I have more than I deserve. If I should die, don't stop Waldorf marrying again as he deserves a far better fate than me . . .[20]

She did not seem anxious for herself but rather for her husband and son, as she expressed in a letter to Bob Shaw's family:

> In about a week I will probably have a baby – naturally I am looking forward to this and my one fear of death is that I shall have to leave Bobbie behind. I am writing you this to ask if anything should go wrong and I should die will you please remember that all of my life since I have had Bobbie he has been first in my thoughts . . . I can't realize how anyone should have so much happiness in life and love so perhaps I am a little bit morbid . . .[21]

However, those sentiments did not chime with her request to Waldorf's sister to 'move Heaven & Earth to keep him away from the Shaws'.[22]

Suggestions that Nancy read little were, at this period of her life, unfounded, and she often recommended to her friends books she herself was reading, or at least looking into. Now, awaiting the birth in her 'glorious room', she read a life of Anne Boleyn, perhaps because her father-in-law's castle at Hever was formerly the Boleyn family's home.

She also read *Tom Jones*, which she found 'delightful' – rather surprisingly as she also maintained, when she had read a life of Ninon de Lenclos and a book on the Holland House set, that she could not get used to 'the scandalous lack of morals of the 18th century and the idle pleasure-seeking ways of the beaux and wits'. Yet even when about to give birth she bridled at a sedentary lifestyle, and would descend to the river, which she found 'delicious in a punt on week days, hardly a soul on it'.

The Astors' first son was born on Tuesday 13 August 1907; he was given the Astor family name of William, but would usually be called Bill. 'Frightened to death,' she wrote in her diary, as the moment drew near. 'Can't say I am enjoying it.'

A little later she wrote with motherly affection that the pains were bad, 'but I would go through them all gladly for one squeeze of Baby. He has Waldorf's nose and eyes & no chin but I can't help loving him. He's very well built & strong & I am glad to say I will and can nurse him – it makes all the difference.'[23] She was to be less glad at the involvement of Princess Marie: 'That lunatic Princess,' she told Phyllis, 'is going to be a Godmother & I *hate* it but gave in to Waldorf . . .'

Her husband was of course delighted with all these events.

It was not long before Waldorf's father announced that he would come over to Cliveden to see what he called 'so important a member of the family as my grandson'. Nancy was horrified at the thought of him seeing the alterations to the house, and took to her bed at his approach. She need not have worried: the old man was delighted with Bill and was sufficiently courteous – a quality he never lost – to say that he liked Nancy's work. 'He thought my room beautiful,' she wrote, 'and the hall & drawing-room much more liveable. Quite a concession from him, I think.'

Waldorf's son and heir was born into a world of peace and luxury, but also into a happy home. The young Astors were content and recognised their good fortune. 'The joy of knowing you are absolutely independent,' as Nancy told her sister. 'It is comforting,' she added. 'I should have married an ogre for that.' She sparkled with confidence. Her good looks and beautiful clothes enhanced the pleasure that she radiated, delighted as she was at the obvious magnetism of her bubbling talk.

Yet remarkably, in view of the image that she presented to her friends, she retained misgivings. With her purity and sense of righteousness she was not at ease with the rich, serene society she had entered: 'I know you didn't like it,' Waldorf commented many years later, 'as you have often told me.'

Most of her friends had no such qualms. It was famously said that no one who had not lived in France before the revolution could know the true sweetness of life, and likewise for many the antebellum age in the American South had aspects of perfection; while in England, the years that followed the death of Queen Victoria were for the rich a brief moment of unalloyed pleasure. For this was the Edwardian Age, and the surroundings in which Waldorf and Nancy lived contained the quintessence of that era: opulence; indolence; hedonism; sunlit summers; long days and nights of fashion and society. Peace reigned at home and in the Empire, trade was good and life inexpensive, as Britain, at the apex of her military and financial power, benignly ruled a quarter of the world. Underlying all was an almost palpable sense of satisfaction that the state of the country was, if not perfect, then as near to that as God could make it.

The way of life established by the Astors at Cliveden, and, in the first years of the century, by many other families up and down the land, gave focus to that image: a carefree era with people largely unconcerned about the state of affairs beyond their own world. It was an understandable reaction to the austere days of Queen Victoria, even if it seemed to some dour souls, such as George Orwell, to have but a garish veneer:

It was the age when crazy millionaires in curly top hats and lavender waistcoats gave champagne parties in rococo houseboats on the Thames . . . when people talked about chocs and cigs and ripping and topping and heavenly . . . From the whole decade before 1914 there seems to breathe forth a smell of the more vulgar, un-grown-up kinds of luxury, a smell of brilliantine and crème de menthe and soft-centre chocolates – an atmosphere, as it were, of eating everlasting strawberry ices on green lawns to the tune of the Eton Boating Song.[24]

Behind that alluring facade, however, erosion had begun; the tide had already turned and was advancing, remorseless if almost imperceptible in the agreeable haze of the times.

The effects of the long years of cheap food imports and stagnant agriculture were beginning to force many of the upper classes, at least those reliant on rural rents, to sell off land, to let or sell family houses, and to draw in their horns radically. Enormous sales of property were ceasing to be unusual, and many ancient names were quietly slipping off the social map.

At the top of society, however, especially among those who had flows of income other than from land, little change was noticeable. The gaps left by the financial adversity of some of the aristocracy were soon filled by rich men who would not have been 'received' in the previous reign but who were encouraged or at least tolerated by King Edward: men such as the grocer Sir Thomas Lipton, German bankers Sir Ernest Cassel and Baron Hirsch, the Rothschilds, and Sir Edward Sassoon, scion of a powerful Indian merchant family, along with rich British merchants, American heiresses, and randlords from South Africa. Such people exemplified a change in society that marked the end of the old century; at the same time, however, by adopting in their pattern of living the traditional framework of that society, the newcomers reflected the general desire at the time for as little change as possible.

In accordance with common practice among people with time to spare, in late summer the Astors went up to Scotland, for sport and a chance of relaxation. Even if the scale of entertaining was smaller than at Cliveden, there were plenty of house parties, some of which the Astors attended, although so soon after Bill's birth Nancy had to spend many hours each day lying low. They took a place of their own near Loch Luichart, in Rossshire, which offered the attractions of a comparatively simple life: a small motorboat, a large garden full of flowers and vegetables, and woods around the house. There were red deer to stalk, and grouse and fallow deer to shoot. Nancy longed to go stalking, but her temporarily frail state prevented it.

In October 1907, Nancy returned to Scotland, having been invited to a party at Gosford House, the seat of the Earl of Wemyss, who had once been a Liberal MP, as had his son, Hugo Charteris, a leading member of the Souls. Nancy had been encouraged to hear that Arthur Balfour was due to be a fellow guest, but before she could join the party she received a frightening shock: she was rushed off to Edinburgh – 'Flat on my back in a nursing home,' she wrote, 'a lump in my breast, might turn to an abscess, I was frightened green . . .' It turned out to be a harmless matter, and Nancy was quickly up, and able to go to Gosford.

There she did meet Balfour, as she had hoped. As he was a leading politician of great influence, it may have been more than his agreeable company that interested Nancy. There were many differences between her character and that of Waldorf: she was lively, stimulating, humorous, irrepressible; Waldorf was altogether more studious, and with a kindlier nature. Their various attributes had jointly hastened their progress into society, and already they were establishing Cliveden as one of the finest houses in England to which to be invited. But at a deeper level they had many similarities, including a yearning to encourage goodness and Christian attributes. By their nature neither was satisfied with mere social activity, however exhilarating. The Puritan strain running through each of their characters impelled them to seek moral fulfilment.

At first they had their hands full with planning and managing life at Cliveden, a complex matter however efficient the servants at their behest. Now Nancy was further occupied by Bill, even if, should she wish it, she could delegate the care of the child to others at a moment's notice. But from the start she had been impressed by the potential inherent in Waldorf's talents, and felt that they must not go to waste. He too was intent on making the most of opportunity, and they had both begun to give thought to the ways in which he might make a generous and proper use of his time and abilities. A political life beckoned.

FIVE

New Adventures

Among the qualities that had originally attracted Nancy to Waldorf were his modesty and wisdom. At first, however, she feared that they were overlaid by an inclination to an idle life, something she was having none of, as she later made clear when expressing the hope that her son Bill would do something useful, and not just settle down to pleasure: 'what Waldorf wanted to do at 27 when I married him – country gentleman and racing – and I told his father that was no life for me; and although I used at times to irritate the old man he was always grateful to me for saving Waldorf from that'.

In reality, it was not in Waldorf's character to settle for a quiet life, even without the stimulating effect of Nancy's company, and there were always plenty of ideas and projects in his mind. In the early years of their marriage, the foremost of those stemmed from his love of racing, a sport linked with hunting, partly through its offshoot, point-to-point racing. Nancy herself loved horses and hunting, but although she had friends who were in the racing set, she disliked the atmosphere of their world, perhaps because of a mutual feeling that she was not part of it. Nevertheless, she was impressed by Waldorf's knowledge and expertise, and encouraged him to develop them.

He had begun his racing activities while still at Oxford, where, like many of his friends, he took up steeplechasing. He soon developed an interest in thoroughbred horses, and at the age of twenty-one he began breeding them himself. In 1900, he paid £100 for his first thoroughbred mare, Conjure, which he mated to premium stallions with the intention of breeding hunters. In the first years all Conjure's foals died at or soon after birth, although a later foal, Winkipop, was to survive and in 1910 bring Waldorf his first major racing successes, winning the 1,000 Guineas, the Coronation Stakes and the Sussex Stakes. In 1904, he bought another mare, Semitone, and some yearling fillies, and sent them for training. He then bought a yearling, Popinjay, for 1,000 guineas from the celebrated owner Lord Rosebery.

When he bought Maid of the Mist in 1911, it was a step up to an altogether higher level. The price, 4,500 guineas, enormous for the time, reflected the fact that the mare was out of Sceptre, the winner of four of the five classic races of 1902. Waldorf had bought her in foal and with foal at foot, and with his rapidly increasing knowledge and what was already proving to be shrewd judgement, he sold on the unborn foal for 1,000 guineas. Conjure, Popinjay and Maid of the Mist became the foundation of the Cliveden stud, which would more than once take Waldorf to the head of the list of winning owners, and which during his lifetime was to produce about 400 foals, at least half of which won flat races, and of which a high proportion could be described as top class.

What had started as the recreation of a twenty-one-year-old undergraduate was before long to place Waldorf among the leading figures in the racing world. From 1907, almost all the horses he entered for races were bred at Cliveden, and the following year the stud establishment was completed with the most modern buildings and accessories. Over the next few decades, horses in the Astor pink and blue colours were to win the St Leger, the 1,000 Guineas twice, the 2,000 Guineas three times, and the Oaks five times. In the mind of the racing public, however, that remarkable record was tinged by the failure of Astor horses to win the Derby, perhaps the best known of all races, although they came second five times – once beaten by only a neck. It was widely believed that Waldorf would have won it on more than one occasion had he been less loyal to a long-serving jockey who was outclassed by his rivals. Nancy shared that view, and commented that 'As Waldorf always insisted on having jockeys with impeccable characters, who were absolutely straight, we never did as well on the turf as we might have done.' If that were so, it would have been entirely in character.[1]

His devotion to the stud was certainly characteristic. In order to acquire a thorough understanding of horses he apprenticed himself to a vet, and his interest appeared to be as much scientific as emotional, apart from a natural affection for the animals that he owned. The convivial side of racing, the thrill of the chase, the urge for a fast buck, passed him by: he rarely went to a race meeting unless one of his horses was running, and he never placed bets; as he would say, 'the horse can't tell you whether he is feeling fit'.

Although Waldorf would very much have liked to share his passion with his wife, it was not long before she lost interest, and eventually indifference gave way to intolerance; she was famously observed reading her Bible as the Astor champion Buchan was pipped at the post in the 1919 Derby. Waldorf was greatly saddened by his wife's attitude: 'Oh why weren't you at Newmarket?' he wrote to her forlornly, after one of Winkipop's victories:

'Half the pleasure of winning was lost through your not being there . . .'
At least he could delight in taking his sons to the stables on the Malborough
Downs when he went to discuss racing affairs with his trainer.

Nor did others in the family pay much attention. In 1904, Waldorf's
sister Pauline had married Captain Herbert Spender-Clay, a Sussex landowner and Conservative MP, and had become busy with her own life. His
younger brother John had joined the army, and would in due course be
posted to India as an ADC to the viceroy, while his father had never shown
much interest in racing, possibly because he was short-sighted. However,
although William did not display much direct enthusiasm for his son's
enterprise, his attitude was benign; not least, he provided the money without
which Waldorf might not have started the stud at all.

In parallel with the stud and racing, Waldorf took an increasing interest
in agriculture. In order to develop his plans, he used some of the $100,000
his father had given him for his birthday in 1906 to buy White Place Farm,
opposite the Cliveden estate. Ideas for the improvement of agricultural
practice, many inspired by his visits to American farms, and introduced on
his own land, were later to be an important part of his political work, and
chimed with his basic interest in ameliorating the conditions of the poor.
At White Place he turned his attention to the scourge of tuberculosis –
traditionally known as consumption – a lethal disease that was at the time
the country's most urgent health problem. It was highly contagious among
cattle, and humans were thought to contract it through drinking raw milk.

In 1901, a Royal Commission had been established to examine the causes
of TB, and the first successful vaccine, although not then ready for humans,
was created in 1906. For Waldorf, the subject was uncomfortably close to
home: his younger sister had died of the disease, he was at risk of it himself,
and it was also in his wife's family. He was aware of the havoc it wrought,
particularly among the poor and undernourished, and especially their children. He therefore turned his new farm over to the breeding of a disease-free
herd of cows, being one of the first in the country to do so.[2] In fact, Waldorf's
insistence on pure milk was such that, when going away for any length of
time, he would take with him on the train a cow and cowman, ensuring
clean milk for the children and cream for the use of the chef.

Despite the fact that Waldorf was already channelling his ideas into
productive outlets, it was in Nancy's nature to spur him on, and she soon
determined to encourage him into another and entirely different path to
achievement. As she recorded:

I had an idea. Lord Balfour and George Curzon were good friends of
mine. We went to them for help and advice, and it was suggested that

Waldorf should stand for Parliament. He thought it an excellent scheme, and his father was delighted. Waldorf went to the Central Office to learn. Like so many people of that day he was at heart a Liberal, but he liked the Conservative programme.[3]

In fact, Curzon and Balfour were not yet good friends of Nancy – Balfour's first visit to Cliveden was not until the end of November 1908 – but both were regular guests of the Desboroughs, and for some time they had been at least acquainted with the Astors. In any event, it was not very long before political plans for Waldorf were hatched, and in due course they were reflected in the Cliveden party list: Henry and Margot Asquith were among the first political guests, staying there the following summer, when Asquith had been Prime Minister for over a year.

The prospect of Waldorf standing for Parliament as a Conservative candidate brought into harmony four sets of interests: first, it offered him a way out of the *Pall Mall Gazette* without too much opposition from his father. He greatly disliked the job, and nor did Nancy approve of it: 'He uses up his energy on the work a clerk could do,' she wrote, 'and it's a great waste.' Second, the idea gratified Nancy: 'He is too good a man,' she told Archdeacon Neve, 'not to help in public things.' Third, it suited the Conservative authorities: they could use the services of a seemingly sensible and personable candidate whose politics, they might reasonably assume, matched the party line, and who was the son of an influential newspaper proprietor. Tory administrators no doubt also envisaged Astor money being injected into the political infrastructure of whichever constituency selected Waldorf, and perhaps flowing more generally to party funds.

Finally, it pleased Waldorf's father that his family should lend all the support it could to the Conservative Party. It gave teeth to his fierce opposition to socialism, which he saw as a grave threat to the way of life he cherished in his adopted country. However, William Waldorf's politics lacked the milk of human kindness that appealed to his son, who had a full measure of social conscience and whose politics in fact set him very much on the left wing of the Conservative Party.

Another reason for his father supporting the idea was that Waldorf's prospective move into politics might help William with his ultimate aim of sealing, through ennoblement, his transformation into an English gentleman. He had made enquiries in that direction soon after his arrival in England, but had been given to understand that in his particular case a peerage was only a remote possibility, which, even if realised, would first require the passage of many years. Undeterred, he laid plans to overcome the obstacles in his way. In July 1895 he had written to the Marquess of

Salisbury, then Prime Minister, with a donation of £10,000 to Conservative Party funds. Three years later, at a meeting with Sir Schomberg McDonnell, the Prime Minister's private secretary, he tackled the matter head-on and directly requested a peerage. Salisbury, however, demurred, saying that he was unaware of any instance in which an alien had been created a peer; unless he was of royal blood. William persisted, and in due course asked McDonnell how long, in the case of his becoming a naturalised British citizen, he would have to wait before his name could be considered for a peerage. McDonnell had replied that even then no period less than seven or eight years would be sufficient, and that twenty years would be a more proper term.[4]

Patient but dogged, William became a naturalised Englishman in 1899. Over the following years, with his own particular mix of shrewdness and generosity, he continued to dispense enormous largesse, not only to the Conservative Party but also to a variety of good causes. When England was suffering military reverses during the Boer War, he gave the government $100,000, which, among other things, was used to procure a quick-firing battery of great value to the fighting troops. In 1902, deeply upset by the death of his young daughter Gwendolyn, he donated the huge sum of $50,000 to the Great Ormond Street Hospital for Sick Children. Taking other donations into account, his charitable gifts at that time amounted to £75,000 – over £7.5 million in current values.[5]

For her part, Nancy's determination to steer Waldorf towards politics was a development of a notion that she had held for quite some time. Even while on honeymoon in Cortina, Nancy had written to her father-in-law about the possibility of Waldorf entering politics, receiving an encouraging reply: 'I fully agree with all your thoughtful anticipations of a Parliamentary career for Waldorf – he will have to wait a couple of years as the political weather, just now, is unfavourable for the Conservatives.' To describe the political climate as 'unfavourable' was a considerable understatement. Conservative prospects had all but collapsed at the beginning of 1906, when, after a highly charged and often violent election campaign, they had suffered a landslide defeat – even the Prime Minister lost his seat – and, after years in opposition, the Liberal Party had taken office.

Among their driving spirits was Asquith, at first Chancellor of the Exchequer, and a thrusting Welsh lawyer, David Lloyd George, the new President of the Board of Trade. With overwhelming power in its hands, the incoming government embarked upon an ambitious and highly controversial programme of social reform unprecedented in British history. Over the following three years it introduced a law to put trade disputes beyond the civil law, arranged for an arbitration process in case of threatened strikes, legislated for workmen's compensation and old age pensions, and planned far-reaching changes in the fields of children's welfare and education.

In 1908, Asquith became Prime Minister and appointed Lloyd George Chancellor of the Exchequer. The latter, with a full stock of satire and verbal vitriol, and intent on forcing through welfare policies, began to build a foundation of popular support, hardly disguising his real intention of using tax to deal a body blow, via their pockets, to landowners and others at the rich end of society. The government's programme threatened to implement a major redistribution of the wealth of the country, and in the process to destroy patterns of English life that had been settled for generations. The Conservative Party, defender of the landed interest and of the established political framework, was determined to prevent this. It no longer had a popular mandate, but it did have a final resort: the House of Lords, still an hereditary body, and by long constitutional usage equipped with real power – to amend and veto legislation passed by the Commons.

For men such as William Astor, the outlook was greatly upsetting, as he later explained to Nancy:

For me it is the fight of my life, and I shall never dare tell you the money I am spending in the good cause & the personal efforts I have been making for months to help rouse the British Lion. Not a day passes I do not ask myself, 'What is the matter with the beast that had such good sense & such fine qualities & now seems so wanting in both?'[6]

It was against this ominous background, although at first it hardly disturbed the peace and pleasures of Cliveden, that Waldorf prepared his bid to enter Parliament.

It happened that in the summer of 1908, the Conservative Association in Plymouth was looking for candidates to enter the contest for what was then a two-member constituency.[7] In the 1906 general election the Conservatives had lost the seat to the Liberals, who were now well entrenched. In the new political climate it was not a good Tory prospect, as parts of the town were areas of intense deprivation, by some measures more so than almost anywhere else in the country, and thus fertile ground for the new Liberal ideas. The Barbican, in the harbour area, and home to the city's fish market, was one of the worst parts:

There was almost no sanitation; families were overcrowded into dangerous tenements built indiscriminately over back gardens, over roofs of old sea captains' houses, anywhere you could fit a human container. It was a place of violence, extreme drunkenness and abject poverty, a Calcutta-like inferno of human misery on the coast of Devon.[8]

On 25 June, Waldorf travelled down to inspect the ground, after which he decided to apply for the seat.

Nancy was at once fascinated by Plymouth, and every bit as strongly as Waldorf. It called to her mind the original settlers of Virginia. Her imagination soared above the narrow, dilapidated streets suffused with the smell of fish and crammed with the wretched poor. She saw instead a vista of swashbuckling Elizabethans sailing off to far horizons to lay the foundations of imperial Britain, Francis Drake defying the arrogant Spaniards, and the Pilgrim Fathers aboard the *Mayflower* setting out from Sutton Pool almost three centuries before:

> What a funny thing that was! The moment I got there I had the strangest feeling of having come home. It was not like a new place to me. I felt that here was where I belonged. I remember sitting down and writing to Father and telling him all this. He wrote back saying there was nothing strange about it. One of the Langhornes was Member of Parliament in St Just in 1697, he told me that a branch of the family had then been settled in Devonshire and Wales.[9]

To those without Nancy's perspective the outlook was less appealing, and the Conservatives, who needed two candidates to contest the seat, were having difficulty in finding even one. The previous Tory candidates had failed to work well in harness and had abandoned the attempt; the cause in Plymouth languished, and the mood was all for the Liberals. There were still no takers when Waldorf arrived to meet the party executives. On the issues of the day – the Liberals' threat to reform and emasculate the House of Lords; education; old age pensions; the army and navy; tariff reform, and the other radical plans of the government – both Waldorf and Nancy agreed, on the whole, with Conservative policies. At all events, they were sufficiently orthodox to gain an initial hearing from the Plymouth Conservatives.

However, the potential candidate had to tread warily. There was the problem of his disapproval of alcohol, which, although less strident than his wife's, was very far from the attitude of many of those whose votes he would have to win. The chairman of the local party was head of a distillery; Plymouth was a leading centre for gin production; and there was a large market for beer, with an alehouse at almost every street corner.

In her support of Waldorf, Nancy took a close interest in general ideas but spent little time on the details of policy. However, with Cliveden becoming a centre of political talk, she was able to relate broad ideas to personal circumstance. One such connection was the threat that a proposed Licensing Bill might make to brewery profits: ever alert to other people's woes, she worried about Waldorf's brother-in-law, most of whose money was in brewery shares. Yet her kindly concern, even for friends and relations, was overshadowed by her underlying conviction that easy access to drink increased violence, accidents, lunacy and family misery, and should be curtailed.

Despite his views on drink, and a rather liberal stance on social questions, Waldorf was welcomed as a candidate: personable, quiet but authoritative, possessed of independent means and willing to fill the post. His selection was unanimous: 'Mr Astor for Plymouth,' cried the paper boys. The Astors' courtship of Plymouth had begun, but the family was also to involve itself more widely with British politics, and over the next few decades nine of its members would sit in Parliament.[10]

Not long after Waldorf's selection, the Astors, redeeming a pledge made during discussions about Waldorf's candidacy, bought a house in the constituency, choosing one of the finest houses in the town, number 3, Elliot Terrace. It was large, tall and comfortable, with the outward appearance of a hotel, and stood in a commanding position on the Hoe, where in 1588, as tradition has it, Francis Drake had coolly finished his game of bowls before putting out to sea to confront the Spanish Armada.

Neither Waldorf nor Nancy could have had a clear idea of the exhausting practicalities of nursing a constituency, yet they had no doubts about the course Waldorf had taken. Nancy saw before her a whole new field of excitement and activity: a constituency for her husband to fight, a new house to furnish and develop as a base of operations, great obstacles to be overcome on the path to winning the seat, but a coveted prize at its end. Nor did she doubt that she was made for the part of helping to bring it all about. For a start, she felt that she had within her the gift, if not of oratory, at least of uplifting persuasion; the chance to express it would satisfy her desire to reach out to people and do them good. She used to recall how she had enjoyed talking to some stokers on a liner going to America. The men, escaping the heat below, were probably glad of the excuse to linger for a moment in the cool air on deck, and to be allowed to talk to an attractive first-class passenger. But for Nancy it seemed to be more than that; it was 'like suddenly finding that I had a skill or talent I had known nothing about'.

From an early age she seems to have had within her an irresistible urge to influence and reform, to a greater or lesser degree, almost any state of affairs with which she was confronted. It is unclear where this came from her parents seem an unlikely source – but it had been with her at least since her friendship in Virginia with the missionary Frederick Neve, who had opened her eyes to inequality and suffering. Now she saw an outlet for the vitality she felt she had always possessed: 'I threw myself into the business of working for the Constituency for my husband and loved every minute of it.'

Her ideas, enthusiastically expressed even if not clearly formulated, included two broad ingredients: to build up Waldorf's political prospects by forging and strengthening the Astors' links with influential politicians; and to give to his constituency both time and money. Money would certainly help the process, but for the Astors the plan was free of cynicism. Nancy took to the spadework of politics as a duck to water. Demonstrating in the often hostile streets of Plymouth her combination of self-confidence, fearlessness and a tender heart, she made a deep and unexpected impression, and the very surprise it caused helped draw a grudging but growing affection from its recipients. She soon found that she loved the life of Plymouth and she believed that she understood its people. She also approached the party leader, A.J. Balfour, and within a few months he agreed to her giving a party in his honour at Cliveden: 'Waldorf very pleased at his coming,' she wrote. 'I am rather nervous.' Her neighbours the Desboroughs, she mused, would hate the idea.

Yet for all this activity, Nancy was still dogged by ill-health. Frequent headaches depressed her and made her worry about how she would be able to help Waldorf with his politics. In October, she went to Scotland to try and recuperate, and anxiously wrote to her sister Phyllis, 'I know that there's no use thinking of Plymouth as in spite of sleeping every afternoon here, at about 7 o'clock I turn green and am only fit for bed, so I could not do anything.'

Furthermore, shortly before Waldorf's selection, Nancy had again conceived. All through the autumn and winter she had to avoid stress and exertion, until, in March 1909, her second child, Phyllis, later known as Wissie, was born, receiving for a short time her full and devoted attention. Although in this period Nancy's spirits would occasionally dip, she took pleasure in the new arrival. She also consoled herself with the Bible, and, perhaps feeling an affinity with those on an earlier pilgrimage, studied maps of the journeys of the Children of Israel, '. . . who went hundreds of miles out of their way to reach the land of Canaan'.

She also consoled herself with thoughts of a tea gown she had ordered from the Paris couturier Worth, convincing herself that it would do her for a year: 'I am being very economical – and can't spend money on clothes – never could & don't think I ever will.'[11] A momentary lapse of memory, no doubt; ever since her arrival in England she had dressed well and expensively, although she occasionally wondered why: 'I wish I had character enough,' she wrote in her diary, 'to dress in a uniform. I wish we all dressed like Japanese, and fashions were stationary. I loathe these yearly changes and silly light skirts and gruelling hats. We are not so far from apes as Mr Darwin would have us believe.' Her taste in clothes was appreciated by others, however, and she began to attract the notice of the local press, who soon found that they had a useful new subject.

Larger than life in everything except her slight body, Nancy knew that if she dressed well, it would give pleasure to the humbler inhabitants of Plymouth, whose women had to make do with rough cloth, and little of it. She made sure that she gave them that pleasure, as over the next few years she made canvassing calls to some twenty or thirty thousand houses, by any standards an enormous effort. During election campaigns the job would be carried out at high speed with only a moment or two at each house. She would mount the rough stone staircase of a tenement building and bang vigorously on a door. After a moment it would open, revealing the occupant, often a stern-faced lady with coarse features, wearing carpet slippers. Nancy, slight, neat and bejewelled, would smile and announce: 'I am Mrs Astor. My husband is standing for Parliament. Will you vote for him?' Then she would move briskly on. She was undaunted by adverse responses echoing down the chilly corridors. Her worst problem, which she controlled only with great difficulty, was her acute fear of cats, which would frequently shoot past her in unlit passages, or brush against her legs.

Having bought a house in Plymouth, Waldorf and Nancy established a staff in it and began to devote a considerable amount of time to nursing the constituency. Nancy had picked up a good knowledge of politics at Cliveden, and at various parties and gatherings, but an interest in social questions came naturally to her. As she helped Waldorf in the constituency, acts of unostentatious kindness and constructive help became characteristic of 'the candidate's wife'. Together they pioneered schemes, especially in the poorest areas, for day nurseries and children's homes, and they established a boys' and girls' club in premises they personally bought for the purpose. It made an impression on local people, who had only ever seen the upper classes, if at all, from afar. The Astors also began to support existing institutions, offering much-needed help that would allow them to grow, and Nancy became an active voice in local charitable enterprises. On a more personal basis, she befriended many voters and their families, comforting them if they were ill or in distress.

The Astors' increasing commitment to politics diminished the amount of time they spent with their children. However, Bobbie was at boarding school for some of the year and was happy at home in the holidays, with all the opportunities and excitements Cliveden offered to a ten-year-old. The arrangements for Bill and Wissie were equally comprehensive. All the children were in the charge of their nanny, Mrs Gibbons, a redoubtable lady who was also a force to be reckoned with by the servants. Edwin Lee, then a footman, but in due course to take the reins as butler, recalled the effects of a nanny on children before they went away to school:

> They are mollycoddled, fussed over, decisions are made for them up until the day they go away, so that they're unready for the Spartan life that follows. And it's the nannies that are paid to do this. To justify themselves they make demands on everyone else's time and patience, and are always allowed to get away with it. It's no good any servant trying to fight them because they have the ear of the mistress of the house. It's 'Nanny knows best', not just for the children but for the staff as well.[12]

At Cliveden, there was no let-up in the scale of entertaining. Politicians were now very relevant to the Astors' life, but writers and artists were also invited, besides others with little in common beyond acquaintance with their hosts. Nancy was happy to play hostess to people of culture. Although hardly a philistine, she was neither intellectual nor artistic, showing little evidence of having original ideas; yet memories of the inspired teaching of Miss Jennie may have encouraged in her a continuing thirst for knowledge. In any event, she now drew to her salon successful men of art and literature, mixing them with politicians who not only might help her husband's career, but who also satisfied her desire to feel well informed and near to the centre of events.

Yet the Astors were no lion hunters; if anything, it was the other way around – many people who had never come across Waldorf or Nancy in their own literary or artistic circles were glad to accept an invitation to Cliveden. J.M. Barrie, whom Nancy admired for a time, was happy to go, and she made a particular friend of Hilaire Belloc, who, with an American wife, was well informed about her country and enjoyed discussing it, and who rather appreciated her clowning brand of humour and fondness for practical jokes. Belloc began to send her rather bizarre and whimsical letters enlivened with inky drawings, usually composed on his journeys through Europe while researching his travel writing, or during his lecture tours to the far corners of Britain. Later, however, Nancy turned against him, regarding him as being too obviously worldly – friends described him as 'a good hand with knife and fork, better still with glass and bottle'[13] – and also because of his strong adherence to Catholicism, against which she nursed a deep prejudice.

Also helping to differentiate the parties at Cliveden from those at most other large houses of the day were the frequent American guests at the house. Perhaps because of that, and the fact that the hosts too were American, many English guests sensed a slight impression of foreignness, or even rootlessness, in the atmosphere.

Some of those invited by 'The Young Waldorf Astors' may not have been charmed by Nancy's brisk and powerful personality, but, as is now clear, her humour largely compensated for that. At any rate, the guests came. A virtuous circle formed, with the view spreading that at Cliveden were sure to be found people who were intelligent, amusing or glamorous, of whom some at least might prove interesting and useful to meet. The Princess of Pless, famous for pearls that hung in rows down to her knees, gave a perceptive summary after staying at Cliveden in July 1909:

> The house is full of people, amongst these being Sophy Torby and the Grand Duke Michael, and Winston Churchill, who sat next to me at dinner. I am awfully sorry for him; he is like a racehorse wanting to start at once – even on the wrong race track; he has so much impetuousness that he cannot hold himself back, and he is too clever and has much too much personal magnetism . . . At present his politics are all personal, the politics of an American advertiser . . . He is not happy if he is not always before the public, and he may some day be Prime Minister – and why not, he has energy and brains . . .[14]

Churchill was at that time President of the Board of Trade, and in the Cabinet, preparing for, among a number of revolutionary proposals, the introduction of labour exchanges, an innovation designed to help the unemployed find work. It was an idea conceived, as he later put it, 'to set a balustrade along the crowded causeway of the people's life . . . to fasten a lid over the abyss into which vast numbers used to fall, generation after generation, uncared for and, indeed, unnoticed'.[15]

Such sentiments matched the broad-minded if paternalistic politics of Waldorf and Nancy. Their conscience, and desire to help people, chimed with Lloyd George's assertions that the poor were entitled to a larger share of the increased national wealth, which had resulted from thirty or forty years of unparalleled industrial expansion. On the other hand, they felt stirrings of unease at the unfolding Liberal programme, inspired by Lloyd George and supported by Churchill's eloquence, and Nancy began to worry that the government's objectives contrasted with the robust American attitude that the state should be kept at arm's length from people's private lives.

Meanwhile it became apparent that, to meet the huge expense involved in the programme, the government was bent on imposing high taxation. However, concern at the rates envisaged proved secondary to growing fears that the money thus raised was apparently to be used not only for its traditional purposes, but also for bringing about the redistribution of wealth, which the Conservatives considered to be an unconstitutional use of taxation.

Matters came to a head when Lloyd George presented his so-called People's Budget at the end of April 1909. It authorised nearly a dozen separate taxes, including three highly controversial land taxes, which the government hoped would lead to sales of land, so cheapening its price and forcing on to the market plots that could be used for urban development.

An extraordinary political upheaval ensued, and on 30 November 1909, the lava overflowed: the House of Lords rejected the highly controversial Budget, saying that it was not justified in passing the Bill until it had been submitted to the judgement of the country. Uproar broke out. Furious MPs claimed that such a thing had not been seen for two centuries, and that the Lords' right to reject a Budget had long ago become 'dormant, moribund and finally dead'. The government determined on all-out attack on the power of the upper House, if necessary asking the King to create enough new peers to extinguish its built-in Conservative majority. First, though, to try and circumvent the prevailing impasse, the Prime Minister asked for a dissolution of Parliament, and an election was called for January 1910.

Waldorf could now put to the test eighteen months of hard work in his constituency, and left at once for Plymouth, to prepare for battle. Although Nancy was deeply tired, she involved herself fully in the campaign, on several occasions addressing the voters, sometimes from the balcony of the Conservative Club. 'I am becoming a mob orator,' she wrote after one such speech, 'a female Lloyd George, God forbid . . .' On that occasion Waldorf's father was among the audience, proudly lending his son support, as was Chillie, who had come over to Cliveden with Nora for Christmas.

The result saw Waldorf placed third – his bid foundering, Nancy believed, partly on lack of organisation. Because of the electoral system prevailing in 1910, whereby Plymouth returned two members to Parliament, Waldorf had to manage his campaign in harness with another candidate, an ageing retired diplomat called Sir Mortimer Durand, who proved to be ineffective. Waldorf was also hindered by a serious attack of consumption in mid-campaign, so that he had to leave the field and rush up to Scotland with Nancy, to expose himself to cold fresh air. Despite his enforced absence, his Liberal opponents' majority was sharply reduced, and there was joy in the ranks of his supporters. 'Meeting of our workers,' Nancy recorded. 'Never have I seen such enthusiasm. They dragged our carriage . . . about 1,000 men and women sang and shouted down. It was all v. personal and delicious and I shall never, never forget them . . .'

After the election, Nancy and Waldorf went off to Switzerland for a well-earned rest – Nancy said that she slept ten hours for the first time in her life – and were soon restored by the mountain air, and happy days of skating, curling and sleighing. They returned to Cliveden early in February, with Lent almost upon them, and Nancy dutifully made her resolutions: 'I have made many vows,' she wrote. 'I shall try my utmost to keep them. Gossip is barred. No kiss and intercourse. No cigarettes . . . all this is but little to fear when I think of manifold blessings.'[16]

She resumed family life, riding in the Taplow woods with Bobbie, having tea with Ettie Desborough's eldest son, Julian Grenfell, playing golf with Waldorf, and going up to London for social engagements. She talked to John Singer Sargent, who agreed to draw her again; she met the King, who expressed regret at Waldorf's defeat; she dined with Waldorf's father, and Prince Arthur of Connaught asked her to lunch at Clarence House. She also met her former love, Lord Revelstoke: 'I like him,' she reflected, 'but all love has gone, gone, gone. I admire his brain and dislike his mind.'

To offset the increasing demands political life had placed upon her, she began to think of alternative ways of finding rest and a change, beyond nursing homes or brief cures at fashionable German spas. Perhaps partly for that purpose the Astors built, in 1910, what Nancy, using one of her American idioms, called a 'seaside cottage'. To design it they turned to Paul Phipps, a friend of Waldorf's from Eton and Oxford. He was an engaging and lively man, half American and considered for a time to be the best dancer in London – no girl, it was said, was really 'out' until she had danced with him. Now he was a struggling architect, looking for work; but a particular reason for the Astors' choosing him for their new project was that Nancy's youngest sister, Nora, after a whirlwind but abortive affair with a Virginian, had, rather to the family's consternation, agreed to marry Phipps instead.

The house was to be a retreat for Waldorf and Nancy when tired or in pain, or just to escape the formality of much of their life. The site they chose was between two golf links in Sandwich Bay, in Kent, partly because golf was a bond between them. It was almost on the edge of the sea, exposed to clear salty sunshine or, alternatively, to the clouds that frequently obscured it – exposure that was difficult to avoid even indoors, as Nancy had some of the front windows nailed open to let in the bracing sea air.

It proved to be rather more than a cottage, generously planned, and with a hint of the Indian Raj. There were fifteen bedrooms, a nursery floor, servants' quarters and a lobby set aside as a telephone exchange – even when they were hidden away in Kent, the Astors' daily life required considerable administration. As was now the practice with new houses of any size, bathrooms were installed, but in this case each bath had four taps – seawater and fresh, hot and cold. There were also five different types of shower.

The atmosphere was light, modern and comfortable, the drawing room furnished with a large chesterfield sofa with pale quilted silk cushions, painted floorboards under a square Persian carpet, white furniture, and numerous book tables and rests. On the shelves were model sailing ships, blue china, and a complete set of the Everyman Library, rarely disturbed; a compass showed the direction of the wind, no doubt useful for deciding on whether to go out and play golf. The main rooms faced the sea, with wide windows that let in abundant light, and let out the sound of the dance music that frequently emanated from the drawing room gramophone. Upstairs, doors led on to a balcony, and the floor, walls and ceiling of some of the bedrooms were painted midnight blue, which Nancy considered restful. A miniature golf course was laid out in the garden, at the end of which Nancy later built a squash court. They called their new house Rest Harrow, the name of a plant that flourished in the neighbourhood and was named for fouling machinery used for harrowing the land, holding up the horses while the weed was removed. The house would soon became another outlet of Astor hospitality, and many friends, particularly politicians in need of a rest, would accept Nancy's offer of a stay in her new haven.

The rise in the political temperature following the rejection of Lloyd George's Budget showed no signs of letting up the following year. Nationally, the election results of January 1910 were inconclusive, much to the government's surprise. Not only did there emerge the first signs of a new power in Parliament – the Labour Party, which won forty seats – but the Liberals lost their overall majority. Now, in order to stay in office, they had to win the support of the eighty-two MPs of the Irish Nationalist Party, with whom they were compelled to enter into a pact. It was to be the precursor of dramatic events.

In May 1910, matters were thrown into further turmoil by the death of King Edward VII.[17] Another election would have to be called as soon as possible, to provide for a government with a clear mandate to govern, unimpeded by the House of Lords, but it was considered inappropriate for the new King, George V, to have to confront at the very beginning of his reign issues as grave as any since the days of the Great Reform Bill. A further election was therefore not held until December.

Again the result was neck and neck, with little change in the numbers of any of the parties. In Plymouth, however, there was a change, partly because of the Astors' hard work during the years since the Liberal victory of 1906. Now, with a very high local turnout, of over 85 per cent, Waldorf was successful. Nancy played a prominent part in the contest also, her performance being described as vital, skilled, courageous and irrepressible. Victory was marked by torchlight processions through the city's streets.

So Waldorf was returned to the House of Commons for what would be perhaps the stormiest, most momentous, and longest Parliament in English history. The storm was to break over the constitution itself, with the government determined to renew its attack on the House of Lords, to radically reduce its powers. A most serious constitutional battle loomed. It was compounded by the fact that the Liberal government had no overall majority in the Commons, and was in thrall to its Irish Nationalist allies. To appease them it would have to bring to the fore the recently dormant but long-running and greatly contentious matter of Home Rule for Ireland.

There was also a more immediately urgent problem. Labour MPs had been elected for the first time in 1906, but they had made little impact on the conditions of the working class, among sections of which resentment was turning to violence. It was not long before the government was faced with riots and disorder that threatened to cripple the country. In November 1910, miners in Tonypandy, in the Welsh valleys, went on strike, and the disturbance soon spread to seamen, firemen and dockers; when railwaymen struck, troops had to be brought into central London, and encamped in Hyde Park and Kensington Gardens.

Violence also erupted in an entirely new quarter. The Women's Social and Political Union, a militant spearhead of the campaign for women's suffrage, was established by Emmeline Pankhurst and her two daughters, one of whom, Christabel, had been enraged by being refused permission to read for the Bar, on the grounds of her sex. In a new and violent suffrage campaign, schools, buildings, letter boxes and telephone wires were vandalised – as well as the orchid house in Kew Gardens, although not an obvious symbol of male superiority. As the campaign intensified, suffragettes were imprisoned, and many who went on hunger strike were force-fed to keep them alive. An angry readiness to challenge authority had displaced the satisfaction that had characterised the national mood for so long. The grace and peace of the Edwardian Age seemed to have vanished.

SIX

Into Battle

The new House of Commons convened on 31 January 1911. The Liberals were determined to stay in office at any price, in order to curtail the Lords' powers. They would abolish the Lords' absolute veto over Budget proposals, in effect over all Money Bills that had been passed by the Commons, and would restrict their veto over Bills other than Money Bills. They could then force through the radical measures in the People's Budget. In order to abolish the Lords' existing powers, the government drafted a Parliament Bill. To get it through the Commons, however, they had to win the support of the Irish Nationalists – Irish MPs being at that time constituent members of the House of Commons.

Ireland had been merged into the United Kingdom by the Act of Union of 1800, among many parts of Irish society a highly unpopular measure, and one that had caused simmering discontent ever since it was passed. Two previous attempts, in 1886 and 1893, had been made to overcome the Act of Union's effects. Both were introduced by the Liberal Prime Minister Gladstone, seeking to introduce Home Rule for Ireland, the long-standing goal of those seeking to conciliate Irish nationalism by giving Ireland a new and largely independent link with Great Britain. Both Bills had failed – the latter being killed off by the House of Lords. In 1911, the upper House, with its enduring Conservative majority, still remained a barrier to the enactment of Home Rule.

Now, the Irish Nationalist MPs agreed to support the Parliament Bill in return for a promise of Home Rule. Once the Bill had passed the Commons, it could be sent to the Lords. If they passed the Bill their power of veto would effectively be lost; if they rejected it, the way would be open to a great constitutional battle over their legislative powers in general, and in particular over their power to reject a Budget passed by the Commons and also to veto Home Rule.

The Conservatives in the new Parliament believed not only that Home

Rule had never left the Liberals' agenda, but also that in order finally to achieve it they would resort to the unscrupulous and unconstitutional means of attempting to destroy the power of the House of Lords. To a majority of the Conservative Party it was anathema.

The Parliament Bill passed the Commons and was sent to the Lords, which applied the simple expedient of amending it by excluding Home Rule from its scope. It was a fatal move, negating the one objective on which the government, if it was to survive, could not concede or compromise. For them, it was all or nothing. The Irish members, on whom the government depended, would have the Bill, the whole Bill, and nothing but the Bill. Sent back to the Commons, the Lords' amendment was rejected.

Waldorf was now caught up in this fierce battle. He had won his seat in Parliament and, independent of means and mind and with a strong liberal streak, he was comfortable on the left wing of the Conservative Party. Consequently, he joined the Unionist Social Reform Committee, a ginger group formed by progressive Conservatives in 1911 to counter what they regarded as the reactionary views of a section of the party, and to urge flexibility both on reform of the Lords and on Home Rule.

He was also more informed than most Tory MPs, and more concerned, about the devastation that ill-health caused to the poor. Although a Conservative MP, Waldorf's anxiety therefore led him to support groups appointed by the Liberal government working on the preparation of what became the National Insurance Act of 1911. Some of the clauses of that Bill were drafted at Cliveden, and when it came before the House, in December 1911, Waldorf, with eight other young Tories, voted for it – against his own party, to the small surprise but great distaste of his Conservative colleagues. This brought him to the notice of the Liberal establishment, which in due course was to reward his support.

A few weeks after his election, he made his maiden speech to Parliament. Delivered in an atmosphere of high tension, it was measured, far-sighted and intelligent, and it was well received. With quiet cynicism he exposed the government's plan to reform the Lords as a sham to disguise its fixation with Home Rule, which he knew had little resonance in the country. 'This Bill,' he concluded,

> appears to be framed chiefly in order to bring into law a measure which has been twice before the electorate and twice defeated. It appears to be framed to carry through this measure over the heads of the electorate of the United Kingdom. I cannot for the life of me see how anyone can support the Bill who claims to represent modern democracy.[1]

The climax of what had become a great constitutional struggle between Lords and Commons came on 10 August 1911. Almost every peer, forming a tide of what became known as 'backwoodsmen', made his way to the House of Lords. Not a seat was empty. It was far from the norm, when a handful of peers might put in an appearance, prompting a famous historian's comment that 'An Assembly that does not assemble is defective in a main political ingredient.'[2] Now, the attendance was the largest ever known, yet despite the unprecedented and colourful influx of peers from far and wide, the government won the day, although with a wafer-thin majority, and the Bill passed into law eight days later.

Partly as a result of the constitutional crises, and sessions in Parliament lasting longer than had previously been the custom, it was becoming a convenience if not a necessity for members of Parliament to have a London base. Although Waldorf's father had a house in one of London's grandest streets, Carlton House Terrace, Waldorf and Nancy decided that they should have a proper town house of their own, even though Cliveden was quite close to London. So, as they had done in Plymouth, they sought out the finest property available, and in 1911 began negotiations to buy number 4, St James's Square. The seller was Lord Lucas, known as Bron, one of the group of people sometimes described as 'the children of the Souls', some of whom were in actual fact children of members of the Souls, and a number of whom were Nancy's friends.

The house stood on the corner of an attractive square of large, mainly eighteenth-century houses built around a private garden. It lay between Piccadilly and Pall Mall, at that time the heart of fashionable London, and was conveniently close to the Houses of Parliament. The design of number 4, on the site of an earlier house burned down in 1725, was influenced by the celebrated architect Nicholas Hawksmoor.[3] It was an impressive building, with a stone-flagged entrance hall, a hooded porter's chair by the front door, and a view from the inner hall through to the courtyard between the house and its stables. Lady Desborough, whose family home it had been, might have felt a twinge of sadness at the thought of Nancy setting about the imposing staircases, moulded ceilings, festooned panels, tall pier glasses, chandeliers and other ornaments from previous centuries, and introducing her modern, American attachment to comfort and light.

Once established in London, Waldorf and Nancy began to entertain on a large scale, and the peace of St James's Square began to be interrupted by comings and goings and general bustle at the door, with a footman frequently standing on the steps and blowing a whistle for a cab – one blast for a motor taxi and two, in the early days, for a hansom. The neighbours had also to get used to the sight of the chatelaine doing physical exercises on the lawn. But it promised to be an ideal base for Waldorf's parliamentary career, and was equally agreeable for Nancy, who of course had a natural liking for dispensing hospitality, and who had by now become as compulsive an entertainer as Waldorf.

The Astors' life had moved into a new phase, with the serious business of politics added to their previously social existence. Even so, their activities were not significantly altered by having to nurse Waldorf's constituency in Plymouth. At that time, the demands on an MP were fewer than they are now, and he had considerable flexibility both as to when he visited his constituency and how long he was there. Even although Waldorf was a conscientious man, he spent long periods away from Plymouth. He and Nancy continued to go to Switzerland during January and February, both for pleasure and for health, and often returned via Biarritz, where, despite Nancy's dislike of the place, they sometimes stayed for up to two months.

Although there was change in the air, the lavish entertainments that had become customary in the previous reign continued. Typical of many was the fancy-dress ball given in 1911 by Lord Winterton and F.E. Smith, to mark King George V's coronation. One of the hosts recalled the occasion, with Waldorf dressed as a French policeman and Nancy happily putting on an act:

> It was in the early days of the Russian Ballet when people went mad about 'Les Sylphides', and an exquisite pair of these fairies, with short tulle skirts, little wings and rose wreaths in their hair, were Nancy Astor and Lady Lytton . . . They joined hands and danced gracefully around dear old Lord Chaplin, who looked at them with a gracious smile, murmuring, 'The darlings, the darlings.'[4]

Like many of her friends, Nancy loved dressing up; she even took a party to a fancy-dress ball given by her rival at Taplow, Lady Desborough, whose children she invited to a similar party at Cliveden, as Ettie's son Billy reported to his mother:

> They had such an amusing party at Cliveden on Sunday, madder than the March Hare's soiree, and no method of telling the guests from the members of the band, and none of identifying the bodies who perished from exposure on board the steam-launch. Nance was so amusing, and Pauline Spender-Clay and Lady Kerry the greatest angels. Pauline is the most fascinating creature alive, with those sad enormous brown eyes. Winston described his escape from Pretoria thoroughly.[5]

The Astors' high life continued through spring and summer, and in August and September they would go to Scotland, Waldorf having bought an estate near Fort Augustus. But their main axis lay through Cliveden, St James's Square and Plymouth, depending on the political diary, and to look after the various houses, the staff now approached 150.

With Waldorf beginning to make his mark in Parliament – the Prime Minister commented that he had 'fine manners, good brains, and, rarest of all, high and worthwhile ideals' – Nancy may have felt a little displaced from centre stage. It would have been understandable, considering how difficult she found it to accept a minor role. She began to display a slightly unappealing selfishness, and for the first time in what seemed basically a golden marriage, her gentle husband became the object of her resentment.

Although she herself sometimes went off on her own, such as when Waldorf's health forced him to go to Switzerland, she liked to suspect him of dalliance. This clearly frustrated Waldorf, as he made clear when writing to her in November 1911:

> Supposing all the ladies *were* in love with me (if such a thing were conceivable), I don't see why you should mind provided I did not return the sentiments . . . I think it only natural that people should like *you* but as long as you don't fall in love with them I don't mind a bit . . . you may like being teased publicly, I hate it & you know it – therefore why do it? You always say I don't make friends easily – then if I do by chance happen to make a friend, why criticize me? Believe me, whatever else you think you're the only person for me & I just ache to see you.[6]

Nancy also insisted on continuing to hunt, which caused Waldorf disquiet, besides being a sad reminder of how his own weak heart had forced him to give up riding. She did not love him enough, he complained, to forsake what was after all only a passing luxury; writing to her towards the end of his first year in Parliament, he appeared to harbour misgivings as to her reasons:

> I always understood from you that Phyllis *had* to hunt to provide some interest in life, some relaxation from a selfish, boring husband . . . I have often thought perhaps that was the reason, that it gave you an opportunity of relaxation from the tedium of married life and home – well it may bring you excitement but it certainly only brings me worry. I wish I did not care so much for you and depend on you, then I would not mind . . .[7]

Even with an increasingly bohemian emphasis, Nancy maintained her rule of having an eclectic guest list, although in fact there often seemed to be no rule at all, with many present merely on the whim of the hostess. On one occasion she invited Dr Jameson, notorious for his abortive raid on Johannesburg in 1896, but subsequently exonerated and eventually becoming Prime Minister of Cape Colony. To confuse, and presumably amuse, the party, particularly Hilaire Belloc, she told Jameson to pretend that he was Waldorf, whom Belloc had never met, and also that he was stone deaf. Belloc, Nancy recalled, was touchingly polite, and much abashed when Nancy treated her supposed husband with contempt and derision. Nancy's catholic tastes in entertaining made her happy to issue invitations to all sorts and classes of people, which other hostesses did not; the recipients were happy to accept her invitations, even those who did not yet know her, partly because they anticipated a high degree of luxury, but also because Nancy herself was such a magnetic and exhilarating figure. Her image was not at all formidable, her supposed formality softened by tales of her wit.

For many years the 'celebrities' of the day might receive out of the blue an invitation to Cliveden or St James's Square: when, for example, the pioneer aviator Amy Johnson returned from her solo flight from England to Australia, she soon received an invitation to Cliveden, as did others risen to popular acclaim, such as Charlie Chaplin and Will Rogers. Such people, and other guests like Julius Rosenwald, the man behind Sears Roebuck, or the motor magnate Henry Ford and his wife Clara – 'Mrs Henry Ford', as she dutifully signed herself in the Cliveden visitors book – would not have been asked anywhere near many of the stately homes of England, which were still confined mostly to the upper classes. Nor would their presence have been countenanced by hostesses such as Lady Londonderry, whose guests were largely if not exclusively political; or by Lady Cunard or Lady Colefax, who preferred the company of the rich or artistic, or fashionable party-goers.

Nancy's eclectic gatherings, however, were soon dwarfed by the increasingly larger, and more frequent, parties held at the London house, where the majority of guests were from the world of politics, and which were useful for Waldorf in developing his political life.

As her prominence as a hostess increased, Nancy drew strength from her exceptional insouciance and natural energy, except when they were temporarily extinguished by her bouts of unexplained illness. However, like anyone else, she had to contend with the natural tragedies and setbacks of life. Some were of more concern to Waldorf than Nancy, as when his cousin John Jacob Astor went down with the *Titanic* in April 1912; others were nearer to her. When Bobbie was struck down by appendicitis, then often fatal, Nancy suffered great anxiety. He recovered, but in the summer of 1912, Bill, aged five, became so ill it was feared that he would die. Nancy fell into deep distress as she thought of her son returning to Heaven, leaving her mourning below:

> As at the gate of Heaven, an angel child
> Might wonder at an outcast's pleading gaze,
> And say, 'Come, be my playmate, here the days
> Are longer, and the ways outside are wild,
> And you shall play with suns and silver stars.

Happily, Bill survived, after nearly two weeks at death's door, and Nancy's spirits returned to their customary sparkling level.

Such episodes emphasised the need, in her increasingly busy life, for good care of her children. Accordingly, when he was thirteen, Bobbie was sent to public school. His parents had chosen Shrewsbury, although Nancy maintained that she had wanted him to go to Eton but had been overruled by Waldorf. She hated parting from her son, and a characteristic image of a loving mother was captured by her friend Lord Winterton when he accompanied her to the station to see Bobbie off to school:

Only 1 vacant place (on train), lady next to it says she has influenza. N says she doesn't believe a word of it, in a loud voice . . . beg her not to have a row, we'll find another place . . . 3 large tears on Bobbie's cheek . . . N also looks tearful but as always happens in moments of emotion her hair threatens to come down . . . By this time we've attracted some attention which is increased when the train wants to start & guard begs Nance to stand away from it but she & Bobbie continue to hug each other. At last I managed to seize N and Wiss and Bill & hold them all back & train departs.[8]

A second son, born to Waldorf and Nancy on 5 March 1912, was named David. Wissie was at that time three, and Bill five. As was then usual in upper-class circles, maternal care was largely at arm's length. Nancy and Waldorf made no exception to the custom, save that, unlike many more formal parents of the time, when Nancy did spend time with the children, which was at least for a short period each day if they were in the same house as her, she displayed intense affection, and showered them with love and laughter. They remained for most of the time in the care of Nanny Gibbons. She had Nancy's ear, and could do little wrong. According to Nancy:

Without her I could not have done the half of what I did, or have carried on with my public life the way I was able to . . . She was my strength and stay and the backbone of my home. She came to us, rather strangely, from Australia . . . she was with us for forty years, until she died.

In tune with the Astors' customary generosity, Mrs Gibbons stayed on in grace-and-favour rooms long after her charges had grown out of nannies.

The Astors' bounty extended beyond servants and family, needy members of which were often fed and housed. It was in character for both Waldorf and Nancy to feel sorry for lame ducks, and once they had settled at Cliveden they began to be generous even to complete strangers:

This a.m. we went to church – walking back we met a blind man being led by a hunchback. They were dressed like and talked like Dickens characters. They live in Maidenhead – a more pitiful couple I never saw. So we took their address . . .[9]

On another occasion Nancy met an old lady tramp, a Mrs King, trudging along the road near Cliveden; after some haranguing, she persuaded her to come in and rest; then followed further advice, freely given, as to what would be best for her, with the result that the woman eventually settled happily into a cottage on the estate and stayed there, much admired by the chatelaine, until her dying day.

Lord Winterton, who had observed with detached amusement Bobbie's departure for school in February 1913, was a member of Parliament, and had helped Waldorf in his successful election campaign. For a long time he was in love with Nancy, and his comments demonstrate the effect she could have on those around her. Staying at Cliveden in 1912, he had written:

What a wonderful woman Nancy is – so excitable and yet so wise in her calm moments, so wild and daring in public, and yet so good and so straight; such a talker and yet such a listener, so apparently irresponsible, and yet so really dependable; such a charmeuse, such a moqueuse, such a woman, and yet such a friend, the best in the world . . . Nancy & Bobbie left for Rest Harrow; did some business in the hall after dinner, but could not take my eyes off Nancy's picture.[10]

Winterton was clearly enraptured by Sargent's portrait of Nancy; the painting certainly shows her to advantage: like many successful portraitists

– Graham Sutherland perhaps proving an exception – Sargent knew both that he must please his clients and also how to do so.

Winterton's account also exemplifies how some of Nancy's qualities – gaiety, daring, interest in friends and determination to help them – bubbled in her turbulent vat alongside the defects that aroused hostility even in her admirers: excitable irresponsibility, caustic humour and sudden changes of mood. 'She was rather quarrelsome & almost shrewish,' he wrote, after dining with her, 'supplying me with another example of the fatalness of the policy of giving women votes. The nicest women are sometimes incapable of being sensible.'

These lapses in Nancy's otherwise generous spirit occasionally exasperated Waldorf, especially if she was not at his side when he felt burdened by his work. In August 1913, Nancy, rather bored, stayed in Scotland rather than accompany Waldorf back to Plymouth, and he wrote to her expressing rare impatience:

> . . . A letter has just arrived from you which I confess makes me feel sad. You know that I'm busy, that I'm tired, that I'm just trying to last out for a few days and do the work that's in front of me – I know you have nothing to do all day long, and yet you have never since I left sent me more than 1 or 2 scrappy little scrawls, and then when you do write, instead of being understanding and trying to cheer and help, your sole occupation appears to be to see what fresh daily complaint you can hurl at my hot head. You appear almost to think that I left Scotland and came south in order to be able to sit down and write you long letters. You wake up at 4 a.m., don't you? Well, so do I, and my limbs ache and I hate the thought of breakfast; you are able to doze and be read to, I have had to bustle along and sit in the House of Commons until I loathed the place. You go to bed at ten; I get there anywhere about or after midnight, and by that time the last thing I think of is sleep . . . You always seem to be so upstanding with everyone else and with me to be sitting just trying to find fault. I'm not suffering from uric acid or anything else except weariness – I'm tired in mind, in body and in stomach – I should have thought you might have grasped this and tried to make these last deadly days down here easier, instead of lying in wait every day to discover some fresh delinquency or failure.[11]

Such occasional tensions demonstrated how unhappy Waldorf was if he was apart from her. 'I do miss you,' he said, when Nancy had preceded him to Mirador at the end of 1913. 'I miss you when I wake up and when I go to bed; when I'm ill and when I'm well . . .'

She and Waldorf spent that Christmas at Mirador, which Chillie had given to Phyllis the year before. While there, Nancy was beset by another bout of neuralgia, and Phyllis was upset by her sister's plight. She discussed it with a friend of hers who had turned to a recently established religion, which had apparently healed her of chronic sickness. The friend then gave Nancy a book called *Science and Health with Key to the Scriptures*. It had been written by the religion's founder, an American called Mary Baker Eddy, later president of the Massachusetts Metaphysical College, who had conceived her idea after recovering from a spinal injury caused by a fall. The book was intended to interpret Christ's teaching so as to make it applicable to all occasions and to offer a harmonious solution to ordinary problems. In fact, Nancy's mother had had a copy of *Science and Health*, and one of Chillie's aunts had been among Mary Baker Eddy's earliest disciples, but to Nancy herself it came as a revelation.

Mrs Eddy, who had named her concept Christian Science, believed that her physical recovery had been a consequence of ideas that had come to her when she had turned to the Bible. One purpose of her new religion was to try and restore to Christianity its potential for healing the sick, to complement once more its power to 'redeem the sinner and bind up the broken-hearted'. She had reached a simple conviction about the human condition: that it is transformed by regarding Man as God's spiritual image and likeness. She proposed accordingly that since God is good, He has not created anything evil, and that evil matter does not exist save in the mind of Man; so purging the mind of the thought of evil should be sufficient to vanquish and dispel it.

It follows, according to Christian Science, that drugs and medicine are superfluous, an axiom supported by the fact that medicine was not prescribed or employed in the healing ministry of Jesus. Instead, anyone sufficiently convinced by the religion's basic concept can by prayer exercise God's power to heal, both themselves and others, even where an illness and its symptoms are physical. In simplistic terms it is a question of 'God's mind over matter'. In fact, Christian Scientists do not wholly reject the use of drugs or clinical help, but their belief, usually born of experience, is that prayer is often a quicker and more effective agent for healing than is medicine. Some do turn to drugs and doctors if Science fails to bring relief, but Nancy interpreted what was to become her new religion in a way that led her to reject orthodox medicine altogether.

While in America for Christmas 1913, Nancy had not paid much attention to her copy of *Science and Health*, but she did so early in the new year, when her health deteriorated sharply.

. . . at one time I was constantly ill . . . I seemed to be constantly in the Doctor's hands for something or other. I could not sleep. I had headaches and I had backaches and I was constantly tired. This tonic and that was prescribed, and did me no good. Finally Lord Dawson of Penn, who was the king's physician, told me I could never hope to be anything but a semi-invalid. He talked to Waldorf and said a quieter and more restful life would have to be planned for me. The thought of a restful life simply horrified me.

Presently, after further probing, internal abscesses were diagnosed, and I had a bad operation. I don't think in all my life I have ever been so miserable as I was then. I suffered agonies. Presently, when I was well enough to be moved, I went down to my sea-side cottage in Sandwich, to recuperate . . .[12]

As she lay on her balcony overlooking the sea, she began to have doubts: 'This,' she thought, 'is not what God wants. It is not what he meant to happen. It couldn't be that God made sickness. It turned people into useless self-centred people who became a burden to themselves and to everyone else . . .'[13] Being useless was at odds with Nancy's robust Virginian ideals, while self-centredness offended her Puritan ethic of loving one's neighbours and doing them good. They were certainly not what she saw or wanted in herself. However, help was at hand.

For Sunday 1 March 1914, Nancy had invited a party of a dozen people, including her sister Phyllis and friends such as Alice Mildmay, whose husband was a Devonshire MP and owned land near Plymouth; Alice Salisbury, whose father-in-law had three times been Prime Minister; and an international banker, Robert Brand. Another guest was a Christian Scientist called Maud Bull, a friend of Phyllis, who had introduced her to Nancy. Although Mrs Bull was not a practitioner, officially listed by the Mother Church in Boston, she did have experience of healing and knew much about the new religion. Phyllis hoped that she might help Nancy recover from the wounds and pain caused by the medical treatment of her abscesses.

On the Sunday evening, the Scientist and her hostess disappeared upstairs. Nancy later said that she could not remember anything about Maud Bull herself but that she had always remembered what she said and the message she brought. In fact, that day Nancy underwent a translation, as is said of the saints, which was deeply to change her life:

. . . We talked for a long time. I told her how much I wanted to be well, but said if it was going to separate me in any way from my religion or shake my Faith, I would not touch it. 'It will not harm your faith,' she said. 'It will give you a greater understanding.'

I asked her what I had to do.

'Read this book,' she said, 'and I will pray for you.'

The book was Science and Health with a Key to the Scriptures, by Mary Baker Eddy. I read the first chapter, on Prayer. It was just like the conversion of St Paul . . .[14]

'I can never forget,' she continued, 'the joy of that first flash into my consciousness that God made neither sin nor sickness, that God created only good, and man in His image and likeness . . . I awoke from a quiet sleep with the thought: God is Spirit, and Man is His Spiritual image and likeness. Therefore, I have no need to fear sickness or what the body tells me.'[15] Her fear had been cast out, and from then on she felt equal to the countless demands of an extremely busy life.

The Christian Science principle that right thinking can heal became a frequent admonition of Nancy's, especially to younger members of her family, to 'get your thinkin' right', and to avoid error. Other Christian Scientists doubted that Nancy ever really understood what the religion was all about, although noting that she occasionally gave the impression of being 'on intimate terms with the management'.[16] Its tenets were close enough to Protestantism for her to feel that she was not rejecting what she had been brought up to believe, and as they were not set in stone, they allowed her to adapt them to her idiosyncrasies, as her son Michael later recalled:

Within this new Church she could have matters more her own way, and could proclaim her faith at the same time. Once she had clasped its banner she held on to it fervently and carried it into every camp. It became part of her strength and part of her weakness. It accentuated both sides of her character: the zealot, the missionary, impelled by love, who longed to help those she met; and the bigot, the woman of overbearing self-will, determined at all costs to get her own way, who at times entertained unusual and unnatural fears about the world and its wickedness. And yet she never allowed her religion to diminish her sense of fun.[17]

The Astors' butler, a perceptive man, had a slightly different take on what happened:

It's my view that it was the doctors' fault. At one time she had a succession of illnesses and while doctors, like lawyers and undertakers, seem on the outside to show deep concern, their ultimate real interest is the money. They also work in droves, so a physician calls in a specialist who seeks a second opinion, and so on and so on. I have watched this sort of thing happening all though my life in service. Then the bills come in, and no matter how rich you may be you begin to sit up and take notice . . . She saw what they were up to, so she was easy to sway when other influences came along.[18]

Nancy regained her vigour almost immediately after Mrs Bull's visit and was to have hardly another day's illness until the decline at the very end of her life. Whatever the real nature of this metamorphosis, she attributed it to Christian Science. But it remained a puzzle to her friends, unable so easily to dispose of the laws of physics or biology:

Bob Brand related a typical discussion at Cliveden, between himself, Hugh Cecil, brother of the Marquess of Salisbury, and Nancy on the new religion. 'I asked Nancy whether as a good CS & as she hadn't a body she wd lie down in front of a steam roller & let it pass over her soul. Nancy was doubtful, but said with real believers it wd be all right. Hugh Cecil then became philosophical and was very good, I thought, but philosophy didn't appeal to Nancy. He said that everything no doubt was only an idea. That Nancy's idea of a steam roller wd pass over Nancy's idea of her body & though it was quite possible neither existed in real matter yet Nancy's idea of what happened when her idea of a steam roller passed over her idea of herself wd be what other people wd call being squashed . . .'[19]

With her knowledge of the Bible, Nancy might have wondered about St Matthew's question, 'Which of you by taking thought can add one cubit unto his stature?' Alternatively she could have accepted the axiom that a person who does not believe in metaphysics is really a metaphysician with a rival theory of his own.

Meanwhile, during his first year in Parliament, Waldorf had met Philip Kerr, scion of an aristocratic, staunchly Roman Catholic, Scottish family. Soon to become the Astors' closest friend, Kerr was a few years older than Waldorf, and also a graduate of New College, where he had gained a first-class degree in history. He had subsequently gone out to South Africa, returning to England in 1910, when Waldorf had invited him to Cliveden. Nancy was attracted by Philip Kerr's personality, and it was not long before he took pride of place among her friends. He was handsome, combining 'both the looks and the essence of purity'; he was charismatic too, and very clever, if slightly inflated by self-assurance. But he was also impressionable, and no one was to make a greater impact on him than Nancy.[20]

It was partly their respective health problems that brought them together. In April 1910, shortly after returning to England, Kerr had been offered a safe parliamentary seat by the Conservative leaders but had declined it. The following year he collapsed with a severe bout of nervous and then physical exhaustion, a recurrent problem with him which he termed 'brain fag', and was advised that the appropriate remedy was a change of air and foreign travel. It took him some two years to recover.

Kerr's troubles struck a deep chord with Nancy; perhaps it was because they seemed so similar to her own that she sent him a copy of *Science and Health* even before she had given it more than a glance herself. The two had become closer friends after the end of a romance that Kerr had pursued with Mima Cecil, daughter of Nancy's friend the Marchioness of Salisbury: 'I once touched her soul,' he reflected sadly. 'I have lived on the memory ever since.'[21]

Nancy invited Kerr to come to St Moritz in January 1913, and to forget his affair in the Alpine sunshine. It was an exhilarating holiday, and by the time the Astors left, Mima seemed but a memory for Kerr, who was smitten by Nancy instead. 'I feel like a lost sheep,' he wrote, 'with no shepherd to answer the tinkling of my bell. It's simply wretched here without you . . . perhaps you don't realise how much I've enjoyed the last fortnight, and how I hated seeing the train steam away this afternoon.'

Their letters became more frequent as the year progressed, especially after Kerr's health failed again, forcing him abroad once more, mainly to India. There, his liberal reflections on relations between the British and their native subjects contrasted with Nancy's view of black men. 'You would soon cease to draw the Southern States' kind of colour line in India,' he told her. 'It's a different sort of line here . . .'

In April 1914, soon after Nancy's evening with Maud Bull, Kerr returned to England once more, only to be struck down with a burst appendix. Nancy at once arranged for him to be treated at Rest Harrow, and there he gradually recovered – after orthodox surgery – sitting out on the balcony, sometimes watching the rows of portentous destroyers steaming up the Channel towards Sheerness, or contemplating the waves breaking white at low tide, the strip of sand and the pale blue sea, or the nearby fields thick with buttercups and daisies, the hedgerows blue with speedwell, the trees glinting with fresh young leaves.

Kerr, who had already toyed with popular metaphysical ideas such as New Thought, in which he had tried to interest Nancy, became more and more convinced by his study of Christian Science, describing it as 'just like a searchlight showing up the road on a dark night. It never reaches the horizon, but it always uncovers the next step or two.' Nancy worried that Kerr's mother might question his writing to her every day, or query the number of letters that she was sending to him; but he was able to reassure her: 'I used to think she was suspicious of you and your influence on me – but now I don't feel a bit that way.' Her doubt might not have been dispelled if she had read the lines that Nancy inscribed in a book she gave to Philip:

> *You and I have found the secret way,*
> *None shall hinder us nor say us nay,*
> *All the world may stare and never know*
> *You and I are twined together so.*[22]

The friendship seemed to have aspects of a love affair, but without its core. As Nancy later related to a niece, one day she and Kerr were suddenly overcome with desire for each other, but rather than responding as others might, they fell on their knees in prayer, and so managed to quell the urge.

For her part, Nancy was by nature honourable, and too frank to deceive. She paid great attention to the teachings of the Church, and besides, in her heart was an underlying affection for her husband, who was of paramount importance to her life. She delighted in her attractive appearance and beautiful clothes, and, in the words of one admirer, exuded, like Queen Elizabeth I, invincible femininity, which helped satisfy her need for men friends. But although innocently flirtatious, she was lowly sexed. 'Never make me believe,' she had once written to Irene, 'that carnal love is anything but lust, and that's Christ's whole teachings.' In fact, she was just not interested. 'How lucky I am,' she once said, 'vice has no allurements for me. My greatest battle is with my tongue: it's far too sharp and inaccurate.' Those who knew her well agreed – exemplified by her old friend Alice Roosevelt Longworth, who, on hearing of Philip Kerr's eventual rejection of Catholicism in favour of Christian Science, commented wryly that for him it was 'merely a matter of swapping Blessed Virgins in midstream'. Nevertheless, the affection between Nancy and Kerr was deep enough to make Waldorf occasionally feel a little perturbed. In fact, the religious turmoil in Kerr's soul left little space for earthly pleasures, and he also soon became too preoccupied with political business to find time for a love affair.

Kerr's political vision, which took shape during his years in South Africa, came to be described as the 'Larger Idea', and encompassed his belief that harmony would not prevail in the world unless political power was dispensed by some form of international organisation, preferably one imbued with

British values. He had consequently formed wide-ranging views on the need for world government, seeing it as essential for the preservation of peace.

To promote his ideas, his paramount interest had become the Round Table, a pressure group and forerunner of the modern think tank. Dedicated to imperial reform, it championed the need for an agreement between the countries under British rule jointly to support and control imperial defence and foreign policy, in order to prevent the disintegration of the Empire. It was in order to found and edit an authoritative magazine promoting the ideas of the Round Table movement that he had turned down the offer of a parliamentary seat in 1910.

Other members of the Round Table, all political missionaries with powerful intellects, were already friends of Waldorf. They included Lionel Curtis, the paramount enthusiast in the movement, and also Ned Grigg, Geoffrey Dawson, John Buchan and Robert Brand.[23] Kerr, and most of this group, had been in the 'Kindergarten' of Lord Milner, High Commissioner for South Africa, in the aftermath of the Boer War. There they had worked as civil servants, helping Milner create a new nation for the erstwhile belligerents. Deploying persuasion and political insight, and supported by rich 'randlords' such as Abe Bailey and Alfred Beit, they had achieved an unlikely but spectacular success in bonding Boer and Briton, at least for the purposes of efficiently administering a new, united country, even if, at heart, bitter feelings between the two races persisted.

For Milner and his young men, the fledgling Union of South Africa became a blueprint for a larger idea, a high-minded vision born of the dreams of Cecil Rhodes, that the nation, rather than the class or individual, was the fundamental social unit, needing a core of thriving, manly people, drawn from the Anglo-Saxon races. The Kindergarten aimed for a close bond between England and its Dominions, convinced that for Britain to maintain herself in the same league as America, Russia and Germany, her political unit must be enlarged from nation to empire – a rationale similar to the modern case for a federal European Union. Success, the group believed, benevolently administered with Anglo-Saxon precepts by the British Empire and America, would lead to peace and prosperity in an ordered world. It was a view with which Nancy concurred, the ideal of Anglo-American co-operation appealing to her narrow but strong sense of history.

While distributing its magazine throughout the Empire, the Round Table believed that its strength lay in discreet behind-the-scenes influence, rather than in appointment to executive office. Lloyd George himself was in time to describe it as 'a very powerful combination, in its way perhaps the most powerful in the country . . . behind the scenes they have much power and influence'.

Waldorf had come to hold a similar view of his own political value. He became an important benefactor of the Round Table, and soon the Astors began to host gatherings of the movement at Cliveden. Although neither he nor Nancy attended their meetings, they were both, through increasingly close acquaintance with the members, exposed for the first time to the broad concepts of imperial and foreign affairs.[24]

Nancy had now been in England for some nine years. During that time, through money and position, and latterly through approaching with Waldorf the edge of high politics, her self-confidence had grown and her character traits had become more entrenched, woven with contrasting strands: assertiveness and an unbridled tongue marring her vivacity, and a love of material pleasures – jewels, clothes, food, hunting, parties – competing with almost Puritan inclinations and a churchy desire to do good.

With her pleasure in social life joined by an increasing interest in political topics, Nancy was delighted by her power to attract the Round Table and to associate with their ideas. She had for some time yearned for more from her life than being a hostess, a feeling fuelled by her growing share in constituency work in Plymouth. Her friendship with the Round Table group, in and out of her houses, was for her an inspiration. She recalled how they 'talked and talked. If I hadn't had that outlet I'd have stifled. My mind was expanding and I was so full of life. I wanted a lot more than Society.'

In the four years following the group's establishment in 1910, the opinions of the Round Table began gradually to attract attention. They provoked thought particularly in respect of the increasing concern at the expansive ambitions of Germany, which many feared had the potential to involve the British Empire in war. The Round Table, and in particularly Philip Kerr, believed that the Kaiser could be dissuaded from overt aggression by a firm and cohesive stand by Britain, which would be sustainable if the government spent enough money on the Royal Navy. However, while peace in England was threatened by Irish nationalists and by suffragettes, that of Europe began to disintegrate as accelerating events took diplomats and politicians by surprise, and plunged their countries into war.

It might never have happened: the Astors' butler told of an incident that occurred when the Austrian Archduke Franz Ferdinand came to Cliveden for the weekend. Chillie, who was also staying, had been deputed by Nancy to meet the royal train:

> Charles Hopkins was the chauffeur and he chose to drive a spanking new Lanchester which was his pride and joy. They hadn't got to the end of the drive when Mr Langhorne cleared his throat and spat straight on to one of the windows – he must have thought it was open.

It wasn't. Charles stared at it at first incredulously, then in rage. Then he stopped staring because he'd driven into the lodge gatepost making a nasty dent in his front wing. He returned in a towering temper. I remember thinking, some months later, that if his driving had been as wild as his rage he might have prevented the outbreak of the First World War by crashing and maiming his passengers.[25]

As it was, Britain declared war on Germany on the evening of 4 August 1914, to the cheerful enthusiasm of the young men of England, and to wild rejoicing in the streets of Berlin. Others were filled with trepidation, and as the Foreign Secretary murmured that the lamps were going out all over Europe, the Duchess of Beaufort, entertaining a house party at Badminton, walked slowly across the hall in silence, and turned to the wall the portrait of the Kaiser, once a welcome guest.

Nancy was playing tennis on the covered court at Cliveden when she was brought the news that war had been declared. She and Waldorf went at once to Plymouth, whose huge naval dockyards made it a place of great military importance. There they set about helping with the organisation of hospital work and with arranging shelter for the influx of soldiers and sailors that began almost immediately, as ships laden with wounded began to arrive at British ports: Belgians in their strange pink uniforms, and more and more British.

Waldorf at once tried to join up, but he failed the medical tests. In fact he applied five times to join the fighting troops but was barred each time because of his weak heart. At length, typically undaunted, he went to the Quartermaster-General and asked for a post, any post, however disagreeable. According to Nancy:

> They made him a major, and gave him the job of trying to check Army waste. In a brand new uniform he went into a cookhouse to learn the job. Then he went round the various units, making checks on the waste. I have often wondered whether people realised the courage it took to do this. There were many who must have resented what they probably called interference by this upstanding and apparently fit young man of military age. It was an almost unbearable position for him . . .[26]

Waldorf also demonstrated his patient determination to place at the disposal of others, in this case the country, his wealth and his own good-natured intelligence. He soon concluded that, besides doing what he could as Inspector of Quartermaster General Services, he should offer Cliveden to the government, who might surely find some use for it. In due course officials arrived to inspect the estate, but the house was turned down as unsuitable. Surprised but undeterred, Waldorf approached the Canadians. The Governor-General of Canada was then the Duke of Connaught, a friend of the Astors, and Waldorf's offer, passed along the line, soon resulted in the Canadian Red Cross sending their own inspection team. They too found the house itself unsuitable for military use, but they saw potential in the covered tennis court with its adjacent bowling alley. They agreed to accept Waldorf's offer and decided to build a hospital in Cliveden's grounds, very soon sending in builders and medical overseers.

It was a perfect stage for Nancy's brisk presence, energy and power of communication, and as the war progressed she was to raise the spirits of large numbers of people shattered in mind and body by the conflict. In hard and grim circumstances, the work she did with the Red Cross authorities and the inspiration she gave to so many Canadian servicemen was to forge a valuable and enduring bond between the two countries. The Canadian Prime Minister, Robert Borden, later praised her for her 'fine ability and high courage, of serious and thoughtful temperament, of immense earnestness, brilliantly clever and witty, amazingly vivacious': the war had brought to the fore the best aspects of Nancy's character, while overshadowing some of the others.[27]

She often visited the hospital twice a day, word of which soon got back to Canada and the USA. An American banker staying at Cliveden at the end of April 1916, three weeks after the birth of Nancy's fifth child, Michael, recalled, 'It was pretty heart rending; Mrs Astor had just had a small son and was out for the first time. It was touching to see the affection with which the men regarded her.'[28]

She kept morale high in whatever way she could, often having a band to play, and sometimes arranging a football game for the staff. Back in Canada, the stories of her rallying the wounded and the dying were told and retold with pleasure and admiration. One example serves for many: when one badly wounded soldier had lost the will to live, and had, as Nancy put it, 'turned his face to the wall', the despairing doctors called in Mrs Astor, who went to the soldier's bedside:

'I'm going to die,' he said.

I said, 'Yes, Saunders, you're going to die. You're going to die because you have no guts. If you were a Cockney, or a Scot, or a Yank, you'd live. But you're just a Canadian, so you'll lie down and die! I'll have them send you up a good supper for your last meal, and I bet you this wrist watch you'll be dead this time tomorrow. You can keep it till then,' I said, 'I'll get it back when you're gone.'

He ate the supper I sent him, and he still has the watch. Later when he got back home he wrote me from the Middle West. 'They're making a lot of me here,' he said. 'They think I'm a hero. Gee, Mrs Astor, they don't know how you had to kick me around to make me live.'[29]

There must have been those who groaned at such a bracing draught and wished it would blow elsewhere, but for the huge majority the air lightened when her neat, slight, smiling figure fluttered into a room, and a small wave of pleasure recharged the battered spirits and soothed the broken bodies. She flitted about the wards, a wounded man remembered, like an eighteen-year-old girl, radiating cheer and hope, with anecdotes and stories at the ready. She was, in her own way but of course without there being any other remote comparison, treading the path once illuminated by The Lady with the Lamp.

She arranged for the long, painful days of the wounded to be enlivened by visitors, inviting leading lights such as Churchill, the Duke of Connaught and the Canadian Prime Minister. She also hauled in an odd mix of stage and literary personalities – Kipling and George Robey, for example – to do their bit and to provide the battered soldiers with a little interest or amusement. She also arranged a rota of local ladies to supply the wards with books and flowers, and to take the walking wounded around the grounds. Even the King and Queen were asked. It was said that Queen Mary was the one person who, then and in later years, could quell Nancy's spontaneous chatter. She certainly seemed sufficiently austere and formidable to do so: on one royal visit to a hospital, Nancy was also of the party, and having comforted a blinded soldier she went quickly over to the Queen and asked her to see him also:

Queen Mary: 'Have you talked to him?'
Nancy: 'Oh yes, of course.'
Queen Mary: 'Then I think that will suffice.'

By the end of 1915, the hospital held 110 patients, and eventually the number rose to 600; overall, some 24,000 casualties were taken in. Some were beyond help, and for them Nancy created a cemetery in a secluded sunken garden near the house. In its green, silent turf were placed forty-two gravestones, and nearby a bronze female figure representing Canada, for which the sculptor used Nancy's features, although she asked him not to make it a recognisable portrait.

The inner strength that Nancy found in Christian Science was sometimes driven out by temper, and it is not clear how she managed to reconcile the claims of her religion with the physical wreckage that she saw around her. There seemed to be no received CS wisdom on the matter, nor guidance on how to meet the violent tide rolling over the country. Philip Kerr, of military age but not yet having recovered his full strength, had not joined up. He wrestled with the problem with a fellow Scientist while on fire-watching duty in London:

> We got talking about the war. I told him I was thinking of taking a commission and he seemed doubtful. He is quite neutral himself. He said that the question for him was whether the time had come to take the sword as the best way of combating evil. He admitted that the time might come, but he doubted whether it had come yet . . . Anyhow CSites are all evidently at sixes and sevens about the war . . . The general conclusion, I gathered, is that if one has enough understanding of the truth one won't go, if one hasn't one will . . .[30]

Kerr, it seems, did have enough understanding, and so realised that he should apply for exemption and stay behind. Nancy was not troubled by such anxious introspection, but even she despaired at times:

> The gas cases were the worst and most distressing. At times I felt I could bear it no more, and I remember one day saying, 'When this war is over, I am going to have nothing more to do with this man-made world. I am going into an old ladies' home, and I shall just sit and knit.'[31]

Early in the war, the rest of the estate was placed on a war footing: the menservants went off to fight and their places were taken by maids, who often filled posts never before offered to a woman. The stately lawns and flower gardens were ploughed and sown; the peaches hung ripe on the old brick walls; and Cliveden shed its calm and beauty for an earlier, more primitive aspect. Gone, for now, was the glamour. The serenity of this quintessential patch of Edwardian England had been invaded by harsh modernity, as uniformed orderlies and nurses hurried about their business, and roaring, spluttering motor lorries jostled with horse-drawn carts and churned up the flinty gravel tracks, laden with the wounded and the para-phernalia of a busy hospital.

Nancy was generous with presents to those at the Front, not least sending food in its season, which must have delighted soldiers reduced largely to eating tinned rations, even if, for many of the Astors' friends, a certain amount of it was caviar. She also became an assiduous writer to her young friends in their hard new life in the trenches, though not all of her correspondents relished her pressing them with Christian Science, which she was quick to do. 'Nancy, you can't think of your soul in this war,' Julian Grenfell told her, after one such attempt. 'It is absolutely at a discount. It is much better for us to leave it out altogether, if one can . . .' She had even tried to convert Waldorf's father, an attempt that fell upon distinctly stony ground, as William disdainfully told her of his going to a Christian Science church in New York ten years previously: '. . . I understood little of the "service", if I may call it that, but its irreverence and blasphemy were shocking. It is the first time I ever met the Almighty on a footing of equality.'[32]

She exchanged many letters with her brother-in-law, John Astor, who showed great gallantry at the Front. He yearned for home and comfort, as he and his friends, so keen to join up, saw the reality of war:

> I had hoped that one might regard coming into action in the same frame of mind as when hunting a fox or riding a pig, but this is a delusion and I don't seem to get any fonder of it . . . if we were only on manoeuvres it would be a delightful picnic – as it is, things are damnably grim. Just to think we might be up at Glendoe now. I wish I could be there, even for a few hours, just to have a long bath and a meal, and put on some white flannels for a bit . . .[33]

Many of those who came to be described as the Young Elizabethans, once carefree guests at Cliveden and Taplow, were soon dead, dying or permanently wrecked in body or soul. Some were killed on the ill-fated Dardanelles expedition, their lives ending on shores whose pictures had adorned the schoolrooms in which a few short years earlier they had first learned about the ancient world, whose stories some remembered as they contemplated battle:

> *I will go back this morning*
> *From Imbros over the sea;*
> *Stand in the trench, Achilles,*
> *Flame-capped, and shout for me.*

Patrick Shaw Stewart, who wrote these lines and who was killed in Flanders, stayed at Cliveden on more than one occasion. He was one of a group of friends that included Julian and Billy Grenfell, both of whom were to die fighting. Billy had formed a great affection for Nancy, and wrote her a number of letters from the trenches, presenting her with a vivid contrast to life at Cliveden:

My Darling Nancy,

Such a Chamber of Horrors we have passed through, shells thicker than flies, flies thicker than air, and our nearest and dearest neighbours 37 English and 22 German corpses of varying age and savour . . .

His last letter, sent only two days before he was killed, closed affectionately, 'Take care of yourself, my pretty, do your hair nicely & do not overload yourself with charitable works in this ungrateful world . . . Toujours a toi, Billy.'[34]

She did have the occasional respite from her wartime load, sometimes at the gatherings of a club christened 'The Ark', established by the Marchioness of Londonderry, who had conceived the idea in order to create some relief from the exhausting, bleak work of wartime. By then Edith Londonderry had become London's leading political hostess, and as such she was to remain prominent for many years, perhaps even more so than Nancy in the period before the Second World War. She knew almost everyone of any political importance in London, and held her unusual entertainments on the top floor of Londonderry House in Piccadilly, the rest of which was being used as a hospital. There, late at night, with dinner and champagne, politicians of all sorts, from Cabinet ministers and Secretaries of State downwards, soldiers on leave, painters, writers and beautiful women could relax and turn for a moment to friendship, and to jokes, verses, skits and childish games.

The Ark was an attempt to continue the pre-war social and political mix; it was a far cry from the Souls, but as near to a salon as could exist in wartime London. It was the perfect milieu for Nancy, who loved the frivolity in a grand setting that was the keynote of the gatherings – especially as they were always suffused with a political essence. Each member was given a special name and associated description; Nancy's was particularly perceptive: 'The Gnat . . . who, although prone to "bites", was still a great acquisition: she quipped and quizzed all around her and, wherever she was, her corner was all a "buzz". . .'[35]

As the war dragged on, such leisure was rare, although Nancy did manage to maintain some of the Cliveden comforts. She travelled frequently to Plymouth, where she worked arduously, helping with hospital work and doing what she could to improve the arrangements, at first chaotic, for housing wounded soldiers and sailors, their numbers greatly increased following the naval Battle of Jutland in 1916.

As telegraph boys bicycled up to countless doorways, fateful orange envelopes in their pockets, Nancy herself must have feared for her beloved son, Bobbie. He turned eighteen on 18 August 1916, by which time conscription had been introduced, and he was called up less than three weeks later. Even in 1916, when the army needed great numbers of re-inforcements, the best regiments were hard to join without a word in the right quarter. Bobbie's case was helped by Gordon Cunard, one of Nancy's friends from her first days in Leicestershire, who put his to the commanding officer of the Royal Horse Guards. He received a positive response:

> Dear Cunard,
> I will certainly put young Shaw's name down for the Regiment. Geoffrey Robinson, editor of the Times, came to see me yesterday about him too and said what a nice boy he was.
> Gerald FitzGerald.

Having attended the Royal Military College at Sandhurst, and the Young Officers' School at Tidworth, Bobbie was commissioned at the end of 1917. He was posted to the Guards Machine Gun regiment in 1918, by which time the average life expectancy of an infantry officer was just over three months.

Long before that, grief had touched almost everyone the Astors knew: 'After two years in that first war,' Nancy wrote, 'we did not look at the casualty lists any more. All our friends had gone.' Separated for ever from their children, and left behind in the familiar surroundings in which they had watched their sons grow up, the mothers mourned: 'I walk in the golden sunshine and calm peace of lovely autumn days, through *his* woods, *his* hills, and tell him that he is not forgotten, that the world is rejoicing because *they* won.'[36]

Philip Kerr, despite losing a younger brother, also put on a show of optimism, insisting to Nancy, as the turmoil deepened, that 'we shall lose a great many things one thought good and worthwhile, but we shall be all the better for it in the end'. Afterwards, when it was all over, that idea seemed hard to grasp, and in Cliveden's cool, green-painted library, Nancy would sometimes wistfully reflect upon her many exuberant friends who had so soon left a world grown old and cold and weary: 'a gallant company of gentlemen who died for England & all that England means on a fine evening'.

The impact on people's lives was so extreme that it could hardly be absorbed, as memories of the distant pre-war world slipped finally over the horizon:

> I see striped awnings, linkmen with flaring torches; powdered, liveried footmen; soaring marble staircases; tiaras, smiling hostesses; azaleas in

gilt baskets; white waistcoats, violins, elbows sawing the air, names on pasteboard cards, quails in aspic, macédoine, strawberries and cream, tired faces of cloakroom attendants, washed streets in blue dawns, sparrows pecking about the empty pavements, my bedroom curtains being drawn apart to let in the late morning light; a breakfast tray approaching my bedside; bandboxes, tissue paper . . .[37]

Before long it seemed that every home had its empty bed, its empty room, its lost love and laughter, and that every pavement bore its maimed or wounded man. Perhaps such sights stirred subconscious images implanted in Nancy's mind in her earliest days, of wounded Civil War survivors in the streets of Danville; it was certainly all to colour her later political development, with her aversion to the prospect of another war.

> *I gave my life for freedom, this I know,*
> *For those who bade me fight had told me so.*

At Cliveden, which remained Nancy's base, there was a new development. As the war dragged on, it became once more a place for Americans and Englishmen to meet, but the gaiety of former days was now replaced by grave discussions of war and of an Anglo-American alliance, all the more sensitive as America still determinedly preserved her neutrality. The American commander General Pershing was a guest, as was the British military supremo Field Marshal Sir William Robertson.

Distant as were the United States from the battlefields, which in the first years of the fighting had almost no impact on any but a small minority of the American people, the progress of the war sparked economic concerns among influential business leaders. They scented opportunity on the turbulent air, as European markets were battered into chaos, sucking down most of the financial institutions that comprised the system of credit supply. On a more emotional level, Americans, with their love of peace and freedom, became increasingly uneasy at the might and ambition of Imperial Germany and at the harrowing tales from the trenches. The war had been brought close to home by the sinking of the *Lusitania* in May 1915, in which many Americans – men, women and children – were drowned in the icy Irish sea.

In the same year, Henry Ford was a guest at Cliveden, arriving shortly after the departure of King George and Queen Mary, whom the Astors had been entertaining. The Americans who visited Cliveden at that time were mostly from a patrician elite of rich men, mainly bankers and diplomats. With their transatlantic interests, they became convinced that a formal alliance, or at least a de facto collaboration, with Britain was not only the honourable course for America but might in the long run be of both financial and political benefit. Prominent among the group were leading lights at J.P. Morgan and Co., at that time the most powerful commercial bank in America, and which at the beginning of the war had become the United States purchasing and fiscal agent of both the British and the French governments. Pillars of American finance, such as Dwight Morrow and Thomas Lamont, followed the lead of their august senior partner, Henry P. Davison, and also of the former president, Teddy Roosevelt – champion of the Preparedness Movement, formed to increase America's military might as the European war developed.

These powerful Atlanticists began to feel the need for a more positive stance than was framed in President Wilson's dreams of an international organisation to foster world peace, which was to be armed not with guns and steel but with hope and the threat of economic sanctions. They also looked beyond the carnage in France and Flanders to the riches and influence that after the war might be America's for the taking if she helped restore the shattered economies of Europe. The Astors hosted many discussions between leaders from the two countries, whose ideas were mutually refreshing, even if they sometimes seemed very different types of people; while staying at Cliveden, for example, Lord Balfour had long talks with the future American president Herbert Hoover.

On the British side, a number of men were ready to join forces with such forward thinkers from America, and, at Nancy's instigation, to come and meet at Cliveden. They included two British diplomats – Lord Eustace Percy, and Lord Bryce, British ambassador in Washington during Theodore Roosevelt's presidency – and some of the Round Table group: not least Philip Kerr, now close to the Prime Minister, and Geoffrey Dawson, editor of the London *Times*.

One of the occasional guests at that time was Dr Thomas Jones, who in 1916 became Deputy Secretary of the Cabinet, and whose work had brought him into contact with Waldorf. He described the growing feeling for Britain among Americans in London, which he had encountered at dinner with the Astors in St James's Square. His account shows how Waldorf and Nancy kept up their style even amid wartime deprivation, and used their wealth and sense of purpose to draw in men of influence:

> . . . a biggish house, with powerful, tall women domestics who take charge of you. The dining room the size of a chapel vestry, all panelled, and at the far end of it a round table laid for seven, lit with candles

and silver. Nancy and Waldorf, Mrs Brooks, Geoffrey Robinson, the American Ambassador and Mrs Page . . . Mr Page an old gentleman of sixty or so, talkative, friendly and most unneutral; his wife even more pro-Ally than he. Indeed this American group were thirsting for war. They told me many tales of young Americans fighting, sick and dying among the Canadian regiments . . . [38]

Jones first stayed at Cliveden in 1917, and was immediately struck by Nancy, whom he recalled as the centre of attraction:

30-something, with a lithe figure, with not a wasted ounce in it, sharp-featured, a face all light and colour; she talks at a great rate, in the cleverest way, with a philosophy free from hate, full of humanity. You feel she has a golden heart and I can understand what a mothering influence she has been on the young Knights of the Round Table . . . [39]

Another who valued co-operation between Britain and America was Willard Straight, also for a time a partner at J.P. Morgan. He had been to Cliveden early in the war, and it was he who now introduced the senior partner, Henry P. Davison, a man of great influence and financial clout. Straight remembered Davison's first visit:

He was charmed by his hostess and delighted by her husband, Waldorf Astor, a member of Parliament, quiet, serious and most considerate and thoughtful . . . Lord Curzon, former Viceroy of India, Lt. The Hon. Julian Grenfell, 'the stalker', a Miss Hozier, just back from Red Cross nursing in Belgium, and Geoffrey Robinson, editor of the Times, were fellow guests . . HPD walked back from church with Miss Hozier on Sunday. She then told him further stories of her adventures and in response to his inquiries said that by 'atrocities' she meant hand-lopping and ear-cutting; she didn't think there had been many but she said that whole villages had been cleaned out, the buildings fired as the Germans entered the towns, and the people, men, women and children inside, butchered. She told the most pitiful tales of mothers, and daughters, husbands, wives, babies, who had lost all those near and dear to them.
     A fine-looking, clean cut young fellow, Lord Titchfield, son of the Duke of Portland, turned up for lunch. Mrs Astor hailed him with delight. 'Sit right down, Sonny,' she said. 'Have a good time. You may be dead in a week.' 'So I may,' said he, and did. [40]

That America should come into the war had become vital if the Kaiser was not to win after all. American public opinion had supported the tradition of isolation without entanglements, and had been equally indifferent to the belligerents. Dislike of Germany, which seemed to many to have been the aggressor, was matched by indignation at the British blockade of Europe's northern coasts, with its consequent restriction of trade, and neutral ships often being diverted by the Royal Navy to British ports. American pride was injured, but the situation took a new, and more dangerous, course when the German submarine offensive began to take an appalling toll of British shipping, raising the spectre of the country being blockaded itself, and starved of fuel, raw materials and vital supplements to its scarce home-grown food. America began to feel affront to its sense of righteousness, besides injury to its trading profits. With a number of leading Americans ready to believe that right was now on the British side, it was a moment that with careful handling might lead to America finally joining in the war.

Meanwhile, Waldorf was active in Plymouth, now a vital naval base, and in 1916 his continuing political work resulted in promotion. Under the terms of the National Insurance Act of 1911, a Medical Research Committee had been established with the prime role of distributing medical research funds, some of which were used to support a Departmental Committee on Tuberculosis. Waldorf had been chairman of that committee in 1912–13, and in 1916 he was appointed chairman of the Medical Research Committee itself, forerunner of the Ministry of Health.

Further preferment came largely as a result of the fall of Asquith. In 1915, following the reverses at Gallipoli, the Prime Minister had been forced to form a coalition with the Conservatives, but his hesitant conduct of the war had led to increasing dissatisfaction, turning to indignation at the exposure of a lack of shells for the artillery at the Front. Feelings were heightened by widely believed allegations that Lord Kitchener, Secretary of State for War, had suggested, as a remedy, that troops venture into no-man's-land during lulls in the fighting and carry back unexploded shells. In December 1916 the Tories lost patience, and withdrew their support from Asquith, forming a coalition government under Lloyd George.

Shortly after taking over, Lloyd George appointed Waldorf his parliamentary private secretary. It was not long, however, before the new Prime Minister's close advisers concluded that Lloyd George, almost devoid of system in his work, would need an organised secretariat led by someone who knew the ways of Whitehall. A War Cabinet Secretariat was set up, but even then it was felt that another secretarial organisation was needed, to buttress Lloyd George's small existing staff, which included his mistress, Frances Stevenson. Consequently, at the beginning of 1917, the Prime

Minister's Secretariat came into being; it was also described as his Intelligence Department, but soon became known as the Garden Suburb, as its work was carried out in huts in the garden at 10 Downing Street.

When the Secretariat was established, Waldorf and Philip Kerr were both appointed to it. Kerr's nomination was the result of the influence of Lord Milner, then in the War Cabinet, but Waldorf's membership was mainly pressed by J.L. Garvin, editor of the *Observer*. Garvin had entered the Astor fold as an indirect result of the dismissal of Harry Cust as editor of the *Pall Mall Gazette* in 1896 – after a vitriolic discussion between Cust and William Astor, which had ended with the editior addressing the proprietor as 'pig'. After Cust's departure, the *Gazette* gradually lost much of its influence, which both Waldorf and his father believed might be restored by finding a good editor. In 1910, they decided that the man they needed was Jim Garvin, then editor, manager and part owner of the *Observer*, the world's oldest Sunday newspaper. Their plan became more feasible the following year, after a split between Garvin and the main proprietor of the *Observer*, Lord Northcliffe, over food taxes. The quarrel led Garvin to look around for a new owner for the *Observer*, and he lighted upon Waldorf, whose politics appeared to match his own, and who, it conveniently turned out, was in quest of an editor for the *Gazette*. With Waldorf acting for his father, who was wintering at his villa in Sorrento, the Astors proposed a typically expensive and grandiose solution: that William would buy the *Observer* for £45,000, in return for Garvin giving up his part ownership and agreeing to edit both the *Observer* and the *Gazette*.

Garvin took up his new duties in 1912. Under his editorship the *Observer* continued to prosper, but after a time William decided to sell both it and the *Gazette*, regarding the latter as one of his 'notable failures'. Unable, however, to sell them to his satisfaction, in 1915 he gave both papers to Waldorf, who was happy to take on the *Observer* but soon sold the *Gazette*.

In the event, Waldorf was far from a hands-on newspaper owner, and for many years it was Garvin who would continue to be the *Observer*'s driving force, working by and large harmoniously with his new proprietor. He soon became a frequent guest at Cliveden, and demonstrated in many political discussions there that he was an excellent strategic thinker, if also apt to inflict upon his companions incessant and seemingly uninterruptible opinions: 'he talked most of the time, and Astor put in a monosyllable most of the time', said one friend, describing a typical conversation. Garvin was supportive of Nancy's ideas on alcohol, giving them prominent space in the *Observer*, although he did not always practise what he preached: 'Jim Garvin's consumption of old brandy,' noted a fellow member of one of Garvin's clubs, 'is in striking contradiction to his temperance articles in the *Observer*.'

As Lloyd George's new administration was being formed, Waldorf's name was also put forward for membership of the Local Government Board. His sponsor in this case was Dr Christopher Addison, a parliamentary under-secretary influential with Lloyd George, who saw the board as an opportunity for laying the foundations of a Ministry of Health, a project close to Waldorf's heart. Although the new ministry would soon be created, at that time nothing came of the suggestion, and Waldorf explained his disappointment to Garvin, demonstrating his political ideals:

> The job which LG wanted for me and which was being considered was practically the creation of a Health Department. One has only to realise that a healthy people is a contented people . . . to see what a genuine chance for constructive and valuable work it would have been for me.[41]

Prospects for the introduction of a health department were not to fade, however, and Waldorf continued to cherish hopes that, if it were established, he would play an important part in it, and possibly in due course become its chief.

It was largely because of high aspirations for his political career that the news that Waldorf received at the beginning of 1916 came as an appalling shock. In fact, it caused an immediate furore throughout the Astor family, and was soon to steer the course of Nancy's life in an entirely new direction.

The first that Waldorf heard of it was on 1 January, when he was tele-phoned by a newspaper asking how his father's news was going to affect his political career – so disclosing to an incredulous Waldorf that in the New Year's Honours William Astor had been elevated to the peerage, as Baron Astor of Hever.

It turned out that throughout the period since his meeting with Schomberg McDonnell fourteen years earlier, William Astor had been patiently pursuing his quest for a peerage. He had discreetly cultivated influential members of the Conservative hierarchy, dealing mainly with Sir Herbert Praed, secretary to the Conservative leader Bonar Law. His methods and purpose are succinctly portrayed in a letter dated 5 June 1912, from Praed to Bonar Law, before a meeting with William in a private room at the Ritz Hotel:

> As you are probably aware Mr Astor is the owner of the Observer as well as the Pall Mall Gazette, both of which papers are edited by Mr Garvin.
>
> In addition to the large sums he has given me for the Party fund, he has subscribed most generously to oppose Communism in other

ways; amongst others he gave me £4,000 for the development of Conservative Clubs.

He is in favour of fighting the Radicals at every possible opportunity, and admires you because you have the determination and capacity to carry out such a policy.

I know he thinks he has been neglected by the Party and that his efforts have not been recognised.

A few compliments will not be thrown away. He became an Englishman eight or ten years ago, it may be longer. His son, Waldorf, is MP for Plymouth, a very bright, popular fellow with an ambitious wife who had been previously married.

I invited Lord Lansdowne who wrote me he would much like to have come but he will be out of London. He is, however, going to ask Mr Astor to dinner . . .

. . . No suggestion of future financial assistance must be made. The principal object is to get over his feeling of soreness at having been overlooked. He thinks Balfour might have put forward his name for a peerage . . . Recognise what he has done for the Party by the Pall Mall and the Observer and great financial assistance.[42]

The coming of war gave William the opportunity to combine these interests with his patriotic feelings. At all events he now stepped up his largesse to astonishing levels: $125,000 to the war fund established by the Prince of Wales; $200,000 to Lord Rothschild's Red Cross; $25,000 to Queen Mary's Fund for Women; $25,000 for the *Daily Telegraph*'s Fund for Bands for the New Army, $125 for a fund for officers' families, besides 'large amounts' to funds raised by *The Times* and St John: donations amounting all together to some £10 million in today's money. He was also the first name on the list of subscribers to *The Times* War Fund.

In his fashion he certainly helped the country in its hour of need, so it was perhaps unsurprising that he was now ennobled. However, while it had been a long-term strategy, William had never mentioned or discussed this impending event with his children; the first any of them knew about it was when Waldorf received the journalist's call. Far from celebrating, Waldorf and Nancy greeted the news with disgust. It was the last thing Waldorf wanted: in keeping with the law as it had stood since time immemorial, when his father died, Waldorf, as the eldest son, would inevitably succeed to his peerage and consequently become ineligible for the Commons. He would then have to resign his seat, and his political career would be all but finished. Certainly there was political and legislative work to be carried out by members of the House of Lords, but already by 1916, as a result of the battles over their veto, effective power had moved to the Commons. Waldorf anyway shared A.J. Balfour's opinion that addressing the House of Lords was like 'talking to a lot of tombstones'.

William's daughter and his younger son had also been taken by surprise. At the time of William's elevation to the peerage, John was away fighting at the Front, with neither the time nor the inclination for conspiracy, yet Nancy was not convinced by his or Pauline's claim that they had not known in advance of their father's honour. She was never to forgive her brother-in-law for not protesting, and for many years afterwards accused him of wanting Waldorf's inheritance. Relations between the brothers' respective wives also soured, which affected those between the brothers themselves.

The prime object of Nancy's spleen, however, and more importantly of Waldorf's, was William Astor himself. Immediately on seeing confirmation of the news, Waldorf, spurred on by Nancy, sent a letter not of praise or congratulations, which his father was expecting, but of very strongly worded criticism and condemnation. On hearing of it, Pauline Astor realised that her brother had overstepped the mark and persuaded him to write another, less abusive and more generous letter. But the damage was done: William was bitterly offended. Until then relations between William and his son and daughter-in-law had been distant but cordial, despite William's occasional irritation at opprobrious remarks by Nancy, but that now changed.[43]

Waldorf deplored not only his father's actions but also his secrecy, objecting that had there been discussion with the family, it would have become clear that he was bitterly opposed to the idea. For good measure he threw in some negative opinions about the peerage and about the decadence of class distinctions in general.

It was certainly not the orthodox Conservative line, and to such a fierce opponent of socialism as William it was anathema. But it seemed that New World egalitarianism, mixed with Puritan inclinations, had temporarily eclipsed Waldorf's appreciation of his fortunate circumstances and his material luxuries, and the fabric of English society that protected them. Nancy agreed with him wholeheartedly, accordingly spicing and stiffening Waldorf's comments to his father, which included his stated intention to try and get the law changed so as to enable him to resume his seat in the Commons. Coming from the habitually reserved Waldorf, it was strong meat. He also disclosed an uncharacteristic concern for his own career.

For the new Lord Astor, pleasure in his peerage exceeded pride in his son's prospects, and he found Waldorf's reactions indigestible. He believed that he had served the family well, finally establishing the Astors in the front rank of the best society in the world, and achieving for them honours that would transcend generations. Furthermore, he did not relish the implication that his son and daughter-in-law, to whom he had given so much, which they had apparently been delighted to receive, had after all little interest in worldly goods, regarding them more as a responsibility than a pleasure.

He considered that his son had behaved disloyally, and, ever ready to nurse a grievance, declared that he was not prepared to see him again. Not only was Waldorf virtually excommunicated, but to some extent he was disinherited: 'It was a little late in the day for William Waldorf to cut his elder son off financially, as the bulk of his distributions had already been generously made. But he now made provisions to leave the residue of his fortune to his other two children and to his grandchildren . . .' As Waldorf had already had very large sums made over to him by his father, he was not greatly inconvenienced financially, save that the change would bring to his own sons a greater degree of independence when they reached twenty-one, which might lessen his ability to exert control over them and direct their ways at an age when they would, in his view, still need his guidance.

Very soon, Nancy seems to have had second thoughts about having addressed Waldorf's father so directly, so she sent him another, more emollient letter. He was a little softened, but as to the main business, unmoved: 'I am sorry that Waldorf takes my promotion so bitterly hard,' he said. 'I cannot think that what has happened is in any sense a decadence, and the course of advancement is as open to me as to him . . . I have never gone in pursuit of this honour,' he added, allowing himself a certain freedom of expression, and concluded, '. . . The love of success is in my blood, and personally speaking I am delighted to have rounded these last years of my life with a distinction. I should be still more glad were it possible for me to meet Waldorf's wishes and convey it away from him at the last . . .'[44]

Waldorf realised that a ceiling had been placed on his political career. Frustrating as that was, it did not seem an immediate problem, although that did not lessen his dismay. William Astor was only seventy-one and appeared to be fit and well, although he himself believed the contrary, that 'the machine' was worn out. Certainly William was insuring that all his affairs were in order. In September 1918, he made over the Hever estate to his younger son, John, partly because of the very great admiration he had for his war service – he had been slightly wounded two months after the start of the war and again, more seriously, two months before its end, when he lost a leg. William then retired to an attractive house in Brighton, where he remained, busying himself both with writing articles and with preparing menus for his Italian chef, estranged both from Waldorf and also from his daughter Pauline, who for the sake of Waldorf's career had also objected to the ennoblement.[45] He was, however, happy to see his grandson

Bill, who often came to stay with him at Brighton, accompanied by his nanny.

As it turned out, the threat to Waldorf's career materialised all too soon. Early in 1919, Nancy had been shocked by the death of her own father, aged seventy-five. During the war years he had turned into an old man: his thinning hair and drooping moustache had become quite white, and he moved carefully, aided by a walking stick; but even so he had been expected to live for some time. Eventually he had left the house into which he had moved after giving Mirador to Phyllis, and settled into an apartment in Richmond. Irene, the only one of his daughters left in America, soothed and flattered him, reminding him of Nanaire: 'His eye followed her around the room, and her beauty enhanced his life . . .'

Nancy had never had the same kind of love and respect for her father as she had for her mother, noting the rough side of his character and frustrated that his hold on the purse strings had enabled him to dictate so much to Nanaire. Yet the soft and emotional part of her character was moved by her 'cranky old Pa', and for a time she was deeply upset at the news of his death, although pleased at the fulsomeness of the public tributes to him: '. . . father of America's most beautiful woman', proclaimed the Richmond *Times*, 'millionaire railway builder, sportsman and gentleman of the old Virginia school . . .'

Grave news of Waldorf's father came just eight months later, and had much greater significance. A swift and sharp deterioration in William Astor's health preceded his collapse and death on 18 October, after a favourite dinner of mutton, macaroni and Beaune. Waldorf therefore became the second Viscount Astor and was obliged immediately to resign his seat in the Commons. A new member had to be found for his constituency, now renamed the Sutton division of Plymouth, following amendments to electoral law made the previous year that divided Plymouth and neighbouring Devonport into a total of three constituencies, returning to Parliament one member each.

Waldorf lost no time in looking for ways to limit or undo this potential damage to his career, either by petitioning the King to extinguish his peerage or by moving a Bill in Parliament to enable him to renounce it. On 23 October, five days after his father's death, he made his case to the King's private secretary, Lord Stamfordham. In his submission, Waldorf reasoned that he could do more good to the state in the Commons than in the Lords, saying that he deprecated his father taking a peerage, and adding that upon his expressing regret about the matter his father had taken offence and declined to see him again. He also told Lord Stamfordham that he had always preached against honours and titles in his political campaigns; titles, he believed, created class distinctions, whereas intellect, ability, character and work were what counted in citizenship.

Whether egalitarian views of that nature appealed to George V's deeply conservative nature may be doubted, especially in the dangerously unsettled times of the war's aftermath. Waldorf also raised the point that on her marriage to a commoner, Princess Patricia, daughter of the Duke of Connaught, had been allowed voluntarily to renounce the style of Royal Highness and the title of Princess of Great Britain and Ireland. But it seemed that constitutional practice was against him: records showed that only one peer had managed to renounce his peerage, and that had been over 450 years earlier and for a reason not applicable to Waldorf's case. The only ways open to him were giving up British nationality or obtaining an Act of Parliament allowing him to renounce his peerage. Waldorf at once set about trying to obtain such an Act, perhaps unconcerned by Stamfordham's rather pertinent comment, made both to him and to the King, that he '*did* venture to point out that his argument about the House of Commons was based on the assumption that his seat there was a permanency . . .'[46]

Meanwhile the Conservative leadership instructed the Plymouth Unionist Association to begin the search for a new MP. As the Astor name was by now well known and popular in the city, the local party officials were keen to maintain the family link. Their first thought was to approach John Astor to invite him to take his elder brother's place, and the constituency chairman, Frank Hawker, was dispatched to London to persuade him to stand. However, partly because of his war wounds, John declined.[47] The question then arose as to who else might serve, and it was only a moment or two before Nancy's name was suggested.

Nancy maintained that it was Waldorf who first suggested the idea of her going into Parliament, and that without his encouragement she might have felt too daunted by the idea of attempting to enter what was still exclusively a man's world, and where she had little detailed information to guide her. In any event, Waldorf was wholly in favour. He wanted to become eligible as an MP once more, and in due course to resume his seat, partly in order to continue with the social reforms that he was promoting in Plymouth. He believed there was a chance he could get the law changed quickly so as to achieve his purpose. 'So it seemed that it was best,' Nancy said, 'to keep it in the family, and for me to try for it, which I did.'

By then the way had been cleared for a woman to stand for Parliament. In February 1918, largely because of circumstances created by the war, the Representation of the People Act extended the vote to women – although only to those aged thirty and over, and with certain other qualifications. Nine months later, as a logical extension of the process, the Parliament

(Qualification of Women) Act was passed, allowing women to stand for Parliament and to sit and vote as members of the House of Commons. Consequently, in the election of December 1918 there had been seventeen women candidates; all had lost their contests except one of the Sinn Fein candidates, Constance Markiewicz, an Irish girl, well born but turned revolutionary, and married to a Polish count. However, in accordance with her party's policy, she declined to take the oath of allegiance to the British crown, and had not taken her seat in Parliament.[48] So by the time Waldorf had to vacate his seat, there were still no female MPs.

At first the Plymouth Unionist Association did not contemplate the possibility of worldwide interest if they put up a woman in a by-election for a seat it appeared they could win. But the idea did cause immediate controversy among their members, with many seeing it as a risky experiment. They thought it quite possible that a woman candidate would lose the seat, as evidenced by the experience of women in the previous election. Further, considerable doubts were expressed about the potential of Nancy herself: people queried whether she was a 'fit and proper person' and suitable as a candidate. Although she had become popular in the constituency through her energy and for the good work she had done both with Waldorf and on his behalf when he was away, she had at the same time displayed what a number of the local Tories thought were socialistic tendencies. She had earned a reputation for being dashing and daring, but 'a bit Bolshie' too.

It was also necessary, primarily for the Astors themselves, to decide whether Nancy, if selected, would stand simply as a 'warming pan' for Waldorf, while he attempted to regain his eligibility. If she admitted that that was the case, she would be emphasising, however unwillingly, the subordinate role of women, and would risk forgoing the potential support of many of the female voters in Sutton. If she denied that role, it could make it difficult for Waldorf to reclaim the seat should he manage to divest himself of his peerage.

The arguments about whether to select her as candidate intensified, and a splinter group emerged, led by a prominent Conservative official. Its members felt that they were being bounced into supporting Nancy; they claimed that the chairman had been sent to London to bring back Waldorf's brother John Astor, but had somehow returned with a woman instead. The Conservative executive was accused of being out of touch. 'Though we admit,' said the objectors, 'that nobody could have done more benevolent work than Lord and Lady Astor, we say that neither a kind heart nor a coronet fits a woman to take her place in Parliament. And, from what we know of Lady Astor, she is more unfitted than most of her sex.' However, it seemed that superior, and perhaps better-financed, forces were already at work: when those opposed to Nancy planned meetings to air their views, they learned that 'the Astor party at once booked up all the halls and the committee-rooms, so that we should have been heavily handicapped'.

Even Nancy's friends were doubtful, and one of her literary trophies, J.M. Barrie, expressed the 'man's view':

> I hear of your presumptuous ambitions at Plymouth. How any woman can dare to stand up against a man I don't understand. What can you know about politics? These things require a man's brains, a man's knowledge, a man's fairness, a man's eloquence. Woman's true sphere in life is to be a (respectful) helpmeet . . .
>
> . . . However, there is no use arguing with you and you must lie in the bed you have made, tho' as far as my experience goes very few people do this . . .'[49]

Poor Nancy; but she was soon to revise her opinion of Barrie, when she felt that he had abandoned what she called his 'homely Scotch ways' and become instead a 'Duchess's Darling'.

The local Unionists, by nature and experience somewhat parochial, believed that Nancy manifested other disadvantages, mainly that she was not English. It was felt that her breezy, outspoken American manner, her lack of British phlegm, and her impish humour – which in any case did not amuse many of the local Tories, who prided themselves on being involved with serious politics – might prove counterproductive in an election campaign. Nor did she demonstrate proper knowledge of, or interest in, the minutiae of topical issues, or lay claim to much learning – with good reason, in the opinion of disgruntled local Conservatives. They wondered whether she had enough concentration to be able to master detail, instead of relying on broad concepts based in many cases on her prejudices. Finally, for all her wealth and grace, she was a divorcee, potential tinder in Devonshire, large areas of which were predominantly strait-laced and Low Church.

Waldorf continued his efforts to get rid of his peerage. He was helped by J.H. Thomas, a Labour MP later to become a good friend of Nancy, who was to give him the use of a grace-and-favour house on the Cliveden estate. Thomas supported Waldorf in presenting a Bill to the Commons that would allow the renunciation of his peerage; however, on 26 November it was defeated by over a hundred votes, partly because Conservative Party leaders would not give their backing to piecemeal legislation that might prejudice them in later action to reform the House of Lords, and partly because they believed that legislating for surrenders might lead to the Lords losing its most valuable politicians.

In the last week of October 1919, with the need to prepare for an imminent election, the Plymouth Conservatives resolved their differences, finally agreeing that Nancy's merits outweighed her disadvantages. She was known in the constituency, she had stood on countless doorsteps, she knew every street and alley and those who lived in them; she had taken over many of Waldorf's tasks while he was at Westminster; in all she had done good work. 'For eleven years,' she would say, 'I helped my husband with his work at Plymouth. I found out the wrongs and he tried to right them.' Those who had heard her speak had begun to realise that she had a flair for gripping an audience. Further, there was the great question of Votes for Women: the Representation of the People Act had added eight million new voters to the register, and over 17,000 of them lived in Plymouth – more in fact than there were male electors.

On Monday 27 October, within ten days of William Astor's death, Nancy received a telegram inviting her to stand. It was the moment for a complex and very important decision. She had great difficulty in making up her mind; she even asked the butler: 'I've talked to so many people about Plymouth,' she said. 'What do you think I should do?' 'I should go for it, my lady,' he replied. At length she did decide, perhaps with an inkling that an astonishing future was opening before her, and later that day she sent a reply to the Plymouth committee: 'Fully conscious of the great honour and grave responsibility. I accept your request that I be a candidate to stand for Plymouth. Nancy Astor.'[50]

Almost as soon as the news of Nancy's selection flashed out, first to London and then far beyond, it was clear that it would be no ordinary election, and might well prove a memorable stepping stone in Western social history. The morning after Nancy's acceptance, more than thirty newspapers ran the story. Messages of support for her 'plucky fight' began to pour in to Plymouth: from sailors, soldiers, Yorkshire miners, Lancashire mill hands; from Welshmen, Scots, from all parts of Britain, and before long from far corners of the Empire; from women, and from men who felt that the time had finally come for a woman to enter Parliament – and who could be more exciting to cheer than a beautiful American of fabulous wealth?

The press got to work at once, and did not all paint her in a positive light. She was described as a Gibson Girl, too graceful and old-fashioned to appeal to the poor voters of Sutton. Although the Astors had gained credit for buying Elliot Terrace and showing generous commitment to Plymouth, not least during the war years, hostile journalists initially tried to belittle their work and categorise Nancy as a 'Lady Bountiful'. More dangerous, less than a year since America had introduced Prohibition, she was accused of wanting a similar ban in England. The views of William

'Pussyfoot' Johnson and the American Anti-Saloon League had received wide publicity in England, and Nancy was now tarred with their brush. The threat from that line of attack was, however, slightly diminished when, after the candidates' nomination papers were filed on 7 November, it became clear that her Liberal and Labour opponents were both also teetotal.

It was not long before the American press also took up the story, sensing that remarkable events were about to unfold. They explained to their readers that although Nancy was called 'Lady', that did not bar her from standing for the House of Commons, though it was because her husband was a lord that he could not stand, and they began to sing her praises as an unusually favourable candidate. In some cases, of course, the journalists could not shed their professional cynicism: 'There is also the advantage,' said a paper in Columbus, Ohio, 'that as she already possesses a peerage she will not have to devote most of her time to swelling party funds in order to get one – an activity which often hampers the ordinary MP's work.'

On 3 November, Nancy issued her address to the voters:

I hesitated long before consenting to stand at the coming Election as I was overwhelmed by the special responsibility which, under the circumstances, would rest upon me as regards Plymouth, womankind, and my husband's past work. I have no personal ambition to go into Parliament . . . If you decide that Plymouth is once again to help in making history by being the first English constituency with a woman member, I shall do all in my power to maintain the high traditions of the Borough, the ideals of my sex, and the credit of Parliament.

On the same day, Waldorf applied to the Chiltern Hundreds, traditionally one of the ways in which an MP can effectively resign his seat in the Commons, and the writ for a by-election was served. That evening, in Plymouth's Masonic Hall, Plymouth Sutton Conservative Association formally adopted Nancy as Coalition Unionist candidate. Her brother-in-law, Colonel Spender-Clay, was among those speaking in her support. The writ was received in Plymouth the next day, and polling was fixed for Saturday 15 November. The votes were not to be counted until two weeks later, on 28 November, to allow for the collection of the votes of eligible but absentee voters, many of whom were servicemen still overseas on post-war duties. Nancy now had to summon up great courage: a by-election throws upon a candidate a beam of limelight more intense than in a general election, and all the more so on this occasion, which would excite interest in many overseas countries besides doing so throughout Britain. In addition she may justifiably have felt that if she failed, not only might she attract personal discredit and embarrassment, but, more importantly, the political cause of women might suffer a heavy setback.

Having been formally adopted as candidate, Nancy now began her campaign. Donning the mantle of the Pilgrim Fathers, she set forth, ready to begin her own pilgrimage from their historic landmark. She also invoked the city's hero, Sir Francis Drake, who long ago sailed out to fight for England: 'You sent out Drake in a little ship to fight for what was right. Now you are going to send a woman, and a little woman at that, to a great place called Parliament where she is determined to be a help and a credit to you.'

From the outset she exuded confidence, clothed in a carefree but attractive appearance: 'Don't send me with a nasty, stingy little majority,' she said. 'I don't want to slip in or slide in. I want to bound in.' She called for co-operation and partnership, to transcend class and special interests, and to meet the country's yearning for reconstruction. 'I do not see much difference between the Parties,' she remarked. 'They all have their ideals, and they all have a lot of scallywags to put them through.' The greatest need, for which the time had come, was for the doors long closed to women to be opened: 'My hope is that I may pave the way for women to enter Parliament. There is not going to be any screaming in the House. If I am not satisfied by what is being achieved by Parliament,' she added, 'I am not going to weep over the disappointment.' Clearly it was vital for her cause, and for her chance of victory, that she win the women's vote, so she arranged a series of 'women only' meetings for each day until polling day. 'I think that women had better put a woman in the House of Commons,' she proclaimed. 'Much as I love you, Gentlemen, you have made a terrible muddle of the world without us.'

Icy cold gripped the streets, and flurries of sleet and snow gusted down from the bleak tors of Dartmoor. Yet Nancy crowded each day to the full: out among the tenements, meetings in halls, on quaysides, on street corners. Her presence could not be missed: immaculately dressed, in a simple black dress to mourn the death of her father-in-law, with a black turban toque on her massed fair hair, she was conveyed around the narrow streets in a gleaming carriage drawn by a dashing pair of sorrel horses. At the reins was a huge silk-hatted coachman, Churchward, a Plymouth man with a beaming russet face, his whip and the horses' bridles adorned with red, white and blue ribands; on his coat he wore an enormous rosette made for him by Nancy. Smiling and full of energy, it was the Nannie of twenty years earlier, on a prancing Queen Bee in the horse shows of Virginia.

The constituency was full of the poor, the huddled masses, but she faced them head-on. There were already 6,000 unemployed in Plymouth, but as the navy wound down from war, the dockyards were discharging more each week. Nancy could argue with anyone on the problems of the dockyards, and proclaimed that even before the election was called she had been taking steps to alert the authorities in London to the plight of good men being thrown out of work.

Against her the Liberals had put up Isaac Foot, a solicitor. He had fought before but had never won. Her Labour opponent was William Gay, who wanted, she said, to destroy the capitalist system. At Nancy's first meetings, Gay's supporters tried to floor her with facts and figures, specially searched out by their experts. Nancy was having none of that. 'I don't claim,' she said, 'to be a political economist or blue stocking, but I have certain strong, and I believe sound, ideals, and I do claim to have practical knowledge.' She was an expert, she cried, on motherhood and womanhood.

Waldorf was always at hand. At press conferences he was quick to switch his wife off when any hard or dangerous topic was thrown at her. 'I don't know,' she answered, when faced with a technical question. 'I am not a paid politician so I can afford to speak the truth and declare straightforwardly that I don't know.' And she would extol her husband's virtues – claiming that the new creation of a Ministry of Health owed much to his work. Maternity, child welfare, housing, Poor Law reform – these were the things she would push for in Parliament.

Word of the beautiful lady quickly spread: her pearls, her fine carriage, her street-corner speeches, her repartee. The halls began to fill, with tough, grimy working men, and even tougher women, wrapped in shawls, clutching children or carrying infants. A rich American, with plenty of houses and servants, she was easy meat, they thought. Then she would mount a table and, hands on hips, start to speak. Catcalls and cries from the back would greet her, but they put her in her element. 'Are you a sportsman?' she called to one heckler. 'Yes.' 'Then shut your mouth until I have finished, and then you can yap as much as you like . . . Now, you Bolsheviks at the back,' she continued, 'just you listen to me. Would I like to live on £2 a week? No, but would you work as hard as me if you had what I had?' 'Why are you doing this?' they cried. 'To keep the Bolsheviks and Labour out of power.' 'What have the Tories done for the country?' they asked: 'Glorious things,' said Nancy. 'They built the Royal Navy.'

At one meeting, at the start of her campaign, three hundred people, many hostile, all curious, crowded into a small school hall. People climbed on to desks and window ledges, and scores more stood outside, clamouring for admission: 'We be coom to 'ear 'er Ladyship,' they said, and would not be moved on. 'Why are we all packed in the room like this?' Nancy asked. 'Because the men arranged it . . .' The press report continued:

. . . Lady Astor, mounting the table-top, began, 'I have been handling soldiers for the last four years – you'd better watch out' – which brought laughter and cheers – 'I just want to tell you some things that I'm going to get done if I get into the House of Commons. What's more, I am going to get there. Just remember that.' There was more laughter and applause, and when the interrupters got busy she exclaimed vehemently, 'Don't give me any of your sass. I shall come right down there to you. What you fellows want is to stop yelling and get to work.'[51]

On the whole, she sounded a high note: 'I believe the time has gone,' she cried, 'for governing on Party lines.' She called for 'co-operation and coalition, which alone can meet peace dangers, as it met war dangers'. She came across as constructive, while Labour and the Liberals began to sound negative, as though their campaigns were based on carping criticism and class warfare. The Liberals stood for a party, it was said; Labour for a class; but Nancy for the nation.

She was undaunted by hostility: 'Few hands were raised,' ran a newspaper report, 'in favour of the woman candidate when she addressed an open air gathering of weather-beaten fishermen yesterday. "What? Not going to vote for me?" she retorted. "Well, never mind. Your wives will even if you don't."' She courted the soldiers in their barracks, favourable territory as neither the Liberal nor the Labour candidate had fought in the war: 'Listen,' she began as she smiled on them, 'you've got the choice of three candidates. You can't get a fighting man out of the other two. So you'd best take a fighting woman. That's me.' In the streets the children sang:

> *Yankee doodle had a son,*
> *They said, 'Now who's your fancy?'*
> *He said, 'I'm off the lower deck*
> *And so I'll vote for Nancy.'*

She also faced criticism for not being local, or even English: 'Are there no social reforms in America,' she was asked in a crowded meeting, 'that you could give your time to?' 'If you're going to be insulting,' came the response, 'I'll have you turned out . . . The likes of you ought to be only too glad you have an American who will stand up and fight for what is right.'

In fact being American and free of English inhibitions gave her the common touch. Her vivacity, repartee and unrivalled energy were carrying the crowds with her. On street corners newsboys sold papers filled with telling photographs of the lady candidate – standing with smiling grizzled fishermen on the quayside, declaiming on a platform, serene in her shining carriage, or in among the crowd watching Plymouth Argyle play its Saturday football match. Not that Nancy much liked being photographed: 'I always look like Rameses' great-grandmother,' she would say. But in those days such familiarity was unusual, and almost unheard of from the rich, upper-class Englishmen typical of Tory candidates.

She was quite willing to go into the poorest, roughest parts of the constituency, into which it had been considered unwise for Waldorf to step. One morning her carriage drew up outside the gates of a gasworks. A newspaper described the scene: the men streamed out for their lunch break, and some gathered around and stood among mothers in aprons and shawls, and curious children. Nancy mounted a lorry and began to speak. Below her, by the wheels, a puppy sat shivering in the snowy wind, its tail in the slush. Later a reporter followed her into a stinking, scruffy room. Inside were six children, and a dog asleep in the bath. She picked up a baby and gave it her necklace. 'I know how working mothers keep their children happy,' she said, 'by letting them play with a rope of pearls. Now then, young Devon,' she added, 'what are you trying to tell me?' In the street outside, she squared up to an angry-looking coal-heaver: 'A woman,' he said, 'should be at home, looking after her children.' 'Well, I want to help you look after yours,' Nancy replied.

She was armed with endorsements from Arthur Balfour and from the Prime Minister, Lloyd George. People were struck by her energy; by the final days of the campaign, far from flagging, she had found a second wind. One day, after long hours of campaigning, she visited the Victory Club, a children's welfare hostel which she had established in a disused factory: 'Dance with us, Mrs Astor,' the children cried, as they chanted their election song: 'She is the one, to have a bit of fun', and she tirelessly joined in their games.

It was a sparkling campaign, full of what the American press called 'peppiness'; it lit up the whole of Sutton, the docks, the quays, the alleys, the dank, grimy tenements. The Labour and Liberal camps were pushed on to the back foot; they had begun to have difficulty in drawing a crowd or filling the halls they had booked. Where had everyone gone? Where were their supporters? Listening to Nancy. 'A circus procession,' they complained, but to no avail. Lady Astor was the centre of attraction.

On Friday 14 November, the eve of polling, she spent twelve hours touring the streets. Teddy bears, silver horseshoes, flowers and laurel wreaths were thrown into her carriage. In the afternoon she held a final rally at the Guildhall, where the Prime Minister's wife spoke up for her.

Two weeks later, the votes were all in, from an exceptionally heavy poll. At two o'clock on Saturday 28 November, the result was announced. All doubts were finally extinguished. In an election now watched by two continents, Nancy had won a sweeping majority, of over 5,000.

Outside Plymouth's Guildhall a huge crowd swayed and waited, noisy, tense, expectant. At last the great balcony windows were thrown open. Nancy stepped forward, and the smile on her face told all. The crowd erupted. The cheers were so loud and prolonged that they were heard even above the rumble of a distant tram, whose conductor turned to his passengers and said, 'She's in!' The risky experiment had come right.

SEVEN

The Power of One

Nancy wasted no time. She would take her seat in Parliament immediately. So after the briefest of respites, she left for London, surging on the crest of her wave. Her departure was supposed to be secret, but now she was news, and the wires began to hum; by the time the Plymouth express steamed into Paddington, a throng had gathered, flowing on to the platform. As she stepped down from the train, she was surrounded by a smiling crowd, pressing forward to greet her. Almost the first to clasp her hand was a severe and ageing suffragette who, only a few short years before, had lain incarcerated in Holloway gaol, pinned down by wardresses as doctors clamped a steel gag on her mouth and forced a long rubber hose into her stomach, executing their duty under the notorious Prisoners (Temporary Discharge for Ill Health) Act 1913, commonly known, even in official circles, as the Cat and Mouse Act. Now, with tears of a different emotion in her eyes, she stood before Nancy, a bright image of elegance quite unlike the hardened fighters for 'the Cause', and smilingly told her that her victory had made all the suffering worthwhile. Nancy was greatly moved. Then, as the crowd made way, a scowling rough moved close and shouted, 'I never voted for you, anyway.' 'Well, thank Heavens for that,' quipped Nancy, to cheers and applause.

On Monday 1 December soon after three p.m., the Commons lobbies were crowded, the chamber was packed and the galleries filled to capacity. At that time there were over 700 members of Parliament, and even without the Sinn Fein contingent, absent on principle, there were nothing like enough seats for all those who had turned up to witness the historic event; sober-suited men were spilling into the gangways, peering from the doors, and gathering behind the Speaker's chair. Two adventurous women reporters had made their way to the Press Gallery, where to their surprise they had for the first time found their entrance unopposed. In the other galleries were friends, family, peers, the American ambassador and other distinguished observers, all eagerly awaiting 'the first woman to be summoned by the Speaker from the Bar of the House to take her rightful place among the representatives of the nation'.

Looking charming and wholly feminine, in contrast to what many disgruntled members might have been expecting, Nancy waited at the Bar of the House, the line that marks the place where the formalities of the floor begin. She was beautifully but demurely dressed in a dark tailored suit, white satin blouse, tricorne velvet hat with cockade, and white kid gloves; asserting that women should dress in a businesslike manner, she declared that 'I shall wear nothing that the poorest woman elected to the House could not wear.'

When the preceding business was finished, the chamber fell silent, and, just before four o'clock, at the Speaker's call, the small, trim figure, looking pale and nervous, bowed and walked slowly forward, flanked on her left by the Prime Minister and at her right hand the Lord President of the Council, himself a former Prime Minister, A.J. Balfour. After more pausing and bowing the trio reached the table with the Mace, and there the two escorts stepped back, leaving Nancy on her own, to take the oath and sign the roll.

From the moment of her introduction Nancy seemed to infuse the portentous atmosphere with a certain insouciance and with her distinctive approach to rules, in contrast to what *The Times* later described as the 'ingenuous shyness' of her two sponsors. Neither Nancy nor Balfour, quietly chatting, had at first noticed the Speaker's summons, so Lloyd George had unwittingly moved forward on his own, before being pulled back by Nancy, to the onlookers' delight at this breach of solemn observance. One or two other small errors in formality also slipped in, but soon the ceremony was completed and Nancy turned towards the corner seat that had been allotted to her. For a moment it seemed that she was going to sit down on the government front bench, which would really have caused a flutter, but on that score all proved well.

The Prime Minister later put his own gloss on events, telling a friend that in contravention of the rules, Nancy had talked all the way up the floor of the House, embarrassing both him and Balfour, and that when she got to the table she wanted to have a chat with the Speaker.[1]

News of this milestone in the long hard road to women's emancipation was soon flashed around the world. It had been a simple but moving scene for those watching from the galleries, among whom was the Prime Minister's mistress, Frances Stevenson, who expressed the emotion she had felt despite her personal antipathy for the heroine of the hour:

> Went to see the first lady MP take her place in the House. It really was a thrilling moment, not from the personal point of view, but from

the fact that after all these hundreds of years this was the first time that a woman had set foot upon that floor to represent the people . . . I had a lump in my throat as I saw her come in at the far end – a very graceful, neat figure – & wait for her turn to walk up the floor . . .[2]

'To me,' wrote the wife of a miners' leader, who had been in the gallery, 'it was a sight that thrilled my very soul. I could have shouted for joy at this mark of the completeness of women's political emancipation . . .' But she noticed the doubts just beneath the surface of Nancy's welcome:

. . . Now and again I had a sense of sharp annoyance because of the coldness of the stodgy old politicians on every hand . . . Why were they so chilly? Did they feel repentant of the Party decision to admit women? Or were they out to give Lady Astor a quiet hint . . . It meant to me that the battle is not fully won, and that Lady Astor has to justify her place in the nation's legislative councils.[3]

Nancy now sat through her first debate, the lone woman in the chamber. She later said that she had been terrified, so much so that she had sat for five hours without even moving. 'They call it the best club in Europe,' she recounted, 'but it didn't seem like the best club to me. I can't think of anything worse than being among six hundred men none of whom really wanted you there.'[4] For most MPs it was indeed an unwelcome change. It disturbed settled assumptions and created a sense of dismay, as though a woman's touch was going to spoil a well-loved club – moving the furniture, replacing leather with chintz. As one member put it, her presence was 'like a butterfly in an old library, flitting about', 'Lady Astor's return,' recorded the Deputy Chief Whip, 'has upset some of our people a good deal. Old Sir Henry Craik was quite livid about it.'[5] Nancy could scarcely fail to notice, but, of course, she was intended to do so.

She may have expected that the older or brasher members would be affronted: 'We have some Conservatives,' she said, 'who belong to the days of Noah. Not only have they not come out of the ark but to hear them talk one would say they have never even looked out of it.' However, she was to find to her distress that the antipathy was not confined to them, but spread across a large portion of the House, including those who were supposedly her friends. Even they, she recalled, who might have been expected to adopt a more gallant approach, could not bring themselves to speak to her. Balfour and Lloyd George said they believed in women, she recounted, but 'they would rather have had a rattlesnake'. After hearing of her selection, the chairman of the Conservative Party, for example, had told his colleagues that 'the worst of it is that the

woman is sure to get in'; Neville Chamberlain, learning that Nancy was immi-
nently to take her seat, recorded it as 'melancholy news'; and other prominent
parliamentarians would, for a long time after her election to the Commons,
go out of their way to discomfit and upset her, not least Winston Churchill,
whose friendship with Nancy soured as a result of his gruff refusal to acknowledge her parliamentary existence, despite Nancy having invited him on several
occasions to Cliveden, and his family to Rest Harrow.

But that evening it was Horatio Bottomley, a heavy, flamboyant dema-
gogue, who dominated the proceedings. Speaking for his own motion to
urge the government to introduce the public to Premium Bonds, he dismissed
the argument that such bonds were a lottery, pointedly saying that 'marriage
is a lottery. Sometimes we know a lady may draw a prize in the shape of a
splendid husband, with the reversion of a seat in this House – but that is
an exceptional case. Everything in life is a lottery . . .'.

Nancy maintained that nothing would induce her to support betting, and
her first vote as an MP was against the motion. It did not go unnoticed.
She was warned that Bottomley, although a remarkable orator, was 'the kind
of animal that spits mud',[6] 'and to tread warily; that not being one of her
instincts she was soon to meet him in bruising collision, before he himself
became entangled in an altogether more notorious clash, with the law of
the land, as a result of which he was to cross the narrows between Parliament
and the Old Bailey, and exchange the Commons chamber for a prison cell,
with a seven-year sentence for fraud. Later she was to say, only half joking,
'That first five years at the House of Commons was Hell. It was full of men
now in gaol or the House of Lords. Those who were found out went to
gaol; the others to the House of Lords.'[7]

Telegrams were now flowing in from all over the world, and even on her
second day as an MP she received 600 letters. She knew she must do her
supporters justice, and make her presence felt in a way that would induce
her male colleagues in the Commons – sure of themselves, averse to feminine
advice – to accept that lady MPs were here to stay, and that legislation must
properly reflect the needs of the nation's women and children. She had now
to tread a difficult and delicate path. Upon her performance might depend
the future pace of British women's political – and therefore social and
economic – progress. Were she shrill or forceful, or if she appeared to be
too astute, she might antagonise the people who counted, especially party
leaders and constituency officials. Their doubts and prejudices would be
confirmed, and barriers placed once more across the path of women; the
political experiment would come to a premature close. On the other hand,
were she mute or too compliant, she might find herself merged into the
existing regimen, failing the hopes of countless women.

Not too hot, and not too cold. She must please and yet cajole.

As it happened, her particular blend of gaiety, wit and resolve – a double dose of life – together with self-confidence, wealth, excellent staff support and the experienced guidance of her husband, exactly met the needs of the hour. At that crucial moment it was probably only someone with Nancy's combination of character, resources and status who could make an impression on Parliament. She was untrained in the arts of debate, but her brain was powerful. More valuable, her intuition was strong: she understood that it was her presence that was important, and that she must make it felt to just the right degree: 'Ever since I entered the "Mother of Parliaments",' she was to tell an American audience, 'I realised that I ceased to be a person and had become a symbol. The safe thing about being a symbol is this – you realise that you, of yourself, can do nothing, but what you symbolise gives you courage and strength, and should give you wisdom.'[8]

Nancy now stood alone between two opposing forces. The first had arisen from the feminist ideas which, accelerated by the circumstances of war, had passed on to the statute book. The broad terms of the Sex Disqualification (Removal) Act of 1919, in particular, seemed to say all that was needed:

A person shall not be disqualified by sex or marriage from the exercise of any public function, or from being appointed to or holding any civil or judicial office or post, or from entering or assuming or carrying on any civil profession or vocation, or for admission to any incorporated society.

That seemed clear enough. Women were no longer to be confined to the home. Those who wanted to do so could in theory now play a full part in the nation's professional life – barristers, solicitors, local councillors, chartered accountants, doctors, civil servants, members of august bodies such as the Royal Society and, most important of all, members of Parliament. Queen Victoria would have been appalled. 'The Queen,' she had written barely fifty years earlier, 'is most anxious to enlist every one who can speak or write to join in checking this mad, wicked folly of "Women's Rights", with all its attendant horrors, on which her poor, feeble sex is bent, forgetting every sense of womanly feeling and propriety. God created man and woman different – then let them remain each in their own position.'[9]

In the other direction came resistance from the incumbents of the professions at last opened to women. But now both camps – women pressing forward, men holding back – stood uncertain as to how they should proceed. Politics and society had entered a state of flux; the ruling class felt the ground beneath it shifting.

It was the legacy of war. Large numbers of the upper and middle classes were dead, or disabled in mind or body, and many landowners were left without an heir. War casualties were not wholly exempt from death duties – sometimes successive levies on one family – with ruinous consequences. To some extent the difficulties had begun even before the war. Although by the turn of the century rents had started to recover from the long agricultural depression, the introduction of land taxes had started an avalanche of land sales in the last few years of peace. Now the trend accelerated, and income was threatened, as assets tumbled in value once more. Untrained as they were in the actual making of money, many of the governing class found their ease and stability beginning to dissolve. English society had been pitched into a period of change on a scale seen only in the Civil War, the Reformation and, before that, the Norman Conquest. The Edwardian Age had vanished, and there was no going back: 'Hurricane-wracked communities are never the same again: the beach has been suddenly eroded, the houses off their foundations, strange new inlets and sandbars have developed, the landscape no longer familiar.' Long-settled country estates were now bought by newcomers, or split up, soon to be prey to developers. Large numbers of London family homes were turned into flats, hotels, offices or clubs. Houses that had long been flagships of politics and society were sold off by their owners: Dorchester, Lansdowne, Derby, Dudley, Portman, Holland, Wimborne – famous names receding with a lost society.

In 1920 alone, a million acres of land in England had been sold; more were soon to follow, besides huge swathes of Wales and Scotland – estimates suggest that in a few short years up to 25 per cent of England and 30 per cent of Wales and Scotland were sold by the 'nobility and gentry' – before a collapse in prices and agricultural depression caused the process to come to a temporary halt, with impoverished landowners forced grimly to stay put, in ever-worsening circumstances, and, where possible, to survive by selling long-held works of art.

Consequently, even as the barricades in the way of women's advancement were dismantled, economic difficulties lessened the impatience for political experiments. Certainly, there was an initial take-up of posts newly opened to women, as magistrates or local councillors, for example, but there was little follow-through, and the Civil Service, vital for giving effect to changes in the law, seemed determined not to alter their ways. The first female civil servant, Mrs Nassau Senior, had been appointed nearly fifty years earlier, but there had been little advance since then.[10]

There was also obstruction from the legal profession, which did its best to prevent women even from sitting on juries. By 1921, there were still no female lawyers, and serving as magistrates or on juries, for the few who managed it, was almost the only practical way in which women could increase their contribution to developing the law of the land. Even peeresses in their own right were not yet allowed to sit in the House of Lords.

Nowhere was there more surly reluctance to budge than among trade unions: with the boys coming back from the trenches – 3.37 million qualified for demobilisation following the end of the war, in November 1918 – they were not going to let women keep their war jobs, and were ready with verbal and physical abuse for those who looked like sitting tight; and while companies relished the chance of minimising the wage bill, to both private and public employers a married woman, who might get pregnant, or whose husband might at short notice prevail upon her to stay and mind the home, was a liability. Further, men resented the fact that women were taking scarce jobs even though many had a husband to support them.

Meanwhile, leading parliamentarians proclaimed that women in work neglected their home-making, undersold their labour and deprived men of jobs. The war had also tarnished the image of domestic service, which did not appeal to a new generation of women whose only experience of work was in munitions factories.

Women demanded a champion, to ignite the moment, to invigorate the calls for change and to give them focus: to be a mouthpiece for women's organisations, enabling them to channel their strengths into one compelling voice, to understand what was happening beyond their own particular areas, to assess prospects and exchange ideas, and so to exert pressure on lawmakers. Determined, therefore, that the momentum of the Sex Disqualification Act should not fail, women's groups, inspired by the very fact of Nancy reaching Parliament, turned to her with their pleas.

She also managed to allay the doubts of the militant feminists, the heirs to the suffragettes, who had hoped and expected that the first woman MP would be a tried and tested suffragist, or at least someone with experience of local government or social service. Nancy had given generous support to their cause before the war, but otherwise had not identified herself with them. Yet she called herself an 'ardent feminist', and she soon showed that in her own way she was as determined as any. Welcomed accordingly, she gradually began to win over hardened feminists to her side, and to dispel doubts that she was just a political hostess with wealth and social contacts riding a wave made by others.

> I knew I had to represent the women . . . I walked in one procession
> asking the Government to allow women to work in munitions. Why
> in Heaven's name men took it that the Christ's message was for men
> I do not know. Men have ruled for 2,000 years.

As I said to the Archbishop, 'When you get to heaven God's not going to ask whether you put on skirts or pants.'[11]

One of her first, and particularly effective, ideas stemmed from her realisation that her position could provide a platform for all sorts of separate interests. She visualised introducing to each other politicians and women's groups that might never otherwise cross each other's paths, but which could foster understanding and co-operation. It would be an enormous task, but she was the one person to whom it was perfectly suited. Others clearly thought the same way. Her impact was recalled by Caroline Haslett, co-founder of the Electrical Association for Women, a pioneer in the use of electricity and how it might benefit women by liberating them from household drudgery:

Lady Astor, full of life and hope and joyous undertakings, swung into my life, then full enough of serious endeavour, certainly, but lacking a little of joyous spontaneity. Before we had proved ourselves she gave us the great benefit of her name and became our first president. Many a time since, her sparkle has invigorated and cheered me, and life always seems to have much more flavour when tasted in her company.[12]

With her fame spreading – her effigy was placed in Madame Tussaud's – Nancy addressed in the ensuing weeks a number of large gatherings, outlining a list of crusades she believed must be undertaken – sometimes revealing unsuspected interests, as, for example, when she opened an exhibition of women's industries: 'I love home life, knitting, butter-making, and the quiet occupations.' Besides speaking on essentially feminine topics, she addressed the need for both England and America to support the League of Nations.[13] She advocated the Round Table line that it was up to the British Empire and America jointly to restore order in the world, now that the rivalries of other nations had proved so ruinous, their failure marked by the lines of wooden crosses stretching across the shattered European landscape.

There soon arose the daunting prospect of her maiden speech to Parliament. She decided to make it in a debate on the removal of wartime drinking restrictions, which had been introduced, supposedly temporarily, principally to reduce drunkenness among workers making explosives. No subject could have been closer to her heart. The fact that successful trading in alcohol had been one of the building blocks of the Astor fortune, which to a large extent had paved her way to success in England and to the position she had reached, had little effect on her hostility to drink in almost all its aspects. For Nancy, drink and poor housing impaired the economic productivity on which national prosperity depended, and was a cause of much of the evil in the world and many of the hardships of women and children. 'I've seen it all my life,' she later used to say. 'I've never seen it improve anyone.'

Hers, however, was the minority view in England, where the freedom to drink at will was considered the source of good cheer for body and soul. Those who advocated its restriction were thought sour and interfering, and, where taken seriously, were deeply unpopular. In those days heavy drinking was widespread, and for great numbers of people about the only relief available after long hours of hard work. In some cities there were over a dozen pubs on a block. There was no shortage in Plymouth, for example. 'I can get my husband past four,' one of Nancy's constituents complained to her, 'but not eight.' At this stage it was the excess to which Nancy objected; she appeared to accept that a man should have at least some consolation from the bottle: 'He wants his drink occasionally,' she said, 'but he does not want the reek of the fifteen pubs which are found on every highway and byway of his city to be the smell which spells home to his children.'

The subject had become emotive as a result of the imposition of Prohibition in Canada. Fears that the idea might spread to other parts of the Empire were increased by its acceptance – at first – in America, which went dry in 1920. There was anxiety that England might suffer the same fate. Feelings on the subject were running high when, on 24 February, Nancy rose to make her maiden speech. Waldorf, who had himself been partly responsible for the imposition of the shackling Act that Parliament was now urged to strike, sat in the Peers' Gallery, along with the Archbishop of Canterbury, ready to see Nancy perform.

It was her good fortune that the mover of the Bill was Sir John Rees, a man generally viewed as old-fashioned, if not eighteenth-century in his outlook. Rees now posed as a champion of the Englishman's liberty, urging that restrictions tolerable in an emergency should be lifted now that the war was over. Nancy had listened to Sir John's assertions with emphatic denials and little ripples of scornful laughter, and when the lady member rose to reply, MPs were more than ready to hear her. Sir James Barrie had suggested to her that she begin her speech by praising what Plymouth and the fighting men of Devon had sent out into the world, and pointing out that at first even Drake, Raleigh and the Pilgrim Fathers had been considered too adventurous. She did so, but then continued, as she was so often to do, by largely ignoring what had just been said and branching out in the broadest of terms.

Attacking her bête noire, the brewing trade, she dwelt on the moral gains to be made by restricting drink. She was open about her preference for the total prohibition of alcohol: 'I hope very much from the bottom of my heart that at some time the people of England will come to Prohibition. I myself believe it will come. I say so frankly.' Drawing from the Bible and Christianity, she used many of the arguments for banning drink that in the coming years she was assiduously to repeat. It was a politically risky approach, but once on her feet she gained confidence, and her demure appeal briefly warmed the hearts of the rows of dark-suited men squeezed on to the benches: 'I do not want you to look on your lady Member as a fanatic or a lunatic. I am simply trying to speak for hundreds of women and children throughout the country who cannot speak for themselves.' As the press put it, parts of her speech were something between 'an easy-going unconventional talk' and 'the harrowing effort of a reformer at a congregational meeting'; Archdeacon Neve might well have approved.

Her speech lasted for half an hour. Her voice was clear and carrying, with a slight American accent, and she persisted in dropping her final 'g's. Her tendency, one commentator noted, was to plead and coax, like 'a missionary to an assembly of inebriates'.[14] She spoke long enough to display the virtues and faults of many of her future Commons speeches: she could not resist the temptation to moralise, and she seemed to leap from idea to idea, often barely connected, as each swam into her mind. As a result, she wandered from the point, even if with eloquence clearly spoken from the heart. Fearlessness in her remarks, without first pausing for thought, was to become a hallmark: 'How do I know what I'm thinkin',' she would often retort, 'until I've said it?' But even if her mental restlessness was evident, the speech was admired. There was a roar of 'Hear, hear' as she sat down. A government minister paid a tribute felt by many of her listeners: 'Whatever may be the merits of this resolution, it has at any rate this merit, it has elicited from the Hon. Member for Plymouth a speech of brilliant and vivid eloquence, which has obtained general acceptance from every quarter of this House . . .'[15]

A less extravagant but perhaps more important reaction came from the party managers: 'Lady Astor made her maiden speech on Tuesday on a drink motion. Quite a good performance. Style rather "street corner" but delivery good, and points made well. Very few members could have done so well.'[16] From a government Whip that was high praise; a maiden speech in the House of Commons is a nerve-racking experience, and for Nancy it must have been particularly so, being the only woman in a chamber packed with men who at heart regretted her presence. But on balance it was a success, even if she was gradually to find that the street-corner style was not to the taste of Parliament, which, like Queen Victoria, disliked being addressed as though it were a public meeting.

Although Nancy soon showed that she would be diligent in attending Commons debates and a conscientious constituency MP, it also became apparent that she was unable, or, as many said, unwilling, to master the rules of the House – all-important in a forum of 600 or so assertive individualists if the nation's business were to be duly transacted. For instance, it was not long before she was responding to members who disagreed with her by heckling them, provocatively pointing a white-gloved finger, or throwing up her hands in despair at some reactionary remark, whether from her own party or her opponents. She also soon fell into the habit of maintaining a more or less audible running commentary when others were on their feet: a newspaper report of a typical day soon after she had taken her seat told of her interrupting fifteen speeches, and breaking off in the middle of her own to shout comments at other members:

> When she did not directly interrupt to explain, comment, deny, expostulate, she interjected. She popped up excitedly. She subsided suddenly. She opened her mouth. She shut her mouth. She turned to this side and that. She shrugged her shoulders. She said 'tch, tch'. She tapped an irritated toe tattoo.[17]

Within not much more than two years, Nancy was to adopt the somewhat cavalier demeanour in the Commons that would last throughout her career there, as was later depicted by a fellow member who often sat in the same row as her:

> She enters the Chamber with short steps, always well-dressed and usually wearing a hat with a sort of Versailles hunting curve to it. She bows to the Speaker, sits down and remarks, 'What's he talkin' about?' . . . Her question having been answered by a neighbour, Lady Astor may then throw a friendly remark at the MP who is speaking – some neat remark such as, 'You don't know what you're talkin' about!' . . . About this stage in the proceedings she gets up and walks out, bowing prettily to the Speaker. She does not leave the Chamber. Just beyond the bar of the house . . . she enters into earnest conversation with some MP or Minister who is standing there. Then she disappears, to turn up by the Speaker's chair, where she has a few moments' chat with its distinguished occupant.

By that time the whole affair has taken on the aspect of a Southern reception. It would not surprise us if negro waiters appeared with mint juleps for all. But wait! The MP on his feet has said something with which our first Lady of the House most definitely does not agree. Back she comes like a corvette in our midst again. 'What *is* he talkin' about?' she says boisterously.

Five minutes later she leaves the Chamber with the demure self-satisfaction of a Pekinese which has innocently upset the calm of a whole kennel of bulldogs.[18]

Many MPs ignored her, and on meeting her around the House looked through her as though she wasn't there. She did her best to minimise confrontation, keeping clear of the dining rooms and smoking room, even though that deprived her of their conviviality and might have brought her new friends in the Commons, to make her early period there more tolerable.

It was to be almost two years before another woman was elected, and in all that time her loneliness was intensified by the glowering hostility with which she was continuously faced across the chamber. Not only did MPs create a palpably unwelcoming atmosphere, but they deliberately made her feel uncomfortable, like someone in a factory being sent to Coventry. Often, when she tried to reach her seat, which was mid-row, she found her way physically barred by adjacent MPs unwilling to let her in. They would move together so that there was no room for her to get by, and she, physically small, had somehow to force herself past them, squeezing through in an embarrassing and undignified manner and scrambling over them as they quietly laughed and jeered. It was enough to destroy the morale even of someone with the ego needed to get into Parliament. For all her vivacity and confidence, Nancy was distressed.

She was often further discouraged in the lobbies or corridors, when, at her approach, MPs would start talking loudly in a rude and gross manner, or begin discussing topics that were embarrassing for a woman to hear, such as venereal disease. No Edwardian lady of her class would have put up with what Nancy had to, but she persevered with determined idealism, fortified by sheer toughness of spirit.

She was soon appointed to a number of standing committees – small, informal groups with the remit to review and amend proposed legislation as the majority thought advisable, before sending it back to the full House for further debate and voting. In the relatively relaxed atmosphere of such committees she expressed herself even more stridently than she was to do in the full chamber, often causing dissension, but sometimes hilarity.

However, it was also awkward for her to take part in some of their debates. The first committee that she sat on dealt with aspects of criminal law, including the age of consent, which was subsequently debated in the House. There were lurid discussions ranging from activities in Shanghai brothels to those on the doorsteps of south London. Her brother-in-law, Pauline's husband, Col. Bertie Spender-Clay, MP for Tonbridge, came up and urged her to leave the chamber, telling her 'how difficult' her presence was making it for the Commons.

> I was sitting there feeling sick and going red and white by turns. The way they were talking was new to me. They were showing indecent photographs around the House of Commons too. I said to them, 'You go tell your friends that if they like they can take off their trousers and parade up and down the House of Commons naked, but I shall sit here.' The things I talked about then . . . often my knees were shaking, so I was glad that we wore skirts, to hide it . . .

Sometimes she was in tears by the time she got home. It was only the thought of what so many women had been through in their long march for representation that made her stick it out. 'I had to do what the women wanted me to do,' she said. 'I had to just sit there.'[19]

She could find little refuge: she was allotted a comfortable room, with panelling, easy chairs, a telephone and a writing desk, but she felt isolated; nor was she offered the use of any nearby washroom, despite the long hours, from early afternoon to the end of the session. The battle was on, as Churchill later told her, to freeze her out, in the hope that she would be forced into playing an insignificant part, so that constituency associations would be confirmed in their prejudice that it was a waste of time adopting women.

Nancy, though, was undismayed by the crack of the party whip. Her duty was to women; it was they who had sent her to Parliament, and she must vote for the reforms that would benefit them and their families. Her independent and liberal stance would often make her unpopular, not least at Tory conferences, where her speeches were sometimes met by noisy hostility. Yet she was sure that she was ideally suited to the task.

From the start, however, her new celebrity exposed her to the pitfalls in public life. Comment had already been made about the Astors' influence in Plymouth, with *The Saturday Review*, for example, pointedly questioning how far Nancy's election victory had been 'due to the spirit of the music-hall, or how far it was procured by the diffusion of golden philanthropy'.[20] In April 1920, two months after her maiden speech, she was the subject of banner headlines and another unpleasant article, when – courageously for a divorcee – she voted against relaxing the divorce laws. A motion had been placed before Parliament calling for equal treatment between the sexes in matrimonial matters – which Nancy supported – and for new grounds for divorce, including desertion, which she vigorously opposed.[21] 'It really was a religious thing with me,' she recounted. 'I wanted the world to get better. And it wouldn't with men alone.'[22]

With Christian zeal, she urged that nothing should be done to weaken the law's protection of the spiritual aspect of marriage. 'I am not convinced,' she said, 'that making divorce very easy really makes marriages more happy . . . Shall we help women and children and men by making divorce easier? I think the world is too loose altogether. What we need is tightening up . . .' Being tightened up did not appeal to many of her hearers, nor did they think that it would go down well with their constituents.

She also claimed that the easy divorce laws in America had brought no gain to women. It was certainly a bold statement: a little sleuthing by journalists would of course show that Nancy herself had benefited from the 'easy divorce' back home. And so it happened: 'Lady Astor's Divorce' appeared on placards all over central London, placed there as advertisements for Horatio Bottomley's paper *John Bull*, which on 8 May 1920 ran a piece describing Nancy as 'A Hypocrite of the First Water'. A further embarrassment was the exposure of Waldorf's entry in *Who's Who* describing himself as married to the widow of Robert Gould Shaw. Even if the Astors took the line that having to supply data and private details to government departments was intrusive and objectionable, it was false for Waldorf to say that he was married to a widow. Luckily, however, the accusations of hypocrisy were soon defused: MPs were outraged by Bottomley's attacking Nancy so aggressively in his newspaper, and when she next entered the chamber she was loudly cheered.

She also championed another of the great causes of the day: equal franchise for women. The War Office estimated that in 1918 there were nearly 800,000 fewer men living in Britain than would have been the case had there been no war, leaving in effect nearly one and a quarter million 'surplus' women, unlikely to marry and a threat to the re-employment of ex-servicemen. There was a current of opinion, therefore – mainly, as it chanced, among men – that the war had left in its wake a shortage of male voters and that no further changes to the franchise should be made until a new generation had reached voting age. Although it was by now conceded to be a matter of 'when', not 'if', Nancy was determined to help keep up the pressure, and equal franchise was to become one of her causes until the goal was finally reached in 1928.

There were also dark thoughts that the majority of advocates of temperance were women, and that if there were more female voters than male, Prohibition might be introduced against men's will. Further, leading Tories claimed that the majority of women did not want the vote, and that to make a fuss about votes for women was a lot of 'sentimental slop and slobber'. Nancy was instantly roused:

> She was astonished by such reactionary speeches as the Committee had just listened to . . . Why were the men voters so frightened of women who wanted the vote? Men had made such a mess of things that women were justified in taking the vote away from them. If women had the vote there would have been no war. Why were men so frightened of what they called 'Pussyfootism?' . . . 'You need not fear women,' she added, 'because we are going to give you what is best for you.' [Loud laughter][23]

However, Nancy found reactionary members a useful if exasperating foil. When, a few months later, a veteran member tried to prevent, by 'talking out', the passage of a Bill imposing a reduction in shop opening hours, Nancy, indignant at the idea of young girls having to work late into the night, marched over and pulled at his coat tails in a vain attempt to make him sit down and stop talking – a most unusual procedure in the House.

From 1920, the framework of her political life began to take shape. She frequently went to Plymouth, sallying forth from her great house on the Hoe to see to the needs of her constituents. Many were poverty-stricken, and a large number were dependent upon the dockyards, where the return of peacetime conditions had led to large numbers of redundancies. Yet the people of Plymouth could see that Nancy was on their side, campaigning, so far in vain, for the government to award ship-repair contracts to the city's dockyards. When she went into the poorest areas of the city, she was sure always to add colour by being well dressed: her clothes were sometimes made by the world's leading dress designers, and sometimes faithfully copied from fashionable styles by her dressmaker at Chez Beth; but the materials and the ensemble owed a considerable amount to her own imagination and excellent taste.

The personal following of 'Our Nancy', as she was often called, although she discouraged it, gathered pace, and not just with the naval men and families of the 'lower deck', for whom she had become something of a champion: the public who recounted the stories of her fearlessness in haranguing the bleak tenement balconies also enjoyed the story of how she had dealt with a burglar outside her own house. Far from giving way, she confronted the man, who quickly turned tail and ran, and chased him relentlessly down side alleys, into a public house, through the bar and out at the back, until he stopped and gave himself up to her. She then declined to press charges but instead, characteristically, pointed out to him the error of his ways. The tale quickly spread.

Her rapidly expanding schedule was filled with speaking up for a variety of good causes, mostly with the common factor of women's and children's welfare, such as equal pay for equal work, and the need for female police officers, under threat of extinction now that their wartime employment was deemed superfluous. In 1920, she was appointed to an official committee examining the role of women in the police force. In parallel she campaigned for prison reform, and for improvements to the probation service. She was told that her ideas would interfere with the dignity of judges: 'Who cares about the dignity of judges,' she riposted, 'where a child's soul is concerned? The dignity of judges lies in their justice, not in their office.'

She also called for more women MPs. Women had stood in two by-elections since Nancy's triumph but both had lost, their party consequently concluding that it would be better after all to adopt men. So Nancy was still on her own. With hundreds of letters continuing to fill her post bag each day, it was vital that she should be able to spread the load: 'As one woman,' she said, 'it was hopeless to try and express what women thought on all the complex matters in public affairs, and I began to feel impatient for the arrival of women of every shade of political thought in the House of Commons.'[24]

In the early summer of 1920, the Prime Minister, Lloyd George, appointed Nancy the official delegate of the British government to a great gathering of the International Woman Suffrage Alliance, meeting in Geneva. The government claimed that her appointment showed that were amenable to giving women a say in foreign affairs. Whether or not that was the case, it is true that other countries, not least America, had fewer misgivings – American women became eligible for foreign service in 1922 – and women were soon to show that their participation in international gatherings caused no surprise or difficulty. Nancy had long had an international outlook, and she was sure her principles had universal application. She was also pleased that the Alliance meeting in Geneva was affiliated to the American League of Women's Voters, whose cause she was soon to espouse on a triumphal American tour.

At the end of May, she set off for Geneva, where she found the press waiting for her:

The slender little lady under the veil was amiably, vivaciously chatting with those about her. One arm was weighed down with a black bag and the other was filled with books and papers. She made light of the difficulties of the trip and seemed to enjoy the experience as part of life. As her secretary straightened things out with the customs, she posed for photographers, petite and thoughtful, with an ever-ready wit and laughter.[25]

Nancy took a particular interest in debates on the League of Nations, believing that it was vital for achieving the reconstruction and future peace of Europe. At a great public meeting attended by female members of European parliaments, she was 'the cynosure of all eyes . . . blonde, wavy hair curled at the back but in something of a halo about her face, particularly suited to her finely chiselled profile. Everyone was a bit tired out but Lady Astor was alive with energy and charming animation as she read her manuscript speech, with off the cuff comments and gestures.' She expressed her creed in a speech on 'Women in Parliament':

> There are of course some spheres which concern women more than men and men more than women. Women are perhaps specially sensitive to the whole question of human suffering; they tend to think of legislation in terms of men, women and children rather than in terms of theories. That lays on us a special responsibility for securing better protection for children, better care for mothers, better factory conditions and better education for the young.[26]

As one reporter put it, a day in Nancy's life during this period was like an adventure with a gale – a friendly whirlwind that 'never stops'. That could in part be attributed to her genes, but the effect was greatly enhanced by her total abstention from tobacco and alcohol, and by physical fitness, which, with her natural vivacity, kept her slender and supercharged through a disciplined morning regime. Her day began at eight with a study of the Bible and the daily Christian Science lesson, her bed littered with notes, and *Science and Health* duly marked up. Her friends sometimes used to ask why she spent so much time with the book, to which her reply was usually 'It means everything to me: it's how I run my life, you know.' After this she had a cold bath and a game of squash – she had installed a court on an upper floor of the London house[27] – followed by physical exercises – a friend remembered seeing her on the bathroom floor, legs in long white knickers, toes touching the floor at the back of her head – and finally a hot bath.

She would usually have breakfast with the younger children, after which she was ready to go, galvanising the atmosphere and any who came into contact with her, not least the household servants. She would spend two hours or so going through the daily piles of letters with her secretaries, and then, if Parliament was sitting, she would go to the Commons and deal with more correspondence before attending committees or entering the chamber.

Her working day was crammed, dealing with myriad requests. With so many calls for her assistance, she needed a complex political and social organisation. She was therefore fortunate that the momentum created by her arrival in Parliament enabled her to conjure up a high-quality secretariat. But it was also her fame and reputation that drew capable people to her service, and she had the intuition to find the best on the market. It was expensive, but that was no problem, with Waldorf patiently managing the Astor affairs.

The London house remained an ideal base for operations, and Nancy used it, and to a lesser extent Cliveden, as a venue for introducing politicians, men of influence and others who could help them to women's leaders and representatives of the causes she endorsed. It was also the setting for the conferences of women's organisations in March and April 1921. At the second of these it was decided to set up a joint consultative body to concentrate on reforms particularly affecting women and children. This was to be the Consultative Committee of Women's Organisations, and Nancy described its aims to her constituency chairman:

> . . . I invited representatives of all the leading women's societies, together with individual women experts on social questions, to confer together and see whether greater co-operation between these organisations was possible and desirable. Two conferences were held, and at the second it was decided to set up a joint consultative body without executive powers, to focus attention on reforms especially affecting women and children . . .[28]

The committee gave further practical expression to Nancy's vision of providing women's organisations with access to those who could further their various causes. An overall umbrella would help the many groups that were ignorant of the work of others with the same goals, and would encourage them to pool their ideas. By the summer of 1921, there were sixty or so groups under the aegis of the Consultative Committee, and she reported progress to the Plymouth Conservatives:

> As I have also found that many Members of Parliament are anxious to know more of women's questions, I have undertaken to hold a series of At Homes once a month, when representatives of the women's organisations and Members of Parliament will have an opportunity of discussing these matters informally. I am glad to say that many MPs,

including members of His Majesty's Government have taken this opportunity of meeting representative women.[29]

Her experienced secretariat was vital in allowing her to put such ideas into practice. Her first private secretary, appointed before her election campaign, had been a fellow Christian Scientist, Miss Bunny Benningfield, but soon after Nancy's election, Ray Strachey, who had been closely involved with women's suffrage groups before and during the war, and who herself had stood for Parliament in the 1918 election, offered to become her part-time parliamentary secretary and adviser for her first six months in Parliament. Ray explained to her mother, 'It is so very important that the first woman MP should act sensibly, and she, though full of good sense of a kind, is lamentably ignorant of everything she ought to know.'[30]

A little later, Nancy appointed another private secretary, Hilda Matheson. She was a former secretary to the President of the Board of Education, Hayes Fisher, the force behind the 1918 Education Act, which had made school compulsory for children up to the age of fourteen. Raising the school leaving age was another cause that Nancy was to champion. She argued that fourteen was too young, as the labour market was crowded with unemployed juveniles for whom lack of a job was demoralising, while keeping children at school for longer would increase their efficiency when eventually they did move into work. Her views annoyed the Conservative Party and flew in the face of the inclination of most poor families to send their children out to earn a wage as soon as possible.

Hilda Matheson had been in the Secret Service during the war, and had then worked for Philip Kerr, so in Nancy's view her credentials were excellent. She soon made far more of the job than just working as a normal private secretary, immersing herself in the issues surrounding Nancy's social and political interests, and taking a considerable hand in drafting her speeches – although that was sometimes a waste of time, as Nancy often ignored material prepared for her and was known to have made a speech using entirely the wrong notes, which had not pleased her audience at all.

At first Matheson's confidence was dented by Nancy's attitude. She found her employer assertive and often bullying, offering her no encouragement; even when Nancy felt sympathy and admiration for those who worked for her, she seemed unwilling to show it. Hilda turned to Bunny Benningfield, who by that time no longer worked for Nancy, Bunny duly wrote to Nancy on Hilda's behalf:

She feels that you have no confidence in her and that until you can trust her a little more she won't be able to give her best or to please you in any way. From what I know of your beloved, bewildering and exasperating character, I think she is right . . . she's used to a certain amount of approval and satisfaction for value received . . . now she gets no sympathy, or encouragement, or patience, or consideration. Her chief faults are ignorance of your character and bewilderment. She's giving you her very best and is trying hard to learn your ways. You'll have these difficulties with any secretary you take on.[31]

The letter apparently achieved its object. Nancy may also have realised where her interests lay, and since she took notice of people who stood up to her, it was not long before their working arrangement improved and became very effective.

Nancy was fortunate to be able to surround herself with specialists, and her various secretaries' political antennae and knowledge of the feminist world played a vital part in enabling her to put some ordered detail into her speeches, and to make them more effective in Parliament. She readily admitted that, as she put it, in the British Empire there were many women with far greater potential as politicians, but she was the one who had actually forced open the doors. Now she could gather the leading groups around her and say, 'You're the experts; I'm the MP: brief me' – rather like a lawyer carrying the public's banner at a government inquiry, articulating and directing the campaign. It was a successful partnership: through her position and her personality she persuaded women's leaders that they could get laws changed, or at least improved, by merging their various ideas into one fast-flowing channel. At the same time she gave practical help by providing money and the space in which to marshal their plans, and by continuing to introduce them to influential men who might respond to their ideas.

She soon had four secretaries: two for home and social arrangements and one each for the House of Commons and the Consultative Committee. Between them they dealt with an unceasing flow of engagements and correspondence. Lunches, dinners and large receptions followed each other in rapid succession. The atmosphere at these parties, although friendly and far more luxurious than most of the attendees were used to, was strictly business: Nancy made short work of people who tried to engage in more than the minimum of small talk: 'See here,' she typically told a guest, 'you've come here to talk about business. You're not talking business now and I've no time for this nonsense. Come to the point and stick to it.'

She was the first – in May 1924 – to introduce name tags, now in general use at business gatherings, for guests to pin on their clothes, giving each person's name, profession, organisation or specific topic of interest. Timid or brave, they were turned loose, complete with labels, avoiding the need for formal introductions. Although at first the badges caused surprise, and some haughty mystification, they were soon accepted and even enjoyed; not least on one occasion at the gentle expense of the lady walking around with a badge saying 'Unmarried Mother'.

For engagements at St James's Square, the large L-shaped drawing room would be banked high with many varieties of flowers from Cliveden, and the quiet liveried servants would keep the tea and barley water flowing for the assembled women's leaders, peers, businessmen, civil servants, MPs of all parties, Christian Scientists, trade union leaders, magistrates and men from the professions. At the top of the stairs the first guests would be met by their plainly dressed hostess, but after a short time Nancy's secretaries would do the greeting, enquiring about a guest's special interest, and conducting him or her up to those whom they might wish to buttonhole. It was a new way of organising receptions, American in its directness. An entrée to 4, St James's gave people a chance to find others knowledgeable on their subject.

The impression Nancy made was just the same at the smaller gatherings she held: colourful, restless, amusing, dominating without a grand manner, charming but determined. Despite her purposeful vitality and the formality of her position, she had a certain quality that made people come to her if they were in trouble. She often entertained in her boudoir. It was small and attractive, with a wide fireplace and, by a window, a large desk over which hung a painting of Cliveden. From deep, comfortable chairs could be seen the garden with its lawn surrounded by paving and lined by tall trees. Nancy would be continually on the move: getting up and sitting down, replenishing the fire with small logs, on and off the telephone, or answering the servants or secretaries who seemed endlessly to bring messages to her door. An American acquaintance recorded the general impression of swirl around a gaily painted rock, at a meeting made all the more informal by the presence of the two youngest children – John Jacob, Nancy's sixth child, was born on 29 August 1918. He became generally known as Jakie, and from an early age was close to his brother Michael, two and a half years older than him.

. . . Lady Astor, looking very feminine in some charming, informal costume, displays the combined talents of director and leading lady. She can in immediate succession toss her guests a gay word, sign letters and documents, arrange luncheons and dinners with the chef, direct the housekeeper as to the exact arrangements of the truck-load of flowers that comes twice a week from the country, and fling a bit of her much-besought attention to the children who are frequently playing on the floor . . . 'Oh, look at Michael: he's kneeling on John

Jacob's chest.' So everybody goes down on the floor and begins to unwind the infant tangle . . . She springs up and hurries to her dressing-room door. Friends, secretaries, nurses and even newspaper reporters, if any, crowd after her. She holds them at bay with a few last words and rushes out . . . The delightful little play is over. Chaotic it may seem, this method of attending to business. Yet everybody has had a good time. The secretaries have settled the main issues and the leading lady has played her role without getting too bored.[32]

The many 'broad church' conferences and meetings that Nancy organised complemented Waldorf's work at the Institute of International Affairs, of which he was a benefactor and later, in 1935, chairman. Initiated at a gathering at the Paris Peace Conference, it was founded by Lionel Curtis, generously funded by the randlord Abe Bailey, and based at 10, St James's Square. Chatham House, as it became known, was conceived to carry on the ideas of Lord Milner's Kindergarten, partly using the Round Table movement as a disseminator.

Waldorf had also been pursuing his own parliamentary career, perforce from the House of Lords. In 1919, he had been appointed parliamentary secretary to the Ministry of Health, under Dr Christopher Addison, who had in June 1919 been appointed the first Minister of Health. As parliamentary secretary, a post he held until 1921, Waldorf had a considerable amount of business to transact in the Lords, and during the early years of the decade he also helped with legislation on subjects including unemployment insurance, proprietary medicines, bastardy, rent restrictions, juvenile employment, slum clearance, factory inspections, inheritance law, and restricting the sale of alcohol.

Nancy and Waldorf also regularly organised what they considered to be useful informal talks at Elliot Terrace and Cliveden, and also sometimes at Hever, with the help of Waldorf's brother John, MP for Dover. Such discussions were successful in building bridges between people on different parts of the political and social spectrum. This was in large part possible because Nancy, influenced by the precepts of Christian Science, at that stage successfully engaged with trade unionists and others far from her own political and social medium. Much quiet, constructive, non-party, non-partisan work resulted. It was later in her career that she was to lose such tolerant impulses, and become unable to meet a trade unionist without, as Waldorf put it, 'feeling he was a Red'.

However, even now, political work was bringing about a change in her character. Beneath all the gaiety that Nancy sprinkled over her many social and political gatherings in this early period of her parliamentary career, her priorities had changed. She had to respond to a shattered post-war world. 'I did not mind,' she said, 'giving up social life. After the war – well you just couldn't be interested in things like dancing when so many of your friends lay dead in France.' On the surface, the magnetism and vivacity were undimmed, but beneath it there was growing a certain hardness, a thickening of the cocoon of self-concern. It was discernible in some of the photographs of the time, showing Nancy smiling and beautifully dressed as ever, but with a hint of command in her eyes, and Waldorf with the almost imperceptible air of a man who was now playing second fiddle.

Each phase of her development had left its mark upon the core of her nature: the child, giggling with Phyllis, a little of the tomboy, fighting her corner; the young woman, so soon scarred by her harsh experience of marriage; the hopeful, zestful Mrs Shaw, in a new country, charming the bloods in the hunting field; the glamorous bride, showered with riches, intriguing society and adored by her husband; the feisty Virginian in the fight for election, proclaiming her message to the dockers and fishwives of Plymouth; the triumphal entry into Parliament.

This latest step in Nancy's evolution came at a cost, and it would be paid by her family, especially, for a time, by Waldorf. Steadfast and loving as he was, and providing an immensely generous and expensive lifestyle, he was not in good heart. Although only forty, he was afflicted by back pain, and his discomfort was compounded by an awareness that, despite his invaluable support and guidance in her political work, his wife did not respond with the soft affection he would have liked.

He had also been presented with a financial problem. It might have seemed strange that anything could threaten the greatest urban estate in the world, but not even the Astors were immune from the new political ideas that had blown into the twentieth century, with economic effects greatly increased by the world war. As that conflict dragged on, William Astor had been haunted by fears of socialist legislation, of having to swap good American securities for British war bonds, and of a capital levy. Accordingly he had conveyed a huge amount of stocks, bonds and New York property into trust for his sons. The arrangements had still left him as New York's largest landlord and immensely rich, but before long he had been confronted with further difficulties as the continuing ravages of war compelled both the American and British governments to impose steep increases in tax rates.

For William, living in England largely on earnings from America, the consequences had been dire: he was squeezed with double taxation of the same money, at the highest rates. So much so that by 1919 the US government was taking nearly half his income, and the British government most of the rest. He was forced into drastic action, and orders to sell began to flow in quick succession from the office on the Embankment: houses, tenements, blocks, whole streets even, built over what had been bought as farmland.

The family policy of buying and holding a crock of gold for a century went into reverse. Before long, the estate office itself, across whose polished parquet floors William had escorted his guests only a few years earlier but in what seemed like another world, was sold to an institution. Fortunately for his family, he had effectively protected the very large amounts of property already transferred. However, in August 1919, two months before he died, he had transferred further property holdings, worth over $50 million, into trust for his two sons. Now the American revenue authorities challenged the move, saying that it had been made 'in contemplation of death' and was an attempt to avoid inheritance tax. Demands of more than $15 million were presented, with the possibility of further duties to be paid in England.

So in the autumn of 1920, gripped by back pain, uneasy at the apparent coolness of his wife, and burdened by immense tax claims, Waldorf had to sail for America to iron out these difficulties with the US authorities. He knew that he might be away for months. 'I just can't think what you'll do without me to lecture and abuse,' he wrote to Nancy from the *Mauretania*, 'for tho' you say you don't want me for your holidays I believe you like to have me on hand at the end of a wire when you work . . . Don't think too harshly of me – I repent me often and deeply . . . don't be afraid to take advice. I wish I were there to give it.'[33]

To whatever extent she took advice, Nancy was not afraid to give it. Worried by thoughts of her ailing husband, she now urged Waldorf to turn to Mary Baker Eddy for help. Her suggestion was made partly, perhaps, because she felt that religion was separating her from Waldorf, although he did not agree, but also because she was an ardent proselytiser of Christian Science, and there was no closer target than her husband. So Waldorf agreed to begin studying 'Mother Eddy', as he called her. He found her hard to understand – 'It is just as if I asked you to study trigonometry in French,' he told Nancy; nor did her ideas have any noticeable effect on his back. But he persevered, so that a few years later, in 1924, yearning for relief after a severe attack of sciatica, he was persuaded, and finally became a Christian Scientist. For Nancy it was a success that perhaps compensated for her failure with Waldorf's father, an altogether tougher nut.

Before his eventual conversion, Waldorf's search for a cure now took him to the Langhornes' old haunt at White Sulphur Springs. There, time passed slowly, unrelieved by any letters from Nancy. 'I know how busy you are and am only hoping you aren't writing to anyone else,' he wrote, while commenting that the local church was 'disgracefully empty'. 'I certainly am thoroughly fed up,' he added, 'with being a childless bachelor.' He then moved on to the Bahamas, in the hope of some fishing, and settled into the Rod & Gun Club in Bimini Bay. In 1920 it was a remote sandy reef, reached intermittently by seaplane, and with one small hotel – although, Waldorf noted, apparently large enough to accommodate $1 million worth of whisky that had been moved there to avoid Prohibition. There also seemed to be plenty of gambling. 'So you see,' he wrote, 'we have come to a choice spot.'

At that distance he was reduced to reading press reports of Nancy's parliamentary activities. 'My only anxiety,' he said, 'is leaving you to paddle your political canoe without me. Remember you have a jolly good staff helping you. Don't get down on them . . .' He was sure that she needed his guiding hand, which he wanted to extend. His feelings were perhaps the converse of those of Arthur Balfour, who, when asked whether he was intending to marry his fellow member of the Souls, Margot Tennant, replied, 'No, that is not so: I rather think of having a career of my own.'

Soon Waldorf had also to face another problem: his stepson. He had always treated Bobbie as his own, and had assumed the role of guiding him and shaping his future – his ability and willingness to do so being one of the things that had originally persuaded Nancy to accept his offer of marriage. However, partly as a result of the extraordinary mix of intense maternal love and the formality of the Astors' routine, partly because of his army life with rich, easy-going fellow cavalry officers, and partly, perhaps mostly, because of his nature, Bobbie had warmed to the attractions of a playboy life, increasingly resistant to the outlook of his serious, if not quite Puritan, stepfather.

He could have remained in the army after the war, but Waldorf saw little evidence in him of the stern, successful soldier, and he felt that Bobbie should make more of himself than 'hunting a bit, playing polo mildly, going to Sandown, marrying later, and having a small country place', which was how he envisaged he would turn out in the army. So in June 1919, Bobbie had transferred to the Reserve of Officers list.

He was entitled to a generous income from his own family estate, and to what would be a very large sum if he outlived his mother, but in the meantime Nancy was somehow managing to prevent him actually receiving most of his entitlement, she and Waldorf feeling that it would be a good idea if Bobbie found a job. With that in mind, he was sent off with a friend to Rhodesia, to study the rudiments of agriculture, with the possibility that he might buy a share in a farm out there, rather than spend his time in England indulging a taste for alcohol, and a fondness for what Waldorf termed idle frivolity.

Hard work in the Colonies did not appeal to Bobbie, who soon started writing home with a litany of complaints, and pleas to be allowed to cut short his stay, telling Waldorf that 'Africa is hopeless, useless' and that he would rather 'sell papers in London'. In response, Waldorf laid bare his own feelings:

> Have you ever thought what my feelings have been during the past two months? I have been as far from the family as you – as lonely – as bored. It is not much fun living alone in a hotel at a watering place – or to be cut off at Bimini where we dined at six and then had absolutely nothing to do. I did not tell you nor did I write to Mother how in addition to all this boredom I was often and daily in acute physical pain. I hardly ever got up from table without having to take hold of myself so as not to let people see what pain I was in. My back is much worse than it was . . . Mother never suspected how I was because I knew she was having a difficult time with all her political work, and I did not want to add to her anxieties by grumbling or complaining.[34]

Engrossed in politics and her causes, Nancy left the lion's share of Bobbie's problems for Waldorf to solve. Apart from sending her son a number of postcards without any clear indication of what she thought he should do next, she seemed disinclined to give deep thought to something that was effectively 'out of sight, out of mind'. She had a great deal to contend with closer to home. By her nature she tended to focus on whatever had swum into her immediate ken, and then usually only if it concerned one of the many interests with which she was involved. That did not indicate any lessening of the intensity of the love she felt for Bobbie, or even of her possessiveness, but she could reasonably believe that he was materially secure, and that no doubt all would be well.

Bobbie, however, now in his twenties, was affected by the curdled relationship between mother and son, alternating unpredictably between intense affection, almost as though the umbilical cord had not been cut, and indifference. At the least he was confused, and he may have felt spiritually, as well as physically, apart. Although brought up as one of the Astors, he didn't bear their name, and while it could not have entered his mind at the time he went away to boarding school, being nine years older than the eldest Astor child, he may have wondered subsequently why he went to Shrewsbury and they all went to Eton. Nor did the Astor children, with the notable exception of Michael, evidence any particular affection for Bobbie, then or later, which may have helped to thicken his defences against life. He proved unreceptive to his mother's blandishments about Christian Science, and she accepted that in his case it was a lost cause; even so, he may have resented it when he was excluded from the other children's lessons, knowing how important religion was to her. In any event, good-looking, amusing and popular, he did not relish being in faraway Rhodesia, among local inhabitants of whom he formed a poor opinion, claiming that most of them were stupid and dull as ditchwater, their sole topic of conversation being dip and cattle.

Nancy's relationship with her five other children was essentially distant. Bill and David were at boarding school for a good part of the year, and during the summer holidays they usually went with their father to Scotland, which Nancy preferred to avoid. At Cliveden, where their parents continued to entertain on a large scale, they were left to themselves for much of the time. When they were ill, Nancy would read to them but forbid them food, to speed their recovery; it was left to the butler surreptitiously to give them suitable nourishment. The arrangements seemed to Nancy to work well, and the children were quite happy living in the nursery rooms, when not outside with their ponies and dogs.

If there were not too many guests, the youngest children, Michael and Jakie, did see their mother briefly at fixed times of the day, and she was loving and sweet and tender and full of fun. Besides being in the overall care of Nanny Gibbons, they were for some time taught by a governess, a Mrs Wallis Walker, who had been passed on to Nancy by her old friend Alice Mildmay, despite proving both tiresome and a 'dead loss' with the Mildmays' own children. When Nancy was away, or the children were on holiday, she would write short, light-hearted letters, or send affectionate postcards, such as one to the six year-old Jakie, at Rest Harrow:

Been to see Plymouth play rugger . . . Mr Jules is washing my hair, and you would think it was a poodle dog instead of a lady, and he is pulling it and going so fast you would think it was a typewriter . . . Tell Nannie that I hope she is playing golf and squash.

But especially in London, her attention might abruptly move to some piece of social or political business, and then she would be gone, and it would seem as though the lights had suddenly been dimmed. The reliable pillar of the children's existence was not their mother, or their father, kindly but usually busy or otherwise remote, but Nanny Gibbons, warm and loving and the centrepiece around whom much of their day revolved.

Ironically perhaps, in her political work Nancy attached great importance to the welfare of the young, especially of poor children, with whose conditions she was familiar from seeing them in the crowded tenements of her constituency. Believing in the need for fresh air and space in which to roam, she welcomed the idea of building nursery schools to enable young children, at least for part of the day, to escape the grime and confinement of their homes; and, for older children, creating playing fields on which to develop their bodies and keep their minds pure. As ever, she was not suited to practical work in such causes: her value was as torch-bearer and door-opener. In the case of nursery schools, however, she was to give time and money to a pioneer in the field, Margaret McMillan.

Margaret and her sister Rachel had begun crusading for children's welfare as far back as the nineteenth century, and in 1914 they had established an embryo nursery school: 'the organic and natural education which should precede all primary teaching without which the work of the schools is largely lost'. They had witnessed conditions in the mill towns of the north of England, where many children were sewn into their clothing for the whole of the winter, with pads of cotton wool underneath. Such children spent a minimum of time at school, and the conditions were anyway not conducive to learning – the teachers generally needed bags of sulphur to be sewn into the hems of their skirts, to keep vermin from 'climbing, sliding or leaping up'. The main concern of families was to send their children to work in the mills – if they survived long enough. At that time in the cotton towns of the north, about a third of all children died in their first year. Those who survived could suitably be described, in the caption of a famous *Punch* cartoon, as 'Sentenced to Life'.

The McMillan sisters gradually wrung from local authorities, first in Bradford and then in London, grudging support for baths and medical inspections, and then for the prevention of infection by moving children for as much as time as possible from foetid houses into treatment centres and then night camps, with plenty of fresh air. From these developments evolved the concept of open-air nursery schools. Claiming that she was driven to do so in a dream, in 1926 Margaret McMillan telephoned Nancy, who accepted her invitation to visit the first nursery school, in Deptford in east London. She saw at once that Plymouth was fertile ground for McMillan's ideas, and besides giving money, she raised the concept with otherwise inaccessible people, such as the Education Secretary, H.A.L. Fisher, and Sir Robert Morant, a former top civil servant in that department.

Through her drive and political position, Nancy ensured that Plymouth soon had its share of nursery schools. She realised that they could hardly exist without trained teachers, and supported McMillan's dream of establishing a fully fledged training college for nursery school teachers. She persuaded Waldorf to buy a site for the college, and assisted in raising £20,000 to build it. At the laying of its foundation stone, it could almost have been Nancy herself speaking when Margaret McMillan told the guests, 'We desire to turn out teachers who will be true gardeners in real child gardens, and, if these gardens are planted in poor areas so much the better. Education should make even the poorest district beautiful, and create gardens in the heart of mean streets . . .'[35]

The various causes that Nancy began to promote both in Parliament and on platforms up and down the country were tied by a strong thread of logic. Children had to be educated, but to have a chance of absorbing what they were told, they must be healthy in body and alert in mind. For that they needed enough food, and clean milk – a fixation with Nancy, and more so with Waldorf, having himself brushed with TB – and if they or their parents fell ill, the nurses who tended to them must have had proper training. They must also be properly housed – she knew too well the shambles in which so many people in Plymouth lived, in contrast to the space and comfort at Cliveden. Their mothers must have the time to attend to their offspring, without being chained to the workbench for long hours until they were exhausted; they needed protection from drunks, in the streets and especially in the home, and their teenage daughters needed defending from ill-intentioned men. That required a body of women police, able to succeed where male officers trod too hard. Where marriages sank into divorce, women and men must have equal salvage rights; the guardianship and maintenance of children should be the right and duty of both parents, and in their absence adoption should be made easier, to 'provide a secure home for many a friendless child'. And, of fundamental importance, women should have equal power in the ballot box.

That was especially necessary in the aftermath of the war, with the coalition government's decision to prioritise a reduction in the nation's debt by slashing spending. To do so it appointed a committee under the chairmanship of Sir Eric Geddes, who, swinging what became notorious as the 'Geddes Axe', recommended cuts in spending on defence, health, housing, pensions, bureaucracy and the dole. The result was lower wages, higher prices and soaring unemployment, leading to a shift in political power as an increase in the electorate contributed to the development of 'mass politics'.[36]

Despite the economic gloom, however, Nancy and the few other women MPs who were to join her in the Commons fought their corner successfully through the 1920s, and after many battles in committee and in the chamber, Bills remedying deficiencies they had highlighted reached the statute book.

That was partly due to the success in changing male MPs' perceptions of what the voters might be interested in. It was becoming apparent that since women had been granted the vote in 1918, members of Parliament had at last come to realise that a large proportion of their constituents were now female, and both MPs and the party Whips seemed suddenly to find in much proposed legislation a women's side that previously they had not appeared to notice. The result was that within the next decade a remarkable amount of legislation of benefit to women and children reached the statute book. Some of it had been the subject of campaigns for many years without any practical result, but now that began to change, and women's pensions, women's property, adoption, legitimacy, guardianship of infants, divorce, midwives, and a register for nurses were all set on their way to being dealt with by Parliament. Women and men were placed on an equal footing in divorce for infidelity; married women were given equal guardianship rights; an Adoption Act and a Legitimacy Act addressed the welfare of children without legal parents; and a number of statutes improved the employment conditions of women, reducing the hours they could be made to work in factories as a condition of keeping their jobs.

Narrower legislation included, in chronological order, the Infanticide Act (1922), the Age of Marriage Act (1929), and the Sentence of Death (Expectant Mothers) Act (1931). Nancy promoted these causes in their early stages, both by the inspiration of her position and in other, more practical ways, often in the teeth of opposition. The Infanticide Bill, for example, was drawn up only after an outcry over the fate of Edith Roberts, whose newborn baby was discovered under some linen in a chest of drawers, unwanted and the result of rape. Edith was sentenced to death, impelling a large number of women's organisations to write to Nancy imploring her to get Parliament to address the matter not just of the unfortunate Miss Roberts but of the urgent need for a change in the law and of sentencing policy.

Nancy, being convinced of the close link between children's welfare and housing, frequently stressed the importance of the latter, both in Parliament and in local councils. She knew that building more and better houses was of little interest to men: 'If they thought as much of housing as public-housing,' she would say, 'we should have had the houses long ago.' She felt that as a woman, she could open the eyes of men to new ideas. In 1923, she and Waldorf set an example with a plan to provide neat model houses for the poor in Plymouth. It was Nancy's brainchild and she put up an initial £10,000; Waldorf arranged technical help and provided a further £10,000 – a total of nearly £1 million in current money. They included the ground-breaking condition that three-quarters of the tenants should be families with young children, whose searches for accommodation were so often met with a 'Children Not Taken' sign. Tenants were also given a share in the administration, and the use of social and recreational facilities.

While wanting to put right a raft of political wrongs – what her detractors called the bees in her bonnet that never stopped buzzing – Nancy had to keep in mind the need to please the Conservative authorities, and of course the voters. All her plans and policies would fail if she lost her seat. Because of the post-war disorder in Britain, the political ground had become unstable, and was to remain so for many years. Governments felt obliged to hold elections more frequently than was usual: in little more than a decade following her first election, Nancy had to fight for her seat five times: in 1922, 1923, 1924, 1929 and 1931.

That she retained the seat with such consistency is testament to her popularity, and when, in April 1922, she and Waldorf went to the United States, for the first time since her election to Parliament, it was clear that she was held in equally high regard there. The enthusiasm with which she was greeted fed on itself and produced a resounding success, strengthening for Nancy the platform from which she would call for Anglo-American solidarity, as clouds began once more to darken the international horizon.

They sailed to America on the *Olympic*. Progress at times slowed to half-speed, giving the passengers an uneasy reminder that it was exactly ten years since her sister ship, *Titanic*, had hit an iceberg on the same route. Nancy was as energetic as ever, rowing on machines in the ship's gym, and running circuits of the deck. The press caught her even before she had disembarked, dressed for arrival in 'coloured pumps, silver buckles, soft black velvet hat, a striking background for her pink-and-white beauty, her grey-blue eyes and soft fluff of blonde hair having an aureole effect like the blonde locks of a child'. With the click of a hundred cameras and the scratching of notepads, they fired their questions at her on the hurricane deck. Waldorf, in spats and a homburg hat, was by her side: 'Lord Astor, looking as though he would like to make a clean plunge over the side, stayed shoulder to shoulder with his peach-bloom lady, and smiled like the brave and kindly soul he is.' 'It's worse getting into New York harbour than into the House of Commons,' said Nancy.

Her original invitation had been to address the Pan-American Women's Convention, in Baltimore, but even before landing she was giving interviews to journalists, and great numbers of other invitations were arriving by radio for her to address meetings up and down the land, including in her native Danville, where it was proposed to name a street after her. Waldorf, her prop and mainstay, began to sway as he tried to maintain some degree of order and to sketch out a plan: 'I feel like the agent, secretary, manager, booster and adviser of a prima donna, Cabinet minister and circus all in one.'[37] Within days of landing, the pace quickened further, as the intensity of Nancy's welcome became apparent, fuelled by ceaseless coverage on radio and in the press:

. . . I sigh daily, nay hourly, for our Secretariat from St James's Square, who know my ways. What with helping with speeches, dealing with the Press, watching papers, tackling endless correspondence, answering cable invitations from every part of the States and Canada, altering dates of meetings, telephoning, fixing cross country journeys, etc., etc., it's like being in a maelstrom in a monsoon in a thunderstorm.[38]

On arrival, Waldorf did gather a team of secretaries to help him catch up with and pin down the mercurial figure darting, slipping and gliding some way ahead of him. She would continuously experiment with methods of preparation, switch her train of thought and change her system of notes. Waldorf soon discovered the value of sending advance copies of her important speeches to the press, so that her message was not obliterated by her impromptu and wayward digressions. Typing the notes – which it was vital for her to have, to prevent her straying too far from the points she wished to make, and which her audiences, often of several thousands, had come to hear – was a thankless task for Waldorf, 'as they are misspelt, abbreviated on no known system, and illegible'. He soon recorded that 'one really requires a traffic manager, a diplomat, a Pelmanist, and a political economist, each in charge of a big staff of secretaries and clerks'. Instead, he was more or less on his own. He felt his hair turning white.

Nancy's speeches, delivered in high, strident tones but with the ring of youth in her voice, were spontaneous and unpredictable: sometimes irreverent, sometimes spiritual; sometimes gently sarcastic, usually witty; intelligent and eloquent. At times they were inconsequential and too long. It did not matter: she was a heroine, a bright star that now shone in the Old World while in their own country, for women, so little progress had been made. A woman had first sat in Congress in 1916, and although several had followed since, never more than one at a time. American female audiences cheered Nancy's pioneering success, and were spellbound by her speeches. They loved the asides that punctuated her serious points, and applause rolled over her like breakers every few minutes: 'No one who heard her will easily lose the picture of a gay, friendly, girlish person telling us all, with a gallant jerk of the head, things we already believe.'

Her performances did need serious content, to take her beyond an initial rapturous welcome, and there was the constant risk, as there was in the House of Commons, that she would say something entirely inappropriate and cause the mood to change. Only recently, both American and Canadian pride had been wounded by a series of tactless and ignorant remarks made by Margot Asquith, the former Prime Minister's wife, on her own tour of Canada and America, including her sometimes giving the strong impression of not knowing which of the two countries she was in. Potential pitfalls gaped around Nancy, yet with mostly the same ingredients – Christianity, the Bible, homilies on temperance – she managed to stir everyone up without striking a wrong note.

She also stressed the need for international co-operation, and for America to play a part, with the British Empire, in policing the world and helping to rebuild Europe. It was a controversial theme. Co-operation was out of favour with an administration that largely represented big business and preferred isolation. Although it had been accepted by the bankers and diplomats meeting at Cliveden during the war, who had perceived its benefits for both Europe and America, it was no longer in the political mainstream.

Yet the respect with which Nancy was held was demonstrated by her meeting President Harding, and by the invitation she and Waldorf received, as legislators in their own country, to come on to the floor of the Senate while it was in session. Although they tested opinion on all sides of the Prohibition question, both Waldorf and Nancy declined to address meetings on temperance or to discuss it with reporters, so as not to compromise themselves by inaccurate reports, in what they saw as a long-term cause.

In Richmond, Nancy had a triumphant reception, right from the outset, when she emerged from her sleeping car and, typically, cheered everybody by telling the grimy, sooty engine-driver, 'I feel as you look.' She was given the freedom of the city and addressed a meeting of over 4,000, with a further 5,000 turned away. In Danville, equally jubilant, she hailed the crowds gathered outside the house where she was born.

After Danville they went north to Chicago, and on to Canada. Telegrams, letters and flowers followed them incessantly: invitations to speak flowed from throughout the USA, from bankers, businessmen, hospitals, clubs, universities and politicians. In a white dress and large green hat, Nancy addressed a packed Canadian House of Commons, which frequently broke into applause, contrary to its rules. A meeting in Ottawa presided over by the Prime Minister was headlined as 'one of the biggest things Ottawa has seen for a generation'.

They found at least some respite on the long trips across the country, travelling in comfortable private carriages lent by well-wishers. One of these had three sleeping rooms, large brass beds, a bathroom, kitchen, dining room and sitting room. 'But,' recorded Waldorf, 'not even with a stateroom can we get privacy – particularly with a honeypot butterfly like N. who flits from rosebud to rosebud [poetic description of fellow passengers] or alternately as a honeyed rose attracting all sorts of bees, butterflies etc . . .'

Yet despite pleas and persuasion to countless audiences, she had only scratched the surface of the question of Anglo-American relations, and of America's future involvement in Europe. And it would not be long before both continents were to be plunged into economic turmoil; in Europe it would herald an international crisis that would cast a shadow over Nancy's reputation.

On her return to England, she introduced into Parliament, at the beginning of August 1922, a private members' Bill, the Liquor (Public Control) Bill. However, because of a general election, caused by the decision of the Conservative Party, under Bonar Law, to withdraw from coalition with Lloyd George, the Bill was abandoned. Nancy was now well prepared for an election, confident in the work she was doing. Each year she set out for her constituency chairman a detailed memorandum of her work in and out of Parliament, including questions to ministers, speeches, voting record, standing committees, special committees, and public and private meetings.

Making the same points in more populist colours, she prepared to fight her first general election, with polling day on 15 November 1922, three years exactly since her first battle. Once the campaign began, she flourished her manifesto before the voters. It demonstrated how liberal and advanced were her beliefs, for the politics of the day, to the extent that in a remarkable show of support, the Liberals did not put up a candidate against her; in fact a number of Liberals, including Mrs Isaac Foot, the wife of her erstwhile Liberal opponent in Plymouth, signed her nomination papers.

The forces threatening her re-election took the form of a Labour man, and an independent Conservative, backed by her main demon, the brewing companies, in those days customarily referred to as 'the Trade'. The ensuing colourful, lively, sometimes violent electoral battles revolved mainly around the personality of the candidates, much more so than was the case in most seats, where the results turned on national issues. The Astors had been building up a following in Plymouth since Waldorf had first become a candidate for Parliament nearly fifteen years earlier, and they had succeeded in identifying themselves with the city. Candidates from other parties came and went, but 'Our Nancy' seemed to remain a fixture. She knew the names of a large number of her constituents, and had at one time or another visited many in their homes. They would joke that they did not dare vote the wrong way: 'Why,' one old housewife told a reporter, 'you never know when Her Ladyship will come into your scullery and put it across you.' She drew support, grudging admiration and fierce hostility in measures that would vary with the years but which never brought about her defeat. The nearest she came to that would be in 1929, an election fought in the turmoil of slump, unemployment and hunger, when she squeezed past her opponents by only 211 votes.

In 1922, she could draw the dividend of the three years' work she had already done in Parliament, and the prominence with which she had fought. Her courage and her ability to speak publicly in a way that made headlines had brought her renown across the political spectrum: she might not please right-wing Conservatives, but their loss would be balanced by the votes of Liberals and of many whose natural home was Labour. She could rely on the support of a large proportion of the women in her constituency, and she also had the church on her side: both the Church of England and the Nonconformists, who were traditionally strong in Devon and Cornwall, and not averse to bringing politics into the pulpit.

Often ringing a 'muffin bell' to bring people to their doors, Nancy canvassed the streets, squares and quays, beautifully turned out but ready for any sort of fun. Coming upon a group of ragged urchins, she challenged them to a race to the end of the street, which at once made her their favourite. In the cold stone passages of the tenements she would do a little dance, striking an attitude, nose in the air, umbrella in hand, until the suspicious, reluctant occupants came out to look. Then she would start talking, establishing with them some sort of a relationship, however brief or unpersuasive; and most of them, even the determinedly hostile, remembered it. Dressed in a fur coat with a huge rosette, on balconies overlooking wet and windy squares, she addressed jostling crowds, sometimes several thousand strong; she would declaim from the platform in Plymouth's Guildhall, where she swung like a censer the silver pencil that she wore on a long chain around her neck, or jabbed it in the air at her opponents.

She was followed almost wherever she went by reporters, and also by an organised pantomime of communist hecklers. Sometimes she was drowned out: 'The reason you don't want to hear is that you don't want to hear the truth,' she shouted. 'I am never allowed to get through an argument without these interruptions being fired at me. It is not fair. It is not cricket.' Quick as she was in the expression of her own opinions, she was often far from tolerant of criticisms directed at her by others. But with hecklers she was in her element, and usually turned the tables on them. 'We're all equal,' shouted one woman. 'My children are just as good quality as yours.' 'Which one?' Nancy called back. 'I have one boy who could sell a horse without legs to any man, and one who could not sell the Derby winner. One child who could make good in Timbuctoo, and one who would not make good anywhere: she is a dreamer . . . Pay no attention,' she cried, 'to darned idiots who come round touting fake promises.'

Her slogans were not new, but still they seemed to match the hour: 'I'm all for the Navy,' she cried. 'There's nothing like a navy . . . I'm not for universal disarmament: that would mean a world without policemen . . .

Mind you, I'm not promising Paradise – most of you wouldn't be at home in Paradise.' Labour threatened a capital levy, which according to one heckler was the solution for all England's woes: 'So you think that is the solution, do you?' returned Nancy. 'Well you don't know enough to run a tripe shop.' She wouldn't mind, she said, if they did take her money. 'It would be a better world if there were no very rich and no very poor, but the capital levy won't make anyone a penny better off.'

She claimed that the defenders of the drink trade were often the opponents of slum clearance and general social and moral work, yet she worried that the independent Conservative, with the support of the brewers and distillers, might steal away her votes. One of her young protégés, Robin Barrington-Ward, later deputy editor of *The Times*, agreed: 'The power of the Trade, and the hyper-sensitivity of the male kind where drink is concerned, must not be undervalued.'[39]

Sometimes the meetings became violent, not least when people had fortified themselves in the numerous public houses whose existence so distressed Nancy. Her supporters would become nervous and try to whisk her away, but she seemed oblivious to the danger of assault by angry inebriates, and carried on regardless. She had in fact been hit once before, in the most surprising circumstances: after the end of the war, she was at Cliveden discussing with some friends those who had been at the Front; among those present was Lord Winterton, whom Nancy began to taunt, accusing him of cowardice. Winterton, deeply stung, quoted his commanding officer's comments on his bravery, but as Nancy continued her rude interjections, he lost his temper and knocked her to the floor. Astonished, but even then not lost for words, she raised herself on one elbow and said, 'You have hit somebody for the first time in your life and it had to be a woman!'[40] Such unusual conduct, however, did not apparently destroy their friendship.

There were times in her election campaigns when it seemed as though she might be hit again. On one occasion a part of the crowd turned nasty: a brawl started and the hall rapidly filled with shouts, cheers, jeers, punching, kicking, chairs collapsing, hats hurled about and general turmoil. As Nancy's supporters tried to drown 'The Red Flag' with 'Rule Britannia', a frustrated male heckler hurled a well-aimed cabbage, which landed at her feet. Quite undismayed, she picked it up, and when the din had subsided a little, waved it aloft, crying, 'Some gentleman has lost his head!' Usually, however, she retained control, as described by a journalist who heard her speak 'dressed in violet, young-looking, winsome':

How she held her audience. How entertained and moved they listened, for an hour, to sweet Lady Astor and stern Lady Astor and light Lady

Astor and genuine Lady Astor and vivid Lady Astor and thoughtful Lady Astor, and play-up-to-'em Lady Astor and Virginian Lady Astor and British Lady Astor, and international Lady Astor and all the Lady Astors of which Lady Astor is made.[41]

The 1922 election result was a comfortable win for Nancy in Plymouth, and for the Conservatives nationally. Although her majority was down on her famous by-election, it would have been well up even on that had not the independent Conservative stood against her; even so, she vanquished him by over 9,000 votes.

Nancy's views on drink had caused her problems during the election, but now that she had prevailed, she wanted to press on with curing people of their bad habits. She would not let up: her tendency, greatly increased now that she had political authority, to identify her principles with those of a higher power made her reluctant to compromise. In February 1923, having been successful in the draw for private members' Bills, she once again introduced a Bill to limit the sale of alcohol, a measure that the press called, despite her denials, 'Lady Astor's Bill'. It was actually entitled the Intoxicating Liquor (Sale to Persons under Eighteen) Bill, and was largely masterminded by Waldorf. It had broadly the same objectives as her original attempt: to ban the sale of alcohol to young people, who at that stage could buy drink in public houses once they were fourteen – with scant attention paid to whether they had reached even that age. The problem was increased by the swiftly spreading fashion for installing wirelesses in public bars, which drew young people to them all the more.

The general sentiments underlying her Bill reflected those of the Liquor (Popular Control) Bill introduced into the House of Lords by the Bishop of Oxford in 1921 but lost in transit to the statute book. Then, history seemed to be repeating itself: nearly two hundred years earlier, a previous Bishop of Oxford had warned Parliament of the dire situation in which it had become famously easy to get 'drunk for a penny, dead drunk for twopence', and, it was said, 'dead for threepence':

> . . . Almost in every street we had two or three gin-shops filled with such company as no sober man could view without horror, and . . . every one of these gin-shops had a back shop or cellar strewed every morning with fresh straw, where those that got drunk were thrown, men and women promiscuously together: here they might commit what wickedness they pleased, and by sleeping out the dose they had taken, make themselves ready to take another . . . till they have dosed themselves into their graves.'[42]

Nancy claimed that the Bill was not her own initiative, but rather the result of a petition from 116,000 teachers, worried about the mental and moral development of adolescents. She had behind her, she stated, 'all organised women', heads of private and state schools, the Church of England and the country's highest medical authorities. She wanted to change the law so that fourteen-year-olds could no longer buy beer in pubs, to drink there or take away. She proposed outlawing the sale of intoxicants to anyone apparently under eighteen for consumption in a public house. It would encourage adolescents to exercise self-control and powers of resistance, and help them keep 'morally straight'.

She was opposed by a diehard array of what she saw as antediluvian members who had put down amendments which, if accepted, would result in her ideas being wrecked. Promoting the Bill, her approach displayed what would become familiar hallmarks of the 'noble lady': a cocktail of morality, help for those in need, sharp attacks on opponents, finger-wagging, spiced with a complete disregard for parliamentary language, and wit. She never made it clear why she felt the need or desire to make people laugh: what originally had been a weapon to help her make her way in childhood and youth had perhaps become ingrained, but it proved its value to her in deflecting the antagonism that she generated along the course of her political path.

Nevertheless, her many opponents remained convinced that she was paving the way for Prohibition in Britain:

> I ask the Noble Lady . . . if this Bill is to be the foundation stone of a new Statue of Liberty which is to be erected within the City of London, or if it is to be followed by other Bills of a similar kind, until the whole edifice is complete, and the unhappy people of this country find themselves in the heat of summer, and during the foggy darkness of winter, confronted with nothing more interesting than a glass, say, of ginger-pop or ice-cream and soda . . .[43]

She continued to be vulnerable to such suspicions. Although she had stated that she was not in favour of complete Prohibition on the American model, she was equally clear that she did not approve it only because England was not yet ready for it. She had also proclaimed that people in Canada and America felt Prohibition to be beneficial, and that they had not been turned into nations of dope fiends and criminals, as the opponents of Prohibition had claimed they would be. Her comments on America were set out in an article in the *Observer* – owned by Waldorf, who was steadfast in his support: 'When I balance these results – when I offset the uplifting of the poor and

Nancy as a debutante.

Irene Langhorne, Nancy's elder sister,
the prototype for 'The Gibson Girl'.

A fine old Virginia gentleman: Chillie (right) with a friend at Mirador.

Nancy's pastoral guide, the Reverend Frederick Neve, on a visit to Cliveden in 1925.

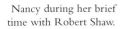

Nancy during her brief time with Robert Shaw.

Lord Revelstoke, as portrayed in the magazine *Vanity Fair* in 1898.

Waldorf, when he first knew Nancy.

Cliveden

Old Father Thames, running softly
below Cliveden woods.

Nancy and 'celebrity'
guests, 1931:
Amy Johnson, Charlie
Chaplin and George
Bernard Shaw.

'Vote for you,
Lady Astor?'

December 1919: with Arthur Balfour
on her right and Lloyd George on her left,
Nancy makes her first entrance into
the House of Commons.

The Member of Parliament,
working in her boudoir.

Nancy on her motorbike, an idea inspired by her riding pillion with T. E. Lawrence; Waldorf strongly disapproved.

Winston and Clementine Churchill with Nancy during the 1941 Blitz on Plymouth.

'The Shiver Sisters Ballet, 1938', a cartoon by David Low which appeared in the *Evening Standard* at the height of the controversy about the Cliveden Set. Nancy is depicted as dancing to Goebbels's tune, along with J. L. Garvin, editor of the *Observer*, Geoffrey Dawson, editor of *The Times*, and Philip Lothian.

WHERE OUR FOREIGN POLICY COMES FROM.

Nancy helping out on a municipal dustcart filled with clothes donations for victims of the Blitz.

'Are we downhearted? No.' Nancy amid the rubble and ruins of Plymouth.

(Left to right) Bobbie, Wissie, Michael, Bill, Nancy, Waldorf, Jakie, David.

Nancy aged eighty: still looking lovely, still feeling strong.

struggling, and the salvation which Prohibition has brought to many wives and children against the alleged degradation of some of the rich – well there can be no doubt that the net result for the country has been good.'[44] It cut no ice with her opponents. Instead it was popularly believed that Prohibition had made the law something to be circumvented, forcing the poor man to go dry while the rich secured what they wanted.

In the event, the Bill was watered down far too much for Nancy's taste; but she had made a start, accepting the various amendments put forward, and in July 1923 it became law. It was her crowning legislative achievement: the first time a woman had piloted a Bill through Parliament in all its stages, and in substance it remains in force to this day.

Yet for all Nancy's success, the heralded advance of women MPs was proving surprisingly far from a surge. In 1922, the only other woman elected was Margaret Wintringham, and she had already entered the Commons, as a Liberal, in a by-election a year earlier. Like Nancy, she had taken over the seat of a husband who had ceded it involuntarily, in his case by dying. The second woman MP was large, stolid and businesslike, the British matron personified – quite unlike the boyish, vivacious and volatile Nancy, who Mrs Wintringham likened to a 'young prancing pony', with herself as 'a slow old carthorse trotting beside'. A Commons reporter described them together:

> Two women of an utterly different type coming along the corridor. One fair, eager, vivacious and young-looking, with her arm linked in her companion's, a motherly-looking lady with a somewhat anxious but very sympathetic face, and gentle manner. The younger woman is speaking rapidly and probably in tones of indignation, and the elder one listens, making a few shrewd comments from time to time . . .[45]

In many ways they were like chalk and cheese: it is hard to imagine the portly Mrs Wintringham starting her day with a cold bath and a game of squash, or sticking out her tongue, as Nancy did at an acquaintance who tried to buttonhole her in the Commons lobby. However, the two ladies warmed to each other and began to work in harmony, soon proving effective in establishing a reformist mentality among politicians, and altering their order of priorities in Parliament, where domestic affairs had always been low on the list. They had similar enthusiasms – both were Christian Scientists, a creed that had found a number of recruits among MPs – and each put cause and principle above party.

The fact that Nancy and Mrs Wintringham were the only two female members meant that they were heavily overworked, as Nancy's success had brought home to so many that women now had a voice at Westminster. Every Bill that touched on their causes – not only the family, but also the professions that women were beginning to enter – demanded their attention, as did standing committees, for which it was now deemed that there should be a 'statutory woman'. They also had to meet the calls of party business and the claims of their constituencies.

The following summer, a third woman, Mabel Philipson, a former music hall star, was elected to Parliament, also in her husband's footsteps, after his election had been declared null for a breach of the election rules. Although in the next general election, of December 1923, there were thirty-four female candidates, twelve of them had stood previously, and only eight were elected. The sluggish pace of new arrivals was partly because it was still very difficult for a woman to succeed in getting selected as a candidate, and most of those who did so were chosen for unwinnable seats. Some agreed to fight simply in order to accustom electorates to female candidates, and to overcome the doubts of women voters about 'bluestocking' and 'society' candidates, which described many of those among the first to stand.

Perhaps as a result of the small number of women returned, it was a considerable time, despite all the noise and publicity, before the Commons authorities accepted the idea of improving the arrangements for female members. Meanwhile the women stoically accepted their discomfort, even though it was in marked contrast to the luxurious circumstances in which a number of them lived at home. One member recorded how the Duchess of Atholl, elected in 1923, 'looking a little like a Victorian governess, would, on changing her frock, present her back to the half-open door to enable her maid, standing in the corridor, to fasten the innumerable buttons which only the maid's practised hand could manipulate'. The lady members' room had 'an adjoining smaller room, which boasted a small Victorian washstand with a tin basin in which stood a jug of cold water. After a chilly wash, one pulled out the plug and the water flowed into an iron bucket standing underneath.'[46] Their enclave was described as a 'boudoir', but the only suggestion of that was a small looking-glass. 'Yet this was where much hard work had to be done and all dictating to our secretaries . . . Often we are in the House from ten in the morning to midnight, with frequent all-night sittings . . . baths are provided for the men, but not for us . . .'[47]

One most unexpected facet Nancy seems to have exhibited, although strictly within the confines of the women's room, was the use of strong language: 'I was astounded at Nancy Astor's crudity,' said one of the female MPs. 'She was completely uninhibited and her running commentary on her life, her friends and her family were almost embarrassing to her listeners. Her language was such that a trade union member, accustomed to the language of the pits or heavy industry would think nothing of responding with expressions equally earthy.'[48] No doubt Nancy had occasionally to release her tensions, and the privacy of her room, shared only by fellow women members, might have seemed to her the only place in which to do so.

Her animated behaviour continued to irritate a large number of members. When, in the summer of 1924, her portrait was hung on a staircase in the Commons, the reaction was distinctly mixed: so much so that the canvas was even defaced. Claims that it breached a tradition that there should be no portraits hung of living members disguised simple animosity, aggravated by those responsible for the idea not having taken 'the sense of the House on the question'. Nancy claimed to have little interest in the matter, but sounded understandably nettled: 'It's no concern of mine. One of the Unionist ministers accepted it more than a year ago. Now another one withdraws it. The picture belongs to the nation and the nation can do what it likes with it.' At length it found its way to Plymouth.

In some debates she spoke with notable force and clarity, but her performance was usually uneven. 'Wild assertion,' an MP told her, 'is not commonly accepted in Great Britain as an equivalent to fact.' In one debate she veered so confusingly around the compass that a Labour member eventually rose to ask her if she could please explain whether she was for or against – a doubt that was never cleared up.

Much as she did achieve on her feet, Nancy's real success remained the inspiration of her reaching Parliament at all, showing women all over the Western world that it could be done, that the doors were finally open.

EIGHT

Centre Court

By 1924, Nancy had been in Parliament for four years, and the gates of Westminster seemed wide open. Attractive and graceful, but provocative and determined, she had forced the pass that led to Parliament, opening the way to power and influence in many other spheres long banned to women. The former masters of the nation's politics had now come to accept a feminine presence, and had turned their minds to domestic and family issues in ways unthinkable a mere decade earlier. She had begun in earnest the work of broadening political life.

Yet women were still a tiny minority. The eight women returned to Parliament at the 1923 election – 'eight little peaches on eight little perches', as the press blithely put it – had a year later, after the election of October 1924, fallen back to only four: three Conservatives and one Labour. That was partly because women were still not as a rule being selected for safe seats, but it was also to a certain extent a result of exceptional circumstances: over half the female candidates had been Labour, a party that had suffered greatly as a result of the publication, four days before polling day, of the 'Zinoviev letter', reportedly a Soviet-inspired plot to stir up agitation in Britain. In the furore, people were put off Labour and swung to the Conservatives, who won a large majority.

Although in the next general election, held in May 1929, fourteen women were returned, there was no real push for a 'women's party' – which had been one of the main fears men had had about moving to equal franchise. Nancy briefly flew that kite, in 1929 giving a lunch party at the Commons for all the female members. There she was in typical form, centre stage, leading the talk, and exhorting all to work together. She received a cool reception, partly as she herself displayed no inclination to abandon the Conservatives. The idea of a women's party was dead by the end of lunch, after which one of the gentlest ladies present made a telling comment, remarking with a sigh, 'If only she did not have to boss us.'

Bossy or otherwise, Nancy was by far the leading presence among them, pioneers and strong characters though they were. She was unfailingly kind to new members, showing them the ropes and quick to help them out of any difficulty. Her zest in that way would sometimes backfire, as she had no compunction about telephoning hard-pressed ministers to push some fellow female MP's case. This did not help Nancy's popularity or her career, and it may have contributed to her not being offered a ministerial role. Being the longest-serving female member, many people, herself included, felt that she should have been given a government job. Ramsay MacDonald, the first Labour Prime Minister, had appointed a woman minister shortly after taking office in 1924, and people wondered if the Tories would in due course do likewise.

Although many MPs accepted that Nancy had a valid claim to office, being able, hard-working and with the most experience of the female members, many others in the party considered her too unconventional. 'She was a Southern Belle with wealth and brilliance and didn't give two hoots . . .' as one of her colleagues put it. It was disappointing to be passed over, after things had gone her way for so long, but she should not have been entirely surprised. Privately she felt briefly downcast, but in public she was as cheerful as ever. Even if she was not included herself, the promotion of other women during the 1920s was a sure sign that the trail she had blazed was being solidly paved.

Although few in number, the quality of the women following Nancy into Parliament was high – in professional ability and experience, higher than Nancy's own – and they soon began to make an impact. However much she spoke from the heart, Nancy's quicksilver but disjointed performances in the Commons were rather the opposite of those put up by the other women members. Although one or two, when standing up to speak, caused MPs to rise 'like a flock of fluttering starlings' and make for the smoking room, as a group they soon succeeded, with solid and well-informed speeches, in dispelling lingering doubts about the contribution of female MPs to the nation's affairs.

During Nancy's first dozen years in the Commons, more than thirty forceful and able women were able to make their mark as MPs. Dogged, industrious, some of them hard-up, they did not all take to the lily in their midst, but they did acknowledge the paramount place she had won by leading the way. Thelma Cazalet-Keir, not hard-up, Conservative, and another Christian Scientist, expressed the mixed feelings about Nancy that by the end of the 1920s were shared by many in Parliament. She admired her great kindness, while objecting to her occasional rudeness, not least when Nancy, in the Chamber, even if intending to be flippant, described Waldorf, as 'practically dead most of the time'.[1]

So, having followed the trail that Nancy had blazed, others were now hard at work applying the nuts and bolts needed to push through Parliament the changes which women, and gradually many men, felt were long overdue. It was work to which Nancy was unsuited, despite her success in piloting to the statute book the Intoxicating Liquors Bill, a remarkable parliamentary achievement. Now it was for other, solid women to get down to detail.

The sharp contrast between Nancy's performances in the Commons and those of the expert women who had followed in her wake was highlighted on one occasion in 1929, shortly after the general election in which she had scraped home with a wafer-thin majority of 211. Nancy was speaking – impetuously, amusingly, but only skirting with reality – on a Ministry of Health Bill. She was followed by the gaunt, austere Labour MP Susan Lawrence. Once sent to Holloway gaol for refusing, as a local councillor, to levy a proper rate on the poor in her borough, her dedication was typical of the women reaching Parliament, and she achieved a ministerial appointment soon after being elected, in 1923. A fellow MP described what happened:

> . . . as she proceeded it was necessary for the Minister of Health again and again to correct her on a point of fact. Slowly it dawned upon the House that Lady Astor had not read the Bill. Lady Astor then abandoned her notes and continued her speech – quite legitimately – attacking the principles of the Bill.
>
> Lady Astor ended and then sat down.
>
> Miss Lawrence rose.
>
> Everyone bent forward, every ear was attentive to catch her words. All knew something worth hearing was about to be said. 'Theologians inform us,' said Miss Lawrence, 'that it is possible to rise to Heaven on the arms of invincible ignorance – the Noble Lady's seat *there* is safe!'[2]

The House dissolved in laughter, but the ever-generous Nancy bore no grudge and laughed as heartily as anyone else.

It was not long before Nancy's girlish flamboyance found its way into popular fiction. One Labour MP, the former communist Ellen Wilkinson, was also an author, and she drew upon Nancy for one of the characters in her novel *The Division Bell Mystery*. Several other writers were inspired by Nancy: most famously George Bernard Shaw, who became one of her firmest friends. Amanda, the 'merry lady' in *The Apple Cart*, was largely based on Ellen Wilkinson, but she also 'has Nancy's particular talent for puncturing male dignity and making her supporters laugh'.[3] Some years later, Agatha Christie also drew on Nancy, at least in part, for her Lady Westholme, in *Appointment With Death*. Nancy's fellow MP Alan Herbert had previously portrayed her, with benign poet's licence, in his 'comic opera' *Derby Day*, as the wife of Sir Horace Waters, surveying the proletariat at the races. There was widespread agreement that the playwright had exactly caught Nancy's blend of humour and intolerance:

Sir Horace (tolerant):	I like to see them merry –
	The People's simple joys!
Lady Waters	They're very vulgar, very –
(vulgarly and loudly):	And what a frightful noise!
	. . . I don't care what their trade is!
	They're making too much noise:
	And why do all the ladies
	Wear hats designed for boys?
	. . . That can't be necessary
	What is the point of that?
Sir Horace:	I'm very often merry
	But I never wear a hat.
Both (greatly fussed):	It's really rather shocking.
	The line where do they draw?
Lady Waters:	Next it will be the stocking!
	This should be stopped *by law*![4]

With a quorum of other women MPs now established in Parliament, Nancy could give more attention to her life outside the Commons. She turned to other outlets for her urge to do good, and to help people escape the 'error', as she described it, in their lives – her crusades, as friend and foe described them. And she could do so in a way that would satisfy her love of large-scale entertaining, which she believed was in itself valuable, and through which she was already gaining an importance in addition to that which attached to her work in Parliament.

When Nancy first became a notable hostess, in the golden Edwardian years, entertaining was conducted more or less continuously in many great houses, and on a lavish scale. At that time, and to an extent right up to the beginning of the Second World War, private entertaining was widespread and often carried to what today might seem extraordinary lengths. In most cases the impetus came from women, but there were exceptions, such as Sir Philip Sassoon, and 'Chips' Channon.[5] Waldorf himself played a great part in the Astors' eclectic and international brand of entertaining: 'But it's

Uncle Waldorf,' said an Astor niece, observing a great party at St James's Square, 'who makes her give that sort of party. He has a sort of self-bestowed sense of Host of England that makes him collect celebrities, and it isn't snobbish really, it's just that he thinks it's his duty . . .'[6] For someone – especially a politician – who was almost devoid of small talk, it was an unlikely obsession.

The company of friends and acquaintances and the pleasurable use of ready money were justification enough for formal entertaining; but a number of famous women had additional reasons for turning themselves into what could almost be described as professional hostesses: Lady Desborough used entertaining as an anodyne to ward off melancholy; Lady Londonderry was determined to further her husband's political career; and Mrs Ronald Greville relished the exercise of power and the indulgence of a little snobbery: she was delighted to have had three kings in her bedroom on the same day – for innocent purposes, of course, and not all at once – and she was famous for saying 'One uses up *so* many red carpets in a season.' In the case of a number of hostesses, it is also possible to discern the lingering effects of insecurity or poverty in childhood.[7]

In Nancy's case, there had been a series of transitions: first she had entertained as a way of consolidating her position in society, and from a wish to share the attractions of great wealth, as well as simply for the pleasure it gave her; those reasons became partly infused with a wish to encourage Waldorf's political career, effectively from 1908 onwards, the purposes of her entertaining becoming more particularly political as her own interest in politics increased, through both her work in Plymouth and her association with members of the Round Table; that process became more focused during the dangerous years of the war. After her election to Parliament, the social aspects of her parties gave way to a paramount wish to crusade one of her myriad projects, or, more often, many at the same time:

The purpose in our entertaining is to give people of every sort and kind a chance to get together and find out the truth about each other's views. You see, I'm a democrat. I believe the world moves on by the working together of all kinds of honest minds, and the more mixed our entertaining the better that purpose is served. What I really like to have in my house is a party which contains thoroughly opposing elements – pacifists and fire-eaters, reformers and die-hards, rich and poor, old and young. When they meet each other they generally make friends, and when they make friends they can find some of the solutions to their problems. That's the general principle I go on; but I'll admit that sometimes there are special and particular purposes in our entertaining as well.[8]

Her political entertaining caught the limelight early in 1924 when she had the idea – startling, but entirely in character – of bringing together, in a social setting, the King and Queen and the leading minsters in the first Labour government, formed in January 1924. Although it was outside normal royal convention, the King reluctantly conceded that it was a wise idea in the new, post-war era. It might increase harmony between him and his subjects, even though the direct contact would be with ministers some of whom were to the far left of the political spectrum, if not outright republicans.

The new Prime Minister, Ramsay MacDonald, needed no persuading – he was a friend and admirer of the Marchioness of Londonderry, London's leading political hostess, to whom Nancy probably ran a close second – but some of MacDonald's colleagues were doubtful about the whole idea. They were in awe at meeting the King other than in an official, formal setting, and their socialist supporters back in the poor industrial valleys and towns might be angered at tales of hobnobbing with Tories, whose wealth, lifestyle and political aims were far removed from their own.

Nancy and Waldorf believed the opposite, demonstrating attitudes about class and politics that had not yet crossed the Atlantic:

> . . . And therefore I can judge that it may be useful, as well as agreeable all round, for me to entertain dukes and even royal personages and members of the Labour Party on the same occasions. I know that they really like that sort of thing, forms and customs notwithstanding, and that it makes easier the expression of that mental and political liberty which is one of the best things in England. And so, coming as I do from Virginia, I go ahead and invite them all. And everything is well.[9]

So on 9 March 1924, King George V and Queen Mary supped with the socialists at 4, St James's Square. White-gloved footmen in full livery lined the walls, and as the guests arrived, Nancy stood ready to greet them at the top of the great shallow staircase. Outside, the square teemed with motor cars, chauffeurs chatting, and a crowd held at a discreet distance by policemen in their brass-buttoned tunics. Inside, the rooms were full, brightened by candlelight, massed double snowdrops brought up from Cliveden, court dress, gleaming buckles, white ties, tiaras, diamonds and general splendour, and cooled by huge blocks of ice placed in the windows and breezes wafting in from outside.

The representatives of the new government were dressed by Moss Bros, the hire company: 'Labor in Knee-Pants' filled the American headlines. Philip Snowden, newly appointed Chancellor of the Exchequer, was exempted on account of a withered leg; he and his wife Ethel had already been befriended by Nancy and entertained at Cliveden. The evening was a resounding success, and the Labour ministers were subsequently invited to dinner at Buckingham Palace.

Nancy was able to use Cliveden and St James's Square as a means of shoring up her own position when she felt her political stock to be slipping – as she did when the Duchess of Atholl began to shine and make a mark very soon after first being elected as an MP. Neville Chamberlain, rapidly rising to power in the party, soon received a call from Nancy:

> Nancy Astor is pestering me to go to Cliveden where she wants to show me a broken heart. She declares that nobody loves her & the Party is going to the dogs & wants to tell me all about it. And I don't want to hear but may not be able to escape. I suspect the trouble is that the Duchess of Atholl has quietly stepped into the front place & Nancy don't like a back seat.[10]

Some months later, when Chamberlain went down to Plymouth to speak at a dinner arranged by Nancy, he was rewarded for his time by witnessing 'the local gentleman who proposed Nancy's health and declared that she was a really tiresome woman, hastily explaining in the gasping silence that followed, that he had meant to say "tireless".'

However, Nancy was certainly not a manipulator for her own advancement, and Cliveden was rather the venue for gatherings encouraging progress and harmony in fields that Nancy and Waldorf thought valuable, or in need of help. Of the many such gatherings a typical one took place at the end of 1927, when a weekend was planned to try and promote a better understanding between the employers and the trade union leaders in all the major industries, to attempt to mitigate the great bitterness that lingered for a considerable time after the General Strike of 1926. Nancy had been appalled by the hardship she had seen on a visit to the mining valleys of Wales, which were suffering from the coal strike that had continued long after the General Strike was called off. She decided not to send presents to any grown-ups for Christmas 1928, instead 'devoting the money to the devastated mining areas'.

Many of the influential attendees at the great international conferences that Britain hosted from time to time also went to Nancy's gatherings when they weren't in session. These included the three Round Table conferences on India, held in 1930–2; the Naval Disarmament Conference of 1930, a cause that Nancy championed, as she became increasingly insistent on the need for Anglo-American co-operation; and the World Monetary and Economic Conference, when she invited leading Americans such as Charles Adams, Cordell Hull, Henry L. Stimson, Charles Dawes, Frank Kellogg, William C. Bullitt, and admirals Stone and Platt. She was later to present her case for Anglo-American solidarity to some of these men, as another world war loomed. The erstwhile president William H. Taft was also a guest, as was, in 1934, Roosevelt's mother, Sarah.

Japanese and Russian ambassadors were among the diplomatic guests, but only a few Germans came. As a people the Germans were still deeply unpopular with many in England with recently dead friends and relations, and their presence was apt to cause difficulties. Nancy's guests did include Andre Siegfried and the former Chancellor Dr Brüning; however, the extent to which she knew any Germans well, or understood the German character, was doubtful and was soon to become highly controversial.

'The scope of the talk at her parties,' said one of her sons, 'encompassed politics, wit, repartee, racing, religion and family rows, principally.' Politics, however, remained paramount. As her butler recalled, 'Being in parliament changed her, of course. She seemed to get a renewed vigour, and heaven knows she'd been vigorous enough before.' The comparatively dour Neville Chamberlain portrayed the atmosphere at a weekend he attended:

Back from Cliveden. Lord! What a party . . . Nancy herself carrying on the most entertaining, witty and imprudent monologue the whole time. She is a little bundle of nerves and is wearing herself out, but I believe she enjoys life. For a long time I disliked her intensely but . . . now I have come to regard her with something like the tolerant affection one feels for a warm-hearted, merry and sometimes naughty child . . .[11]

In mixing the ingredients, Nancy showed intelligence and artistry, injecting a degree of surprise and avoiding too much consistency or convention. Even when her guests were people of great standing, her sense of the ridiculous was never far from the surface, although she did occasionally misjudge the mood, as Harold Nicolson recorded in his diary: 'After dinner, in order to enliven the party, Lady Astor dons a Victorian hat and false teeth. It did *not* enliven the party.' There was nevertheless a degree of consistency, notably with politics, particularly through the 1930s, when Nancy carried less weight in the Commons.

A subsidiary theme in the guest lists was artistic, particularly literary. However, practical expression did not seem to find much outlet – there was barely the sound of piano or violin, although the singer Paul Robeson once made an appearance. Nor were there recitals of verse, or readings of literary works by their authors – with the notable exception of George Bernard Shaw, who, spending Christmas 1928 at Cliveden, wrote some of *The Apple Cart*, a play that encouraged some people to think of him as an inspiration for women's rights. Other writers and fashionable artists came to stay, such as the illustrator Rex Whistler and his brother Laurence, in time the country's leading glass-engraver. Painters included the portraitist Philip de Laszlo, and Alfred Munnings, who had gained great success after the war as a painter of horses – Waldorf gave him a number of commissions.

As her earlier relationship with J.M. Barrie made clear, Nancy loved to hunt literary lions, and she continued to hold weekly salons. To her den came, among many, the Irish communist playwright Sean O'Casey, 'Lawrence of Arabia', Rose Macaulay, Humbert Wolfe, A.P. Herbert and Lytton Strachey. She seems to have delighted in O'Casey, perhaps stimulated by his politics:

Dear Comrade O'Casey,

'You don't know what pleasure your letter gave me. I agree with you there is something in Communism; and there is certainly something in Capitalism; but there is nothing in Socialism. I would like to take you to Russia – I don't know anybody who would be less fitted to live under an autocracy than you, unless it is myself . . .'[12]

O'Casey and his wife stayed at 4, St James's for several weeks while his play *Within the Gates* was rehearsing for the London stage, and once or twice Nancy entertained the full cast. She found O'Casey exhilarating company, even if he cut an incongruous figure among the chandeliers: 'He never wears a shirt, merely a polo-necked sweater in dingy brown. I should think washing was pretty rare with him, and a comb has never touched his grey hair.'[13]

As it happened, Nancy was able to speak of Russia from experience, having gone there in the summer of 1931. Her highly publicised expedition originated in an invitation extended by the Soviets to George Bernard Shaw. Nancy had first met Shaw in 1927, and at one of her receptions he had expounded on Russian spirituality, suggesting that their example should be followed, that worship of the idle rich should cease, that America had but exchanged black slaves for white, and similar flights of fancy:

> . . . All of which called forth the banter and rebuke of Lady Astor, who did everything short of beating Shaw with the loose arm of her antique chair, which she actually at one point removed. Finally, with that fearlessness which made her such a terror in the House of Commons, she turned to him and said, very spiritedly: 'The trouble with you, GB, is that you think you're clever: you're not clever, you're only *good*! Isn't he, Mrs Shaw?'[14]

Shaw, however, shrewdly judged Nancy's merits and faults, commenting that 'if she could think consecutively for sixty seconds she would be the greatest woman in the world'.

By July 1931, when he and the Astors set off for Moscow, Shaw's only popular play over there was *Mrs Warren's Profession*, a work once banned by the British censor. It was strange, therefore, that the famous playwright was something of a hero in Russia: 'He meant little even to those Russians who had knowledge of him. He was described by the critics as a typical, middle-class Englishman.' Having been invited, however, he had felt the need for support, and turned to Nancy. The Russians acquiesced in his bringing some friends, and the party eventually included Waldorf and Nancy, David Astor, then aged nineteen, Philip Kerr, by now the Marquess of Lothian, Charles Tennant, a Christian Scientist friend, and the writer and Russian expert Maurice Hindus. Their path was eased by encountering, on the train journey out, Maxim Litvinov, the Soviet Foreign Affairs Commissar, whom Nancy had met in Geneva.

They put up at the Metropole Hotel in Moscow, and there was certainly something of Shaw's particular brand of humour in the fact that the ardent socialist should take with him to meet the humourless Soviets, only a dozen or so years after their great revolution, a Tory MP, a great landowner, and one of the world's richest men, each with an aristocratic title.

The celebrated biologist Julian Huxley happened also to be in Moscow at the time, and saw the party in the Hermitage picture gallery: 'They passed in front of a huge painting depicting a female saint giving suck from her ample breasts to a hungry beggar. "You couldn't do that, Nancy," said GBS to his flat-chested companion, and they passed on, giggling.' Shaw felt that he was treated as though he were 'Karl Marx in person', and revelled in the attention. He was apparently filled with admiration for communism. At a banquet he rose to his feet, announcing to the delight of the assembled dignitaries that '"My travelling companions are all very rich capitalists indeed." At this Lady Astor claps her hands in genuine pleasure, and the audience, not understanding English and imagining that it must be something revolutionary, again reacts with a new burst of applause.'[15]

A high point of their trip was an interview with Stalin, of which Waldorf later made a record:

> After going through endless passages in the Kremlin we were shown into a room where a neatly dressed Stalin shook hands. He was in uniform with boots . . . everybody else we saw had been untidy in their appearance and dress . . . We spent an hour talking with Stalin, asking him questions, and then got up to go. Stalin said that unless we were in a hurry, he would like to ask us a few questions. So we sat down and had another hour. I forget what most of his queries were, but remember one which was interesting in view of subsequent events. Winston Churchill was at that time out in the political wilderness, and Stalin wanted to know whether in our opinion he would regain position and influence . . .
>
> . . . Nancy asked if she could put a question to Stalin, namely, how long does Mr Stalin intend to continue the Czarist methods of dealing with political opponents by exiling them to Siberia? Stalin replied as quick as a flash 'Only so long as may be necessary in the interests of the State.' He had quite a sense of humour . . . Stalin spoke with pride of the great social work being done and quoted the Nursery Schools. Nancy laughed at him, and said if he wanted to see how they should be run, he had better send someone over to England. This he did later on, and she was able to show him a Margaret McMillan Day Nursery . . .[16]

Stalin also asked why they thought the English-speaking peoples governed most of the world:

> 'I think I know,' said Nancy.
>
> 'What do you want to say?' asked Stalin.
>
> 'Well, look at the map,' Nancy replied. 'You can hardly see those little islands on the map; they're so small. It couldn't have been *might*; it must have been something right in their thinking . . . and I might tell you another thing; it couldn't have been the climate.'
>
> 'Why not?'
>
> 'Well, because if you'd lived there you would think that they couldn't grow anything except seaweed.'
>
> 'Well, what do you think it is?'

'I believe,' said Nancy, 'when they translated the Bible and kindled it into the common language, and read it, and studied it, they became an *un*common people, because they had a measuring rod, and they thought for themselves, and they had a sense of justice, and mercy, and a sort of generosity and bigness . . .'[17]

Although David Astor had dutifully accompanied the party to Russia, he was beginning to yearn for independence. He had suffered from his parents having a failing they shared with many others, of being unwilling to loosen the reins as their children grow up. Nancy would not adjust her behaviour in this respect: it was fixed – shaped by her rise to fame, by the power of the wealth at her fingertips, by her position in the political firmament, by the centre-stage nature of her life, and by a chronic inclination to run other people's lives. Underlying all that were the characteristics she had been born with, and, relevant particularly to her relations with her children, by now also an urge to dominate.

The result was that her relations with her children were easily strained. The love and warmth and laughter shared by Nancy and her children when they were small had cooled a little as childhood moved into youth, even though there remained sporadic mutual expressions of intense love. The superficial fact of their having, when young, been left so much to themselves and Nanny Gibbons by their parents did not alter the direction of their underlying emotions. But as they grew older they all came up against what David called 'the eternal parent and child complex'. They wanted to choose when to act freely and independently, and when, on the other hand, to be close and affectionate with their mother. Waldorf had their best interests at heart, but he remained a slightly severe figure, and did not spontaneously offer a compensating welcome for them when their mother was being difficult. At heart a good German, he was like the Prince Consort, and felt that he should plan his children's lives.

Something in Nancy's make-up also gave her an uncanny knack of choking off intimacy, or sidestepping difficult family issues, extinguishing a spark that would have been better left to grow into a flame. In the Astor family, disagreements were often solved, but often only on the surface, by Nancy's ability to amuse, to make everyone laugh, to laugh herself, so that the children's unhappiness and the occasional family rows dissolved into laughter, often at Nancy's own expense, which did not perturb her at all. She liked to tell the story of one of the children's Eton friends saying, 'It must be terrible having your mother in the House of Commons', and receiving the reply, 'Yes, it is bad, but if she wasn't there she would probably be in the Salvation Army, which would be worse.' In time the children, in their respective ways, also learned how to manage the duels: Bobbie and Jakie would answer back, while the others would shy off, closing arguments with 'Well, Mama, that's your view . . .'

Shortly after the Russian visit, David went up to Balliol College, Oxford. There, he grew increasingly unhappy. On one occasion he wrote to his mother, expressing the feelings that beset him:

'. . . I know it 'never entered your mind to dominate me': you do it instinctively and unconsciously. It is the basis of your attitude: that is just the difficulty . . . I repeat what I said before: if you will take me as I am, if you will not eternally regard me as your child, if you will allow to my thoughts the same importance as yours, then we shall be able to get on all right . . . I am grown up, I am different to you, I have got a life, and I want to lead it. We are very near to getting on very well, and it is only the eternal parent and child complex which spoils it . . .'

Nancy always tried to defuse too heavy a discussion with a light remark, and it rang true when she said, during a debate in the Commons on birth control, that 'one of my sons told me recently that I had not taken enough interest in him before he was seven. My reply was that if I had known as much as I do now, I should not have had him at all.' She often managed to pour salt on an open wound, perhaps a characteristic inherited from Chillie, who had a similar disposition. Nancy would not have thought of herself as an unkind woman, but, like her father, her underlying kindness did not seem to preclude moments of surface cruelty or bullying. She was therefore sometimes puzzled by her children's reactions to her attitude towards them. It was a peculiar mixture, as her niece observed, and probably the result of great wealth combined with a dominating personality.

As it turned out, David broke free sooner and more decisively than the other children. Eventually he steeled himself to confront Waldorf, at Cliveden, telling him that he had had enough, that he could not accept his mother's dominating behaviour, and would no longer do so. Waldorf listened in silence, pained but without uttering any rebuke. He probably wished that such matters would just quietly subside: Nancy created more than enough turbulence by herself.

Michael, four years younger than David, was for a time to be similarly unhappy. He had an artistic nature and a creative spirit. When he in his turn went up to Oxford, he felt downhearted and ill, and was unable to do much work. In 1936, his last year there, he took a week's leave, but when it was over he could not face returning. Bertrand Dawson, one of the few doctors whom Nancy was prepared to countenance, at least for other people, advised him to have a fortnight's holiday and then take his degree. Lord Lothian[18] also talked the problem through with Michael, subsequently reporting to Nancy:

> But when one probes the troubles it's the old family complex: Michael admits that the real trouble is the worry about parental authority and interference. He wants to create his own life for himself; he refuses to go in the army; he says he wants to work and is determined not to be an idler but must choose his own life. Apparently he was upset by some interviews he had with Waldorf and some talks with you this autumn. He didn't look well, though there is nothing wrong with him physically. His eyes just looked worried and unhappy and disturbed. I think you will have to be careful with him or he might get like David. Put him in Mind and know that Mind will guide him aright. He is twenty and must assume responsibility for his own life. At the moment he is frightened of pressure from the family, and you will have to make it clear to him that he is free . . . I don't think there is anything to worry about. It's the usual family complex at work again.[19]

The belief that 'Mind' would provide the solution required the great trust that both Lothian and Nancy placed in Christian Science, but which Michael did not, despite at a young age having being given daily instruction and sent to a Christian Science school.

Such difficulties had also affected Bill and Wissie, both of whom were brought up in Christian Science. Waldorf sometimes gave the impression that his son and heir was not as clever as his younger brothers, although objectively the evidence rather pointed the other way: Bill had been awarded a first class in his Honour Moderations exam at Oxford, while David, in some ways the most intellectual of the children, had left Oxford without a degree, although that was largely as a result of his depression. Bill had long been unhappy at the thought of being compared unfavourably with Michael or David, and when Waldorf had suggested that he should demonstrate that he moved among intelligent people, he had introduced his father to Frank Pakenham,[20] a friend from New College, generally considered as very clever – he was for a time an Oxford don.

They met at a point-to-point meeting in Oxfordshire at which Pakenham was due to ride. Bill arrived in his Bentley, and joined a crowd of friends, the girls in the fashion of the day: 'Teddy Bear coats, Joan Crawford haircuts, silly, pretty faces, pillar box mouths and thread-wide eyebrows.' Unfortunately,

Pakenham was unseated at one of the fences, and although he skilfully managed to remount, he had been momentarily concussed by his fall, and by the time he was back in the saddle the rest of the field had disappeared from view. Slightly confused, he gamely set off once again around the course, but this time going in the wrong direction, a fact that was gleefully pointed out to him when he eventually reached the starting post. Waldorf was too generous a man to greet all this with hilarity, but he did make it clear to Bill that it did not say much for his ability to choose intellectual companions – 'If *he's* your cleverest friend . . .' If Waldorf was joking it was lost on Bill, who was abashed: 'My father never trusted me after that, because I brought this man to Cliveden as the brightest of my friends.'

Nancy also had damaged Bill's confidence – in the summer of 1925, when he was still at Eton. He had been asked to cox the Eton Eight at Henley, the high point of the Eton boating season, and a coveted accolade. All went well until in the final, most important race, Eton were overtaken before the winning post. It was a moment of great disappointment, with glory snatched away. Nancy, waiting in the enclosure, beautifully and fashionably dressed, looking at her most attractive and drawing the admiration of Bill's friends, offered no sympathy, but instead blamed him for causing the race to be lost by paying insufficient attention to his Christian Science.

Nancy's determination that her children should embrace her religion, and in other respects dance to her tune, had a very serious and tangible consequence for Wissie. On 12 December 1929, aged twenty, she had an accident out hunting in Leicestershire. Her horse rolled on her after falling at a fence, and pushed her spine out of alignment. She was carried back to a nearby house, and although she did not seem to be in much pain, a doctor was summoned. He found no evidence of serious injury, but a man who had seen the fall, and also Ronald and Nancy Tree, with whom Wissie was staying, remained uneasy, and sent for Dr Whitling, a specialist from London, experienced in hunting accidents. Ronald Tree telephoned Nancy, who said that she would come at once, bringing Waldorf and also a Christian Science healer. When the specialist X-rayed Wissie, he saw that her condition was serious and that immediate medical attention was required if permanent damage was to be avoided.

When Nancy and Waldorf heard the specialist's opinion, they were faced with a crucial and, for them, appalling decision: should they allow Wissie to receive medical attention, contrary to their religious beliefs, or should they stick to Christian Science and put her solely in the hands of a healer. Natural love and human instinct pulled them in one direction, the core of their faith in another. It seems that the basic feeling for a daughter was the stronger, and they agreed to send for medical help. However, Nancy insisted that it be from Sir Crisp English, the doctor who had looked after her at Rest Harrow shortly before she embraced Christian Science and cast doctors from her mind.

When Crisp English did arrive, he saw that the injury was not one with which he, an abdominal surgeon and not a spinal expert, was qualified to deal. He was furious. The Astors' intransigence had caused dangerous delay. At that, Nancy was finally persuaded to agree to the summoning of an orthopaedic surgeon. He arrived the next morning, but even then she was reluctant to accept what she was told must be done immediately. Eventually the appropriate measures were taken, but a precious twelve hours had been wasted. Nancy was beset by 'appalling anxiety' for many months afterwards.

In the event, Wissie never fully recovered, and her relations with her mother, long strained by Nancy's sometimes abrupt and harsh utterances to her daughter, were chronically affected. When, before long, she moved into a house of her own, she tried to keep her mother at arm's length: 'Wissie is in her house,' Nancy wrote to Waldorf, 'and seems to like it, but has not once asked me to a meal, which is a little peculiar, to say the least . . .'

After his unhappy time in exile, as he considered it, in Rhodesia, Bobbie had returned home and in September 1921 had rejoined the Household Cavalry. Like his mother he was excellent on a horse, and he had done very well in regimental steeplechases, winning several notable races, including the coveted Grand Military Gold Cup on his horse Lee Bridge. However, in several races he had fallen badly, and on one occasion, at Hawthorn Hill in April 1923, when he was twenty-five, he had cracked his skull – on hearing of which Nancy cancelled all her immediate engagements to go to his side. He also sustained concussion two years later, racing at Lewes, and severe concussion at Birmingham races in 1930. After that, he designed and constructed the hard hat that is now universally worn by jockeys, and was the first person to wear it. However, the damage had been done, one consequence of which was that alcohol began to affect him adversely.

On the surface it seemed that Bobbie had achieved some happiness at least. He was popular in his regiment, and had a large circle of friends outside it. People were amused by his wit and repartee, even if it contained a hard, teasing element similar to his mother's. Exchanges between the two of them often seemed to reach high flights of humour; in fact he seemed to some to be the only person who could stand up to Nancy in full flood, often with a disarming comment that overwhelmed her with laughter. Yet he had a troubled streak, largely because of his intense but difficult relationship with his mother – 'Miserably attached to her,' as Michael Astor described it, 'by an invisible, unbroken, umbilical cord.'

The counteractive forces that seemed to swirl deep in Bobbie's mind could make his conversation dangerous, particularly if guests were present. On one occasion at Cliveden, when Nancy was dominating the talk in the dining room, he interrupted her in a loud voice with 'Why did Mama marry Uncle Waldorf? Because she wanted a millionaire who said nothing.' After a moment's very awkward silence, Nancy smiled down the table and caustically observed, 'There he is; there's my son. Wouldn't anyone be proud to have him?'

Someone who might have been proud to have him was one of Lord Curzon's daughters, Alexandra, known as Baba, whom Nancy had rather taken under her wing and who frequently stayed at Cliveden. She was in love with Bobbie, who was exceptionally good-looking besides being very amusing company. In fact she wanted to marry him, and on a number of occasions she made her desires clear, but eventually Bobbie had to explain to her that much as he liked her, there would be no point in their being married. For while he appeared to be physically attracted by women, and had several affairs with girls in the 1920s, he was put off by the trouble it caused with his mother. More fundamentally, he was bisexual, and men, he said, were altogether easier. However, Bobbie was also to run into difficulty: not physically damaging, as with Wissie, nor a casualty of adolescence, as with the four Astor sons, but something altogether more serious.

Attraction between men was a problem in army circles, not to mention, if it found physical expression, to the law of the land. For Bobbie, trouble came to a head in the summer of 1929, when he was detected with a soldier in conduct unbecoming an officer and a gentleman. He could not remain in his regiment, but to minimise unpleasant publicity it was put about that his adjutant had found him drunk when on duty as orderly officer, and had placed him under house arrest. The story was credible, as although Bobbie's various steeplechase falls had weakened his resistance to drink, they had not apparently diminished its attractions, and the combination had become noticeable. His commanding officer offered the alternatives of resigning his regular commission or facing a court martial; it was an unpleasant choice, but not a difficult one, and Bobbie was retired with a gratuity.

In spite of this experience, he proved unable, or perhaps unwilling, to mend his ways and gradually fell under the suspicion of the authorities. Two years after leaving his regiment he was apprehended for importuning a guardsman. He received, from the police, notice of impending arrest, giving him time to flee abroad, an escape route hallowed by custom ever since the eighteenth century, when a notable proportion of the populations of Calais and Boulogne consisted of English debtors and others unlikely to retain their liberty in England. However, like Oscar Wilde, Bobbie decided to stay and face the charge, even if, as was likely, it meant that he would soon be in Wormwood Scrubs.

Nancy was told of this awful development on the eve of her 1931 departure for Russia. Even if, or perhaps because, she had by then some understanding of Bobbie's inclinations – when he had been ejected from the army, both Nancy and Waldorf had been good-natured and kind to him – the stark fact that he might go to prison could have been hard to bear. But she was nothing if not strong, and anyway, it was agreed that it was now too late for the Russian arrangements to be altered, and that doing so might lead to unwanted enquiries into the reason.

On Friday 17 July 1931, Bobbie was duly tried at Vine Street magistrates' court and sent to prison. It was all rather swift and final. He resigned from his clubs, settled up with the landlady of his flat, gave his spaniel to a cousin, paid off his servant and his chauffeur, and sent his car and clothes to Cliveden. Struck off the Reserve of Officers, his last connection with the army was severed. On 21 August, a bleak announcement appeared in the *London Gazette*: 'Lt. R.G. Shaw, having been convicted by the Civil Power, is removed from the Army, his Majesty having no further occasion for his services.'

As Waldorf owned the *Observer*, and his brother John had a controlling interest in *The Times*, the Astor family could wield an enormous amount of influence in press circles. In fact, Waldorf had always given his editor, Garvin, a long leash; he did not feel that he himself had the skill to direct the paper in detail, nor did he have the inclination; in any event, he wanted to retain Garvin, an editor of the highest ability, which he recognised would not be possible unless he gave him, within broad and agreed parameters, a free hand. As the political views of Waldorf and Garvin coincided at this time, the potential consequences of any fundamental difference of opinion had not needed attention.

For his part, John Astor had been MP for Dover since 1922 and believed it inappropriate for a politician to attempt to influence a newspaper. However, in Bobbie's case, arguably a personal matter without public relevance, the Astors had little difficulty in deciding to keep the news out of *The Times* and the *Observer*, and beyond the bare comment in *The Times*'s London Gazette column, there was no other mention of it in those papers. In a further indication of their ability to influence the press, Waldorf and Nancy also managed to persuade Lord Beaverbrook to keep the news out of his various publications; the editor of his Plymouth paper was most reluctant to withhold it, but felt obliged to respect his employer's instructions in the matter. On the day Bobbie was sentenced, Nancy sent Beaverbrook what was in part rather a strange letter:

My dear Lord Beaverbrook,

I am deeply grateful to you for the trouble you have taken to keep my name out of the papers. Nothing matters very much about me – but I felt I should like to spare the other children. I know you appreciate that.

For the first time in years I am really fond of my son – Bobbie.

Thank you very much.

Yours,

Nancy Astor.[21]

Nancy was deeply upset by the revelations that led to Bobbie's imprisonment, and even if unable properly to understand all the aspects, she did visit him in prison and on his release went alone with him to Rest Harrow. Plans were then made for him to buy land at Wrotham, in Kent, where he would start anew and farm. In his greatest need, Nancy proved supportive. Both she and Waldorf treated him with generosity of spirit and made no reproach. However, the grief that she apparently felt for a time, and the exhaustion the matter caused her, stirring her own latent feelings of insecurity, were followed by her seeming to cast thoughts of Bobbie's flawed character from her mind and return quickly to her usual liveliness. However much Bobbie was relieved to feel that, despite all, his mother and stepfather were treating him with kindness, he soon returned to drink, and his other ways of finding consolation.

Despite Bobbie's difficulties, and Wisssie's accident, and periods of underlying strained relations caused by Nancy's possessiveness with her children, there were good times of family harmony. One such occurred two years later, when, in the summer of 1933, Wissie became engaged to James Willoughby de Eresby, an MP, heir to great estates, and generally regarded as a wholly suitable and agreeable man. Warmth and pleasure at the prospect brought the family, and in particular, mother and daughter, happily together:

. . . Aunt Nancy is a new woman, and wreathed in maternal smiles. Wiss says that now she and Aunt N are inseparable. Peas in a pod. They do nothing but discuss trousseau, dressing gowns, a few simple little frocks, dozens of sets of lingerie and a coat or two. Literally everybody is pleased . . . Aunt N wants to have gold in her wedding-dress; she may be right as Wiss is very dark . . . Bill is all brotherly and offers jewels, furniture or cheques as choice of present . . . so far Aunt N has behaved beautifully and James and she are great pals. She has teased him about being rich and says she's going to skimp Wisssie's trousseau as she will afterwards be so wealthy . . .[22]

The wedding took place at Taplow church on a hot summer's day, with the reception at Cliveden. In the bright sunlight 2,000 guests sauntered in the perfect gardens and restored themselves in a marquee below the terrace, as a band from the Guards played at a discreet distance and a masque was performed at the Fountain of Love.

Nancy received a letter of congratulation from T.E. Lawrence, then serving incognito in the Royal Air Force and masquerading under the name of Aircraftman Shaw. She had met him through Bernard Shaw, and they became fast friends after Lawrence had been posted to RAF Mount Batten, at Cattewater in Plymouth Sound. They exchanged a number of bantering letters:

Dear Peeress,

Three things, my memory says, on which to congratulate you: order of merit:

[1] Personal. Your tact in ceding at golf to the Prince of Wales . . .

[2] Social. Your good fortune in having the new National Sporting Club as your neighbour in St James's Square. When an evening falls dull you can just slip in and see a little boxing.

[3] Dynastic. The engagement of Wissie as the future Lady Ancaster. Not an easy peeress to succeed, let me say. Enough said . . .

My own affairs march well, but it should have been Epstein not Strobl . . .

Yours proletariately,

T.E. Shaw[23]

Nancy's reply was typical, and rather in the same vein:

Dear Aircraftsman,

I could not resist showing your letter to Geoffrey Dawson. We think it is the best thing you have ever done – better even than the Odyssey . . .

. . . First, about HRH, I vow it was not tact or gallantry. I did my best. The only thing that I did do was to put him at his ease, and the minute I did that he began to play good golf. Secondly, you are quite right about boxing. I have a passion for blood sports. Thirdly, my daughter's marriage. I make no bones about it. I am absolutely delighted . . . because when a young woman gets that age she ought to have her own life, and as I saw no signs of her making her own life under my roof I rejoice she is going to make it under her own . . .

May I ask if we are ever to see you again? May I tell you that I

truly miss you at Plymouth? If you are free on Monday or Thursday
next could you come up and dine with Bobbie and Philip and me . . .
My grammar is bad but my affection grand, enduring, and well worth
your keeping.

N.Astor, Peeress, Mother of peers and peeresses.[24]

Lawrence liked and admired Nancy, but 'for living beside', he told Bernard
Shaw's wife, 'commend me to some vegetable'.

Cliveden continued to be a forum for all types of gathering. One subject
that was frequently discussed there, especially by members of the Round
Table, was the political development of India, which was of fundamental
interest to the group – in 1931, Philip Lothian had been appointed
Undersecretary of State for India. It had long been a controversial topic,
especially after the possibility of an advance to some measure of independence had been given impetus by the Government of India Act in
1919. Feelings were strong, for and against introducing Indians into
government, and were heightened by appreciation of the service given
by the large number of Indians who had fought for the Empire during
the Great War.

In March 1929, a pact had been signed between the Viceroy and Mahatma
Gandhi, by then the representative of a significant section of Indian opinion,
and in 1930–2, the British government convened a series of Round Table
conferences to consider proposals for political change in the subcontinent.
Gandhi came to London to take part in the second conference, which began
in September 1931, and it was not long before he was brought round to 4,
St James's by Philip Lothian, to be introduced to Nancy. The Astors' friend
and admirer Thomas Jones, at that time Deputy Secretary to the Cabinet,
was at the house when Gandhi arrived:

She introduced me and then fired away: 'So this is the wild man of
God!'
Gandhi: 'I hope I can live up to that certificate.'
Nancy: (clapping her hands in his face) 'Think of the trouble you have
made in the world.'
Gandhi: 'I have been warned to beware of Lady Astor – perhaps she
is a wild woman of God.'
I left them bantering each other in the friendliest fashion . . .[25]

Gandhi's description seemed rather appropriate.

Nancy had been hostess to those attending a similar conference the
previous year, and had invited some of them to lunch at Cliveden. Not

knowing much about them caused her little concern, as her political secretary observed:

> Nancy gave a women's luncheon for women delegates to the first Round Table Conference . . . Of course, we didn't know each other at all then, and it was rather stiff . . . Then Nancy said all of a sudden, to the whole table, 'Well now, you ladies, just tell me what you really do when your husbands get troublesome. Do you give in to 'em, or how do you manage 'em, or what?' Of course, this was just the one subject you wouldn't think they would talk about. There was a kind of stiffening all round the table, and they were horrified. I did feel a sort of black cloud. And then Nancy made some sort of joke against men, and they couldn't help laughing; and after that they all began to talk quite freely about their homes and their views about men and women and all sorts of things, and that was the beginning of the real friendship we had with them, and meant a great deal.[26]

'Fortune favours the bold', as Nancy proved on so many occasions.

The political future of India was a seemingly intractable problem, but less so than the worldwide slump, which had begun in 1929 and showed no signs of ending, miring Britain and Europe in economic difficulty. The war had given great impetus to mass production, which in turn had spurred enormous economic change by creating new needs for much wider circles of population; cheaper and easier methods of production then led to overproduction, with dramatic consequences for prices: first inflation and then sharp falls when demand collapsed at the end of the decade.

America had her own troubles. In the wake of the sudden and dramatic crash in world stock markets after October 1929, a bleak economic era began, bringing the post-war 'Jazz Age' to an abrupt end – and leading, among other things, to a steep loss of momentum for the social change Nancy had sought in housing, health, education and the home.

America had provided a great deal of finance during the boom years, but after the onset of the slump she found herself left with enormous amounts of unpaid debt, and shrunken markets for her exports. In the three years following the initial crash, nearly 5,000 United States banks failed, and five-sixths of the wealth represented by securities was wiped out. America was all the more determined to remain politically isolated, at least from Europe. On both sides of the Atlantic markets for real estate were practically paralysed, while in England agricultural depression was ruining many long-established families – agricultural estates in many parts of England had fallen to less than 10 per cent of their value sixty years previously, before the long depression in land prices began. The Astors' income was derived mainly from urban rents, so they were not much affected by rural depression, but the appalling economic conditions were causing great anxiety to rich and poor alike. The dire international situation had convinced Waldorf of the need to economise.

Nancy suggested letting Cliveden for a year, partly in order to release funds to contribute to some of the Astors' charitable initiatives, especially the Margaret McMillan nursery schools. Waldorf agreed that there must be some reduction in the scale of the family's living, although he did not want to close Cliveden entirely. Early in 1931, he expressed his feelings in a letter to Nancy:

> Never have I had anything so hateful and unpleasant to do as applying the economy axe to Cliveden. We shall have to get rid of all the casuals . . . I shall also make an all round reduction in wages. This will be fair as our wages are rather higher than those paid at Dropmore, Taplow Court and Hedsor. Hopkins suggests putting the old Rolls by. It is an expensive car to run. His suggestion is that we have in London during the spring only the new Rolls, your new Humber and Wissie's Ford . . .
>   . . . I have not touched the house, leaving that to you to deal with the indoor staff. I, however, had a long talk with Lee. We both agree that if we go to Cliveden with the family for a fortnight at the end of the Easter holidays so as to enable the boys to be there for a bit, the best arrangements would be for you to use the secretary's rooms, and for me and the boys to sleep in Greenwood Cottage, coming up to the house for meals. We could eat in the Steward's Room. This would enable us to keep the main building closed. I think it would not be at all a bad thing for the children to have this experience.[27]

To Waldorf's dismay, Nancy now changed her mind about any variation of their life at Cliveden. Worried by the financial climate and greatly disturbed by having to cause hardship to anyone who worked for him, he urged her:

> Please don't start discussing again whether Cliveden must be closed . . . I've seldom had a more painful and distasteful job than when I had to speak to all the men . . . Now don't make believe that we've acted precipitately or without need – you sometimes don't realise how much worry you give when you change your mind . . . Psychologically

it's wise to close Cliveden – it would be impossible to reduce staff at this moment of unemployment unless one did.

Feeling 'battered', Waldorf found solace in his daily Christian Science studies – 'harmonising', as he put it.

NINE

Downhill

Though Waldorf had been beset by illness and financial worries, and seemed somewhat to play second fiddle to Nancy during the whirlwind of her early parliamentary years, he was certainly not inactive. Besides his work in the Lords, he also devoted himself to his stud, and to his interest in agriculture, on which he had published a number of books and specialist articles and become recognised as an expert. His output was full of imaginative ideas, ranging from a call to develop smallholdings, 'to increase our healthy, thrifty, vigorous land population', and an attack on the National Farmers' Union, advising them 'to drop their pose of infallibility and not to behave like touchy operatic singers whenever anyone treats them like mortals instead of demigods. This will enable them to move with the times.'

He was also, in his painstaking way, spending a considerable amount of time on League of Nations affairs, having been appointed a British delegate in 1931. The League's remit, rather broad, was to promote international co-operation and to achieve international peace and security, in search of which it was conferring, interminably it seemed, in Geneva. As early as 1918, Waldorf had spoken up for a League of Nations, urging countries to share their resources 'as in a great family . . . at a moment when the world is looking anxiously for signs of a brotherhood of nations'.

'Brotherhood' had about it the ring of Christian peace and understanding that ran through Nancy's politics, and she too supported the idea of a League of Nations as a vital part of a new system; like the Round Table, however, she was Atlanticist rather than European. In any case, her ideals rose above mere nations, and she shared Waldorf's belief that the 'basic cause of all wars is the existence of separate sovereignties. It is the anarchy or absence of government in international affairs that makes wars possible and probable.' Again, it was the Round Table view: 'Alexander Hamilton realised this question was fundamental when the constitution of the USA was being drawn up. War between the different states in the Union has been eliminated because the question was dealt with, and only because it was dealt with' – although, of course, it did take a civil war to finalise the matter. 'Though the era of a world state is not yet,' Lothian wrote, 'the war has marked one definite advance on the road to it.' As on so many subjects, Waldorf, Nancy and Philip Lothian were agreed.

Despite talk of the brotherhood of nations, few people conferring in Geneva or elsewhere seemed keen on fraternity in practice, and in the real world nationalism was stirring once more, particularly the German variety; it had in the event been only temporarily quelled by a defeat which, it could not now be denied, had not been decisive enough, leaving Germany too strong. The country's resurgence spurred an increasingly anxious debate in England about whether Germany should be welcomed back into the comity of nations, on terms of equality with the victors, or whether she was to be kept down, largely unarmed and economically weak, in order to prevent yet another European conflict.

In the aftermath of the First World War, the victors had at first been in broad agreement: someone had to pay for the war, and make amends for the indescribable amount of damage that had occurred since 1914. The Covenant, or terms, of the League of Nations was therefore based on the age-old principle of human justice that when damage or suffering has been inflicted, the perpetrator must make amends to the full extent of his capacity, and the peacemakers attempted to incorporate in the Treaty of Versailles recognition that the Great War was a monstrous wrong for which Germany and her allies were responsible. At first it was widely held that although the peace terms were harsh, had the Germans won the war they would have been very much harsher, but in due course that sentiment began to fade. While Germany remained a festering sore in the centre of Europe, the 'Hang the Kaiser' emotions that initially prevailed at Versailles were replaced by a sense – especially in Germany – that the terms imposed on the vanquished were unjust and too severe.

Nancy's opinions were often based on emotion rather than analysis, and she was quick to form strong views. However, having little relevant experience of European political affairs, she was open to influence, from Waldorf and especially from Philip Lothian – partly because of her deep affection for him, and partly because of admiration for his political wisdom. Even though Lothian had played a part in drafting the peace treaty, he and Waldorf, like many others, now began to have second thoughts about the peace terms, and to feel a sense of guilt.

On European matters a paramount influence upon Nancy seemed to be an aversion to the French. There were no obvious reasons for that; she had had few encounters with Frenchmen, although the Astors regularly took houses in France, and no direct cause to dismiss France, as she did, as one large brothel. She seems to have harboured a disapproval of Latins in general, as well as the French in particular: 'I hate the Latin mind,' she said, 'it's so bent on the wrong track', the result, perhaps, of anti-Catholic prejudice.

Yet there did not seem to be any obvious justification for her antipathy to Catholicism either, except perhaps that she regarded it as a spiritual dictatorship and therefore running counter to her individualistic instincts. It is doubtful whether her childhood religious instruction had been strident enough to have instilled in her such feelings. Nor were the tenets of Christian Science anti-Catholic. At the time Nancy embraced her new religion, there was a suspicion, fortified by the prejudice of Jesuits among others, that Catholic thought was antagonistic to Christian Science, but it seems unlikely that Nancy would have noticed. She studied the writings of Mary Baker Eddy almost daily, so she would no doubt have been familiar with the leader's assertions that 'a genuine Christian Scientist loves Protestant and Catholic', and that 'Christian Scientists have no quarrel with Protestants, Catholics, or any other sect'. Her prejudice may have been heightened by her discussions with Lothian, and his eventual rather agonising rejection of Catholicism.

However, as she began to pay more attention to international affairs, she began to comprehend the depth of hostility between France and Germany, and she soon concluded that unless the friction was removed, Europe might one day again be plunged into war. She also shared the view, increasingly widespread among her friends, that if another war were to break out, Western civilisation, such of it that had survived the Great War, would collapse, ushering in anarchy and Bolshevism. At the same time, logical or otherwise, Nancy's general suspicion of France led her increasingly to feel sympathy for Germany. Her paramount wish was that people and nations should live in amity together, though that had to accommodate her antipathy to communism.

As a result, what people came most to perceive was a pro-German bias in her views on European politics. She had been indignant when, in 1923, France occupied the Ruhr, despite being implored by the British government not to do so. This had come about because Germany had fallen behind with her war reparations to the victors, and France understandably took the hard line that her old enemy could not be trusted and must stick to what she had promised. However, the Ruhr was Germany's industrial heartland, and by commandeering its production, the French further impeded Germany's ability to earn the money with which to make the payments the Allies demanded.

France's action highlighted the divergence between French and British attitudes. Besides the mutual antipathy of the two countries at that time, there was a fundamental difference in policy objectives: the dominant instinct in Frenchmen was for security, while that in Englishmen was for peace. For the French, security meant the protection of her eastern borders, while for England peace had a much wider horizon, that of a huge empire, and the protection of her routes across three oceans. As Germany rose from her debasement in 1918, the French grew unsure whether England might side with her against them, while for their part, the British began to worry that France's actions, in particular her system of alliances, might drag them into another European war. The disquiet caused by France's occupation of the Ruhr had not waned a dozen years later when the French entered into a pact with communist Russia, an agreement deemed by many on the British right to be almost a betrayal of Western civilisation. Meanwhile Nancy announced that no English party or British statesman of any importance agreed with the French entry into the Ruhr. The occupation reinforced her opinion that Germany's grievances must be addressed as the only way of achieving lasting peace in Europe.

At the same time, by instinct and emotion she remained drawn to America, sure that peace in Europe required America to abandon its policy of isolation and play an active part in reconstructing the continent. She had expressed her view in many of the speeches she made on her 1922 US tour, telling the English Speaking Union in New York:

> America, I am told, draws back with horror when she looks at Europe. I don't blame her. Certainly, it is a sad enough sight to make one draw back. I cannot believe, though, that standing back is the right way to help, and I don't believe that any part of the world can go forward in the truest sense while another part is suffering desperately. The war has shown us that the world is really round and is part interdependent . . .[1]

Ten years on, that seemed to her to be just as true, yet there appeared to be little prospect of a new direction in American opinion, even after the shock of the 1929 stock market crash, the onset of the Depression, and Roosevelt's 'New Deal'.

By early 1933, Germany had walked out of the League, apparently set on a belligerently expansionist course, although for some time after taking power the Nazis devoted much of their attention to internal affairs, and to cutting out what seemed to them the decay that had befallen their country. Their trumpeted crusade against communism, which lent their movement its first coherent form, gave them a pretext to start vilifying all sorts of people and institutions of whom they disapproved. One such group was the Christian Science Church, which, only a few months after the Nazis took office, was accused of distributing Marxist propaganda.

It was for that reason that Waldorf was one of the first men from England to have an interview with Hitler. Worried by events in Germany, the board of directors of the Christian Science Church invited him to lead a delegation to Germany to discuss the Nazis' complaints, and in September 1933 he flew to Berlin, where he met Wilhelm Frick, Minister of the Interior.[2] Frick offered comforting words, and promised that as long as Christian Scientists practised religion and not politics they would remain undisturbed. Before the delegation left the country, Waldorf was offered an interview with Hitler. Their meeting lasted for twenty minutes, leaving Waldorf satisfied with the Führer's confirmation of his minister's assurance.

A twenty-minute meeting might be enough to form a first impression, but it did not give Waldorf much insight into what Hitler was really like; nor, it seems, were politics mentioned at their meeting. Yet the fact of his going to Germany at all marked Waldorf out as reputedly having special knowledge at a time when, in Britain, experience of the country was scant. Relatively few Englishmen had travelled there during the 1920s, and fewer still had an inkling of the nature of the men who came to power in 1933.

In March 1936 a crisis erupted that forced the problem of Germany firmly on to the centre stage of British politics, and began the sharp polarisation of opinion in Parliament and the country at large as to how the new Germany, thrusting its way stridently up the political agenda, should be treated. On the morning of Saturday 7 March, Cologne's famous Hohenzollern Bridge echoed to the rumble and tramp of German columns as they re-entered the Rhineland, to be greeted by adoring crowds, the women weeping with joy and showering the soldiers with flowers. It was a clear breach of the Versailles treaty, and, following Germany's resignation from the League of Nations and its announcement of conscription, the third of what came to be called 'Hitler's weekend surprises'.

However, with what in hindsight proved to be fatal lack of resolve, there was no military response from either England or France.

> *Pale Ebenezer thought it wrong to fight,*
> *But Roaring Bill (who killed him) thought it right.*

Describing their measures as 'purely defensive', the Germans cited their anxiety at the pacts signed between France, Russia and Czechoslovakia, and declared themselves ready to conclude new agreements for the peaceful security of Europe. The British government, unwilling for a host of reasons to fight, were only too anxious to believe Hitler sincere. The Führer also proposed that the League of Nations should become a consultative body rather than an international policeman – at which it had proved wholly unsuccessful, notably in failing to deter Mussolini from invading Abyssinia or from effectively sanctioning him after he had done so.[3] It was a masterful diplomatic manoeuvre on Germany's part, and gave Britain her excuse for not drawing her sword to enforce the Versailles treaty.

In Germany, the occupation of the Rhineland was regarded as a dangerous gamble. The German service chiefs had warned their government to abandon the plan, fearing, correctly as it turned out, that a march over the Rhine would destroy the goodwill that the soldiers and diplomats had been trying to build with their British counterparts.[4] That did not at all deter Hitler, however – the Reich needed defences on the west bank of the Rhine to protect its major industries in the Ruhr valley – and he was triumphantly vindicated. The response in England was far more muted than might have been expected from one of the victors of 1918, with a glorious history as a mighty nation. Lothian captured the country's new mood when he described the reoccupation as Germany entering 'her own back garden', a cry taken up in clubs and pubs, with typical English sympathy for a former aggressor now seen as underdog.

When news of the occupation reached England, Nancy and Waldorf were staying with Lothian at his stately home, Blickling Hall, in Norfolk.[5] There was a mix of influential guests, including Canadian and American diplomats, a British Cabinet minister, and the editor of *The Economist*. They all remained quite calm. Hitler's offer of a pact was welcomed, and the entry of German troops into the German zone was 'not to be taken tragically', but seen as an assertion of a recovered status of equality. It was a sad example of man's ability to believe what he wants to believe. The vast majority of thoughtful and intelligent people in England at that time sincerely thought that no stone should be left unturned in order to find an accommodation with the dictators, and so, as they saw it, pave the way to a lasting peace. Few were willing to test the age-old concept that bullies bow to strength.

France, on the other hand, massed troops on the German border, causing anger in England, heightening irrational and emotional feelings that France was unreliable, and reinforcing the anxiety aroused by her recent pact with Soviet Russia. Members of Parliament reported that there was no public appetite for another Passchendaele to eject the Germans from their own land; instead there was a widespread fear that England might be drawn into war on the coat tails of France, a possibility in view of aggressive Japanese behaviour on Russia's eastern borders, which had the potential to involve

Russia in hostilities. The electorate would not stand for Britain fighting as an ally of the Bolsheviks, who were widely demonised as even worse than the Germans.

On 10 March 1936, Parliament debated the Rhineland news. The mood was uncertain. The pacifist Labour MP George Lansbury, whom Nancy described as 'a dear old soul, but muddle-headed and half-witted', asked the government how it would defend the slaughter he foresaw if Britain stood up to Germany. 'Many of us,' replied Nancy, 'feel just as strongly on this matter as the right hon. Gentleman, but will he tell us – unless you get the real brotherhood of man and the fatherhood of God – what on earth any government in England can do . . .'6

Soon afterwards, Winston Churchill placed the issue before the House in graver, more measured tones, repeating the warnings that he had begun to give, with increasing urgency, ever since Hitler had come to power:

> . . . The gravity of the situation is in no way diminished by the fact that it has become less exciting than it was two or three weeks ago. When you are drifting, floating, down the stream of Niagara, it may easily happen that from time to time you run into a reach of quite smooth water, or that a bend in the river or a change in the wind make the roar of the falls seem far more distant; but your position and your preoccupation are in no way affected thereby . . .7

A short time later, the Germans embarked on an exercise in improving their relations with Britain. They had several objectives: they were anxious to play down the anti-Semitism that had received what they considered to be disproportionate attention in the world's press; they wanted to ensure that there was no delayed military reaction to their Rhineland reoccupation; and Hitler was determined that the 11th Olympiad, in which Germany was to be host to fifty nations, should be a triumph.

> Much of this exercise was aimed, particularly, at Great Britain. The theme of anti-bolshevism, the theme of France's decadence, the theme of Germany's just demands, and the hard deal she had received at Versailles and Locarno – all these things were accompanied by a comprehensive approach to the British, spearheaded by Ribbentrop. England and Germany were natural allies, and should be friends.8

At that time Joachim von Ribbentrop was Hitler's 'ambassador-at-large', and he did have some initial success in establishing a relationship between Britain and Germany, though it proved to be of short duration. He had encouraged the foundation, at the end of 1935, of the Anglo-German Fellowship, and its German counterpart, designed to promote business links and closer understanding between the two countries. He had also scored a notable diplomatic success with the signing of an Anglo-German naval agreement, in June 1935.[9]

Two weeks after the Germans entered the Rhineland, Nancy gave a large dinner party at 4, St James's Square. The guests included the German, American and Russian ambassadors and a large number of League of Nations delegates who had gathered for a conference in London. The party had all the hallmarks of Nancy's carefree and direct way of treating people, however supposedly important. When the meal was over she announced that they would all play games. Amid mixed reactions of delight, bafflement and perhaps some embarrassment from the foreigners, she whispered to the English that they should let the Germans win, a scene recorded by her niece:

What do you suppose Aunt N did after dinner? Made us all play musical chairs. She really is a remarkable woman, for who else could think of such a thing? Some of the older ones stood by thinking, no doubt, that the English are mad, quite mad. But they smiled benignly and were amused. After this, group conversations took place . . .[10]

The German Ambassador, Von Hoesch, declined to take part, and in fact was dead within a month. One of the objectives of his eventual successor, von Ribbentrop, had been to get Hitler to meet the British Prime Minister, Stanley Baldwin, and in May 1936 he had for that purpose invited Thomas Jones to Germany. Jones, who as Deputy Secretary to the Cabinet had gained Baldwin's respect, duly had an interview with the Führer, who sent him back to England with a personal message for the Prime Minister. Baldwin, a keen reader of thrillers and detective stories, exclaimed that the message read like 'an Oppenheim story', although giving no indication of much further interest than that.[11]

Undeterred by Baldwin's apparent lack of any serious intent to take the matter forward, Ribbentrop continued his efforts to arrange for Hitler and the British Prime Minister to meet. Although Thomas Jones had retired from the Civil Service in 1930, he remained close to Baldwin, and Ribbentrop once more sought him out. They met for lunch early in June 1936. Ribbentrop offered to arrange a secret meeting between Hitler and the Prime Minister – perhaps off the English coast, near Dover or Folkestone, as Baldwin had never flown in an aeroplane and did not much like the sea, while Hitler would not be prepared to go so far as actually to land in England.

To take the matter forward, Jones suggested that Ribbentrop accompany him that very day to Rest Harrow, to meet Sir Thomas Inskip, who had just been appointed Minister for the Co-ordination of Defence. The plan was agreed at once. It was the sort of occasion that few people in England other than Nancy could, or would, host at short notice: a serious top-level conversation between a highly placed German and a member of the British Cabinet, in discreet and informal surroundings of great comfort.

Later that afternoon a sleek silver 5.4-litre Mercedes-Benz, containing Ribbentrop, his valet, and an aide, drew up outside Jones's flat to collect him, and they headed out towards the Dover Road. On the two-hour journey to Sandwich, Jones warned Ribbentrop that Inskip was an evangelical churchman who might question the Nazis' persecution of the German churches. Forewarned, the urbane German was able to satisfy the minister's doubts, and after dinner they set to the main business:

> We talked till nearly midnight and when the others had retired Lothian and I talked on till 12.45 with von R in Waldorf's study. There Lothian impressed upon von R that in any agreement with us it must be made plain that it contemplated the peaceful revision of the Treaties as they affected Austria, Memel and the rest. We must not get into a position of a breach of faith should Austria fall to Germany. Von R, of course, agreed . . . At breakfast Nancy chaffed von R about the 'bad company' he kept when in England – Lady Londonderry and Lady Cunard. Von R pleaded that they had both always been extremely kind to him and to his friends . . . Later in the afternoon von Wussow came to the PT office and we arranged a short secret code, for communication between us when he returned to Berlin. I rang up Geoffrey Dawson and arranged with Wussow that he should see von R this evening between 6.30 and 7.30.[12]

Ribbentrop clearly made a favourable impression, and the next day Lothian sent a long commentary on the discussions to the Foreign Secretary, Anthony Eden. Declaring that the country was faced with the most dangerous and critical decision since the war, he asked whether Germany was to be given the 'position in Europe and the world to which she is entitled by her history, her civilization and her power', or, alternatively, whether Britain was going to continue to support the group 'led by France and Russia which seeks to prevent her from obtaining those adjustments without which she will not have equality'. There were distinct echoes of Ribbentrop's own eloquence of the previous evening, a benign view of Anglo-German friendship that Nancy was to support wholeheartedly, but which unsurprisingly was misinterpreted by many, causing her, for a time, a discouraging loss of friendship and support.

Meanwhile the indefatigable Jones arranged a further meeting for Ribbentrop, with Geoffrey Dawson, a pillar of the Round Table, who had long been editor of *The Times* and a doyen of the newspaper world. *The Times* was now entering a period of influence enhanced by its reputation for enjoying the confidence of the government, who in turn paid it close attention. The fact that the paper's main shareholder was Waldorf's brother John was one of the reasons for the damaging campaign that was soon to be directed against the Astor family, accusing them of undue influence in the machinery of government, and of using the paper to promote the appeasement of the dictators to a degree that was destructive of Britain's interests.

By now, widely read sections of the press, in both England and America, portrayed many politicians and leaders of society as being sympathetic to Nazi ideas, including anti-Semitism. The fact that this was in many cases a distortion of their views did not mitigate the ill effects upon the people concerned. Some of the victims of this misrepresentation were, through naivety, the architects of their own misfortune, while many were genuinely friendly towards the new regime in Germany but heedless about how they might be seen by others. For a time, the warmth towards Nazi Germany felt by leading hostesses such as Lady Londonderry, and Mrs Greville, who had the ear of several influential Cabinet ministers, was reflected in the determination of many in Parliament to offer friendship to the dictators as a way of finding enduring peace. Through much of the 1930s, most English people, even those who had fought in the trenches, felt that they had no quarrel with the Germans, were benignly disposed towards the Italians, had no interest in the Spanish Civil War, and no curiosity about Japan. On the other hand, there was a widespread belief in the need to resist communism.

Unfortunately for a section of society identified as both rich and right wing, the desire for peace, although very widely shared, came to be seen more as a wish to keep their privileges and wealth free from disturbance, whether the dictators were a threat to England or not. Chips Channon, an American MP, exemplified what was to become a deeply unpopular image once the prospects of peace began to fade and the public mood changed:

> The Channons have fallen much under the champagne-like influence of the Brunswicks, the Wittelsbachs and the House of Hesse Cassel . . . They think Ribbentrop is a fine man, and that we should let gallant little Germany glut her fill of the reds in the East and keep decadent France quiet while she does so.[13]

Nancy was not of that stamp. With an independent, robust spirit, she was the last person to fawn on Ribbentrop, German aristocrats or dictators, but she was convinced that nothing should impede the search for a permanent peace, and she would not accept that the Germans might be insincere and malevolent, or that Britain should try and rein the Nazis in.

The misleading impressions that arose were caused in part by the difficulty many sections of the press, even with the freedom they enjoyed in Britain, had in gaining access to primary sources. Instead, newspapers often resorted to second-hand information, causing them to paint incomplete or erroneous pictures, and misconceptions were easily transmitted from one magazine or newspaper to another. As a result, large numbers of readers were fed the same mistaken facts and rumours. So it was that Nancy and her friends were caricatured, first in the British press and then in America, with sufficient plausibility to make the public suppose that there was 'no smoke without fire', a doubt encouraged by Churchill's wary speeches echoing ominously through Parliament. Further, the press knew that stories of behind-the-scenes influence were good for sales, so the tales began to spread.

Time and Tide was a respected independent political weekly magazine, to which, although it was a strong supporter of Winston Churchill's uncompromising approach to the dictators, both Waldorf and Nancy occasionally contributed. A month or so after Ribbentrop's discussions at Rest Harrow, the magazine suggested that there were two distinct camps, and firmly placed Waldorf and Nancy in one of them:

At the present moment we have in influential quarters two pronounced and opposed sets of opinion as to the right course to pursue in Europe, both equally dangerous. There are those – Lord Londonderry, Lord and Lady Astor, the Earl of Dudley, and others in the most influential positions are amongst their protagonists – who, half fascinated by the surface tidiness of the Fascist regimes of Central Europe, stand for a rapprochement with Germany . . . on the other hand, we have the realist politicians such as Mr Churchill, Mr Duff Cooper, Sir Austen Chamberlain, who remember 1914, who know that Germany wants to grow, and believe that sooner or later she means to grow at our expense, and who, however they may have hated Bolshevism in the past, are prepared to join with Russia and with France today to play power politics against Hitler . . .

Nancy was having none of that, and replied at once:

I have desired to restore a sense of security in Europe by treating Germany as an equal. I have worked for a reversal of the policy of goading her people and rulers into restlessness by trying to keep them in a state of inferiority and of perpetuating the settlement imposed on Europe by the Versailles Treaty in a moment of passion . . . I do not blame France for having feared Germany after her experiences of 1870 and 1914 – I do blame those British Foreign Secretaries who have helped France to reject every German proposal for an honourable settlement. This policy has not succeeded. It has fomented a sense of injustice and hatred in Germany. Treating Germans decently and as members of a great nation might have failed – but I still think this policy would have been more likely to lead to an atmosphere of peace in Europe. Is it too late to try even now?[14]

A much greater impact than that of *Time and Tide* was achieved by a nondescript news-sheet called *The Week*. Edited by a communist, Claud Cockburn, it rapidly made a name by speaking out against the dictators, at least the right-wing ones, and those in influential circles whom it perceived as their friends.

The Week hardly merited the attention it received, with Cockburn admitting that he considered rumours to be just as valid as facts. Yet by fearless editing he attracted copy from respectable newspapers who fed him material they dared not publish themselves, and he was able to barter stories, true or otherwise, with correspondents of foreign newspapers. *The Week* soon punched well above its weight, and found its way to influential quarters, especially foreign media, which were incapable of winnowing fact from fiction but could recognise a story that might interest their readers. People soon began to think that Cockburn's warnings of the intentions of the Nazi regime and the state of the British defences were reasonably accurate, and accordingly there was a ready market for the magazine's rumours when, towards the end of 1937, it began to shine its limelight in a most disagreeable way on Nancy and her close friends. As much as a year earlier similar gossip had reached the ears of the American ambassador in London, at that time Robert Bingham, who reported to President Roosevelt that 'There is a pro-German cabal led by Lord Lothian and actively fostered by the Waldorf Astors. This carries with it the "Times", as the Waldorf Astors have more influence with Geoffrey Dawson than John Astor has, who is the real proprietor of the "Times".'

The glare of publicity that Claud Cockburn managed to direct towards the Astors naturally upset them considerably, so much so that when John Strachey, a journalist and Labour MP, tried to introduce Cockburn to Nancy in the House of Commons lobby, she responded by spitting at him. 'I had rather to admire her for that,' Cockburn later commented.

Dismayed as she may have been by the smear campaign, Nancy held firm in her pursuit of what she believed to be right. In September 1936, she had crossed to America, for the first time in four years. Accompanied by her niece, Virginia Brand, she set sail in the *Bremen*, on which the passengers received a relentless diet of Nazi propaganda. It had no effect on Nancy. Interviewed on arrival, she urged the importance of bringing together her 'two countries': 'Unless England and America stand together there will be chaos in the world. They would be a sort of moral police force and it would say to belligerent countries, 'Well, here we stand.' It would have a sobering effect, a terrific effect on Germany, for one . . .'

'Europe is in a terrific state,' she continued. 'I am perfectly sure the democracies of the world are up against it.' She saw Europe as beset with Bolshevism and communism: 'They can thrive only where there is ignorance and poverty, and there is less of it in England and America than anywhere in the world.'[15] Even so, she maintained that 'There is nothing in the European situation to arouse fears of war.' She saw no danger in fascism, as it was not international: it was the communists who wished to spread their creed abroad. They had ruined Russia, and now she saw them threatening both Spain and France.

She went first to Mirador, before progressing around Virginia and North Carolina, seeing relations, including her brother, Buck, now Mayor of Warren, attending parties and giving talks, where she 'completely vamped' the locals, according to the press. She was invigorated by the optimism she felt all about her, and announced that the Depression was over. Having gone down to Florida to see Nora, for whom she had bought some land near Tryon, she and Waldorf went to Bermuda, to stay with Vincent Astor, one of Waldorf's American cousins.

She was away from home for three months, but was able to keep on top of her political interests in England, and the requirements of her constituency, largely through having an exceptionally able, knowledgeable and thorough political secretary, Barbara Brew, who kept Nancy informed about government business, the parliamentary calendar, Commons committees, political meetings, news, invitations, and applications for employment. She also drafted amendments for forthcoming Bills for Nancy's approval:

> Enclosed is a draft of your speech for Pathé Films on your return. You said you would like to have something to tear to pieces while you were away. I don't think myself it has a sufficiently American 'slant', but I expect you will alter it as you wish.

We have had a message from the Duke of Kent's secretary, saying that HRH would like to have a talk to you about the Plymouth visit on your return. You will be glad to hear that Virginia House have now been able to arrange the Country Fair for Friday, 3rd July, at 3 p.m., and are delighted that you will open it then . . . Everyone seems quite reconciled to your being away, although they are very anxious to see you immediately you come back, and will want as much attention as you can give them, as *no one* takes your place.[16]

'I hope you're getting a really good rest,' she added. With her political administration in such competent hands, Nancy had a chance of doing so. It was vital support for someone who had so much to deal with yet who had a butterfly mind.

While in Bermuda, Nancy was deeply upset by a family tragedy: on 16 November, her nephew David Brooks, known as Winkie, one of Phyllis's sons by her first marriage, fell from the fourteenth floor of his Park Avenue apartment. The news devastated Phyllis, not least because of her fear, later confirmed, that it was a case of suicide.

By then, though, the talk of the town was the King's affair with Mrs Simpson. The English newspapers had loyally kept their silence, but it was the reverse in America, with sensational nationwide coverage exemplified by the famous headline in a Chicago newspaper 'King's Moll Reno'd in Wolsey's Home Town'. On her return to London, Nancy found that the news had finally broken there as well. Her own feelings were mixed. She had met the King on a number of occasions, and in 1933 had played golf with him at Walton Heath before a large crowd, when he had defeated her on the seventeenth hole. Whatever her feelings for her King, Nancy soon decided against his favourite: asked what she would do when introduced to Mrs Simpson, she replied simply, 'I am a Virginian. She is from Maryland. She would as soon meet a rattlesnake.'

When Nancy had met the King at official engagements of the type he loathed so much, he had clearly appreciated her breezy presence. The previous year, for example, she had sat next to him at a dull fund-raising event. During dinner it became obvious that they were getting on well together and apparently enjoying the evening, but there then followed a number of lengthy and monotonous 'money' speeches, and the guest of honour became visibly bored. When the appeal for the cause was finally made, Nancy suddenly sprang to her feet and announced, 'I have His Royal Highness' permission to say that unless you give generously to the appeal, and raise the full amount asked for, he will command that all the speeches we have just heard be repeated, in full, once more, before you go.'[17]

Within a week of the King's abdication, Nancy wrote to friends living abroad:

> We got back in the middle of it all. It is quite obvious that nothing could have moved the King from the course he has taken. The general opinion here is that he is really not sane on that subject. I saw Princess Alice last night and she said that every time they implored him to give her up he just replied, 'You would love her, if you knew her.' . . . It has been a staggering blow, but I don't believe that a single person would want him back now.
>
> It is quite wonderful to see the House of Commons so wholeheartedly behind Baldwin. Winston Churchill, true to form, for one mad moment thought he could form a King's party, but he saw it was no good.
>
> The Yorks are terribly miserable, but I believe that they will do a good job, and the country seems to be truly welcoming them. Poor Queen Mary weeps all the time, and who can blame her? One's heart aches for her.
>
> It seems the more they hear of Mrs Simpson the worse she appears. That part of it is so tragic it doesn't bear thinking of. It is awful to see the look of heartache on all the people's faces. I've been in the House of Commons all the time, but my secretary says that she was in a big restaurant the other night, and on all the hundreds of faces there was not a single smile. I do feel that a certain section of Society are largely to blame for the whole thing. If she had not been accepted by them and run after, the King would have realised that he could not possibly get away with it. I saw it all going on at Ascot this year, and spoke hotly and loudly then . . .'[18]

'Really,' she added, 'she seems to have turned out an arch-adventuress of the worst type.'

The BBC asked Nancy to explain the abdication in a broadcast to Canada and the United States, partly in order to help counter American fears that the British did not want Wallis Simpson as Queen because of her origins. Thomas Jones helped her draft it, before she went on air at two a.m. 'She had a pad and was dabbing sentences on it as if she was throwing darts at a target and she kept shouting them at me. Waldorf came in with a draft which an American had prepared for her because he knew what America would like . . .' Her broadcast took the official line, with which she broadly agreed – 'Those who will not obey the rules can't rule,' she said, in the rather high pitch she tended to fall into when broadcasting – but, occasionally sobbing, she softened the script a little with her own feelings:

England is like a mother who sees her best beloved son place his personal affections before his public duty. The king is a monarch but he is also a man with a fallible personality, as we all have. His passions are the same as other men's. He is tempted, as they are. But in accepting the crown he accepted the symbol of the Constitution, and had promised obedience to it . . . There was no class issue but fundamentally a moral one. Mrs Simpson was rejected because of her previous history . . . not because she is not of royal blood nor because she was an American.[19]

Earlier that day she had been less emollient: walking past one of the King's most fervent admirers, Chips Channon, in the House of Commons, she observed pointedly, 'People who have been licking Mrs Simpson's boots should be shot.' These various facets of Nancy, by now in her late fifties, were captured by a fellow MP, and Christian Scientist, Victor Cazalet, who noted in his diary that she was:

Still a very remarkable woman. Lives on her nerves. Possesses every contrast possible – good, bad, full of angles, incredible insights and unbelievably bad judgement. One minute offering deepest confidence, next day saying the most insulting thing she can think of. Very religious. Terrific energy.[20]

With the new year of 1937, Nancy continued her many crusades, one of which was the Ten Year Plan for Children, of which she was both president and a driving force, together with Waldorf, Margaret Wintringham and Ray Strachey. Its basic premise was that the children of England would not grow up into good citizens unless at an early age they received a foundation of physical health and education in an environment that provided them with healthy food, milk and enough sleep. She gathered support by cajoling fellow female MPs Eleanor Rathbone, Irene Ward and Mavis Tate, and some left-wing Conservative MPs with a social conscience, such as Harold Macmillan. With one eye on politics, she also drew the party's attention to how much building work the plan would generate for the unemployed, by the rebuilding of slum schools.

In February 1937, she staged a large reception for the cause, filling the rooms of her London house with models and drawings, and with old photographs of ragged schoolchildren of the previous century in what she called the 'airless, sunless "three-deckers" in which thousands of our children are cooped up like prisoners today'. In ringing tones she portrayed children 'with bloated stomachs and cruelly-misshapen legs' whom new schools full of air and sunshine would transform into glorious specimens of manhood. As a third of all children had developed some physical defect by the age of six, her arguments rang true.

Her ceaseless activity helped temper her grief at the death of her beloved sister Phyllis, who in January 1937 had died of pneumonia, perhaps never having recovered from the death of her second son. With typical generosity, Nancy thereafter took responsibility for many aspects of the lives of Phyllis's three surviving children. Her feelings for Phyllis, as they had been for Nanaire, whom Nancy claimed still to think about every day, were intense, and when she heard of her sister's death she gave way to a rare display of emotion. It was witnessed by her loyal maid Rose, a gruff, no-nonsense Yorkshirewoman who began working for Nancy in 1928 and who was to spend the rest of her career in her service, in a formal yet frank and curiously intimate master–servant relationship, despite having to endure what often turned out to be an eighteen-hour day for seven days a week, and also despite never being offered a pay rise:

> Lady Astor screamed and prayed. The butler came to me and said, 'For God's sake, Miss Harrison, go to her ladyship.' I went and I said, 'Now, m'lady, it's no use screaming and crying. Nothing that you and I can do can bring her back.' And then she put her face next to mine and I put my arm around her. I knew then that she had the affection but couldn't give it, but that then she gave it to me. I knew it.[21]

For some time afterwards Nancy remained unusually nervy, although fellow Christian Scientists considered that her religion ought to have prevented her minding so much about her beloved sister's 'departure'.

Despite this rare display of grief, Nancy's deeper emotions still tended to be subdued for much of the time, both by her nature and by her frenetic daily life. By now her relationship with Waldorf was, although still loving, rather restrained, as it continued to be with her children, although in their case interspersed with sporadic displays of love and affection.

Although she remained tireless in her good works, not least in Plymouth, by 1937 her political career appeared to be flattening out. At the opening of Parliament, the previous November, her supporters had been hurt that the honour of replying to the King's Speech was given to Florence Horsburgh and not to Nancy, who they felt deserved it from her position of seniority as the first woman MP. On the other hand, in June 1937 she became a Companion of Honour. It was a considerable political distinction, perhaps some compensation for not being given a government job, even if that was mainly a consequence of her own waywardness. She herself claimed not to mind, maintaining that she preferred the freedom of the back benches from which to castigate ministers: 'Nobody wants me as a Cabinet Minister,' she later said, 'and they are perfectly right. I am an agitator, not an administrator, and right-thinking women do not want to be where they do not belong. We do not want to take the men's places, but only to have our place by their side.'

In March 1937, Nancy was asked by the Six Point Group, founded in 1921 by Lady Rhondda to press for changes in six areas of the law relating to women and children, in order to help rescue two women imprisoned by the Nazis. They had been expelled from Brazil for alleged subversion, and had imprudently fled to Germany, where they were arrested and charged with communist activities. Nancy deflected the group's initial idea of a delegation to the embassy, saying that it would only stiffen opposition; instead she agreed to have a private word with Ribbentrop, now ambassador. At the same time she warned them that left-wing opinion 'goes on too much about Fascism and not Russia'. She consistently maintained that one dictator was as awful as another:

> I do not want to hold any particular brief for Nazi methods against those who do not agree with their political faith, but I really do not think that the methods vary very much in any of the Dictator countries. After all, if persons holding strong anti-Communist feelings had settled in Russia, certainly in the early days of the revolution, they would have received a far from warm welcome.[22]

Nevertheless she did take up the cases of the incarcerated ladies, first with the counsellor at the German embassy and then with Ribbentrop himself, writing him 'a private and confidential letter as I know you will do anything you can to help'. He soon did so:

> My dear Lady Astor,
> . . . As far as these two women are concerned, I hear that they are both most active Communists, but they are reported to be in good health, and there is no reason whatever for any alarm about their condition.
> You will understand that for reasons of principle I cannot consent to discuss such an interior German matter with any Woman Association or any other body. But as I have the privilege and great pleasure of

knowing such a delightful personality as Lady Nancy Astor, and as you seem to take a personal interest in these two women, I shall be pleased – if you can find the time to come and see me sometime or at another occasion which we could arrange – to give you some particulars about their unpleasant activities. You will then see how unjustified the allegations, which some Women Associations have evidently placed before you, are, and how little such women deserve their and your sympathy. I think the dreadful example of Spain should have taught a definite lesson to all those who cannot or will not believe the truth of the terrible consequences of the disintegrating work of such Communist agitators . . .[23]

In return, Nancy invited the ambassador to 'lunch or dinner' on 20 April; but as that was Hitler's birthday, a day of celebration in the Third Reich, Ribbentrop pleaded previous engagements. In spite of her failure on that occasion, she continued through the year to ask the Germans for help with cases put before her by the Six Point Group.

In May 1937, Neville Chamberlain took over as Prime Minister from the easy-going Stanley Baldwin, and at once keener, more bracing air swept through the corridors of power, in particular those in the Foreign Office. In fact, as Chamberlain told Nancy, he was determined to be his own Foreign Minister. He was quite unaware that the outlook and values of the dictators were wholly beyond his experience, and he now introduced the policy of appeasement proper. For most of the following two years it matched the mood of a very large majority of the British population, who were uneasy at the belligerence of Hitler and Mussolini, and, for those who took any notice of events in the Far East, of the Japanese. The people still seemed to want agreement rather than war: 'Right or Left,' the Foreign Office believed, 'everybody was for a quiet life.' On 1 June, within a month of taking over the government, Chamberlain told Ribbentrop that one of his principal tasks would be the improvement of relations with Germany, an essential basis of appeasement.

Meanwhile the United States remained contentedly isolationist. Despite the determination of US policy-makers to stick with neutrality, however, American dislike of fascist ways and of Nazi sympathisers was vociferous. In the summer of 1937, when Nancy went over to visit Buck, who, like his two brothers, was to die of TB, she became embroiled with the newspapers, having to deny reports that on leaving New York she had said that she was 'amazed at the anti-German feeling in the United States'. In America, it seemed, a picture of Nancy as sympathetic to the Nazis was being brightly, if misleadingly, painted. She explained her views to the press:

. . . I said that, having supported the Zionist cause, I felt bound to issue a note of warning about the anti-German propaganda which was being conducted in America by the Jews (and by the Communists) and the bitter anti-German feeling being created. One would imagine from this propaganda that Germany was the only European country with a dictatorship in Europe, and alone had attacked religion . . .[24]

Waldorf, who was now feeling almost constantly ill, was frequently in Geneva on League business. He had been upset at Nancy's departure, and yearned for some private peace with his wife, 'on a yacht – or an island – or a canal boat – anywhere away from the crowd, and from friends – and even from the family'. But if not with her in the flesh, he was with her in spirit, 'which, as you so often emphasise, is what matters'.

Chamberlain had never served in the armed forces, and military and naval matters were to him distasteful. Nor had he come across anyone in Birmingham, the power centre of the Chamberlain family, who in the least resembled Hitler. Instead, the people with whom he had dealt in the past were like him – reasonable, honest and, after customary give and take, open to a deal. Chamberlain believed that the German and Italian dictators must also be reasonable men. He accepted that they might want concessions, and there were some that Britain could afford to make. He believed that they had done a great deal for their respective countries and he was sure that therefore they could not possibly desire war, which would nullify all they had accomplished. The sooner he could get to grips with them, he felt, the better. Crucially, however, as David Margesson, the Tory chief whip and close associate of the Prime Minister during the difficult times ahead, noted, he mistook a wolf for a sheep.[25] Unfortunately it seemed that the same applied to Halifax, when Foreign Secretary, and to Dawson, editor of *The Times*: they had no first-hand experience of Germany, and little comprehension of the attitudes of ruthless murderers like Goering and the other German leaders.

Sections of the press, however, now began to raise a vocal opposition to the bypassing of properly qualified ministers and senior civil servants by Chamberlain and his inner cabal, while also sensing the beginnings of public unease about too enthusiastic a pursuit of appeasement. They presented an image of decisions taken by influential groups at country house parties, behind closed doors. *The Times*, though, remained aloof, and, seemingly uncritical of Chamberlain's policy and methods, it began to be considered as almost an organ of government rather than rigorously independent, probing and questioning.

Elsewhere in the press, conspiracy theorists soon found grist for their mill. On Saturday 24 October 1937, a large house party gathered at Cliveden.

Thirty sat down to Sunday lunch: they included the newly appointed British ambassador to Berlin; Alec Cadogan, soon to take over as the top official at the Foreign Office; Geoffrey Dawson, editor of *The Times*; and Lord Lothian. The chief guests were the Foreign Secretary, Anthony Eden, and his wife. The fissures in government were apparent in the almost unceasing political talk, a normal feature of Cliveden parties, which exposed the conflicting views of the Foreign Secretary and the new ambassador to Germany, Sir Nevile Henderson:

> Politics all day and all night . . . Henderson struck me as sensible and informed without distinction. He has lived in the countries we talked about and Eden has not, and this was apparent . . . Eden thinks the Cabinet very weak and the armament programme far in arrears. On the other hand he seems to argue that we can't do business with Germany until we are armed – say in 1940. This assumes that we catch up with Germany – which we cannot, and that Hitler takes no dramatic step in the meantime, which is unlike Hitler . . .[26]

News of the weekend gathering soon found its way into the press, initially via *The Week*, which, according to its editor, often received leaks from those attending Cliveden parties – unlikely, but just possible in view of the variety of the guests, some of whom would not have agreed with the Astors' politics. Alternatively, judging by the fact that the press sometimes received accurate forecasts of the guest lists, information may have come from some member of the Cliveden staff in need of a few extra shillings. Nancy herself, vigorously defending her way of entertaining, stressed the diversity of her guests as proof that accusations of some cohesive group of people wielding undue influence were quite without foundation.

However, to others, outside and at a distance, the idea seemed plausible, and when, in its issue of 28 November, *Reynolds News*, a popular left-wing newspaper, coined the phrase 'Cliveden Set', it stuck, and quickly gained wide circulation. The allegations in *The Week*, and in the newspapers that copied its account, included the suggestion that it was at Cliveden that plans were agreed for Lord Halifax, by then second only to Chamberlain in guiding Britain's foreign policy, to go to Berlin to make a bargain with Hitler giving him a free hand in central Europe in return for Germany dropping, for a time, her demand for the return of the colonies that had been removed from her after the First World War; and further that the plan led the Foreign Secretary to threaten resignation. 'For eighteen months,' said *Reynolds News*, 'Cliveden has been the centre of friendship with Germany influence.' The house, it was said, had become 'a second Foreign Office'.

Similar suggestions had been aired by *Time and Tide*, in an article entitled 'Wire-Pullers', which claimed that there could be no more admirable instruments for the cynical Nazi realpolitik than the Christian Lord Halifax, and Lord Lothian, the equally earnest Christian Scientist with a bad conscience about the Treaty of Versailles.

He sees himself as the man who will quietly prevent the next war with Germany. His powerful allies are the Astors (*Times* and *Observer*) and Lord and Lady Londonderry . . . It is a formidable combination in itself. But this group behind the scenes controlling the papers, regarded as peculiarly responsible in English life, becomes dangerously forceful through its associates in the Cabinet.

The waywardness of many of the newspaper accounts was demonstrated when it was alleged that plots had been hatched at Cliveden at a weekend party in January 1938, a time when the Astors were in fact in America. On that trip they had visited the Senate and been invited to tea at the White House – Nancy cabling her acceptance, 'Tell President I don't take tea but if it's all he can do we will drink it. Many thanks. Nancy Astor.'

People with inbuilt prejudice against the upper classes found it easy to believe that their main concern was that communism, if unchecked, would sooner or later threaten their control of the tools of power in the democracies. From that, it was a simple step to equate antipathy to communism with sympathy for the Nazis, who were determined to prevent the spread of communism. Further, the impression that government policy is being influenced by unelected people or 'behind closed doors' almost always arouses anger. In the case of the Astors, the perception was false, but it harmed them nonetheless As Nancy's son Michael described it.

The danger of Philip Lothian's position was that although he had no actual responsibility for government policy he had the ear of men who wielded power. In Germany he, and the rest of the Cliveden 'set', helped to fortify the notion that the pro-German faction in Britain was stronger and more influential than it really was.

To that extent, it ran the risk of encouraging the Germans to take steps from which they might otherwise have refrained, and which increased the possibility of war.

Ultimately, that danger did not have the consequences feared. When, at the end of 1937, Ribbentrop sent to Hitler a long report on the prospects for Anglo-German relations, he did include Lothian, and the 'Astorgruppe', meaning, broadly, the so-called Cliveden Set, in the 'circles that want a fresh understanding with Germany and who hold that it would not basically be impossible to achieve'. By then, however, he had been disillusioned about the chances of a durable agreement between England and Germany, at least one that would leave Germany with the free hand that she wanted, initially in eastern Europe.[27] Whatever baleful influence the detractors of the Cliveden Set might accuse them of wielding, in the end Ribbentrop proved impervious to it.

The thrust of the press was not wholly fair, but without well-informed inside information it was easy for the papers to draw wrong conclusions from what they perceived from the outside, and in doing so they articulated the fears of those beginning to question the wisdom of appeasement. Halifax himself had previously assured the Germans that the British people would never consent to go to war because two German countries wanted to merge; it was a belief perhaps consonant with Halifax's mistaken impression of the German leaders – he did not for some time seem to realise that with the Nazis he was dealing with brigands rather than with gentlemen, or that the Germans by their nature might not be as averse to another war as were Englishmen.

To the press, the government's policy looked like feeding the wolves with a diet of sovereign, if minor nations:

> Give the Third Reich all it wants that does not belong to us – Austria, a bit (or all) of Czechoslovakia, a free hand in Russia, and so on (and perhaps just a little of what does belong to us and the French – Tanganyika, the Cameroons, Togoland). The Third Reich will then be busy digesting its spoil, and may, if we are lucky, find it indigestible. But it will, in any case, leave us alone through sheer gratitude, if not for any other reason.

Nancy did not press her views on the newspapers, save by writing letters of defence against allegations, and attempting to correct false impressions. She was interested in government opinion, rather than public opinion, for which she had never shown much concern, always excepting that of her constituents. She put up a less thorough defence than she might have done because she felt that the allegations against her were blatantly untrue. Her natural reaction was to shrug them off light-heartedly, as she later expressed in a nutshell, debating at the Oxford Union:

> There are three Lady Astors. The first controls the fate of politicians, and the destinies of nations, and is mythical. The second makes

glittering speeches, and debates with devastating wit, and is mythical. And the third is a born social reformer, a crusader against idealists who will not face reality, the most loyal and exacting supporter of the National Government, a hard-working public servant, a feminist, and a mother.[28]

If she had to agree with everyone who went to Cliveden, she said, she would have to be 'a lightning quick-change artist'. Nor, she maintained, was Cliveden's guest list any indication of her personal opinions: 'We do not entertain with any plan or plot. With a purpose, yes; but not a plot or a plan. I am too impulsive to plot or even to plan ahead.'[29] The latter point was certainly true, yet it would be hard to deny that Nancy did orchestrate the parties at Cliveden: she always had subliminal control over whom she asked to her house, directing seating plans at meals, raising topics of conversation, and ensuring that particular points or lines of argument were made to particular guests.

Tension rose steeply the following spring, after Germany's notorious Anschluss of Austria on 12 March 1938, a drama that finally, in Churchill's words to the Commons, confronted Europe with a programme of aggression, nicely calculated and timed, unfolding stage by stage. However, since it appeared initially to be jubilantly welcomed by the Austrians themselves, and – which was of great importance to the British government – remained within Hitler's stated aim of bringing into the German Reich only populations of German stock, what amounted to an armed invasion of a sovereign state could still be explained away without too much disturbance to the conscience of Englishmen brought up to respect fair play and the rule of law. Yet in Britain the Anschluss did finally begin to raise a more urgent and widespread questioning of government policy. Understandably, in Europe's capitals it seemed a much darker development.

The blood of the Nazis' opponents now flowed fast in Vienna, yet England remained at peace, and two weeks after the 'rape of Austria' Nancy held a house party for the Prime Minister. She invited also the government Chief Whip; the Speaker of the House of Commons; Mavis Tate; Clarence Dillon, an American financier whose business partners had from time to time held high positions in the American government; Dr Thomas Jones, and assorted friends and Astor relations – in fact a typical Cliveden gathering.

Despite the high offices occupied by some of the guests, which would no doubt have contributed to rumours of deals and influence, the atmosphere was light and informal: 'Instead of long secret corner discussions, after dinner they played Musical Chairs and The Game. Mrs Chamberlain put her heart and soul into being "Battleship" winning the National, on all fours, at moderate speed . . . We heard Myra Hess' broadcast . . .'[30] In the dining room the shuttlecock of talk and banter flew ceaselessly and noisily between Nancy – quick-witted, slightly aggressive, and not listening very much – and her guests, however important: 'There are times,' she called over to Speaker FitzRoy, 'when I get so fed up with the House that I wish I were dead.' 'There are times,' replied the Speaker, 'when I wish you were too.'

With Austria annexed to the German Reich, it seemed more than possible that Hitler would now turn his sights on Prague. That would pose an altogether different question: absorbing willing Germans into the Reich was one thing; doing so by force was another; invading land that had no bond at all with Germany was something entirely different. No one knew quite what would happen next. Addressing the news cameras, in his quiet, squeaky voice, the MP Harold Nicolson summarised the new danger confronting Europe:

We say to Herr Hitler, 'We don't mind your taking your Germans, your Sudeten Germans, and putting them in your Reich. That, we say, on the whole, is a reasonable thing to do. After all, we hadn't even heard, most of us, of Czechoslovakia above three weeks ago. But we *do* mind when you seek to achieve your aim by violence. Because that is placing violence above the law. And by trampling on Czechoslovakia you are seeking to achieve your aims by violence.

And *we* say, 'If you use force to achieve these aims, we shall meet you with force.'

And Herr Hitler says, 'But you don't really mean *that*.'

And *we* say, '*Yes we do*.'

In America too, even with the Neutrality Act firmly in place and the preference for isolationism apparently still strong, the press were closely following British reactions to the events unfolding in Europe. American suspicion of Britain was growing, because of her ardent pursuit of appeasement, and because of tales of the Cliveden Set and its supposedly malign influence, and and articles from *The Times* and what the American press usually described as 'Viscount Astor's *Observer*' were widely read and popularly believed, their opinions frequently attributed to the Astors, as owners and, it was assumed, hands-on directors of editorial policy.

The attention of Americans was further aroused when, early in May, Nancy gave a lunch party at 4, St James's Square for Chamberlain to meet a group of journalists from American and Canadian newspapers. This was to have extremely embarrassing results. The atmosphere was conducive to open talk: in the beautiful dining room, its long oval table dominated by a great silver centrepiece in the form of a silver Chinese pagoda with tinkling silver-gilt bells, the guests hung on the Prime Minister's words.

Perhaps incautiously, he allowed himself to speak freely of matters that had not yet been set before the House of Commons, revealing why, a few months earlier, Anthony Eden, the Foreign Secretary, had abruptly resigned, to be replaced by Chamberlain's closest colleague, Lord Halifax. The sensational reasons for the change, it turned out, had included not only Eden's objection to the policy of courting the Italians, of which Parliament had been told, but also a fundamental disagreement about the extent to which America should take part in European discussions, and the rejection of an offer from the White House to preside over an international conference. At the time, Nancy had welcomed Eden's departure, damning him to the press with faint praise: 'I think Mr Eden made an unwise decision, but I put it down to his being overwrought. We all hope and pray he will get a rest, because he is a brilliant young man, high-minded and loved by all.'[31]

One of the reporters asked Chamberlain if he would consider secession a solution for the Sudetenland, and the Prime Minister answered in a plain, common-sense way that he would not refuse to consider it, and also that the country's 'adjusted' borders might then be guaranteed by a Four Power Pact.

Chamberlain later recounted the matter to his sister, Ida:

. . . the Astors arranged a luncheon at which I met a dozen hardboiled toughs and I addressed them on the situation in Europe and then answered questions. So far as I can tell from what the Astors and Kennedy (the American ambassador) heard afterwards the experiment was a success. They concluded that I was sincere, reasonable and moreover had a sense of humour . . .[32]

Yet although the lunch was off the record, the dishes were hardly cleared before the hardboiled toughs were at their teleprinters, flashing out to Canada and America the Prime Minister's disclosures. 'Britain preparing land sacrifices for Reich accord', ran the headlines in New York. In England, it was rapidly concluded that the Prime Minister's remarks were a calculated indiscretion. Parliament was in uproar, as the nation's representatives, even those who had welcomed the rolling of Eden's head, realised that they had been kept in the dark. Chamberlain was not amused. To compound matters, one of the journalists had told the whole story to an MP, who had put it to Chamberlain in the House: 'That would not have mattered,' he wrote to his sister, 'if Nancy had not shouted that there was not a word of truth in it. The consequence is that she has got to make a personal statement on

Monday to explain that in fact it was all true! Heaven save me from my friends.'[33]

In a rare departure from custom, Chamberlain was forced to attend a late night debate in the Commons to explain himself to recalcitrant members demanding to know what had happened. Testy and dismissive, he failed to satisfy them.

Making a personal statement to Parliament is a rare occurrence, and is often indicative of transgression or a fall from grace. Nancy strove to come up with a convincing explanation, but failed to do so: 'I never,' she said, 'had any intention of denying that the Prime Minister had attended a luncheon at my house . . . What I did deny, and still deny, is the suggestion that what took place on this particular occasion was an interview . . .'[34]

She then reminded the House of the definition of 'interview', but failed to dissolve the hilarity that arose on all sides – except where the Prime Minister sat. It was another indication that in the increasingly serious political atmosphere, Nancy's popularity in the House was falling. Her audiences were becoming hostile even when her points were sound and logical. That was the case with her intervention in a debate on refugees from the Sudetenland. While the government was being pressed, even by its own MPs, to let in more such refugees, Nancy suggested that Russia should be asked to take its share, especially those who were communist. Members shouted that it was an 'insulting' suggestion, although both parts of her proposal were valid – Russia had admitted no refugees at all. Harold Macmillan, for whom she had in the past campaigned strenuously in his constituency, sent her a long letter of complaint, saying that the Sudeten refugees that his family had taken in were not communists, but civilised people – which entirely missed Nancy's point.

Her habits in the Commons had not changed much over the years, but in the increasingly tense atmosphere members were becoming less sympathetic towards her. Further, the severe hardship caused by the Depression rendered Labour MPs all the more virulent in their dislike of Conservatives, particularly those, like Nancy, whom they regarded as plutocrats who did not understand the troubles of ordinary people. It made no difference that much of what she said was true, even if uncomfortable: she was dismissed as unfeeling. Her problems were typified in a debate in a Commons committee about distressed areas, when her various interruptions, particularly one to the effect that hardship could not be avoided in an imperfect world, incensed the opposition and led the chairman to ask her to sit down. She then left the meeting, after which a Labour MP voiced the antipathy on his side of the House:

She comes to the House, hears nothing of the Debate, neither the opening speech nor the speeches that follow, and then tells us what she knows about the distressed areas having visited them, on her own showing, only once in four years . . . She says that she knows South Wales much better than the hon. Members who were born there and who are its chosen representatives, sent to this House to speak for them. She tells us that most of these people will never work again . . . and what is her remedy for that? She says, 'After all, it is an imperfect world; what do you expect?' . . . It is all very well for people living in highly comfortable circumstances, who have never known any trouble or anxiety, to apologise for the misery that society inflicts upon these people by saying that it is an imperfect world.[35]

To level such criticism at Nancy, a true philanthropist whose hard work in Plymouth caring for the poor, for dockworkers and their families and for naval personnel stretched far back into Edwardian days, was unjust, although a typical example of human nature; but it was by now the common reaction to much of what she said, and to her distorted image in the press.

As might be expected, the long reign of an habitually outspoken MP had fostered resentments. It perhaps explained why Waldorf had received the freedom of Plymouth in 1936, but Nancy had not. Opposition to her was increased by her unwillingness to pull her punches with opponents, constituents or otherwise, especially those she suspected of communist inclinations. When, for example, Eden's resignation spurred the council representing 30,000 Plymouth trade union members to question the fascist sympathies of 'the Astor group of politicians', she offered no soft words, instead hitting back: 'I notice that in spite of their democratic principles your members never send me resolutions of protest against the mass murder under the Russian dictatorship; I wonder at their omission . . .'

Although at this time Germany and Italy were the main political pre-occupations, Nancy remained a tireless worker for good causes – it was quite usual for her to attend three or four bazaars and public meetings in a day – and her political interventions were in many cases far-sighted, anticipating issues that became topical many years later, such as the dangers of smoking, and of driving under the influence of alcohol. She also continued to campaign for improvements in education, in conditions for working women and youths, and in prisons.

Yet it was undeniable that her stock had fallen. The impact of her being the first woman in Parliament had been absorbed, and impatience at her repetitions, as well as the stridency with which she expressed opinions and the evident lack of forethought that attended many of them, added to a certain weariness. She did not let up on her attacks on the evils of drink, and widened her arc of fire to include betting, contraceptives and smoking, urging that tobacco should be prohibitively taxed, if not banned altogether. People found her desire to improve their habits and morals increasingly irritating as, week by week, the situation in Europe added anxiety to their domestic difficulties. At the same time, the implementation of many of the improvements for which she had long campaigned seemed, paradoxically, to lessen the merit of her crusading zeal. In the increasing tension, recognition of those achievements did little to help her image.

However, as the prospects for peace began to dim, the paramount cause of her loss of people's affections stemmed from her becoming more vocal about foreign affairs, and from the public's perception of the Cliveden Set. The Astors saw that it was high time to mount a defence, and to bring the speculation to a close. Nancy wrote to the *News Chronicle* and the *Daily Herald*, and Waldorf to *The Times*, Waldorf's letter was restrained, and no doubt persuasive to the large majority of his readers:

> For years my wife and I have entertained in the country members of all parties (including Communists), members of all faiths, of all countries, and of all interests. To link our weekends with any particular clique is as absurd as is the allegation that those of us who desire to establish better relations with Germany or with Italy are pro-Nazis or pro-Fascists. Lady Astor and I are no more Fascists to-day than we were Communists a few years ago when we supported the trade agreement with the Soviet, nor do we sympathize to-day with Communism because of a desire to preserve good relationships with the Russian dictatorship . . .[36]

Nancy responded to a considerable amount of what would now be called hate mail by enclosing a copy of Waldorf's letter. But, clear and persuasive as that was, a far greater public relations effort would have been needed to dispel the widespread perception that had settled in the public mind. Nancy put similar points, in a more populist style, in an American magazine, *The Saturday Evening Post*, in an article headed, with presumably unconscious irony, 'Lady Astor Interviews Herself':

> We're deeply interested in social reforms. We're democrats in the widest sense. I'm not a Communist; I'm not a Nazi; I'm not a Fascist. I'm a passionate believer in democracy. I believe the world moves on by putting together all kinds of honest minds. The object of our parties is just that – to give people of all sorts a chance to get together and hear one another's views . . . Now I'm almost an ancient monument

but I'm still a Virginian, and still a democrat, and an ardent believer in women's rights and social reforms. Well, how on earth should such a combination as that believe in Mussolini, or Hitler, or Stalin, or in any dictator?[37]

The international problem reached a crisis in September 1938, when the Germans threatened to use force to subsume the Sudetenland into the Fatherland. The dangers were temporarily averted by the Munich Agreement, which, even with hindsight and many decades later, remains a matter of controversy. At the time, doubt and danger seemed to attend both further appeasement and also a firm stand against Germany. In any event, few people thought that England could fight and win alone, and as Thomas Inskip, then a Cabinet minister, noted, 'everything showed that the French did not want to fight, were not fit to fight, and would not fight'. The Cabinet had also been warned, by Britain's service chiefs, that 'no pressure we and the French could bring to bear, by sea, land or air, could stop Germany over-running Bohemia and inflicting a decisive defeat on Czechoslovakia'.[38]

Into this feverish atmosphere stepped Charles Lindbergh, the Minnesota farm boy who had become an American hero for his pioneering feats of aviation. During the previous month, August 1938, he had been to Russia to inspect Soviet air power. He had not been impressed. On the other hand, on a similar tour of Germany, he had been awed by the strength of the Luftwaffe. 'Germany,' he had reported, before Chamberlain left for Munich, 'now has the means of destroying London, Paris and Prague if she wishes to do so.' It was a highly inaccurate piece of forecasting, but at the time, the British authorities did not have the data with which to test it. Also potentially disquieting for Chamberlain as he prepared for his meetings with Hitler was an intercepted German telegram, addressed to Ribbentrop, containing detailed plans to unleash an air raid on London before the Munich meeting. Each hour through the night, it stated, a hundred planes would arrive over London, to devastate the city. According to President Roosevelt, the British authorities said that they had power to ward off the first two or three attacks, but not more. 'This knowledge,' said Roosevelt, 'made Chamberlain capitulate at Munich.'[39]

The Lindberghs had become good friends of Waldorf and Nancy, who had known Anne Lindbergh's father, Dwight Morrow, since he first came to Cliveden during the Great War. Unfortunately for the Astors, their association with Lindbergh was taken as further confirmation of their pro-German image. The air ace made no secret of his belief that Germany's might was overwhelming, and that war must be avoided at any cost. Nancy saw the allegations against her as yet another political intrigue.

On 26 September 1938, the fateful weekend when Hitler was due to give a speech that might decide the fate of Czechoslovakia and the peace of Europe, the Lindberghs went to Cliveden. In Berlin, swastikas fluttered high above the Sportpalast, filled to overflowing with adoring *Volk*, and the cheers of the massed crowds reverberated around the stadium as Hitler paused after each harsh crescendo. At Cliveden, a wireless was erected in the hall, and as the Führer's voice echoed across the crackling airwaves the guests became uneasy. 'Lady Astor,' wrote Anne Lindbergh, 'says that she would die for freedom, but it is not freedom we would be fighting for . . . Lord Astor argues that Germany must be stopped now, before she is any stronger . . . that England will be forced to fight sooner or later, and that if she waits and backs down further she will have no friends left when the day comes for her to fight.[40]

The Munich settlement injected great ill-feeling between Churchill's small band of supporters and the vast majority who still followed Chamberlain. The government line taken by both *The Times* and the *Observer* greatly added to the frustration of those who longed for Germany to be stopped in her tracks. *The Times*'s owner, John Astor, appeared to think that as the proprietor, and an MP, he should not interfere with his newspaper, and that anyway its opinions broadly represented the view of both government and public. Even so, John Walter, the minority shareholder, lodged a formal protest at the policy of the editor, Geoffrey Dawson. The *Observer*'s editor, J.L. Garvin, like Dawson a long-standing habitué of Cliveden, would continue to write staunchly pro-Chamberlain centre-page articles, very much in accordance with the ideas of Waldorf, the paper's owner, until, in March 1939, Waldorf finally changed his view. Both newspapers infuriated their opponents. While London awaited news from the Munich talks, Garvin went to a dining club in the Savoy Hotel:

> As the tension grew, the atmosphere in the room became increasingly acrimonious. The editor of The Observer, J.L. Garvin . . . was forced to defend himself; he had, he pointed out, written a 'stiff article' in the previous Sunday's paper. 'What is the use of that,' asked Bob Boothby, 'after forty flabby ones?' Garvin stormed out of the room . . .[41]

However much Waldorf and John Astor refrained in practice from influencing their newspapers, the public did not give them the benefit of the doubt, and the belief that the family wielded undue power was fuelled by their close relations with the editors of their papers. Moreover, it was noted with some suspicion that while Waldorf sat in the House of Lords, not only were Nancy and John Astor both in the Commons, but Bill Astor was MP for East Fulham, Lord Willoughby de Eresby, Wissie's husband, was MP for Rutland and Stamford, and Ronald Tree, married to Nancy's niece, Lizzie's daughter, was MP for Harborough. Further, Bill Astor, after only one year in the Commons, had been appointed parliamentary private secretary to Samuel Hoare, one of Chamberlain's closest associates.

Nancy was sure – as, for a few months more, was most of the country – that Chamberlain had triumphed at Munich, his vision and personality saving the day. She was vociferous in his support in the tense debate in the Commons early in October, and when Churchill forced reality before an angry House, pointing out 'what everybody would like to ignore but which must nevertheless be stated, namely, that we have sustained a total and unmitigated defeat, and that France has suffered even more than we have', she shouted, 'Nonsense.' Churchill turned back to the Speaker:

> When the noble Lady cries 'Nonsense' she could not have heard the Chancellor of the Exchequer admit in his illuminating and comprehensive speech just now that Herr Hitler has gained in this particular leap forward in substance all he set out to gain . . . This is only the first sip, the first foretaste of a bitter cup which will be proffered to us year by year unless, by a supreme recovery of moral health, we rise again . . .[42]

Two months later, the Foreign Secretary gave the Cabinet a memorandum from Bill Astor, who had travelled around Germany and Czechoslovakia in the aftermath of Munich. His report would have been music to Mr Chamberlain's ears, as it indicated that the German people wished fervently for peace: 'The atmosphere of Berlin,' it began, 'is not of rejoicing in a glorious bloodless victory but of relief at the escape from an overwhelming disaster.' However, the report also confirmed Chamberlain in his belated acceptance of the need for rearmament, and that Britain needed time to catch up: 'Everything I saw,' Bill Astor concluded, 'confirmed the view that we must proceed with our armament with maximum possible speed and extent . . . Only by our being formidable will the moderates be able to produce results within the German framework.'[43]

Illusions about Hitler were all but shattered at dawn on 15 March 1939, as the German army crossed the Czech frontier and advanced on Prague, invading the parts of Czechoslovakia that had escaped being ceded at Munich. Whereupon the British government convinced itself that as the country it had guaranteed now no longer existed, it could not take up arms in its defence. Hindsight rose to a premium, and what so few had understood or accepted suddenly seemed after all to be the logical conclusion of 1919: Germany rising anew, and her armies descending once more, uninvited, unstoppable, onto other people's territory. An American critic of the Astors' circle wrote

> I felt strongly that their theories were founded on a false estimate of the Gallic character, which was rotten and undependable when compared with the honest intentions of the trustworthy German. Even in the winter of 1938–9, when Lady Astor came to Florida, she was preaching the surrender of Sudetenland to Germany and assuring her hearers that Hitler would never encroach on the liberties of the Czechs. It is curious how personal prejudice can blind even intelligent people to the most evident conclusions.[44]

With the march into Prague, however, Nancy did finally change her mind, as did others of the most convinced appeasers. The new mood was apparent at a large lunch party she gave at 4, St James's the day after the German invasion of Czechoslovakia:

> Garvin and other established appeasers had made a *volte face* and were demanding that we should at once declare war on Germany. The guest of honour was Maisky, the Soviet Ambassador. As he left the room after lunch Lady Astor said, 'Of course I hate the Russians but I've got to be nice to that little man because he may become our ally in the war.'

Nancy and Waldorf began to campaign for Churchill's inclusion in the government, on the grounds that it would act as a deterrent to Germany. The looming danger also increased their conviction, along with that of Philip Lothian and the Round Tablers, and fortunately, in time, of powerful men in Washington, that the preservation of freedom would soon require an Atlantic alliance. For Nancy's reputation, however, the damage had been done: her previous stance was fixed in the public's mind – and in that of many Germans: 'Not only Lady Astor's Cliveden Set,' recalled one Nazi diplomat, 'but also Chamberlain and Geoffrey Dawson . . . showed complete sympathy for the German standpoint and nothing but utter contempt for Benes and his clique . . .'[45]

Lothian was about to play a leading part in working towards that alliance. To the surprise of many, in August 1938 he had been offered the post of British ambassador in Washington. A year later he took up his duties, beginning the job of drawing the United States out of its haven of neutrality. It seemed a difficult if not impossible task: a nation peopled by so many who had left Europe for a new world did not see why it should again become involved with the old one.

On 2 January 1939, Lothian had had an interview with President Roosevelt, his first for more than two years. On the surface, the exchanges seemed cordial enough. Lothian, building on a theme he had expressed to Ambassador Kennedy in London, maintained that 'as a result of Munich the real questions that the United States had to face were the possibilities which would confront it if the British Empire were to disappear'.

As regards the future, I said that I thought that the centre of gravity of the democratic world was now bound to pass from England to the United States, as Cecil Rhodes had foretold . . . I added that I thought that in the long run the United States would be driven to choose between two alternatives, of retiring in isolation to North America, and underpinning in its own way the command of the seas which hitherto has been maintained by Great Britain alone.[46]

Roosevelt felt that Lothian was an admirable choice as ambassador, but he did not like what he heard at that initial meeting. His former history tutor at Harvard had recently forwarded to him a letter from the Regius Professor of History at Cambridge, explaining away Chamberlain's reluctance to fight for Czechoslovakia but stating that England would nevertheless 'die in the last ditch' if necessary. Roosevelt, however, whether or not he attached much importance to the author's status, read into his letter the implication that Britain would not stand firm without prior assurances of assistance from the United States. Lothian's attitude had confirmed Roosevelt's view, as he wrote to an old associate:

I wish the British would stop this 'we who are about to die, salute thee' attitude. Lord Lothian was here the other day and . . . went on to say that the British for a thousand years had been the guardians of Anglo-Saxon civilisation – that the sceptre or the sword or something like that had dropped from their palsied fingers – that the USA must snatch it up – that FDR alone could save the world – etc., etc.

I got mad clear through and told him that just so long as he or Britishers like him took the attitude of complete despair, the British would not be worth saving anyway.

What the British need today is a good stiff grog, inducing not only the desire to save civilisation but the continued belief that they can do it . . .[47]

The President's letter found its way to various Foreign Office officials opposed to appeasement, and also to the Foreign Secretary, Lord Halifax. Whether or not Halifax resorted to a good stiff grog on reading it, Lothian, for his part, was soon to replace his initial line of argument with an altogether more robust and persuasive one.

Later that year, in August, while peace still, just, endured, the Astors went up to Scotland as usual, but without Nancy, who chose to go to Rest Harrow with Bobbie. Waldorf was left feeling rather lonely, but within weeks they would be together in Plymouth. The build-up to war had done great damage to the Astors' name in Britain – but, as they were about to prove, it was not irreversible. Nancy and Waldorf were soon to embark on their finest hour.

TEN

War on Two Fronts

War between Britain and Germany began at 11 a.m. on 3 September 1939, forty-eight hours too late for England's honour, according to a House of Commons outraged at the government's delay at fulfilling its pledge to Poland. The Astor family was ready to do its bit: Bill, while remaining an MP, had joined the Royal Naval Volunteer Reserve and had been posted as an intelligence officer to Middle East Command, in Cairo; Michael was in the Territorial Army, as was Wissie's husband; and Jakie had joined the Household Cavalry. David had just started working at *The Times*, but would soon join the Royal Marines. Bobbie found war work with a barrage-balloon detachment, his various riding injuries preventing him from being considered for service overseas; 'But they'll be bound to take him later,' Nancy said, 'when they need people . . .'

The war touched Cliveden from the outset, as a crowd of evacuees arrived from London, spilling into the beautiful house and its tranquil grounds, before being housed on various parts of the estate. Soon the great tapestries would be taken down and the gardens become unkempt, although the family would entertain in parts of the house, maintaining them in their pre-war condition. But for Waldorf and Nancy there was a more urgent problem even than preparing Cliveden for war. For the Germans, intent on destroying the means of protecting Britain's Atlantic supply line, an obvious target was Plymouth, with the naval base at Devonport, and its dockyards and warships. Waldorf and Nancy at once went down and established themselves in Elliot Terrace. Steel barrage-balloon cables were already moored in front of the house, which was in the middle of a danger zone, standing directly between the naval base and the Mount Batten airfield.

A brief semblance of normality was restored to Cliveden when the family gathered there for Christmas 1939. Lee and the footmen, never obtrusive, were always at hand, and the house was made ready by housemaids in brown alpaca uniforms, organdie aprons, high collars, and bandeau caps tied with velvet ribbon. Even then there was an atmosphere of comfort and plenty: bright boxes piled on chairs and tables, glass birds in little tin cages, evergreens wound around banisters, a faint aroma from little pots of Nancy's favourite humea. The famous dressing-up box was opened, and the customary games were played: murder, sardines, musical chairs, and charades. The latter included family favourites such as Bobbie preaching a sermon, and Nancy mimicking servicewomen on parade, or parodying a racing tout in an ill-fitting coat, or a horsey English lady inveighing against 'Emmericans' in the hunting field. She also had a memorable imitation of Americans arriving for lunch at Cliveden: 'Lady Astor, this is a *real* pleasure . . .' Such fun and games showed, as perceptively described by her niece, Joyce Grenfell, herself a successful actress, that Nancy's gift was not so much for her wit as for 'more accurately, her comedy, which is different'. In fact the type of humour in which Nancy particularly excelled, and which most amused her guests, was mimicry, at which she was a past master.

Yet inevitably, with the country at war, the underlying atmosphere at Cliveden was slightly strained. The uniforms of Nancy's sons evoked memories of friends long dead in Flanders fields, and were a reminder of the chance of new disasters, especially with Jakie and Michael exposed to potentially dangerous operations with the desert patrol that became known as Phantom, a special unit formed to provide operations information about forward patrols, and sending out patrols itself in support of airborne troops and the Special Air Service. 'An' I've got four sons in the fightin' Services,' Nancy would sometimes sigh, as the war proceeded and the casualty lists lengthened.

A degree of restraint had also been created by the economy drive that Waldorf had instituted after the summer's emergency Budget had increased income tax by two-thirds. Gardeners and some of the servants had been laid off, and for a time Waldorf again considered closing the house entirely. In the end he decided, just as twenty-five years earlier, to offer the house and grounds to the Canadian government, for use as a hospital.

In the early part of the war, Nancy did manage to arrange occasional weekend parties, when thoughts of fighting and of the threat of invasion were put briefly to one side. There were still plenty of servants, although after a time they were mostly maids, taking the place of the men who had been called up. Guests would drive up to the front steps, park and ring the bell; in due course the door would be opened by the imposing but always friendly Lee, still with a slight Shropshire accent, addressing people with the same courtesy, whether they were very grand or of no particular importance. Soon Nancy would arrive – sweater, silk shirt, tweed skirt, sensible shoes – animated, her lively face always in movement, at once imposing her presence.

The meals were delicious despite wartime shortages, much of the food going straight from the gardens to the kitchen. At first the atmosphere was rather intimidating, especially for her sons' friends. The proceedings were peppered by Nancy's habit of firing questions down the dining table, suddenly exposing some young guest to everyone's gaze, whether or not she had been paying attention to the conversation: 'What do *you* think of that, Elizabeth?' she would call out. 'C'mon, let's hear your views.' People occasionally detected an element of bullying: she had a sharp eye, and even when there were a large number of guests around the table, she appeared to miss nothing. She certainly had a knack of exposing weakness, and paid little thought to the awe that some of her children's young friends might feel among Cliveden's important guests: on one occasion, a shy twenty-year-old girl was placed at lunch between the American ambassador and Brendan Bracken, the Minister of Information, to neither of whom, as lunch proceeded, had she been able to think of much to say. Suddenly Nancy's voice rang down the table: 'Jean, you have been put there to entertain the people on either side of you, and so far you haven't said a word.' Tears flowing, the girl rose from the table and left the room.[1] But equally suddenly some thought or remark would start the hostess on another topic, which she would take up as though nothing had happened.

Occasionally there were tears below stairs too, as wartime conditions increased the strain of getting things right. Lee, long faithful, had to bear the weight. In addition to having to tackle Nancy's habit of making last-minute arrangements, and changing existing ones, he was pressed into acting as cellarer to her sons. They would arrive for a weekend surreptitiously bringing bottles of various shapes and sizes for their own use and that of their guests. Lee had to hide them away where Nancy would not find them, and then cope with repeated requests by the boys to produce them. Eventually even the habitually unperturbable butler felt he had had enough. Nancy was talking to one of her guests in the hall, amid the general coming and going, when Lee came up to her and murmured, 'Excuse me, m'lady, I'm sorry to say this, but I can't go on any more. I must go.' Nancy looked at him calmly and with no apparent surprise on her face, and quietly replied, 'You goin', Lee? In that case, tell me where, as I'm comin' with you.' Lee withdrew, but was later persuaded to stay on. 'What can you do when someone says a thing like that?' he recalled. 'She was easier in her behaviour towards me for quite a while.'[2]

It was partly Nancy's unpredictability that was disconcerting, as she would just as readily put her children's friends at ease and bring them out of themselves. She also liked to join in their games of tennis, at which she remained remarkably successful: she had an effective underhand serve, and many opponents even thirty or forty years younger found it hard to get a shot past her. Her youngest sons, Michael and Jakie, added to the general liveliness; they seemed to be very close, and were funny together, complementing each other's humour. After dinner the younger guests would often drive down to nearby Bray, where the Café de Paris had become famous for its bands and dancing.

Waldorf, on the other hand, seemed slightly forbidding: tall, good-looking and rather florid, and often clearly in pain from rheumatism and a slight difficulty with breathing. Conversation with him was frequently heavy going, and although he was impeccably polite, he could make young guests nervous. His knowledge of politics was of course immense, but he didn't like casual political talk, especially with those whom he thought probably did not know very much. He liked to have a definite subject of conversation: for example, his horses, which he was usually very ready to discuss. He would be on hand at formal moments, and when it was appropriate, but would then slip off quietly to his study.

It sometimes occurred to guests that Waldorf and Nancy did not have much conversation with each other. Like many couples who have been together for years, they seemed to take each other's presence for granted, not needing much particular comment or recognition. Yet they gave the impression of being very great friends: Nancy would often fondly quote him, or say that 'Waldorf thinks such-and-such'; or 'Waldorf says that . . .'

Far more crucial than the time he spent making arrangements for his stud and his model farm, Waldorf now had a large amount of work to do in Plymouth. In August 1939 he had been sounded out about becoming Lord Mayor, an office created as a result of the town being granted city status in 1928. At first he demurred, telling Nancy that he could not combine it with his work as chairman of the Royal Institute of International Affairs, nor with helping her at the general election that was expected in 1940. However, with the coming of war in September he agreed to the suggestion, as 'a war duty': it was certainly not an honorary role, and would require arduous and continuous attention, as a member of the city's emergency committee. His stipulation was that the invitation must come from all parties.

One noisy sign of wartime was the auto-bike that Nancy acquired. Describing it, accurately in Waldorf's view, as 'my latest indiscretion', she adopted it for driving speedily between Cliveden and London, without too much use of her petrol ration. In acquiring it she was following the lead of T.E. Lawrence, who some years previously had been riding one in Plymouth when from a passing car 'a peahen voice screamed "Aircraftman"', and

Nancy flagged him down. After that, ever keen to have a go, she had occasionally ridden on his Brough machine, heedless of Waldorf's disapproval. So besides being the first woman MP, she became, probably, the first woman MP to ride to work on a motorbike. Even driving a car she was not as calm or patient as some drivers, and it was as well that she was usually driven by a chauffeur. A friend recalled an incident when her erratic driving near Maidenhead resulted in a vigilant policeman stepping into her path with his hand up to stop her. She just managed to halt in time, but not before the policeman had been forced to jump sharply to one side. 'Didn't you see my hand up?' he angrily enquired. 'If you'd known who was drivin',' Nancy replied, 'you'd have put both hands up.' So it may have been a relief to other road users, at least in the vicinity of Cliveden, where her disregard of the rules of the road also caused occasional upset among drivers of hospital vans, that the increased need for her presence in Plymouth led her reluctantly to put the machine aside.

Her tireless vitality was perfectly suited to the exigencies of war, and almost as soon as she returned to Plymouth she immersed herself in the myriad requirements of preparing the city for the demands it might have to face. Her whirlwind presence was felt at once, in the council chamber, in committee rooms and in the streets, as the city readied itself for action: coping with the total blackout – to be imposed for the next five years – and implementing the rationing of petrol, gas and electricity, all to be done while disturbing the town's business as little as possible.

An early problem was the arrival of some 20,000 evacuees from London. Despite requests from Waldorf and Nancy, the government had not declared Plymouth to be an official evacuation area, unsafe for children, so the Plymouth authorities were left with the job of finding homes for the sudden influx. As soon as she realised what was needed, Nancy began to telephone around the county, asking people she knew to find space. She also asked friends in America to help, an appeal that was in due course met by offers through the Anglo-American Relief Fund.

As the war developed, rationing, high taxes and the Blitz were to kill off social activity, despite the unexpectedly tranquil Phoney War that lasted through the winter and into the spring of 1940. Up and down the country the entertainments of peacetime had to go, and in Plymouth, one by one, they fell into abeyance: fireworks plans abandoned, sports fixtures suspended, and doubt settling over the future of Plymouth Argyle football club.

With a distant echo of 1914, when the fighting had been widely expected to be 'over by Christmas', Nancy made a speech at Virginia House explaining why the war would not last long, but warning of the perils that might in the meantime befall unwary citizens: in particular, their moral tone must not slip. One of her first wartime interventions in Parliament was to appeal for a cut in licensing hours and a tightening of drink regulations, which she followed up with a request for the return of the Liquor Control Board and the rationing of barley for brewers – convinced that others could make better use of it. She also called for the protection of youth by means of a 'girl curfew', which complemented her ongoing objection to 'immorality' in parks, make-up – what she called 'paint' – and what she saw in the same light as abbreviated skirts. She also suggested placing restrictions on football pools companies, and described Parliament's decision not to allow theatres to open on Sundays as 'a direct answer to prayer'. 'I have never,' she maintained, 'found that people mind being preached to if you care enough about them.'

Meanwhile she was alert to the mischievous use of loopholes in the mass of new regulations that began to bind Britain in wartime red tape. Although she was courting unpopularity with the public, who were already chafing under irksome restrictions, her intuition – widely seen as an itch to interfere – was better than her detractors would admit. With the best intentions the government proposed introducing financial allowances not just for the wives of servicemen, but for ladies who lived with them even if unmarried, and even if their co-habitation was for a short time only. Nancy objected that the proposals were not conducive to decent married life, claiming that 'We shall find all sorts of people getting hold of these young men and living with them for six months, and then demanding the marriage allowance . . . The proposal shocks one profoundly, it is not in accord with our way of life.' She also aired her views on the matter in a Commons debate on Army Estimates. It was carrying pity too far, she added, and would weaken the moral fibre of young men and women. She also claimed that evacuated women were already asking for a lot of comforts that they did not have in their own homes. Despite cries of dissent in the Commons, her warnings that the government's proposal would open the door to what would today be called benefit fraud carried the ring of truth.

For the Plymouth naval community, the earliest war news had been of a disaster, when the aircraft carrier HMS *Courageous*, manned by local men, was torpedoed with great loss of life. Three months later, at the end of 1939, the same citizens took especial pride in the navy's famous victory at the Battle of the River Plate. In January 1940, the cruiser *Ajax*, with a Plymouth crew, completed the long voyage back from Montevideo. The ship's mainmast had been sliced in two by a German shell, and she was battered and torn, but when the bands struck up 'Home Sweet Home', jubilation erupted among the crowds lining the quayside. 'We are all very excited and pleased about the naval news today,' Nancy wrote to Pem Shaw in America, adding, 'I do hope the Republican prejudice against Roosevelt won't let it blind them to the menace of Nazi-ism and Communism in Europe.'[3]

Meanwhile, in Europe, the British armies were about to find themselves in the front line, standing between the enemy and the homeland of England itself. For a time the Germans had devoted all their strength to attacking Poland, but by early 1940 their New Order had been established, and the first German settlers had arrived to evict the Poles from their farms. The Wehrmacht was ready to deploy in the west, and at dawn on Tuesday 9 April it descended upon Denmark and Norway.

The German success was swift, and a hurriedly dispatched expedition sent by Britain to block the enemy advance met with failure. Barely a month later, Parliament, demanding explanation for the disaster, held its famous Norway Debate. It developed into a motion of confidence in Chamberlain, and an awkward, ailing, defensive Prime Minister was stung into accepting the challenge to his leadership. 'I welcome it indeed,' he cried. 'At least we shall see who is with us and who is against us, and I call on my friends to support us in the lobby to-night.'

Nancy was no longer one of the friends. For years the Prime Minister's staunch supporter, undaunted by the acrimony latterly attending his policy of appeasement, she saw that war called for a new approach, and it overrode inhibitions she might have felt from personal loyalty. She told the House:

I am one of those who criticise the Prime Minister to his face and not behind his back. Sometimes I feel it would be almost better politically to talk against Ministers behind their backs rather than just to say, 'Yes, yes' to their faces, but I cannot join that group, dead or alive . . . Our job as Members of Parliament and as citizens is to do what is disagreeable if it will help the country – no matter how disagreeable it may be . . . In war-time we should have no feelings about persons, it is principles which matter.[4]

She joined the group of Tory rebels taking the rare step of voting against their party leader. Although fewer than forty, their dramatic action reduced Chamberlain's majority to an unsustainable level, and Leopold Amery's famous plea to him, 'In the name of God, go' was swiftly answered by his resignation. On 10 May, Winston Churchill was appointed as Prime Minister of an embattled country, on its own.

When Churchill took over, he offered Waldorf a post in the Ministry of Agriculture, a position he declined partly because he did not see eye to eye with Robert Hudson, the new Agriculture Minister – though he would not have let personality issues alone deflect him from his duty. He gave more weight to his fear that his health was not robust enough for him to take on a government job as well as his new work in Plymouth. There, one of his first acts was to launch what quickly became a highly successful fund for use by the city authorities: the Lord Mayor of Plymouth's Services' Welfare and Air Raid Victims' Relief Fund. It spawned clubs for officers and men, mobile canteens, makeshift restaurants and a host of comforts that proved invaluable when the population came to endure the German Blitz.

As the pace of war quickened, Nancy began a gruelling regime of work in both London and Plymouth, travelling by overnight sleeper on uncertain and frequently delayed journeys, her train often motionless in a siding to avoid attracting the attention of German bombers overhead. Her work at Plymouth became urgent when, within a few short weeks of the British Expeditionary Force embarking for France, it was forced back to the beaches of Dunkirk, from where ships sailed to Plymouth laden with British, French and Belgian troops. There, Nancy was manifestly on hand, going round the hospital wards, cheering the wounded and exhausted troops, and raising spirits, as she had done years before in the Canadian hospital at Cliveden.

The dramatic events on the beaches of France opened her eyes to the reality of England's plight, and filled her with indignation. Until then, the spirit of resistance had been lulled by the Phoney War – by early summer only eight people in the town had volunteered as air raid shelter guardians, out of the 800 needed, and conscientious objectors working for Plymouth Council had to be threatened with the sack to induce them to take on war work.

The escape from Dunkirk lit the fire of resistance. While France's new government in Vichy was sending hundreds of aeroplanes to Germany and protesting about the British blockade, Nancy cabled to America telling Lothian that she was willing to speak from one end of America to the other if there was anything she could do to prevent America sending food to occupied Europe. With David Bruce, a diplomat at the US embassy in London, she set about directing propaganda at America, broadcasting to the States that there was 'not a day to lose'.

At the beginning of June 1940, she wrote to Pem Shaw in America:

Things are not easy. It would be futile to say that they are, but our spirits and our heads are high. We know that we are fighting for our principles, and because this is a moral war we cannot lose. I believe that the rescue of the BEF is prophetic . . . by the grace of God they are nearly all back again . . . It is no use treating the Germans as though they thought or lived on the same plane as we do, they just don't and that is all there is to it. You send us planes and ammunition and we will give them their own medicine to your hearts' content . . .[5]

Pale-eyed, plausible von Ribbentrop had receded over the horizon.

In the Cliveden hospital there were soon 250 patients, while in the main house Nancy entertained Americans and others whom she thought might, each in their own way, help the war. With an eye on the wounded Canadians, she invited Billy Butlin to stay, describing him as 'nice, with a young wife from Devonshire'. Butlin, who had previously lived in Canada and had been a bugler in the Canadian army, entertained the soldiers by setting up a 'holiday camp' in the Cliveden grounds for a fortnight.[6] Even in wartime, Nancy, it seemed, was irrepressible: on one occasion the venerable Field Marshal Wavell came to lunch, and afterwards Nancy took him into the garden; suddenly she raced off through the box hedges that crossed the great lawn, hurdling each one with sprightly verve. The field marshal gamely trundled along in her wake, as best he could.

'Cliveden looks unbelievably beautiful today in the sunshine,' Nancy wrote, during the clear, hot summer of 1940. 'One dare not think of this lovely land being invaded by barbarous hordes.' Rest Harrow, in the expected path of the invader, was closed for the duration, looked after by a gardener when he was not on duty with a nearby searchlight battery. Wire, mines, and crocodile pipes filled with oil, ready to set the sea alight if the Germans arrived, now filled the beach where only a year earlier the children of Prince and Princess Bismarck, friends of Nancy, who were serving at the German embassy in London, had played in the sand, little swastikas emblazoned on their swimming clothes.

It was not long before the violence of war had a direct impact on the Astors. On the same day that a bomb landed on 4, St James's Square, partly burning it out, Bobbie was seriously injured when a bomb fell on a pub at Wrotham, where, he told Nancy, he was buying cigarettes. He was out of danger a month later, but with injuries that kept him on his back for some time.

It would soon be Nancy's turn to feel the heat of war herself, but in the meantime she took especial pleasure from the crowning success of the career of her closest friend, Philip Lothian. At the end of September 1940, there appeared on the Plymouth horizon the heartening sight of American warships. They were old, four-funnel vessels, greased and laid up for twenty years, but they had now been made ready once more, a vital addition to Britain's fleet. Manned by British crews, they had sailed from Canada, part of the fifty old warships in the 'destroyers for bases' deal that Lothian had negotiated with the American government, persuading Roosevelt that Britain's need, and perhaps that of America also, was now worth the risk of alienating American public opinion, even in an election year.

Nancy had not seen Lothian since he left for Washington, but in the autumn he returned briefly to England, and in October joined a party at Cliveden – a reunion with his old friends Dawson, Brand and Lionel Curtis, who had remained close since their empire-building days in Lord Milner's Kindergarten, forty years earlier. A mere two months later Lothian was dead, gripped by an infection that could have been treated had his Christian Science beliefs not stopped him from calling in medical help. For Nancy, it was a deep and painful loss.

By that time, the war was gathering pace. On the day the American destroyers reached Plymouth, the city suffered its hundredth alert. As ominous as the sirens were, for every raid there had been many false alarms, and the apparent ability of the people of Plymouth to carry on more or less regardless had lulled the authorities into a false sense of security. After eighteen months of war, the city authorities had still not put in place the air raid precautions, or measures to cope with the results of raids, necessary for the proper protection of the city should a major attack develop; and with Plymouth next to the huge Devonport naval base, that was sooner or later likely to happen.

It was on 20 March 1941, the day the city was host to the King and Queen, that the first heavy raid finally came. All seemed relatively peaceful when the royal train arrived. Lined up to greet it were the full complement of civic dignitaries, headed by Waldorf and Nancy, as Lord Mayor and Lady Mayoress; with them were numerous senior naval officers, and also Robert Menzies, Prime Minister of Australia, who was staying with the Astors for a few days' break in a visit to England. The streets were filled with crowds cheering and waving Union Jacks as the party toured the city. At the Virginia House Settlement, the social and welfare centre the Astors had established in 1925, the King, dressed in admiral's uniform, sat between Nancy and the Queen as a crowd of mothers sang 'All the Nice Girls Love a Sailor', and after tea with the Astors the royal couple returned to their train.

As the party reached the station the air raid sirens sounded. No one was quite sure what to do, but after some indecisive discussion the railway authorities urged that any further delay in sending out the train would cause dangerous confusion to the railway schedule at one of its busiest times, and so it set off.

A bare two hours after the royal train had departed, the sirens sounded again. This time they were in earnest. Just after dusk, a hundred enemy aircraft, largely untouched by fire from the anti-aircraft batteries, dropped thousands of incendiaries, raising fears that further waves of bombers would soon follow, their targets by then ablaze. As the raiders turned and flew back towards the sea, showers of fire bombs landed like hail on the rooftops of the city below, the sound of their patter mixed with the occasional louder thump of high-explosive bombs. Fires began to burn, and soon the whole city centre was engulfed in a roaring blaze, the air sucked from the streets, the night sky illuminated by great flames shooting high into the darkness.

Entire streets were set alight, the searing glow sporadically made whiter by flashes of terrific violence. Churches, cinemas, warehouses, commercial buildings and shops collapsed, throwing out timber, bricks and shards of red-hot steel. One bomb hit the maternity ward of the City Hospital, obliterating nurses, mothers and babies alike. The incessant bombardment continued beyond midnight. One by one the famous, long-loved city sights turned to cinders: Spooner's store at St Andrew's Cross was the first, followed by the Royal Hotel at Derry's Clock, destroyed within minutes as flames poured through its roof and windows. Post office, county court, landmarks and household names were all consumed in a night, and by dawn were nothing but heaps of smouldering rubble.[7]

There was to be little respite: the next night brought an attack of equal intensity, when a further twenty to thirty thousand fire and high-explosive bombs rained down upon the city: 'Buildings seemed to burst into flames much as one lights a gas mantle. Fire ran down the walls of the Guildhall, swept over pavements, licked and curled round doors and windows.' For three hours an inferno raged, until dawn revealed the havoc wrought to the shopping area in the centre of the city. In one street not a single building remained standing, reminding old soldiers of war-scarred Ypres; corpses and wounded lay on the ground, across pavements, or buried under debris, where once there had been a house but now was only a heap of stone and timber. In some places all that was left was an empty space, with nothing human remaining that could be collected for burial.

On the morning of 23 March, Nancy received a telegram from the Queen:

Since early yesterday morning when I first heard of the savage attack on dear Plymouth, I have been thinking of you all without ceasing . . . I know how you love the people and how much you have striven to better their lives in Plymouth, and my sympathy is very deep and sincere. I long to hear how Virginia House fared, also the Club and Toc H, as I fear they were in the shopping centre. Oh, curse the Germans. With love and thanks for your devoted service to humanity.[8]

As an exhausted city observed the National Day of Prayer, in many churches congregations overflowed into graveyards and adjoining streets; others, however, were empty, burned to a blackened shell or in danger of imminent collapse.

How rapidly the sunshine and cheers of the royal visit had turned to ash was described ten days later when Nancy broadcast to America:

On March 21, Plymouth had a gala day, the second gala day since this ghastly war began. The first was when the *Exeter* returned from the Battle of the River Plate, when the bells of St Andrew's Church rang just as they did over 300 years ago to summon the townsfolk to welcome Drake home after one of his famous voyages – voyages which made the Atlantic Ocean an English-speaking pond; and I pray God it will always be one.

This second gala day was the first visit of the King and Queen to Plymouth . . . I believe you in America realise what the unfaltering courage and goodness of the King and Queen means to us over here at this time . . . Before leaving that evening the Queen, looking over Plymouth Harbour, remarked how peaceful and beautiful it was, and that she would like to gaze on it for hours. Three hours after their Majesties had left, Hitler's New Order had arrived . . .[9]

She also broadcast a message to the people of Plymouth: '. . . Today Plymouth knows the meaning of total war. Mercifully we have suffered only half of what Hitler's other victims have suffered. At least we have not been driven out of our country. Our sailors, soldiers and airmen will see that we never are.'[10]

Throughout March and April the raids continued intermittently, unpredictably, and with great ferocity. Sometimes there was no warning, but only sudden deafening explosions that plunged the city's life into confusion. Gas and electricity failed, leaving only candlelight; water was polluted, so that every drop had to be boiled before drinking, and heat found to do so. Water gushed into the streets from smashed wells, pipes and sewers. Exposed to wind, rain and the sometimes freezing March temperatures, great numbers of people were reduced to abject misery, with no hope or knowledge of when, or if, it might all end.

Yet in those grimy, dreadful days, amid the wounds, the pain, the burst sewers and the blackout, among the rats, the bodies and the crackling of burning houses, there were occasional smiles to release the tension. On one occasion Nancy took with her on her daily tour a visiting admiral. Sure that it would cheer people up to see a little glamour, she instructed him to put on his finest uniform. She herself also dressed up, with beautiful coat and a full complement of pearls, and thus adorned, with a young officer in attendance, they walked through the rubble-strewn streets. After a time they noticed a side alley that seemed quite untouched by the raids. Nancy went up to the end house and banged on its faded green front door. After a moment a net curtain twitched at the upper window, disclosing the face of a small girl; she looked down upon Nancy, the gorgeously dressed admiral and the young naval lieutenant, and then withdrew. A few moments later she was back, and, raising the window, called down, 'Mam says, if 'tis a sailor, 'e's to put five shillin' in the box by th' door and 'er'll see 'im directly.' After a moment's stunned silence, all three below dissolved in laughter.

The Astors proved adept at organising relief, as Waldorf's calm, methodical management matched Nancy's inspirational zeal. Somehow they conjured up water and hot meals, and found housing for the homeless. Even when the warnings had sounded, they both walked calmly out into the city, with Nancy visiting shelter after shelter: 'Breezy, noisy . . . banging people on the backs and making jokes. The people themselves stoic, sometimes resentful of her but generally affectionately tolerant.'[11] Long afterwards, people would remember the extraordinary sight of her cavorting across the floor to try to cheer up children crammed into airless shelters or on mattresses laid out in schoolrooms: 'Look, children,' she would say, 'I bet you can't do this'; then, in her well-cut clothes, clasping bag and umbrella, she would somersault and cartwheel. 'Oh my,' said the mothers, looking up, astonished, as the children clapped their hands. 'Hark at Lady *Astor*! Well I never . . . My dear soul . . . did you ever . . . *look* at 'er. Oh my!'

By dint of pressure, persuasion and cajoling of the civic establishment, friends and contacts in America, and government ministries, Waldorf, with his authority as Lord Mayor, and Nancy, as MP, managed to bring some order to the chaos. No one knew how long the Blitz would last, or how intense it might become. The future was wholly obscure. Forecasting seemed hopeless even two and a half years later: then, Waldorf had just finalised a report for the government showing that the accumulated destruction would take eighteen months to put right; that night another heavy raid took place, destroying a further three thousand homes.

An operations room was established below the town hall, with telephones, wall maps, secretaries, officials and messengers, each with a task to fulfil as bombs fell on the city above. Thirty food depots were set up, in schools, halls, and any buildings untouched and large enough to be of use. School teachers were recruited as cooks, and mobile canteens were sent down from London – the original 'meals on wheels' – their cost found largely by the

British War Relief Fund of America and other charities to which Nancy had described Plymouth's fate. Gradually, food parcels, christened 'Bundles for Britain', began to arrive from the United States and Canada, sent for those without a roof or walls to their homes.

Buildings burning like matchboxes with people trapped inside, and other harrowing sights, drove hundreds from the city, trekking into the country-side, sheltering in barns and outhouses, or randomly knocking on doors, having nowhere to go but determined not to be caught in the raids. It became urgent to find homes for the dispossessed, and after the first few nights of bombing Nancy tirelessly set about trying to house children away from the danger area. Far more needed to be done than could be achieved without more help, and an obvious solution was for the government to register Plymouth as an evacuation area, facilitating the large-scale removal of chil-dren from the Germans' target zone.

At length, partly as a result of Nancy's urgent pressure, Plymouth was declared an evacuation area, and arrangements were at once set in hand for evacuation and billeting. Soon, through a combination of death and evacu-ation, the city's population had shrunk by a quarter, and numbers continued to fall:

> Teachers must keep cheerful, although desks were empty where yesterday sat tiny children, now, alas, numbered with Hitler's victims . . . Three classes were without teachers, for they too had joined the dead. The next night fewer schools were left, and fewer pupils to use them when daylight came.[12]

It had become clear that peacetime organisations were unable to cope with the effects of the sustained heavy bombing. Plymouth had been taken by surprise. After dealing successfully with the small air raids that had taken place early in the war, the civil authorities had come to believe that their organisations could meet any emergencies that might arise in the future. It was a mistake of enormous consequence. Nancy and Waldorf laid the blame at the door of the government, particularly with its failure to arrange for adequate fire-fighting systems. They felt that their complaints were being disregarded, and so, ignoring accepted procedure, Nancy raised the matter in the columns of *The Times*, while pressing Plymouth Council also to berate the government until it responded.

Meanwhile, large undamaged buildings not used as hospitals or feeding centres were turned into rest centres, Waldorf believing that people were less frightened when they were together with others. He also disclosed a streak of genius when, searching for ways of raising devastated morale, he arranged with the council to invite military bands to play stirring music on Plymouth Hoe. At least, he hoped, it might for a brief moment help the people forget their awful predicament. Accordingly, on 6 June 1941, a notice appeared in the local press, announcing:

> Cornish Floral dancing to the music of a military band on the Hoe tomorrow night when the Lady Mayoress (Lady Astor) will be present . . . dancing will start at 7.30 p.m. and it is hoped that a number of dancing pupils in the city will give a demonstration, and the public would then be invited to take part. Next week a band will play on the Hoe every afternoon and evening, and on Wednesday the Royal Marine Band will give a concert at 3.00 in the afternoon.[13]

Word spread rapidly, and it was not long before the approach of evening would see great crowds of people streaming up to the Hoe, intent on escaping for a time the rubble-filled chaos below. Even in extreme discomfort people drew courage from music. The barrage balloons glowed in the setting sun, and on the broad expanse below, people swayed and danced in their hundreds and sometimes thousands, for an hour or so shedding their cares. Then dusk would descend, and with it reality, and the fear of deadly enemy formations speeding towards them from the coast of Europe, a mere hundred miles away.

Sometimes the bands were supplemented by a group of Welshmen who came to help out. 'Lord Astor got them to sing,' said one report. 'Their voices carried over the water, and they might well have reached Germany, to tell the Nazis of the defiance and of the endurance of this city.' On the first evening, Nancy led off the dancing with a naval rating. Morale soared: 'They knew that the raider would be over later, but this was their way of telling him to do his worst.'

As the bombing intensified, the imperative task of getting the population to work and home again in the evening became fraught with danger. The main bus depot received a direct hit, totally destroying fifty buses and damaging many more. Blitz or not, the buses had to run, through the 'mad medley of crashing, screaming, roaring; through flooded streets, over hose-pipes and all kinds of grotesque debris'. One driver was caught in a raid as he nosed one of the few remaining buses slowly through the blacked-out, cratered streets: 'We got it proper,' he said. Turning a corner, he found himself in an avenue of flames, bombs raining down upon it. 'There was fire all around us and it blistered the bus all over. There were many women aboard and they all sang, "There'll always be an England". They were great.'[14]

On its smaller scale, 3, Elliot Terrace reflected the busy activity of Cliveden, and to cope with all their work, the Astors had also occupied the house next door. Right from the start of Plymouth's Blitz the bombs landed around them as much as on the city below – flattening, among other buildings, the nearby Grand Hotel. On the first night Nancy stood outside watching the enemy aircraft bear down from the eastern horizon, in her air raid clothes of tin hat and fur coat. Just in time, she was ordered back into the house by a warden, throwing herself on the floor as the front windows were blown in. The blast force of the bombs cascading down upon the city was intense – sufficient in one case to lift a seven-ton bus on to the roof of a nearby building – but neither Nancy nor anyone else at first fully realised the power unleashed upon them.

On the first evening of the bombing the household trooped down to the basement, with Nancy, as her maid later recounted, reciting Psalm 91: 'A thousand shall fall beside thee, and ten thousand at thy right hand, but it shall not come nigh thee.' Outwardly she was calm – and inwardly too, perhaps, sustained by her trust in God: 'She seemed serene as she sat there, and quite without fear. She chatted about her childhood days in Virginia as though she was trying to put the fear out of our hearts. I occupied myself picking the bits of glass from her hair which had lodged there as the door pane smashed.' [15]

In the dark, damp, cold basement, the fear of the huddled inmates was almost palpable, as the tall old house shook with the pounding of incessant bombs. It was certainly a far cry from Nancy's childhood – September afternoons at Mirador, the hall cool and silent, shuttered from the bright afternoon; a bowl of lady apples on a corner table, and her father asleep on the horsehair sofa.

The entry of the United States into the war, following the Japanese attack on Pearl Harbor in December 1941, realised the hopes that Nancy had cherished since England had been left alone to fight, and the beliefs she had held ever since her first understanding of what the Round Table stood for. Her dislike of greater government at home had not dimmed her enthusiasm for the Round Table's concept of 'the Larger Idea', and for the future need for the world to be policed by the United States and the British Empire together. 'We are delighted,' she said, 'about America coming in, and now we must love all mankind, and try to build some sort of world police force, and understanding. But when I see the people of one nationality dislike each other it makes me realise more than ever that only by the fatherhood of God understood, and the brotherhood of man practised, can we ever hope to get peace.'

She had long hoped to go over to the States herself to campaign for

American support for the war, as she had told Lothian, and at the end of December 1940, she had written to Eleanor Roosevelt asking 'if it would perhaps do good if I came over, sometime in January perhaps, to talk to the women'. The Astors had long been acquainted with the Roosevelts, and Franklin, exactly three years younger than Nancy, had visited Cliveden in 1918, when he was thirty-six, and assistant secretary to the navy. On that occasion, with easy-going American informality, he had gone out to the garden and helped mow the lawn. 'The nicest moments of my whole trip,' he had subsequently told Nancy, 'were the ones at Cliveden, and I so wish I could have been down there again *even* at the possibility of having to make a speech at your hospital . . . however, you will probably have me on your hands again soon as I have a hunch that I shall be back again this Autumn – and I like Rebels very much . . .'[16] Then, in 1941, having received Nancy's letter, the President had replied: 'About your coming to America, you alone can be the judge of the wisdom of such a move at this time. I do not feel that Eleanor or I should ask you to make the sacrifice it would surely be to leave England in these critical days. You have so much at stake . . .'[17] It had proved wise advice, as, exactly one month later, the Blitz on Plymouth began.

Still, this did not diminish Nancy's longing to instil and encourage in Americans a desire to work as one with England, and she felt compelled to make her case directly to them, as she wrote to Pem Shaw six months after Pearl Harbor: 'I want to go from one end of the country to the other, not speaking to the English Speaking Union, but to farm hands, factory girls and everything in skirts, to urge them to get the USA and the British Empire working together, not for the sake of themselves, but for this miserable, wretched world . . .'[18]

In 1942, with their country in the war, American servicemen began using the Plymouth base. Nancy became assiduous in helping them in whatever way she could. Many Americans were guests at Elliot Terrace. Among them was a journalist, Ben Robertson, who recorded his impressions of England in her darkest year, when she was fighting alone. He arrived in Plymouth in March 1941, just as the Blitz began, and recalled an evening when Nancy chatted to him alone after dinner. She called him 'Brother' – 'she calls everyone "Brother"', he noted – and seemed to him very different from the Nancy Astor who appeared in public, confirming his opinion that she put on an act if there were more than three people to listen to her. When she took him down to inspect the bomb-scarred docks, he noticed that everyone came out to chat to her, and that she appeared to know them all.

One part of his account rang particularly true, and it illustrated how Waldorf and Nancy worked as a team. She had taken her guest on her daily tour around the city, storing in her mind all the details, small or large, that had impressed her as needing attention. 'That tour,' recalled Robertson, 'was like accompanying a fishwife. She talked to everyone, went anywhere.' Back at Elliot Terrace, she told Waldorf what she had discovered and what she felt must be done: one street needed a new shelter, not at the top of a hill, where the existing one was; a train compartment must be booked for a wounded Frenchman, to rejoin his brother before his ship left for France – 'Ellen Wilkinson ought to be telephoned in Liverpool, to see that the ship did not leave till he got there'; Polish soldiers needed an English teacher; blind boys she had visited must be taught how to use their hands . . . 'I saw then how Lord and Lady Astor worked – she found out what ought to be done; he did it.'[19]

By 1943, the now abundant Lord Mayor's Services' Fund was providing for dances for American soldiers, often six days a week, and Nancy also had American officers lodging at Elliot Terrace. At the request of the Prime Minister, her guests included the first black American general, whom Churchill wanted to ensure was entertained just like any other guest. By now an old hand in air raids, Nancy also proved a great support and encouragement to Americans billeted in nearby houses when they had their first experiences of bombing:

> . . . when she talked to American troops she reverted, part consciously, to Virginian: 'What's goin' on here?' she said, as she entered the billet. 'The city's watchin' you and wonderin.' She marched into every room. 'Come on, men,' she said, 'get out of it an' do somethin.' . . . She seemed impervious to fear as she pushed them around.[20]

'I know how much you do for Americans when they are here,' the United States ambassador told her, 'and it is deeply appreciated.'

Cold and heat, fear, anxiety and stress all accentuate people's character traits, and in doing so often expose their strengths and weaknesses. Nancy was all along conscious of having 'four boys in the fighting Services', as she told Eleanor Roosevelt, but during the Blitz she endured conditions of relentless strain and at times fear. Predominantly they brought out her finer points, in particular her constant desire to help people. However, at the same time the urgency of her war work in Plymouth seemed to harden her attitudes and opinions, as well as her tendency to disregard the feelings of others. Consequently, as the war continued, admiration for her determination and the inspiration she had given to people during the Blitz began to be offset by her apparent insensitivity, and by her strident and often inaccurate views. Her image again began to suffer.

The aggressive side of her character seemed inevitably to emerge in the presence of Winston Churchill, and there had been no exception to that rule when, back in May 1941, he and Clementine had inspected the aftermath of the air attacks on Plymouth. At that time Nancy must have been one of the few people in the country who did not wholly revere the man who had given, as he put it, the lion's roar of defiance at the invaders assembling beyond the English Channel. The public feeling was reflected by the people lining the streets and what in many cases had become mere pathways through mountains of rubble. Tears streaming, Churchill surveyed the desolation, and acknowledged the cheers of the undaunted crowds. Between him and Nancy, however, the atmosphere remained tense, only partly eased by the presence of his wife. Waldorf was absent, and his emollient influence was missed.

In fact he was not well. He had developed a deep affection for Plymouth in its hour of trial, and he and Nancy had made an emotional decision, which Waldorf revealed only after the fighting was over: 'During the raids I faced, like others, the possibility of death. So close was my union with the people of Plymouth that I left instructions, in the event of disaster, for communal burial with my fellow citizens.' The unrelenting strain and danger of the Blitz did not deter him, as he later recalled:

> Once more we hear the doleful wail of the siren in the night, and remember again the moments of indecision. Shall we turn over, cover our heads and try to sleep? Shall we, however raw and cold the night, follow official advice and seek a shelter? Or is it best to go out, to see the searchlights probing the sky, the glow of the tracers, the sudden blaze of the flares, and – with raiders overhead and guns cannonading – do all we can to help?[21]

His dedication had led him out into the streets, at all times of the day and night and in all weathers, and sometimes in conditions of great danger, to give whatever help he could. It had taken its toll on a man in his sixties already weakened by years of sporadic ill-health, and at length he had been forced to leave the strain of his work and try and find some rest. He had found it at Rock, a small village on the coast of Cornwall, but by the time of Churchill's Plymouth visit he was not sufficiently recovered to return to the city even to help the Prime Minister rally and encourage its people.

Unfortunately, increasingly, and accentuated by her extraordinary exertions in war-torn Plymouth, Nancy failed to cherish Waldorf in the way that he both needed and longed for. His illness at the time of Churchill's visit had apparently been brought on by a sharp exchange between him and

Nancy, both of them tired and strained, however energetically they seemed to be carrying on their work.

Like many teetotallers, Nancy had a predilection, at times a craving, for sweet things, and she almost always had with her a small stock of sweets – 'a bag of taffy', as she used to describe it – or if that was unsuitable for any particular occasion, then chewing gum, which was easier to conceal, and which she habitually chewed without apparently moving her jaw. When, therefore, in rationed Britain, starved of delicacies, a consignment of delicious sweets arrived at Elliot Terrace, a present from some Americans intended to be distributed among the needy, Nancy was determined to have some for herself. It caused a furore. What happened next is described by Nancy's maid, Rose, and although her story of life with the Astors is partly hearsay, written down many years later, and sometimes wishful thinking, in this case it does sound accurate, especially as it comes from someone who was loyal to Nancy through many tempestuous years.

When Waldorf firmly declined Nancy's request for a sample of the sweets sent from America, he received a volley of vituperation and rudeness, in front of lunch guests, together with a refusal to continue with their plans to go to Rock. Seemingly shaken, he left the room. Shortly afterwards, as Rose was putting away the clothes that had been packed for Rock, she was summoned to Waldorf's presence:

> When I went to his office I could see at once that he was in a dreadful state: he had difficulty with his breathing and his face was high-coloured. I thought he must have had a stroke and to this day I'm convinced I was right. 'Rose,' he said, 'Lady Astor has upset me badly. She now refuses to go to Rock. She must go and I need your help to see that she does.'
>
> Rose then apparently squared up to her wayward mistress and said, 'I don't know what you've done to his lordship but he's very ill indeed. You'll go with him to Rock, and if you don't I'll write to all the boys and tell them that his condition is your fault because you were greedy and selfish over a few miserable sweets.'[22]

In the ordinary run of things such events would seem unlikely in the extreme, but the world had been quite overturned, exposing the frailty in characters even on the Astors' formal stage. In the event Nancy did go with Waldorf, but returned to Plymouth after only twenty-four hours. He, however, stayed at Rock for a further six weeks, attended by Rose, and out of harm's way when, at the end of April, a further series of intense air raids battered what was left of Plymouth.

While at Rock, Waldorf tried to devise solutions to the shortcomings that had been exposed in the measures for the city's civil defence. Frustrated by the usual channels, he had become determined, like Nancy, to bypass them, and in June 1941 he had accordingly sent a note of his ideas direct to Clementine Churchill, in the hope that she would set them before her husband. His letter had concluded, 'There is so much red tape, departmental jealousy and inertia due to divided responsibility that no decision gets rapid execution unless it has the backing of the Prime Minister himself.' Mrs Churchill did not respond directly, but at least she sent an encouraging reply: 'Winston and I were much disappointed not to see you the other day, and we were very sorry for the reason . . . We were painfully impressed by the smash-up of the town. Everywhere we went, however, I was struck by the look of love and admiration which came over the faces of all when they saw Nancy.'[23]

Waldorf remained in poor condition, and at length Nancy realised that she must make a proper attempt to help him; three months later, in August 1941, she went with him to their house on Jura, for ten days of rest far away from the stress of war. She herself maintained that she could find rest, if she needed it, by being on her own. As the war progressed, she usually defied attempts to make her leave Plymouth, or to stay with friends elsewhere in Devonshire, although she did go to Rock for the occasional week, when she would play golf by herself, at nearby St Enodoc. 'I am only going to Clovelly,' she told Waldorf in May 1943, with a typical response to his pressure, 'as I promised you to. It is really much more restful for me to stop here in my room, as I needn't see a soul and have beautiful times for reading. So don't be surprised if I return earlier than you would wish.'

On this occasion, however, she forced herself to go up to Jura; it was an indication of how worried she was about Waldorf, as she wholly disliked the island. The rest of her family had always loved it, but there was little there that now appealed to Nancy: there were no people to mix with, the house was too small for entertaining, and she had almost nothing to do. She would walk along the only road, restless and impatient, clutching a golf club behind her back. Waldorf had built a special small 'lighthouse' for her, on a hill and looking out to sea. It had a room with walls mostly of glass, for her to use as an office or for reading in peace. It did not appeal. 'Yes, I'm going to Hell,' she would sometimes say, when asked if she was off to Scotland. But if Waldorf really needed her, she suppressed her preferences.

Meanwhile, resting at Rock, and on occasional stays at Cliveden, Waldorf's mind turned to the future. He could discern a new spirit in the air, with politics moving towards a more collective age, of high taxation, greater state control, and a much larger share of Parliament's time and public money being devoted to the welfare of 'the people'. To a considerable degree this reflected his own inclination, and it was with the new mood in mind that he first conceived his ideas for the rebuilding of Plymouth, designed for a post-war world. Accordingly he encouraged the city council to find and engage architects and planners receptive to a vision of the future, in the spirit of a new age.

Deeply affected as both Waldorf and Nancy were by the destruction of the ancient city of Drake, for Waldorf this was a moment to look ahead. The first suggestions for the new city provided a blueprint of hope, and over the next two years, with the war still raging, the ideas began to take detailed shape. Waldorf was invited to explain to American radio listeners the vision of Plymouth that was beginning to emerge:

. . . What about Plymouth as a place to live in – the modern city, the Plymouth of the future? Our main sources of employment are ship building and as a shopping and market centre for the counties of Devon and Cornwall. So the new plan features a boulevard (for pedestrians only) firstly through an area earmarked for Government offices, next through a shopping precinct, then past a new Guildhall and Council Chamber, and, so, rising up the hill to the esplanade which overlooks the Sound. Motor cars, naturally, must have access to the shopping centres and to housing estates, but through traffic will be made to circle them; we want children to go to schools and their mothers to shop in safety. We want, too, proper living space – for all the needs of citizens living in a modern town . . . so the plan offers us at Plymouth a City where the daily life of the ordinary man will be more spacious and dignified . . .[24]

'The people of Plymouth,' he continued, 'have danced on the Hoe during the darkest days of war. They will dance there again in peace – as they did after Waterloo – but the boys who come back from this war will dance on a Hoe which overlooks the building of a new city, a city which has been planned for them, for a wider, freer, healthier, and more prosperous life.'

The object of the plan, Waldorf explained, was to reconstruct the city, to preserve all that was best in the region, to safeguard the beauties of the coast, moor, valley and lanes in the West Country, and to present a model for planning for all similarly situated cities. With Plymouth still reeling from air raids, it was a far leap of the imagination, but it also angered those who saw large swathes of road and concrete as rather the opposite of a safeguard for moor, valley and West Country lanes. In fact, although during 1943 Waldorf was the chief force behind developing the plans for post-war

Plymouth, he had to rely on strong Labour backing in order to overcome an enraged Tory caucus. His newspaper, the *Observer,* however, looked on the bright side, and discerned 'a new spirit of civic feeling' flaming up under the inspiration of the Lord Mayor and Lady Mayoress.[25]

Nancy was much less at ease with such visions. Her reaction to the increase of government control of so many aspects of life, accepted by the majority as necessary in wartime, was to shift her politics to the right, while Waldorf was moving in the opposite direction.

Waldorf's reflections on the future had long included thoughts of his family. In 1929, he had protected the Cliveden woods, he hoped in perpetuity, by entering into a Private Open Space Agreement with the neighbouring estates, a special arrangement available under the law at that time. In 1942, he went further: doubting that his family's past way of life could be restored even if the war were won, and suspecting that in a post-war world few people, whether as masters or servants, would be able or would want to live in houses like Cliveden, he gave the estate to the National Trust. The arrangements were similar to those pioneered by Lord Lothian, when he realised that death duties would make it impossible for his heirs to live at his Blickling Hall estate. As current income tax rates were extremely high, the agreement relieved Waldorf from paying a great deal of tax – he told the Trust's agent that on the endowment of £200,000 that he proposed adding to his transfer of the estate he would be losing post-tax income of only £150.

However, besides fiscal considerations, Waldorf was concerned for the future of the house and its surroundings, which he thought should ultimately serve a public purpose. He believed that giving them to the National Trust was the only way to ensure their long-term preservation from developers and to provide a suitable and sustainable future. For the family, the pill was sugared by Waldorf's stipulation that they should be allowed to live at Cliveden for as long as they wished. The endowment associated with the transfer would make it relatively easy for Bill in due course to reside on the estate. He was also given the White Place farm, and paddocks that would have a future value as building land. The arrangement was particularly pleasing for Bill, who had expressed his love for Cliveden in a poignant letter from his faraway overseas posting, when he had thought lovingly of home and pre-war days:

I can hardly believe that it ought to be Ascot Week, with a big party at Cliveden, tennis and riding in the morning, and all the girls in their best dresses, and men in grey top hats, fixing on buttonholes and sprays of flowers in the hall at twelve, and the cars all lined up, and the Royal Procession, and Father's colours on the course; and polo in the evening, and swimming, and all the rhododendrons out, and for once my parents forgetting politics and giving themselves over to social joy. I hope so much that I won't find a new order when I get back: I enjoyed the old order so much.[26]

Nancy had understood the necessity of providing for the future of Cliveden at a time when, as she put it, 'tax left you sixpence in the pound'. Nevertheless, she did not relish such a distressing harbinger of the future, and bridled at the thought of public access: 'Whatever you people do,' she briskly told the National Trust representative when she met him in Waldorf's office, 'I cannot have the public near the place . . . at any rate their hours will have to be clearly defined.' Her attitude now began to put her at odds with the mood of her close family.

She was beginning to find herself similarly isolated in the Commons, where her speeches and interventions, her pointing white-gloved finger, became less benignly tolerated. When one MP said that 'the Noble Lady should listen more and talk less', he was voicing an opinion that had become widespread. The logic of many of her points became clouded by her chronic tendency to ramble, but more fundamentally, her values, and the direction from which she approached many of the topics debated in Parliament, now ran against the sense of the times. With hindsight it can be seen that on many occasions what she said was valid, but the predominant weight of politics was dragging to the left, and she did not wish to move with it. Fearless and outspoken as ever, she was beginning to lose the ear of the House, and also of government ministers.

At the height of the Blitz, in May 1941, she had embarked on a drive for a radical improvement in fire-fighting arrangements, which the bombing of Plymouth had shown to be urgently needed. Her plea had been expressed with typical directness, but it had sounded to most MPs too much like an attack on the government at a time of national emergency. In this field the administration was represented by Herbert Morrison, Minister for Home Security. At that particular moment he was considered an indispensable member of the administration, especially as the Prime Minister felt it essential that in time of war the government should be broadly based, and Morrison was one of the leading lights of the Labour Party. Attacks on Labour ministers were therefore unwelcome, and most Conservative MPs toed the line.

Nancy, however, was not one to mince her words, and two weeks after Churchill's visit to see the damage in Plymouth she assailed his ministry's plans for improving the country's fire-fighting services. She caused particular

anger by making her attack a personal one on Morrison, suggesting in effect
that he was putty in the hands of peacetime local politicians – 'the very
worst people in the world to fight a battle' – and that he should be sacked.
She also issued a thinly veiled reproof to Churchill, so losing the sympathy
of the House:

> . . . this respect for local authorities has really been the cause of an
> absolutely useless waste, not only of lives but of property and all things
> that matter most . . . The Prime Minister is a magnificent military
> leader, but we want a home-front leader as well . . . it is weakness on
> the part of the House of Commons to have gone on so long and not
> protested and helped him. I am here to help him . . . I never wanted
> a Government job until lately, but I have come to the conclusion that
> men are timorous animals. They are always 'passing the buck' on to
> someone else. Women are not like that . . . There are plenty of women
> standing about idle when we have doddering old politicians in all
> parties who ought to have been buried long ago. Government is still
> too much on party lines . . .[27]

The press had a field day, airing its prejudices and probably a latent jealousy
at the paramount position occupied by *The Times* and the *Observer*. It was
said that Nancy's speech was the first of definitely fascist tendency to be
made during the current war; there was nothing to justify such a comment,
but her outspoken ways and high visibility exposed her to attack and misrepresentation, as in the days of the 'Cliveden Set'.

Her reception was similarly cool when, early in 1942, she accused the
government of lacking spiritual values in its overseas broadcasts, potentially
an immensely important weapon of war. She blamed the BBC, saying that
the anti-German nature of their broadcasts discouraged anti-Nazi opinion
within Germany itself, dampening any flames of resistance: 'Do not let us
be afraid to tell the people abroad that we are fighting as much for them as
for the people at home. So far, you have not done that, and I believe the
reason is that you have not got the right kind of people to do it. Words
without feeling are like clouds without rain.' Her basic argument had force,
but it was hard to discern it in the way she presented it.

In calling for the BBC to reach out to anti-Nazis in Germany, she no
doubt had in mind people like Adam von Trott, a young German friend of
her son David who had been invited to Cliveden shortly before the war.
Typically, Nancy had shown him generosity, sending him to one of London's
leading tailors at her expense. He had come to England to try and explain
that there was a spirit of resistance in Germany that Britain could and

should encourage, and he had been taken to express this view to the Foreign Secretary, Lord Halifax, but without result.

Nancy was now having to fight on several fronts. A few months later she also crossed swords with President Roosevelt, who, aiming his words at influential Americans who were lobbying for the United States to remain neutral at all costs, had raised the bogey of the 'Cliveden Set'. Nancy gave the American ambassador a letter to hand to the President, saying how distressed she was that Roosevelt 'as a friend' should have coupled the term 'Cliveden Set', a cruel and communist lie, with American isolationists and defeatists.[28] The President was advised not to become involved; instead he drafted an emollient letter for Eleanor Roosevelt to send to Nancy. He continued to believe that the Cliveden Set had become, as he told his foreign policy adviser Sumner Welles, a symbol not just of appeasement but of a failure to evaluate the world as it really was; Nancy and Waldorf were not unpatriotic, in his view, but mistaken, as were many influential people in Washington.[29]

Nancy continued to set herself at odds with the public mood in a number of her speeches outside Parliament. On 1 August that year, in Southport, she spurned the popular fervour by questioning the Soviet Union's motives in joining the Allies. On that occasion she had initially, due to an administrative error, been under the false impression that she was addressing an Anglo-American audience, rather than what was in fact a United Nations rally. Perhaps that increased the liveliness of her reception:

> I am grateful to the Russians, but they are not fighting for us. They are fighting for themselves. In the Battle of Britain it was America who came to our aid. The Russians were allies of Germany. It is only now that they are facing German invasion that they have come into the fight. To hear people talk you would think that they came to us in our own dire need. Nothing of the kind. It was the United States of America.

Taken on their own, her comments, though accurate, might have seemed ill-timed and unnecessary. However, the other speeches made from the platform were singing Russia's praises as though they were indeed fighting as much for Britain and America as for themselves, and Nancy's speech was made in that context. Clementine Churchill reported unfavourably to her husband on Nancy's performance, but it was not long before Churchill himself came to the same conclusion as Nancy, realising that the Russians had little regard for Britain and were only out for themselves.

In Nancy's case, clamour at once broke out, as at the time it was taboo to criticise the Soviets. It was not then conceived, even by the most suspicious, cynical or worldly-wise, how comprehensively the Western Allies, in particular President Roosevelt, would be duped by Stalin after the war's end, and how, in Goebbels's phrase, later made famous by Churchill, an 'iron curtain' would descend across Europe. Yet no matter that what Nancy said was wholly correct; she was speaking out of turn. It confirmed the opinion of those who had come to regard her as a loose cannon. Her wit and good nature, which had so often diluted resentment at her 'shooting from the lip', seemed to have given way to a hard-hearted stridency.

In any event, there was at that time of stress little humour in the atmosphere, and Nancy was exhausting the sympathy of her friends. Their reaction was typically expressed in an indignant letter from Thomas Jones, complaining of her 'outburst about Russia'. Jones was himself left wing and an egalitarian, and perhaps shared the general sentiment about 'Uncle Joe' Stalin. Although, having been a leading civil servant, he was by temperament discreet, he did now express an opinion:

What an ungracious speech and at this moment. Do you think this is the way to increase sympathy for America? You achieve the exact opposite. I have no reason to love Bolsheviks but I hope I have some magnanimity and some pity left in me. You are the despair of your friends and we all deeply miss Philip's restraining hand.[10]

Typically, Nancy stuck to her guns: she had spoken the truth as she saw it; she suggested that Jones read the whole speech, not just selective press reports, and she cited *Observer* editorials written by their old friend J.L. Garvin supporting her view. Jones did so, climbed down and withdrew his complaints: Nancy had won on points, but she was beginning to need more than that.

The various ways, often all combined in the same speech, in which she was failing to carry her arguments in Parliament were exemplified in a Commons debate on opening up Britain's foreign service – the first appointment of a woman to the Diplomatic Service had not been made until 1939. Now, in March 1943, despite the exigencies of war, reform was in the air, and Nancy's intuition had drawn her to a new target. Once again she undermined valid points and good suggestions with repetition and overemphasis, straying along a confusingly broad range of hilltops before reaching the end of her speech. Tired as she might have been, arduous as was the task of gathering the facts necessary for a persuasive speech, even with the help of her excellent staff, and daunting as was its delivery in the Commons, she had nevertheless usually mastered the detail. It was in logical presentation that she faltered, lacking a sufficiently disciplined mind. The patience of the House was wearing thin.

Into her sights came France, followed by the Latins:

> . . . We have had Foreign Office Permanent Secretaries who have been dominated by what we call the Latin point of view . . . France was their spiritual home . . . If we had a foreign policy not dominated by France – well, I do not want to say anything about a country when she is down. France is a shell-shocked country and has been so since the last war, and I suppose everybody knows it except the Foreign Office. We had a Foreign Secretary, Sir Austen Chamberlain, who said he loved France as a man loved his mistress. Men have no business to have mistresses. It shocked me at the time . . .

'I should like to remind the House of Commons,' she continued, 'of the number of Ambassadors who marry people from other countries . . .' The Deputy Speaker blanched: 'It may be very hard upon us if the Noble Lady should read through the list of names of all the representatives of the Foreign Office. I hope that the Noble Lady will not take too long over that.'

Advancing a number of sound though general reasons why women should be admitted to the Diplomatic Service, Nancy concluded: 'If women had run this country for as long as the men, we no doubt should not be in the mess we are in to-day. If God's gifts and talents belong to one sex and not to the other, then it is to the mothers of the race and not to the fathers.'[31] She was followed by Harold Nicolson. He was himself a former diplomat, and was not persuaded, later describing the experience of following Nancy as like 'playing squash with scrambled eggs'. In fact, Nancy found herself up against a state of mind similar to that which had for so long resisted the entry of women into the professions and into Parliament itself. However valid her arguments and forecasts, she seemed to have lost her powers of persuasion: 'The Noble Lady gabbles and gabbles all the time,' complained the Labour firebrand Aneurin Bevan, exasperated at being interrupted. 'We really ought to have some protection.'

Not long afterwards, to the embarrassment of her family, Nancy got into hot water for asking the wife of an American Red Cross representative to buy her a fur jacket in America, for which she needed a licence under British rationing arrangements. In July 1943, government officers, not without a certain relish, took her to court for breaking the rules, with the result that she was reprimanded and fined. Although the matter soon faded from people's minds, it was momentarily awkward, and her spirit must have rebelled at the example of a country increasingly in the grip of what she deemed petty regulations.

At least her beloved Virginia hams were not restricted, and they occasionally found their way to the larder at Cliveden or Elliot Terrace. To a Virginian who had stayed at Cliveden she wrote:

> Your husband has given me the ham and you have no idea what a God-send it is. A new American admiral turned up to supper last night and it saved the situation. It is hard for you to understand our food problems, but when you do you will realise that a pound of lard, a ham, or a few fresh eggs mean more than a diamond tiara to us.[32]

Virginia was never far from her mind. Its image had been poignantly recalled for her earlier in the war when she had received a letter from Angus McDonnell, staying at Mirador on leave from his work at the British embassy in Washington. Haunted by the memories that the house had revived in him, he sat on the veranda in the still of the night, thinking of Nancy, and remembering wistfully:

> . . . going home for the first time after five and a half years, miserable at having left a letter from you in the rack over the upper berth, having got it out of my pocket to read for the twentieth time, just before I went to sleep. You sitting in the chair right of the table facing the fireplace in the sitting room. I certainly was deadly in love with you then. I could bring back every detail of how you looked, down to the little chicken pockmark on your cheek on the right side. Well, all the ghosts of what we were 38 years ago came, and I had quite a party, and the world was back in those days when it was a pleasant place to live in . . .
>
> . . . You may think I'm crazy and it's all maudlin sentiment, but I sort of felt last night sitting on the porch that you might just like to turn the clock back for a while.[33]

Bill Astor occasionally felt his own particular sense of discomfort as a result of the mother-and-son team, or at least presence, in Parliament. It was a unique and rather inhibiting situation, especially when he found himself associated with opinions stridently expressed by his mother that did not reflect his own more moderate inclinations. In February 1944, he raised a question in the Commons about why an official pamphlet, which he considered contained important information about the Far East theatre and was long overdue, had not been printed and distributed. He received bland government explanations about the national paper shortage, the lack of printers, the fact that they were all busy; in general a typical Civil Service response. Nancy's intuition gave her a more accurate assessment of the situation. She claimed that the shortage of printers was fantasy, and that there was plenty of paper if people chose to find it:

> Yesterday I walked down a street in Plymouth and bought two pounds' worth of the filthiest books I have seen for a long time. All had been printed in the last six months. I mean to take these books back to the House of Commons and show them to some of the Members, and ask them if it isn't about time we stopped allowing this stuff to be printed. I am convinced I'll have every decent father and mother in the country behind me.[34]

Still in missionary mood, she had in the same week opened a concert evening in Plymouth but in doing so had informed the audience that if she had had her way the programme would have consisted instead of hymns, prayers and a Bible reading. The audience, it was reported, became 'a bit impatient'.

However, despite its decline on the national stage, Nancy's popularity remained high among the Americans in Plymouth, their numbers greatly swelled in preparation for the D-Day invasion of France, set for the beginning of June 1944. Three days after her exposure of the printing presses busy in the world of salacious books, she visited an American army depot in order to be promoted from her honorary rank of private first class to corporal, and was ceremoniously handed some stripes to sew on her sleeve.

Having for a time lost the ear of Parliament and the sympathy of some of the press, Nancy also came into collision with her own family, whose occasional requests for her to be less controversial had upset her. Gone were the days, it seemed, when she had fulsomely admitted how valuable was her husband's support and guidance, when she had told him how much she missed it when he was away: 'You can't conceive how difficult it is for me to carry on my public life without you, or my private life either, for that matter . . .' After three years of the stress of war, the amity had receded. Waldorf reproved her, as a good Christian Scientist: 'You really must not malpractice by constant repetition that your family don't love you. It's not true, and it certainly is not good science . . .'

Acrimony now arose among the family over developments at the *Observer*. The newspaper was an obvious outlet for the talents of David Astor, who had been drawn to journalism and in 1936 had gained practical experience by working for the *Yorkshire Post*, having previously done a two-year stint at Lazard's, the merchant bank in the City, in which his uncle, Robert Brand, was a leading light.

Although Waldorf had owned the *Observer* since 1915, the editor, J.L. Garvin, in his post since 1908, had a large degree of independence, guaranteed by his employment contract. He had long made the paper a reflection of his own opinions, dominating it in a way unmatched by any of his rival Fleet Street editors, of whom he was the longest serving, but for a number of reasons he had during the 1930s begun to lose his sureness of touch, without however loosening his grip on the paper.

By 1941, David had started writing for the *Observer*, through a new column entitled 'Forum', with contributions from a group of young, idealistic, iconoclastic writers who shared his relatively left-wing ideas. This was anathema to Nancy, though it is perhaps not surprising that with five sons, one at least should rebel against his mother's political emphasis, and escape the atmosphere in which he had grown up. Politically, Nancy and David had been some distance apart for a number of years, and they grew more so as Nancy moved to the right, gradually abandoning the liberal element in her particular brand of Conservative politics as she felt increasingly at odds with the developing spirit of the age.

Nancy was incensed by the leftward trend that was becoming apparent in *Observer* articles, and disliked the increasing influence that Waldorf seemed to be allowing David to have in the workings of the paper. Early in 1942, matters came to a head when Garvin's contract with the paper ran out. The ensuing dispute as to whether it should be renewed resulted in his leaving and David becoming, in effect, editor-in-waiting, his new work being facilitated by his moving to Whitehall as press officer at the newly established Combined Operations Headquarters, headed by Lord Mountbatten.

These developments also upset Bill Astor. Early in the war he had been posted to the Middle East as an intelligence officer, although that had not prevented him from retaining his seat in Parliament. When he returned to England in 1942 only to find his younger brother entrenched at the *Observer*, he felt aggrieved, having believed that it would be he who would take it over in the fullness of time, and concluded that David had taken advantage of his absence overseas.

Waldorf's vision was that the paper should rise above party politics, thereby becoming free to promote new ideas and concepts, many of which might have a left-wing or at least a cross-bench emphasis: Bill, as an MP, would find it difficult to encourage fulfilment of that ideal, even if he wanted to. Waldorf's was a wholly reasonable position, supported by the fact that he had already perceived that David had great ability as a newspaperman, which was his natural bent as much as politics was Bill's. Unhappily, Bill saw other currents swirling below the surface. He believed that his father considered David more able than him, and that he did not trust his judgement, remembering the Frank Pakenham affair, when his supposedly cleverest friend had managed to ride the wrong way round a racecourse. These divisions reinforced family discord at Nancy's performances in Parliament and on platforms around the country.

Waldorf tried to accommodate Nancy and bring her alongside – in planning a transformation of the *Observer* into a non-partisan trust, he agreed to insist that it be controlled by Protestants – but he refused to give her any rights over the direction of the paper: 'As to the *Observer*, I wish you would understand that I desire your counsel and opinion, but – and it is an important but – no editor could edit efficiently if he had several people who had the right to tell him what to do, a right given through status.' Waldorf believed that the paper had improved since Garvin's departure, mainly as a result of David's success in collecting a good team, including George Orwell, at a time when it was difficult to do so. Nancy, true to form, held firm, continuing to deplore the opinions the paper was beginning to embrace, at a time when Conservative values seemed to have lost popular support and needed a champion. David recounted the problems to Thomas Jones, who had become something of a mentor:

> I learn today re the Observer and Bill . . . that part of the trouble is my mother. She apparently says [a] I am too 'Bolshie' and [b] she resents the way my father and I have got together to her exclusion. Egging Bill on and advising my father to take him into the Observer is apparently her reply . . .[35]

As the war dragged on through 1944, drably and painfully for those at home, many contemporary ideas and visions of the post-war world seemed colourless and collectivist. The gulf between the life that had vanished in 1940 and post-war prospects yawned wide. Spiritually, Nancy and Waldorf had moved to opposite sides of the gap. This was soon to have far-reaching results.

It had pained Waldorf on several occasions to see the various ways in which Nancy seemed to have lost her magic and instead attracted hostile fire. In his mind such demonstrations had by now gradually coalesced into a serious problem demanding a radical solution. He responded with what came to Nancy as a shattering surprise, which reverberated back upon him, shaking him more deeply and for far longer than he could have anticipated.

By 1944 they were both sixty-five; they had worked together in Plymouth for thirty-five years, and Nancy had been an MP for twenty-five: a memorable anniversary was drawing near. In the political field they had complemented each other perfectly: against the feminine impulsiveness and intuition of the one pressed the calm, tact and diplomacy of the other. But change was in the air. The end of the war would obviously be followed by a general election, and Waldorf was daunted by the thought of the effort that would be required for Nancy to fight it. Even as long ago as the 1935 election he had decided that he would thereafter concentrate on Chatham House rather than party politics, and however deep was the love he had for Nancy, he now felt that she had become too much for him to handle on the political stage. 'When I married Nancy,' he said in a speech at a dinner for female businesswomen, 'I hitched my wagon to a star. And then when I got into the House of Commons in 1910 I found that I had hitched my wagon to a shooting star. In 1919 when she got into the House I found I had hitched my wagon to a sort of V2 rocket . . . Nancy,' he observed wryly, 'is apt to say what another person would only think – and apt to say it without consulting a lawyer.' He strongly believed that she now had a great opportunity for service to the country beyond the political arena, for which he was prepared to give her his full support, but he would no longer countenance her continuing in the heart of politics itself.

Despite his wife's exceptionally powerful character, Waldorf's ultimate status as autocrat of the family and arbiter of its fundamental decisions remained unchanged; that was the natural order of things in such a family at the time, and he offered no flexibility, even if he naturally inclined to the velvet glove. He had discussions with the family, besides taking soundings from Nancy's friends in Parliament and from those whose knowledge of the political outlook he valued, and whom he felt could advise in her best interests. Both family and friends concurred. 'Most of us,' Waldorf told her, 'think you should have retired some time ago . . .'

There was also a growing feeling among the Plymouth Conservatives that it was time for a change: the world had been very different in 1910, when the Astors first came to prominence in the city, and after so long a reign, many thought that they should step down. Waldorf himself recognised the straw in the wind when it became clear that the Conservatives on Plymouth Council resented the plan he championed for the city's future, and that consequently, in 1944, they refused him the option of continuing for a further term as Lord Mayor – an unwelcome withdrawal of support even if in fact he wanted to resign the office, as he had told Nancy the previous year. It began to seem quite possible that Nancy might not even be readopted as candidate for Plymouth Sutton.

Waldorf realised that the times were changing, but were not taking Nancy with them. The moment had arrived for him to definitively speak his mind:

> . . . At first you invited my advice and took my guidance. Of late years you go out of your way to oppose them. Most of us think you should have retired some time ago – DD – Philip – others. At present your spiritual individuality is clogged and blinded by your political person-ality. It is impossible for you to be both a good CS and an MP . . . I feel that if you persist you will let down your other supporters just as I feel you are now letting me down . . .[36]

Yet he hoped that all would come out well, and he remained as steadfast for her as he always had been: 'But if by any mischance the demon hardens your heart or if by bad luck a doodlebug contacts me I want you to know that you have been all to me, and that with both eyes open I would pop the same question to you once again.'

At the beginning of December 1944, the silver jubilee of her entry into Parliament, the news was announced in banner headlines: 'Lady Astor not to fight again'.

> Last winter, after the strain of five years of war, with its numerous heavy responsibilities, Lord Astor informed Lady Astor that he did not at his age feel physically able to go through the heavy strain and stress of another contested election. Lady Astor and he have fought seven elections together, and including the period when he was MP for Plymouth, have supported each other closely in the political arena for thirty-five years. It would be difficult for Lady Astor to stand again without his help.[37]

It was all too obvious from the wording that Waldorf and Nancy had failed to agree, and that Waldorf was making the decision. At first her local party officers were taken aback. They asked Waldorf to come and see them, but when he said that he could have no part in supporting her in a new fight, they realised there was nothing more to be said. With only one dissenter, they voted to accept the letter of resignation without further discussion either among themselves or, significantly, with her. It was a body blow. 'Still, there it is,' she told reporters. 'My Lord and Master has made the decision, and I am as obedient as ever. Never in this whole time have I failed in my duties.' In a way, having to bow to a man's decision went to the core of her career's purpose, a factor in the prolonged ire that she was to direct at Waldorf.

She could not bear to think of her political life coming to an end; nor did she see why it should. 'I would like to go on fighting for Plymouth,' she said, 'until the day I die, just like the soldiers, sailors and airmen are doing.' Indeed, such was her spirit and self-confidence that she believed she would win another election if she stood. Even if she were to stand and not win, she told the BBC the following month, 'I would rather go down fighting than retire.' In the event, however, she did not insist upon applying for the candidacy, and this fact was to affect her for the rest of her life: she felt then, and ever afterwards, that the electorate should have had the chance of giving their own verdict.

ELEVEN

Aftermath

In the wake of the Allied victory, a caretaker administration, with Churchill as Prime Minister, was formed to govern Britain. Parliament was then dissolved, on 15 June 1945, having sat for almost nine and a half years. Three weeks later a general election was held, and the result, declared on 26 July, gave a landslide victory to the Labour Party. Until shortly before polling day it had seemed certain that Churchill's immense stature would ensure a Conservative victory; but there then began to loom the possibility that, contrary to the widespread expectations, Labour might win. As had been the case after the Great War, confidence in the old order was lost, with attitudes hardened by resentment of the class that had ruled through the Depression and brought near ruin to the country with another war. The people wanted a new start, and Labour's campaign slogan of 'Cheer Churchill, Vote Labour' captured their imagination and expressed their mood perfectly.

In Plymouth Sutton the Conservatives replaced Nancy with a soldier, which in hindsight was deemed an error in a constituency so closely connected with the navy. Labour, championed by a woman, overturned the large majority Nancy had won in 1935, polling a little over half the votes, slightly ahead of the national average.

The results were dissected and debated and subjected to intricate analysis, and the great question was whether Nancy, with her charisma, fighting ability and outstanding constituency record, could after all have defied the national trend. She of course had few doubts about the matter, and anger about what had happened welled within her, directed first at her constituency executive, and then at her husband for not pressing her case. Waldorf, wholly honourable, could not dissemble: 'What I did not do,' he told her, 'and could not honestly do, was to say that I thought it would be a good thing for you to stand, and that I hoped the executive would invite you to stand – I was much too fond of you to be able to do that honestly.'

A little earlier, Waldorf's wish for a quiet interlude had taken him back to Jura, where the news of the war's end reached him. From there he sent a letter to Nancy, full of sweet words but, fully aware of the volcanic mood in which he had left her, betraying faint signs of misgiving:

What mars my return to health is the feeling that you are dissatisfied or in any way unhappy or resentful . . . I shall look forward to your cherishing me in our old age – I followed and tended you when the pace was hot, and now that it has slackened it's for you to solace me . . .

. . . You can think me guilty of every sort of folly during the past ten years but just remember one thing: you are still my guiding star; you are still what is most precious to me; what I have done at any time has been to protect you according to what seemed to me best . . .[1]

Her last utterance in the Commons was on 14 June 1945, intervening when a question had been raised about fox hunting – not for the last time a subject of controversy in Parliament – and then her twenty-five-year career was over. It was probably as well: she was an individualist, whereas the turmoil of war had opened the door to a grey, conformist, planning age. The closing of her career hurt her deeply, but her well-known valediction was attractively poignant: 'I'll miss the House, but the House won't miss me. It never misses anybody. The House is like a sea. MPs are like little ships that sail across it and disappear over the horizon. Some of them carry a light. Others don't. That's the only difference.'

With a final act of generosity, she hired a special train to take 400 members of the House of Commons staff and their families to Cliveden for the day. It was an action redolent of an already faded age, when MPs treated their constituents to an annual outing at the Big House, but it was a fitting parliamentary finale for someone who had made entertaining so much a part of her political career.

Soon after standing down, Nancy had conceived the hope that she might become a peeress in her own right and continue her career in the House of Lords. In the 1920s Waldorf had put his name on three Bills proposing that the Lords should be opened to peeresses in their own right, but none of them had reached the statute book. Although in 1945 there was next to no chance that the matter might be revived, Nancy, specifically relating the suggestion to herself, had suggested it to Churchill while he was still Prime Minister. He was not persuaded.

Rebuffed, she seemed finally to accept that her parliamentary career was at an end. Consequently, and slightly petulantly, she gave out that she would take no further part whatever in public life – although she did at the same time complain to Waldorf that she now had nothing to do, whereas he had Chatham House to keep him occupied. Without consulting him, she declined the offer of heading up the National Council of Women, a well-regarded fifty-year-old organisation for promoting women's interests. It indicated the direction she intended to take.

Knowing how well she was suited to all sorts of public activity, and fearing that she would become bored if she did not take on some commitments, her friends were dismayed. So was Waldorf, when he belatedly realised what might happen, even if his particular reason had a narrow focus. Writing, it would seem, in terms that he felt might persuade Nancy, rather than expressing any anti-Catholic prejudice of his own, he asked:

> Is there anything more important than that you should help to keep RC influence out of the Women's Council, and that you should steer them on Anglo-American and other big problems . . . You would have more influence in many respects than you have had, though it would be a different sort of influence. If you reject this I don't see what you will be inclined to consider . . .[2]

Nothing, it seemed. And the matter was now becoming pressing. Besides the family, foremost among those addressing the problem were those whom Waldorf had consulted before handing Nancy the loaded pistol. Among them was her friend and champion Edith Lyttelton, known as DD. Prominent in many women's causes, she was a long-time campaigner with Nancy – for the wives and children caught up in the 1920s coal strikes, for the victims of white slavery, and for the success of the League of Nations, to which she had been a delegate.

Edith Lyttelton now urged Nancy to consider what paths she might usefully tread: she had achieved much already, but there was still a great deal to do, especially in fostering Anglo-American friendship and co-operation, for which she was 'quite specially created . . . There is no woman in these islands who could have tackled it as *you* did at the *beginning*, with your mixture of charm, courage and wits.' Nancy remained in excellent health, and Edith believed that her special faculties and flair were now needed outside Parliament.

Nancy, however, did not agree. She remained resentful, still feeling that a foolish sacrifice had been forced upon her. With her character and from past experience it seemed unlikely that she would waver in her view, but Edith persisted, pointing out that many other prominent women agreed with her, and that it would be disastrous if Nancy shut herself 'inside a shell, like an oyster': 'Don't spoil it now by these rather childish threats of never doing any more public work; it is the wrong attitude from every point of view, and I should have thought most specially from a Christian Science one.' Parliament was not the only platform, she added, and Nancy was causing distress to her friends; besides, in respect of Waldorf, her stance was a kind of blackmail.[3]

Eventually Nancy's feelings softened. Waldorf's health was continuing to decline – he was by then nearing his seventies – and so she decided to go with him to America, which they had not seen for nearly seven years. England in 1945 was a bleak place, and Dixieland was an enticing thought. So the plans were laid, and it soon became apparent that in America they would be much sought after, by friends and family.

Many others, however, were also yearning to escape the drabness of post-war Britain, and the long waiting lists for aeroplanes and the major liners forced the Astors to sail on a meat carrier. At 6,000 tons, the boat, repaired after being torpedoed during the war, was very small for a midwinter Atlantic crossing, and the voyage was slow and uncomfortable, with the ship at times reduced to a speed of four knots. Nancy spent much of her time in her cabin – usually with the portholes open, but with the door firmly closed, as the ship had a cat which she feared might slip in to pay her a visit. Uncompromising as ever, she also stuck to her habit of having a cold bath each morning.

Despite the main purposes of the visit to America being to quietly meet old friends and to give Waldorf some peace, Nancy charged the air with her old energy right from the start – on arrival, she marched down the gangway head-on into a barrage of flashlights, and, after declaring herself to be an extinct volcano, proceeded to erupt before the reporters crowding around her.

In Washington, where they stayed at the British embassy with the Halifaxes, Nancy addressed another large group of journalists. It was a time when very many Americans regarded Britain with some disdain as an exhausted former ally who owed them a great deal of money and was now asking for more. Nancy, however, wholly disagreed. She turned to attack as the best means of defence against hostile questioning, and it did not take the newspapermen long to recognise once more the character of press legend. They fell into amazed silence as she seized the initiative, answering all their questions, and several others that she asked herself: 'Now, look here, I want to interview you for a change . . . What has Britain done that is wicked? What is Britain's crime? Why all this criticism?' she cried. 'You should get down on your knees and thank God for Britain . . . Who started this country anyway?' she added, as a sweetener.[4]

Soon, Waldorf managed to escape what seemed once again to have become the tour of a whirlwind, and set off for the sunshine of California, after which Nancy took him down to Florida before he sailed for England. She herself remained in America until midsummer, as vigorous as ever. In Charleston she addressed a joint session of the two houses of the state legislature, and in Richmond, on 4 July, she squared up to another large posse of hard-nosed reporters, only to find that they had softened their stance:

> Two wars and all their woes have not marred Lady Astor. She looks incredibly young . . . the fine lines of her profile have not been dulled by weight or blunted by scowls . . . If she ever is hurt by any retort, her pride and her humor are her link-armor against any deep wound . . .[5]

She was feted wherever she went, although at many public meetings and press conferences she did trigger some lively crossfire: more so than previously, and certainly when compared with her triumphant tour in 1922. However, at least she could to some extent give the lie to misconceptions about the Cliveden Set by revealing the fact that, described as 'Enemy of Germany', she had been included on the Gestapo's 'Black List' of over 2,000 people due for arrest after the invasion of England. Despite that honour, however, she had also received an 'interrogatory' from Ribbentrop in his Nuremberg cell, asking her to support the erstwhile ambassador; it was promptly rejected.

To Waldorf's sorrow, Nancy decided to return to the United States again in May the following year, but this time on her own. He craved companionship from her: 'I miss you very much,' he wrote, when she had been away nearly two months. 'I'm too old to be left alone during my few remaining years. I hope you will soon be thinking of the present and the future, instead of concentrating so absorbingly on the past . . .' A few days later he added, 'The sands are running out, and I hope you will awake soon – it would be so nice to have a harmonious old age . . . I bemoan the last months of this year – and last year. Here is the Spring gone, the summer half spent . . .'

While Waldorf lamented at home, in America, where she also spent the first five months of 1948, Nancy seemed once more amusing in a friendly manner. Her pleasure at being in Virginia and her love for the South, as well as the effervescence of New York, made a refreshing combination and added surely to the relief, perhaps subconscious, that she was free of the hectic round of duties to which she had for so long been accustomed. As much as she loved Parliament, as much as politics had been at her core for thirty-five years, turning her back on their constant, unrelieved pressure must have added some spring to her step. Meanwhile, far away in England, it seemed to her as though, except for Waldorf, much of her family could get along without her, loving as they were in their various ways.

By and large, that was probably correct. David did not relish her criticisms, and kept his distance, while Bobbie's relationship with his mother remained in a class of its own – intense, unpredictable, prone to upset. Certainly Michael and Jakie managed well enough with her, helped no doubt by their versions of her wit: Nancy relished people who amused her, and Jakie in particular had inherited her repartee. 'Don't forget, racin' brings out the worst of all classes,' she had said, as he was setting off for the races. 'Just like the House of Commons,' he had replied – some time, admittedly, before he was to enter it himself.

She was, however, upset by the deaths of two close friends: Archdeacon Neve, who had maintained to the end a faithful monthly correspondence with her, died in 1948, aged ninety-two. She had written to him on his last birthday, the previous December: 'I shall always remember my father saying that he thought I was in love with you because I worked so hard for you, but he didn't understand, did he, that you and I were working for the love of God, and not man.' And the previous June, Mavis Tate, former MP for Frome, for long a companion in arms in Parliament and at Nancy's side on many of her crusades, had committed suicide.

Mavis Tate had suffered greatly after an official visit to the German concentration camp at Buchenwald, which she had undertaken with fellow MP Archibald Southby. Shortly after returning, both she and Southby had been struck down by a mysterious disease: Southby almost completely lost the power to walk or talk, lingering on in that condition for a further twenty years, while Mavis became crushed by depression, which by the summer of 1947 had become too hard to bear. Nancy was at Mirador when she received from Bobbie a letter that could have brought her only pain; coming from him, it was also sadly prophetic.

Oh, Mother Darling,

Mavis committed suicide in her poor little home yesterday. What is this life? Perhaps it is only a sort of dream anyway. Death to me is so final, suicide so tragic, as, say what people may, I know the black misery that precedes the thoughts of life being no use to one any more. I know them only too well, poor, poor creatures who are driven by despair . . . I know no one who is or was a better friend than Mavis to you. She loved you more than anybody. Friends like her are rare

. . . Oh mother, what should I do, when, and if, I am some day separated from you for ever?[6]

Nancy was of course rich, even independently of Waldorf, with capital
of her own and income from both her marriage settlements. Freed of politics,
she was her own master, and she acted as such. Yet it seemed that she could
not decide whether to settle down, and, if so, to what. Back in England her
behaviour seemed unpredictable; it caused Waldorf further upset, and when
she threatened at short notice to abandon an engagement to open a
Conservative bazaar, he put to her a few home truths:

. . . If the Duchess of Kent were to promise to open a show for you
and then run out at the last moment you would feel justly indignant
– sometimes you fail to realise that to these people you are as important,
and that when you decide not to go it creates a lot of inconvenience
and disappointment.
   Of course you may decide that your mission is to go around abusing
the Labour Government . . . I think you will feel unsettled so long as
you do not know whether to concentrate on that sort of activity or
whether to take up something less controversial . . .
   . . . You sometimes talk as though you could not control your
volcanic temperament inherited from your father. I refuse to agree
that CS can be of so little help to you . . . and also I know that your
true self reflects life and is not volcanic, whether suppressed, explosive
or extinct.[7]

She now began spending much of her time at Rest Harrow, and some of
it in Plymouth, while Waldorf remained at Cliveden, becoming less mobile,
with asthma causing him increasing difficulty in breathing. He nevertheless
carried out many duties, although they were no longer attached to any official
position, falling to him instead simply because of who he was: Christian
Scientists at Cliveden, garden parties for economists, meeting newspaper
directors at Elliot Terrace, taking the chair at Chatham House, attending
meetings of the Reconstruction Committee in Plymouth, and seeing many
other people and organisations who required his advice. He also helped
administer the Plymouth American Trust, an ingenious device that enabled
him and Nancy, after they had left mayoral office, to retain a large share in
directing the application of funds earmarked for the rebuilding of Plymouth.
It was a lot of work for an ailing man.
   Meanwhile Nancy returned to fretting at her exclusion from the cut and
thrust of politics, even if, after standing down, she had told Freddie Knox,

her erstwhile unofficial agent and stalwart supporter in Plymouth, that she never wanted to see the Houses of Parliament again. She maintained that stance for some time, and yet she still felt the tug of anything to do with the Commons; when, in February 1950, another general election was called, Waldorf tried to apply some balm to her wounds by urging his sons, three of whom were fighting seats, to consider inviting her to help them in their constituencies.

The Labour landslide of 1945 had missed Michael's seat at Surrey East, enabling him to maintain the family connection with Parliament even during the post-war years of Tory rejection. Standing in 1950, he eventually succumbed to his father's pressure to let Nancy make an appearance in his campaign. It was not long before he had misgivings: discussing with her what sort of a speech she might make on his platform, she responded immediately with entirely characteristic proposals, which with their mix of humour and appalling directness would probably have destroyed any appeal he might have had for the voters.

> 'Whatever else you do,' said Michael, 'omit all reference to me.' Nancy's response was instantaneous: 'You've given me a good idea. I'm going to make my speech about you. I'll pay you out, Michael, I'll tell the meeting that politics bore you stiff, and that all you really like is painting. I'll tell them you're just a Lothario, an artist, and not a very good husband; and that you make fun of them all behind their backs and that they shouldn't vote for you . . .'
>   . . . Once Nancy was launched on her speech Michael admitted that she spoke like a political veteran . . . She used all the old techniques: 'laughing, scolding, giving them the benefit of the doubt . . . they cheered and called for more'.[8]

Michael won the contest, but at the following election, in October 1951, he willingly stepped down to take up professionally his interests as an artist.

In the 1950 election, Jakie, despite having taunted his mother about the House of Commons, attempted to get there himself. He had been selected for Nancy's old seat, but had resisted his father's suggestions that she should come down and speak for him, fearing that, for better or for worse – which of the two was unpredictable – she would fill the headlines. In fact, he had little option in the matter: when seeking selection for the seat in 1947, he had undertaken to the local selection committee to fight alone and without his mother's help. In the ensuing election, the Plymouth Conservatives insisted that he stick to that promise; he was told that if his mother did try and take part it would alienate those, a significant number, who had been incensed by his adoption as their candidate. However, he did invite her to come round with him on the afternoon of polling day, and at a final meeting the audience called upon her to speak, which she gracefully declined to do, save for a few parting words: 'He'll be a better Member than I, but he won't love you as much as I do.'

In 1950, Jakie was narrowly defeated, but in 1951 he won back his mother's old seat, which he was to retain until he retired from Parliament in 1959. His elder brother, Bill, who had lost his East Fulham seat in the 1945 election, was in 1951 elected MP for Wycombe – the seat formerly held by Lady Terrington, one of the first women to join Nancy in the Commons.

Despite Nancy's ongoing temptation to make political waves, Waldorf remained unrelenting about a return to active politics, either for himself or for her, restating his reasons in a letter to her in August 1951:

> I said it in 1945 and I repeat it, that I am not going on in partisan party politics. The world problems, political and economic, are very complicated and complex. I have done my bit. So have you. Others now can have a go . . . I can take interest in politics as an onlooker, but not as an active fighter . . . To dabble in a minor capacity in the dog fight of party politics when one has been in the front line is wasting one's talents. It may be amusing, but it is relatively ineffective. There are many as important questions, social, moral, economic, national or international, which require settlement outside party politics. I want to play an active part in them. There are similarly other occupations and pastimes other than party politics.[9]

Nancy's unrest was also made evident in the increasing strain in her relations with her children and their spouses. Except for Bobbie, by the end of the war all Nancy's offspring were married, which itself was a cause of tension. Despite her lyrical happiness at the time of Wissie's marriage, she had resumed a rather critical attitude towards her daughter, strangely misplaced in respect of someone who was widely considered attractive and highly intelligent. Marriage brought a different problem for her sons, as her impulse was to resent her daughters-in-law, lumping them together as intruders in her relationships with her children who had replaced her in their affections: 'As for when they marry,' she said of her sons, 'you might just as well say goodbye.' The wives and girlfriends who suffered most were the ones who allowed themselves to be overborne: they unwittingly encouraged Nancy's inclination to bully, which had been with her in varying degrees for most of her life. However, like many bullies, Nancy liked it when people stood up to her: in her case it touched a chord and paved the way for friendship. Bill's first wife, Sally Norton, whom he married in 1945, proved the point, finding that when she answered back, Nancy warmed to her:

'Can't you ever say anything nice, Aunt Nancy? Pull yourself together,' she said after a bout of criticism directed at one of her children. 'Oh, you're always tickin' me off,' Nancy replied. 'Well, you deserve it; I wouldn't do it if you didn't deserve it.' Nancy softened and agreed. 'Automatically,' her daughter-in-law recalled, 'she would say, "What'ya talkin' about?"' unrelated to anything I had just said. I don't know how, but we just stepped into that relationship. I adored her.'[10]

Sometimes, however, she became actively aggressive. One of her-daughters-in-law tried whenever possible not to be alone with her; on one occasion she could not avoid it, and Nancy came up and stood over her chair and said, 'Where have you come from? The gutter?' The young wife, who was pregnant, fled the room before she gave way to tears. 'It was very important not to collapse in front of her,' she said, 'because then she had a knife to use.' The wife of one of her other sons often did collapse in front of her when browbeaten, and Nancy would frequently make her cry. She agreed with Jakie when he half-humorously suggested that the only daughter-in-law she was prepared to like was Bobbie's boyfriend, Frank, whose existence at the edge of the family she had come to tolerate, after her original consternation at her eldest son's revelations had gradually subsided. 'Frank,' she remarked on one occasion, 'is the prettiest of all my children's girlfriends; the rest of them are just overpainted hussies.'

As was the case with her daughters-in-law, Nancy's relations with some of her children's close friends were not always cordial, as she never lost her aversion to her family forming groups in which she was not a dominant, if not the principal, member. Where she felt that they were in error, in particular in respect of religion, she remained free with her views: 'I have had Kick Kennedy here for three days,' she wrote to an old friend during the war. 'She is a very nice girl and I believe that if she says she will not bring up her children RCs that she will honourably keep her promise. I had a most interesting talk with her on the subject, and warned her against the traps that would be set.'[11] She took her attitude to extremes in 1944, when Jakie married an Argentinian girl who, although considered by all who knew her to be both beautiful and sweet, was a Latin and a Catholic. With a remarkable display of obstinacy, Nancy refused to attend the wedding and managed to persuade Waldorf also to stay away. Jakie was greatly put out: 'I never felt quite the same about her again,' he recalled. However, responding perhaps as Nancy herself might have done in a reversal of roles, he announced that for his part he would not attend her funeral.

Relations were not eased by her disapproval of what she saw as the lax morals of the younger generation: 'I think you boys are very silly,' she told her sons one day. 'You have perfectly good wives and yet you go jumping into bed with other people. It is not as if it's so wonderful: sex is just like going to the lavatory.' This met with general amusement: 'A sort of Number Three, then, Ma?' Jakie replied – and thereafter, tales of infidelity among their friends were often described as 'a little Number Three'.

Although Nancy's mix of intuition and usually unerring perception could prove painful for those who did not react robustly to her darts – and she seemed remarkably able to find an open wound and pour salt on it – deep down, and beneath the highly charged surface, her nature remained kind. It was laughter and wit that people remembered, rather than hurt or embarrassment. But while she herself was quick to change from seeming harshness to gaiety, others often did not or could not move at the same speed, and were left nursing a wound that had not been intended. She was, for example, very fond of Helen Mildmay, daughter of her old friend Alice, but often proved disconcerting in ways she herself would hardly have noticed:

> To me she was amazingly kind, thoughtful and loving. She never came to Plymouth without telephoning me and getting me over to luncheon. She gave me lovely presents . . . I was always being asked to stay at Cliveden and to parties at St James' Square. But she was curiously insensitive. Shyness was a thing she had never felt, and she simply couldn't picture or understand it. She didn't realise that suddenly to have the attention of a roomful of strangers called to you by a remark like 'Helen! Where on earth did you get that awful hat?' when you entered a room could be embarrassing not only for you but for the others there as well. Then, after the luncheon, she would take me out and buy me six new hats.[12]

The kindliness in her nature did not seem obvious in her continuing resentment at David's success at the *Observer*, and her fury at her exclusion from influence over the paper, which also continued to widen the gap that had emerged between her and Waldorf. For a time she was encouraged in her attitude by Jakie, but Waldorf remained firm, sure that David was the right man for the job of editing the paper, which he was determined should be independent of party politics. He pointed out that the trust into which the *Observer* had been formed was a legal contract, and could not be altered: 'Why do you continue raising the question of the policy of the *Observer* and trying to make your mother believe that it can be changed?' he asked Jakie, adding that he was 'as obstinate as Neville Chamberlain'.

It may be that if this point of dissension had not arisen, some other might have filled its place; however, it fed Nancy's increasing intolerance of socialist, egalitarian attitudes, towards which David seemed tentatively to be leading the *Observer*. Hers was a natural reaction in view of the sudden and unexpected ascendancy that the left had gained in Britain: 'Lower than vermin' was how, in 1948, Aneurin Bevan, then Minister of Health, had gleefully described the Conservatives, while the Labour government was imposing its radical welfare programme with, in many cases, a truculent contempt for its once mighty opponents. Nancy had always loathed communism and totalitarian regimes, and for her son to be furthering even a mildly left-wing creed infuriated her. But she also seemed to be fighting on a broader front, and her antagonism towards the *Observer* was perhaps a symptom of the malaise both in the country and in her own political and personal life.

Although Waldorf was not willing to alter his intentions towards the *Observer*, he patiently tried to reason with Nancy, repeating the stance that he had justified to her in 1947, after David had become foreign editor and was soon to take overall charge:

> With all my shortcomings my chief desire has been and still is to support you. You act by instinct and inspiration – this is fine – but at times it prevents you being willing to reason. You are naturally combative and have developed a habit of increasing your combats . . . You have always been my inspiration, and if you refuse to co-operate because you are not able to direct, then I shall withdraw from my commitments, hand them on to others and come and hold your hand.[13]

He continued to hope that her intransigence would wear itself out:

> . . . remember that you have repeatedly told me and your family that you were going away because you could not direct the *Observer*, or because you could not bear to see your son make a success of the paper, or because you were not in Parliament. All this you have repeated over and over again till one saw it had got a sort of mesmeric obsession over you. I know this can't last and I pray it has broken by now . . .[14]

Although Waldorf continued his attempts to find a role for Nancy and persuade her to fill it, she did not respond. She had built up what the family called 'an array of dragons', including socialism, Roman Catholicism, psychiatry, the Jews, the Latins and the *Observer*, and it seemed that it might be hard to induce her to become constructive again. The best chance, Waldorf considered, was to refuse to support her when she started being aggressive in politics, and to unite in 'begging her to be benevolently constructive', as was her nature and as she used to be.

She could find some satisfaction in her life at a new base in London. The Astors had not occupied 4, St James's Square, scene of so many triumphs in the heyday of their political life, since 1942, when it had been requisitioned. Although they had kept a flat and office space in a building at the back, until the end of the war the main house had been used as the London headquarters of the Free French forces. The family's long and famous connection with the house ended in 1948, when Waldorf sold it to the government, on condition that it was preserved as the headquarters of the Arts Council of Great Britain. As with his transfer of Cliveden, he was determined that such a fine building should be assured of a suitable future, and should not fall into the clutches of speculators.

The Astors then bought 35, Hill Street, Mayfair. The house was on a typically grand scale, with six storeys and a basement. It had been redesigned for Nancy by the fashionable architect Claud Phillimore and had a richly comfortable feel. Nancy's main room, known as the Boudoir, had blue satin walls, tall Georgian windows, and a large gilt-framed looking glass over a marble mantelpiece, on which stood an antique French clock. There she would repair in the morning to glance at the papers and magazines – *Punch*, *National Geographic*, *Illustrated London News* – before moving to the telephone to discuss all manner of subjects, and to arrange plans for entertaining, to which she remained addicted. It usually took the form of lunch or dinner parties, as she did not much like tea, or seeing people at that time of the day. When, occasionally, people did come then, Nancy would drink Ribena, or sometimes Dubonnet, which Lee had persuaded her did not count as alcohol.

At Hill Street her parties had great style, as had been the case more or less throughout her life. Her guests were drawn out by her undimmed sparkle, and by the eclectic company – literary lights, politicians, and the occasional crowned head, usually Scandinavian. Her pleasure in seeing friends, and theirs in being captivated by her, was enhanced by the accompaniment of excellent food, in which her interest, inherited from Chillie, was maintained by the skills of Otto Dangl, a Viennese chef, and his two assistants. Early in the morning the chef would go up to Nancy's room with a menu of the day's suggestions, and hand it to Rose, who would take it into the inner sanctum, where it would be agreed or altered, according to whim. Old habits died hard, and Virginia hams, with their honey and cloves, would regularly arrive from America, besides copious amounts of chewing gum, pineapple brittle and other favourite sorts of 'candy'.

Despite not preparing dishes herself, Nancy could instantly detect if anything was not as it should be, rarely as that happened. On one occasion she was acting as hostess at Jakie's house, with a number of politicians among the guests. The cook for some reason had added margarine instead of butter to the hollandaise sauce. Nancy was incensed, and after dinner she descended to the kitchen like a typhoon, flattening the trembling chef with a stream of well-chosen abuse, in French. Albert Roux, later a celebrated chef and restaurateur, was at the time working for the Astors as a scullery boy. He was in the kitchen when Nancy burst through the door, and was both amazed and impressed as the guilty chef withered and perished before the blast: 'She knew what she was talking about,' he recalled.[15]

At both Hill Street and Rest Harrow, telephone exchanges were established on the ground floor, and one of the servants would act as operator, pulling and pushing the wires, quickly making connections so that Nancy could be put through without having to hold the line. She gave the occasional television interview, when she would usually range inconsequentially through her life's interests, obstacles, successes – the drink trade, the scurrilous scribblers who wrote about the Cliveden Set, women, religion, morality, entertaining, goodness, Virginia, the Civil War. She would firmly take command of the proceedings, with the interviewer soon relegated to bystander, before abruptly ending the discussion: 'But I don't believe in talkin' to you all day, so goodbye.'

After her trips in 1947 and 1948, Nancy did not again spend long periods in America: in 1950, Mirador, one of her emotional anchors, had been sold by her niece, Nancy Lancaster, who had bought it from Phyllis before the war. She still spent time away from London, however, and this continued to sadden Waldorf – indeed, without Nancy's presence, Hill Street had no particular appeal for him, and he soon gravitated away from it, to become firmly based at Cliveden. 'What is the good of putting me in a large house,' he wrote, 'and then running away to be soothed and flattered by distant admirers?' She did spend periods at Cliveden with Waldorf after this, but it was geographically rather than emotionally.

It seemed that they might move even further apart when, in the autumn of 1950, Waldorf had a stroke. Fortunately it was not fatal, but its effects were severe. Grave as that was, another upset for Nancy was the death, in November 1950, of Bernard Shaw, for whom she had long felt deep affection, regarding herself as the closest of his friends. Only a week before he died she had visited him at his home, soothing him by rubbing his head with healing hands, and keeping him amused with stories; he particularly liked her tale of a coloured woman in hospital who, when questioned about how many husbands and children she had had, answered: 'I'se had two husbands an' six children: two by John, two by Mose, and the last two I had by myself.'[16]

Curiously, these woes, both very painful, although of course for Nancy one far more fundamental than the other, seemed for a time to release in her an unexpected element of serenity, certainly in her attitude to Waldorf. It was as if, slowing up physically – she had now moved into her seventies – she also felt less obsessive emotionally, better able to accept the conditions that had settled about her.

Her relations with Waldorf now thawed a little. His mind was not affected by his stroke, but he became more immobile. And although he was troubled by the way the family pattern had developed, he had become resigned to it. His children found that his impairment brought them some balm in making him seem less austere; as his son Michael described it, 'He enjoyed a short Indian summer in the evening of his life.'

Waldorf moved into ground-floor rooms at Cliveden and generally used a wheelchair. To ease his breathing, the temperature of his surroundings was kept as low as possible, with the windows opened wide. Nancy, who had long been happy with fresh air, may not have noticed the cold, though Waldorf's visitors found it uncomfortable. Perhaps her thoughts strayed back some forty years, when in the middle of Waldorf's first election campaign his TB had forced him to leave Plymouth in order to recuperate in Scotland, where he and Nancy had spent the pure but icy northern nights on a balcony.

Now, Waldorf liked to feel that she was nearby, ready to talk and read to him if he wanted it: 'You often say,' he wrote to her, 'that in your youth you read a lot – you are probably more literary than I am – I am sure you are more musical – yet circumstances compel me to turn to music & books for enjoyment now. Is there anything unselfish or selfish in my suggestion that you should read and listen on the radio to music, because we could do this together?' They seemed at last to be at ease with each other once more. Waldorf had always accepted Nancy for what she was, and although the pain of adjusting to her anger and her long absences during their post-war life was severe, he had never ceased to adore her. Now, each had settled into a pattern, and for the last few months of his life Nancy showed him the affection he wanted so much.

Having re-entered Parliament in 1951, Bill was spending most of his time in London, although his home was at Bletchingdon Park, in Oxfordshire. But he was at Cliveden when, at the end of September 1952, his father died; ever faithful, Waldorf's last words to his son were 'Look after Mother.' At the end he wanted and needed only her, and in his final days she was close at hand, and he seemed happy. 'Glad he was like his old self the last ten days,' Nancy wrote, 'and oh how it makes me grieve of the years wasted . . . But I just want to look back not forward, and thank God I had such a long and happy life and that Waldorf is now safe . . . No two people,' she reflected, 'ever worked happier than we did.'[17] Later she reflected sadly, 'Waldorf was no good without me, and, alas, I am no good without him.' Nearly fifty years of partnership were ended.

A few months later, she quit Cliveden. Bill had offered to let her stay on, but the London house was comfortable and there she could reign supreme. She adored Cliveden but was aware that her time there was up. Through the high point of its luxury in the days before the Great War, and in its heyday at the apex of political entertaining between the wars, she had been the house's dynamo: people used to say that Cliveden in her absence was like a great ocean liner with its engines turned off, or, in Lord Curzon's description, 'like a church without a chancel, a nosegay without a flower, a wedding without a bride'. In those days, when she entered a room it had been, in her niece's words, as though an electric light had been switched on in a room lit by candles. Now she no longer had any great purpose to her life, and for all the energy she still generated, the ship was drifting.

With Waldorf departed, her restlessness to some extent returned. She moved regularly through the year from Hill Street to Rest Harrow, attended by her large staff, with annual journeys to America. She retained her domestic support despite the fact that she had never seemed able to express praise to her servants, although occasionally she would obliquely edge near it: on one occasion at a Christmas staff dance, held in Cliveden's covered tennis court, a footman who prided himself on his dancing asked her to dance – encouraged by Lee, who said that Nancy would expect the request; after a few expert circuits of the floor, waltzing and reversing, Nancy suddenly stood still: 'Now I'm going to get a rocket,' thought the footman, wondering what was coming, but Nancy merely said, 'Let me tell you something, Charles, if you did your work as well as you dance, you'd do your work a lot better.'

Bill's first wife had left him for Tommy Baring, whom she married in April 1953. Nancy, who had grown to like spending time with younger people, frequently stayed with the new couple, attended by her loyal maid, Rose. Doggedly devoted to Nancy, Rose now became more a companion, accompanying her everywhere; she was herself strong-willed, and if ever her mistress became too demanding she readily expressed forthright views: 'This won't do, m'lady, this won't do . . .' Tommy Baring, a descendant of Nancy's former admirer, Lord Revelstoke, recalled how Nancy would come down to dinner, dressed in black, her hair beautifully done by Rose, wearing the magnificent necklace Revelstoke had given her long ago, in the days before Waldorf. She would put her thumb under the pearls, 'as thick as pigeon's eggs, some of them', and say, 'See these pearls, Tommy? They're the Baring pearls. But you ain't goin' to get 'em, Tommy, you ain't goin' to get 'em . . .'

By then she seemed rather bird-like, but she still liked to spar with her hosts and their guests: her eyes would sparkle – 'piercing, but full of laughter' – and she seemed as full of vim as ever. Her wealth gave her the confidence still to stand up to other people, however important: 'If she needed to get something done,' recalled Baring, 'boy, did she get it done!'

Yet she still had time to fill. In June 1953 she travelled to Africa, replacing her initial idea of a pan-African tour with a visit to Rhodesia. It attracted the publicity that might have been expected, given Nancy's views on race, which by then were considered prejudiced, at least in newspaper circles. A lively controversy was anticipated when a discussion was arranged between her and a collection of progressive Africans. Nancy rose to the occasion, and although the Africans arrived ready to bristle and confront, she delighted them with her forthright and honest views, and the meeting turned out a considerable success.

In 1958, Hill Street was sold, and Nancy moved into a flat in London's Eaton Square. She didn't really like the idea – 'What is the butler to do with his front door opening onto a landing?' she would complain. 'I walk down the stairs and don't know half the people I see.' It was also said to be haunted, although ghosts seemed reluctant to manifest themselves while Nancy was in residence.[18] It was nevertheless one of the nicest flats in London, extending laterally through three houses, and Nancy soon made it attractive and comfortable, with French furniture, Old Masters, eighteenth-century landscapes, fine china, lacquer screens, and a drawing room lined with pale blue silk. The butler managed the front door without apparent difficulty.

Besides annual visits to the United States, and occasional trips to the south of France, Nancy also began regularly to stay with her niece, Nancy Lancaster, at Haseley Court, near Oxford. The house was exceptionally attractive and comfortable, as Nancy Lancaster was a famous interior designer, and she had placed at her aunt's permanent disposal a bedroom that almost rivalled the magnificence of her room at Cliveden. Aunt and niece used frequently to battle, and exchange views with a frankness that sometimes appalled other guests, until they realised that their words were hardly meant to wound and had no effect on their mutual affection.

When in London, Nancy's brother-in-law, Bob Brand, had also lived at Hill Street, although after breakfast he would usually disappear in the

direction of the clubs of St James's, or to other rendezvous with old friends
or business associates. When Nancy moved to Eaton Square, he used that
as a pied-à-terre for a time, and he also frequently stayed with her at Rest
Harrow, where she spent many summer weekends. Another close companion
was the Marchesa de Casa Maury, who, as Freda Dudley-Ward, had been
an intimate of the Prince of Wales before the advent of Mrs Simpson. She
was by then divorced, but her former husband sometimes stayed at the
nearby Guilford Hotel, and would come over and join the party at Rest
Harrow. Bobbie also frequently came over to stay, from the house in nearby
Deal that he shared with his boyfriend, Frank – whom, however, he judged
it best to leave behind. The two were happily living together, and in her
later years Nancy seems to have resigned herself, with mildly detached
amusement, to the strange way in which her beloved son's life had worked
out.

She referred to Bobbie, now in his fifties, as 'an old gentleman with a
bay window'. His main base was in Fulham, at a house called Pineapple
Priory, which he had filled with Georgian furniture, and where he amused
his friends with a wit that almost matched his mother's – sometimes with
an equally sharp edge, much to the discomfiture of his targets. Bobbie, with
the relative independence of mind that middle age had brought, retained
many of his mother's virtues and vices: kindness and generosity were his
hallmarks, and he was entertaining, full of gossip and generally considered
to be very funny. Yet he had Nancy's knack of noticing any vulnerable points,
and exposing them to uncomfortable ridicule. Friends knew that they had
to be on their guard.

The various ambivalencies that had affected him throughout his life had
crystallised. Although he had a series of fast and luxurious cars, and other
accoutrements of the rich, he had adopted an attitude of smart rebellion.
Just as the grandson of the Prime Minister of the time used to wear jeans
– strictly forbidden – under his school trousers at Eton, Bobbie was inclined
to appear at Cliveden or Hill Street dressed slightly like a Teddy boy, in
clothes that would have bewildered his former brother officers in the
Household Cavalry; he would likewise roll his own cigarettes with cheap
tobacco, but carry them in a Fabergé cigarette case or a jewelled gold one
from Cartier.

Besides having Bobbie, Freda Casa Maury, Bob Brand and other family
members and old friends to stay at Rest Harrow, Nancy, perhaps for old
times' sake, undertook some local public duties: each year the Mayor of
Sandwich would be summoned to the house so that Nancy could arrange
a party in the Guildhall for the town's old age pensioners; and sometimes
she went into the local villages or town and distributed extravagant presents

to people she thought were in need. Back at Rest Harrow, she would spend long hours on the veranda, talking with her guests, at her feet a corgi called Madam, a present from Bobbie. If she was by herself she would sometimes take out a harmonica and play old Southern tunes. The dog would howl.

She remained as fit as someone much younger, and although she no longer used the squash court at the end of the garden, well into her seventies she played the occasional game of tennis. Every morning she bathed in the sea, however cold the water. She would not let anyone go with her, but the gardener was detailed to keep an eye out from a discreet distance. After her bathe – more of a plunge, quickly in and out – she would walk up and down on the pebbles. Ever the politician, she would call to fishermen near the beach and joke with them, or order some of their catch to be sent up to the house:

> One day, my brother and I were fishing on the beach when Lady Astor came out, wearing a swimming costume: 'Come on you chaps,' she said, 'don't just sit there, join me for a swim.'
> 'We haven't any trunks,' we replied.
> 'Never mind that. I'm not prudish. Come in your pants.'
> We did, and much regretted it, as it was early April, not a good time for sea-bathing.[19]

Otto, the chef, would prepare the fish for her guests in the evening, or produce other favourite dishes, such as sweetbreads, and bananas cooked in rum – although alcohol other than as a cooking ingredient remained strictly forbidden. The atmosphere at Rest Harrow was as peaceful as anywhere could be with Nancy around, but the sense of calm was only achieved by constant and considerable activity behind the scenes.

She remained an enthusiastic golfer. Small, neat, and with sprightly step, she would arrive at the course usually dressed in blue, with visor or veil, and brown shoes with laces criss-crossing her ankles. Rest Harrow was almost adjacent to three famous golf courses: Royal St George's, Prince's and Cinque Ports, all of a high standard and well kept, even if play was often hindered by wind and rain scudding in from the sea.

In the aftermath of war, when their own private conflict had unfolded, golf had provided a loose bond between Waldorf and Nancy, even though he used to say that for her golf was not a game but a contest. They would play a few holes together, each attended by a caddie. When they had had enough, or the rain set in, they would call for their car, the two-tone Rolls-Royce having followed them at a discreet distance along a track by the edge of the course. Then they would be driven home, and the car sent on to return the caddies to their hut.

Waldorf had been a member at St George's, but as the club did not permit ladies to play unless with a man, Nancy went there usually only with him. They both kept clear of the clubhouse: the pink gins, Egyptian cigarettes and jovial banter at the 'nineteenth hole' was not to their taste. Now Nancy played frequently with her niece Alice and her husband Reggie Winn, who had a house nearby, and also with their son David – subsequently drowned, after long hours of brave endurance, in a sailing accident off the coast.

Nancy liked to have a senior caddie with her, to carry her clubs and to advise: 'She walked quickly and spoke quickly, a bit sharp,' was how her usual caddie described her, 'very likeable, but a little like a cat on hot bricks at times.' The bricks were sometimes heated by the presence of a nudist colony on the beach near the course. It was a continuing annoyance to Nancy, who would berate the presidents of the various golf clubs, demanding its removal, while also sometimes pressing her complaints through the columns of the *East Kent Mercury*. Her caddie recalled the problem arising one day while he was carrying her bag as she played with the Winns:

David Winn was a bit of a terror and Lady Astor used to get at him quite a lot, trying to keep him under control. She used to send him back off the course if he didn't behave himself. I remember one afternoon we were playing at Prince's, on the 9th tee, and by the green there was the water wagon which used to be pulled round the course in those days, for the greens; and this chap was walking over the course towards us, from the nude huts by the beach. He was wearing a straw hat, but nothing else at all, and carrying a billic-can to get some water. And I thought to myself, you know, Oh dear. I tried to avoid her seeing it. Goodness knows what would happen, being the sort of person she was. She didn't like the day being interrupted by all those nudists down there, you see, she used to be very hot on that sort of thing, propriety, and that. Mercifully for some reason she didn't notice.

She enjoyed her golf, but she wasn't a really good player. She didn't play on her own, hitting the ball round, but always with a party, usually a foursome, but she would play eighteen holes, easily. Very smart and attractive; delicate-looking. And she was always in a hurry. Even as she got out of the car she was almost running. She used to play quite quickly, wanting to get on with it. She usually played at a quiet time, when there was nobody in front, or behind her.[20]

Seemingly content, Nancy would hit the ball, reliably if not hard, straight down the fairway.

For many people her way of life after Waldorf's death would have been interesting, and at a comfortably slower pace after so many years at full speed. But Nancy needed some project to pursue, despite declaring that she had set her face against any more public life. Waldorf had encouraged the idea of her writing her memoirs, and had held discussions with American publishers, and with people in England who might help her to channel her memories. However, she soon lost interest in the idea; she had in any case dismissed as worthless the concept of writing an autobiography, and likewise anyone who wrote one: 'There is nothing to tell about my life,' she said, 'no secrets, no sensations . . . I don't care if people accuse me of adultery because it is not true, but I do care if they accuse me of talking too much, because it is true.'

Her sense of humour remained undiminished. A niece recalled meeting her, in carefree mood and sucking a toffee, on her way to discharge a duty that she had agreed to undertake:

'Hello, Aunt Nancy, what are you up to?'

'Well, I'm goin' up to *Cumberland*, to unveil a plaque to George Washington's *grandmother*.'

'Goodness! What are you going to say?'

'Can't imagine, except that I'll certainly say that I wish she'd lived nearer London.'[21]

Although her previous idea of a peerage had not got past the edge of Churchill's desk, she retained thoughts on the subject, and her interest was renewed in 1957, when the proposal to introduce life peerages gained momentum. The moving force behind that was Harold Macmillan, by then Prime Minister, and in 1958 Parliament approved the appropriate Bill. Nancy was not chosen, although there were four women among the first life peers, including Curzon's daughter Irene, who as a young girl had been a great friend of Nancy, and who had spent much time at Cliveden. Nancy seemed rather put out at being omitted from the list – 'I've done enough for *him*,' she said of the Prime Minister. That was true, as Nancy had often made speeches for Macmillan in his constituency in the far north, when he was a young man. However, by 1958 she was seventy-nine, and even apart from her age there was no compelling reason why she should be selected, as she was no longer on top of the detail of politics, or closely involved in public work, as were the women who were chosen.

Nancy and Macmillan had corresponded a few years previously over another honour, when Nancy had urged the government to give a knighthood to Waldorf's Deputy Lord Mayor, who had done a great deal for Plymouth in the war, while Waldorf was ill:

After the war, neither Waldorf nor I ever asked for or expected anything from the Government, though Plymouth was the worst bombed of any place in England, and it was because of what we suffered here that you got the National Fire Service which really saved Bristol, Bath etc . . . So I am writing to ask you, could you possibly right this dire wrong?[22]

In 1959, the civic leaders in Plymouth themselves righted a wrong by conferring upon Nancy the freedom of the city. Many people thought it was rather overdue – Waldorf had received the honour twenty-three years earlier. The ceremony was on 16 July, at the Methodist Central Hall, which was packed with all those prominent in Plymouth life:

Presently it was her turn to reply. The assembly had been waiting patiently for this moment. Their eyes had been fixed on her as she sat on the platform, a very small figure in a blue dress and hat . . . At her first words the ceremonial gravity which had governed the proceedings so far was dissipated by a breeze of merriment and warmth. Pointing to her sons she declared that to speak in front of them put her on her mettle. Her stories came out one after the other, without other relevance than that they were very characteristic of her, were expected, and that not to have told them would have caused grave disappointment . . .[23]

That evening she attended a dinner in her honour, with about 250 guests, at which she gave another much-applauded speech; at its conclusion, with a gesture of characteristic generosity, she removed the diamond necklace that hung down to her waist, and put it around the neck of the Lady Mayoress, as a future badge of office.

She continued to stay regularly with Bill at Cliveden. She was inclined to take control of the proceedings, in a way trapped by her diva act, but happy to be in her accustomed seat once more. 'She did dominate the dining table,' Bill's wife recalled, 'but it was because people listened to her; either because she was telling them something they didn't know, or because she was being amusing. She was full of information, and with a view about everything. That rather delightful voice, and she loved it when you laughed with her.'[24]

325

Her desire to be in on everything was less popular when directed to the tables of bridge that were sometimes laid out. She could not play but insisted that she wanted to learn: 'This is not a success with the bridge players,' a guest commented. Bill's wife also teased her about her blue-blooded friends: 'She loved Royalty – and the odd duchess or duke: that would be lovely. She would never admit it. I'd say, "You're a bit of a snob, Aunt Nancy," and she would say, "Never. Certainly not. And don't you cheek me, anyway."'[25]

Bill liked to maintain Cliveden in the manner to which it was accustomed, and within the restraints of the 1950s there was some reflection of the formality of earlier days. A custom that had lingered since Victorian times was that of the men taking the women in to dinner, in a queue arranged in proper precedence. In general, Nancy liked old-fashioned customs, and doing things in the proper way, although in her own case she was sometimes happy to override them. She would stand in front of the fire, warming herself with her skirt raised behind, and then unconcernedly turn to pay due respects to some crowned head that she had invited to Cliveden. One evening she asked a shy young guest to take her in to dinner, in order to put him at his ease, as she saw that he was a little daunted by so many old and important people. He felt honoured to be asked but was mildly surprised when, as they reached the dining room doors, she took some chewing gum from her mouth and tucked it down the front of her dress. In the same spirit, as a young hostess of dinner parties at the height of Cliveden's formality, she had often pushed back her tiara as if it were an old hat, cooled herself with a plate as though it were a fan, or put her pearls in her mouth as though they were teeth, speaking through them as if everything was normal.[26]

Throughout her seventies she remained young at heart, and, for her age, spry in body, carriage erect – 'Mind' seemingly preserving the good Christian Scientist from ill or ailment. She continued to switch with little difficulty from formality to girlish fun, and remained kind to children and to teenagers, at least those who had not yet reached an age at which they might resent her dominant ways. In the 1950s, when she stayed at Cliveden with Bill, she would often send a car over to Eton to collect the children of friends. One young guest remembers how Nancy would greet him on arrival and then disappear for a time after sending him off with a footman to collect the golf balls she had driven off the terrace, or while Lee gave him lessons in putting. When Nancy reappeared there would be lots of 'jokes and teasing', and on being driven back by the chauffeur at the end of the day he would find a very generous tip which Nancy, perhaps in hope rather than from experience, had tucked into a copy of *Science and Health*.[27]

She seemed to have lost little of her skill as a hostess, 'getting hold of all sorts of people, giving them the best food in England, drawing out whatever they have to say of interest, and pulling their legs as soon as they show any sign of becoming pompous or boring'.

Her still restless spirit, with youthfulness so near the surface, was evident in the pleasure she took in seeing her grandchildren, of which, by the time she was seventy-five, in 1954, she had five, from the ages of one to eleven. She was usually informal and full of fun with them, just as she had been with her own children when young. They would be taken in to see their grandmother while she was still in bed, looking to them rather strange, sitting up with greased face or with special kinds of make-up paper sticking to her forehead, and she would read to them short Christian Science passages, and urge them to 'hold the right thought'. At Rest Harrow, in the morning, when she had swum and dressed, she would often go and play with them as though she was a child herself, either in a large sandpit at one end of the house, or outside in the garden. While her elderly friends were seating themselves in the drawing room and turning to the newspapers, Nancy would be riding in 'the Astor Express', her grandson William's fairy cycle with a trolley attached to it, in which she would be pulled all around the garden, even down the steep slope at the front: 'She was quite fearless.'[28] Nor did she lose a youthful sense of mischief: one grandson remembers her standing at an upstairs window with glasses of water at hand, ready to pour on the children emerging below and take them by surprise.

She combined such reversions to childhood with apparently treating old age with detached serenity. 'Years ago I thought old age would be dreadful,' she remarked on her eightieth birthday, 'because I should not be able to do the things I want to do. Now I find that there is nothing I want to do after all.'

She was at Rest Harrow in 1963, at the time when the nation was indulging itself in the scandal of the Profumo affair, for many months the leading news story. Some of the trouble had arisen on the Cliveden estate, where one of the principal villains, the fashionable osteopath Stephen Ward, was the tenant of a cottage, gathering around him an exotic group of people, including John Profumo, the Secretary of State for War, and Yevgeni Ivanov, a Russian spy, whom he would introduce to selected 'ladies of indifferent character'.

Bill, as Ward's landlord, was receiving advice from all quarters. His brother David urged him not to keep silent, as he and Cliveden were receiving a considerable amount of unfavourable publicity – even though Christine Keeler, the girl around whom most of the talk swirled, had set foot in the main house at Cliveden only once: Bill's wife had seen her sitting in the hall, and had offered her a drink, which she declined before soon departing. But the germs of the story were so sensational – beautiful girls, naked bathing, Cabinet ministers, Russian diplomats – that they needed the barest touch of a news hawk's typewriter to ensnare Cliveden, before leading eventually to the resignation of the War Minister and the fall of the government.

By then Nancy's short-term memory was failing a little, but it is anyway doubtful that she would have paid attention to the matter for very long even if she had been aware of it. However, her sons and daughters-in-law feared her reaction, feeling that there was quite enough drama being played out around them without any addition from Nancy. They also felt protective: however unpredictable Nancy was, a likely result of her hearing about the scandal would be that she would be unhappy and upset. Her intuition was fabled, so elaborate schemes were concocted to try and prevent her stumbling upon the tales that were filling the news columns. For a time they appeared to be successful: the butler at Rest Harrow filleted her newspaper to remove all references to the story before it was taken in to her – sometimes she had a pretty small paper, observed the housemaid[29] – and telephone calls were arranged to distract her from listening to the news on the wireless. However, when she did eventually discover what everyone was talking about, there was no dramatic reaction; instead her first instinct was to help those in need by setting off at once to Cliveden to offer comfort to Bill.

A year later, in March 1964, aged eighty-five, she was staying with Wissie in France when she was given news that truly did upset her. Something grave had befallen Bobbie, and he was lying unconscious in St Stephen's Hospital. Again, Nancy's family could not gauge her likely reaction or its degree, save that they wanted to spare her from being badly hurt. Unable at first to decide what to say to her, Wissie said nothing at all. Meanwhile, Bill flew back from America.

At length, persuaded that she must say something, Wissie explained that Bobbie had had a stroke. In fact he had attempted to kill himself with sleeping pills. For many years he had tried to manage inherent unhappiness by resorting to the well of humour he had inherited from Nancy, but his intense and volatile relationship with her, and the effect on her emotions of excessive drinking, had overwhelmed him. Now he was in a pitiful state, attached to wires and tubes and other ominous bits of apparatus. David urged his sister to bring Nancy back to London, and against the better judgement of some of the family he then took her to the hospital, thinking that seeing Bobbie would make Nancy understand that he might well die. Whatever might have been the benefit of that, the shock to her was immediate and severe. Although with her extraordinary resilience she seemed very soon to recover some liveliness, it became evident that her vitality had finally slipped away.

The following weekend, she went to stay with Wissie and her husband at Grimsthorpe Castle, their home in Lincolnshire. After her arrival, she herself had a stroke. She was put to bed, and it was not long before it became apparent that she would not emerge from her bedroom alive. Meanwhile, however, Bobbie had recovered enough to leave his hospital bed and go to his mother's side. While she remained in bed at Grimsthorpe, he was constantly with her, more miserable than any at the prospect of her death: 'Poor Bobbie,' wrote Michael, '. . . he will feel utterly lost. Their lives were terribly linked, linked certainly to Bobbie's destruction.'[30]

Nancy's children and nieces came and went, and there were people constantly with her. Occasionally her mind seemed to clear a little, and she would sit in a chair, looking at *The Times.* She had never lost her neat and attractive appearance, and even in old age her fine bone structure lent beauty to her face. But she seemed quite aware that she was dying – informing the doctor so each morning. Her children would read to her: Kipling, Wavell's *Other Men's Flowers* – authors who once upon a time were her guests – psalms, and 'The Battle Hymn of the Republic'. She was too weak to talk, but she acknowledged her family's presence, and liked to hear their voices. The well of impish humour was not quite dry: when something fell from the bedside table, and the nurse bent down to pick it up, Nancy 'extended a frail arm and gave the nurse's posterior a little slap'. But there were heartbreaking moments too. Once she cried out, 'Waldorf, Waldorf, wake me up. Please.'

She had travelled far from the days of the Blitz on her beloved Plymouth; from the blandishments of von Ribbentrop; from the Cliveden parties that brought together all sorts and conditions of men, spawning so many ideas and initiatives; from her tireless work up and down the country for social causes and needy people; from her fierce campaigns, undaunted in the bleak back streets of the Barbican, ending with her triumphant admission to the House of Commons; farther still from the days of King Edward riding out from Windsor with his entourage to inspect the new star in the social firmament, arrived from distant Virginia.

Of course she had failings – in particular her neglect of the man who had for so long adored her and stood by her side; and her naive confidence that there must surely be some good in the dictators who in the event were preparing their attack upon all that England and America valued – but they were more than matched by her determination to strive for the good of others, careless of what people thought of her. Above all, perhaps, was the inspiration of her entry into Parliament: holding firm to the thought of what so many women before her had suffered, resolute against discouragement and aggression, she had stood her ground.

Nancy died in the early hours of the morning of 2 May.

She was buried in the Octagon Temple at Cliveden, a Confederate flag folded and placed nearby. Next to her lay Waldorf, with whom, before he died, she had found contentment once more, and, if her beliefs were correct, would do so for ever after.

One evening many years earlier, in a distant, different world, at the end of the Victorian age, when life in England seemed pleasant and serene, the Souls were gathered at one of Lady Desborough's famous house parties. After dinner they had talked of the form that heaven might take:

> To be laid out to sleep in a garden, with running water near, and to sleep for a hundred thousand years; then to be woken by a bird singing, and to call out to the person one loved best, 'Are you there?', and for her to answer, 'Yes, are you?', and so to turn and go to sleep again, for another hundred thousand years.

Perhaps it is at Cliveden, in the quiet temple, near the ancient yew trees, high above the Thames.

NOTES AND REFERENCES

Chapter One: In Dixie

1 Scidel.
2 Winston S. Churchill, *A History of the English-Speaking Peoples*, Vol. iv, Cassell, London, 1958, p. 121.
3 Margaret Mitchell, *Gone With the Wind*, Macmillan, New York, 1936.
4 Astor, *Lightning Sketch*.
5 W. Carroll Headspeth, *Battle of Staunton River Bridge*, The Record-Advertiser, Inc., South Boston, Va., 1949.
6 Note by Nancy Astor, Astor Papers, University of Reading, MS 1416/1/6/86.
7 Astor, *Lightning Sketch*.
8 Gibson. Lang Gibson is Nancy Astor's great-nephew.
9 From notes prepared by Nancy Astor for a press article, Astor Papers, University of Reading, MS 1416/1/6/86.
10 Gibson, op. cit.
11 Astor, *Lightning Sketch*.

Chapter Two: Silver and Lead

1 See *Chesapeake & Ohio Historical Magazine*, Vol. XXIV, No. 6, June 1992; Vol. XXV, No. 1, January 1993.
2 Irene Langhorne, published memoir, 1943.
3 About $2.1 million in 2009 prices. For a description of Nancy with her friends in Richmond, see *Ladies Home Journal*, April 1920.
4 Astor Papers, University of Reading, MS 1416/1/6/86, see also Astor, *Lightning Sketch*.
5 Nancy Astor memoir, 30 July 1909, Astor Private Papers.
6 See Sykes, p. 32. Aunt Liz had been an acquaintance of Abraham Lincoln.
7 *Harper's New Monthly Magazine*, quoted in Gibson, p. 53; and see *Harper's*

New Monthly Magazine, August 1886. The White was also, in 1858, the birthplace of the mint julep, a cocktail of which Chillie Langhorne was particularly fond; the recipe included French brandy, cut-loaf sugar, limestone water, crushed ice and young mountain mint. The hotel stood until 1922, its successor being the renowned Greenbrier.

8 Percival Reniers, *The Springs of Virginia: Life, Love and Death at the Waters, 1775–1900*, University of North Carolina Press, 1955.

9 Ibid. p. 251, quoting the *New York Daily Graphic*.

10 Ibid. p. 264.

11 Chillie tried without avail to encourage a match between Irene and Longworth, who later married the daughter of President Theodore Roosevelt and in time became Speaker of the House of Representatives.

12 Astor, *Lightning Sketch*, p. 17.

13 Ibid.

14 Recounted by the Hon. Angus McDonnell, who frequently stayed at Mirador, and quoted in Becker.

15 For detailed descriptions of Mirador, see United States Department of the Interior, National Register of Historic Places; Alice Winn, *Always a Virginian*, J.P. Bell, Lynchburg, 1973; Fox; Becker.

16 Astor, *Lightning Sketch*, p. 14. Michael Astor compares Nancy at this time to Irene: 'Her small, firmer, more aquiline features, which conveyed a feeling of vitality and strength, also revealed an epicene quality that was not evident in any of her sisters.' See Astor, *Tribal Feeling*, p. 27.

17 Astor, *Lightning Sketch*, p. 16.

18 Gibson, p. 74.

19 BBC interview with Lady Astor, 1954, British Library, ref. CDA 24051, and see note by Nancy Astor, Astor Papers, University of Reading, MS 1416/1/6/86. See also Neve Papers, University of Virginia. See also Dr Ralph Davison, *Frederick W. Neve: Mountain Mission Education in Virginia, 1888–1948*, University of Virginia, 1982.

20 See Spargo, pp. 146 *et seq.*

21 Astor Papers, University of Reading, MS 1416/1/6/86.

22 Fox, p. 45. For Keene's exploits, see Gibson, p. 41.

23 See Sinclair, p. 2. The Four Hundred were the people considered by *the* Mrs Astor, no doubt encouraged by Ward McAllister, to be eligible for society, although on the occasion of the party to which this numerical stricture first applied, only 317 of them turned up, whether for reasons of illness, mourning, absence or inclination. *The* Mrs Astor was known as such partly because her calling cards bore the legend 'Mrs Astor', without further embroidery. Descriptions of Ward McAllister make him seem somewhat neuter and his charm of the surface variety; his strong

views on etiquette included the importance of keeping engagements, but as he was said to have once decreed that in the case of someone dying after having accepted an obligation his executor should attend in his place, he may have had a sense of humour after all. For an amused insight into the Gilded Age, see Mary Cable, *The Top Drawer*, Athenaeum, New York, 1984.

24 *New York Times*, 14 December 1893.

25 Astor, *Lightning Sketch*, p. 24.

26 Ibid., p. 27.

27 Richmond *Dispatch*, 7 November 1895; see also Gibson, pp. 116–21.

28 Gibson, p. 132. Dana did his sketches for the *London Graphic* from memory, as he was not permitted to sketch at the actual Drawing Room.

29 Astor, *Lightning Sketch*, p. 29.

30 Nancy Lancaster to Barbara Brown, David Brown Archive, Danville, Virginia. Nancy Lancaster was the daughter of Lizzie, the eldest Langhorne daughter.

31 Nancy Astor diary, Astor Papers, University of Reading, MS 1416/1/6/76.

32 Robert Gould Shaw to Nancy Shaw, Astor Papers, University of Reading, MS 1416/1/3/40.

33 As told by Nancy to her niece, Nancy Lancaster; and see Fox, pp. 58–9.

34 Astor, *Lightning Sketch*, p.30.

35 Nancy Lancaster to Barbara Brown, David Brown Archive, Danville, Virginia.

36 Astor, *Lightning Sketch*, p. 32.

37 Mary Shaw to Nancy Shaw, 2 July 1902, Astor Papers, University of Reading, MS 1416/1/3/40.

38 Pauline Shaw to Nancy Shaw, 16 July 1902, Astor Papers, University of Reading, MS 1416/1/3/40.

39 See Fox, p. 65.

40 Hon. Hector McDonnell to author.

41 *Boston Daily Globe*, 7 February 1903; also see *Boston Herald*, 24 August 1916, in which an article describes an accident that befell Robert Shaw while playing polo at Newport. Following his second marriage he seems to have mended his ways, and lived contentedly until his death in New York in March 1929. He had four children with the former Mrs C.H. Converse, and shortly after his second wedding bought a 300-acre farm near Georgetown, turning it into one of the best-equipped stock farms in Greater Boston and building on it what was described by the press, meaning well, as a 'pretentious mansion'.

42 *Boston Daily Globe*, 18 February 1903.

43 Colonel Astor was a man of many parts: an article on his invention of a

'Vibratory Disintegrator', for producing gas from peat, had appeared in the respected journal *Scientific American*, and the Patent Office records contained examples of his suggestions for 'practical and useful devices', including a bicycle brake, a pneumatic road improver, and an 'efficient marine turbine'. But his life was cut short by his decision to sail on the *Titanic*. When the great liner began to founder, Astor lifted Madeleine, his second wife, whom he had married seven months previously and who was then five months pregnant, into a lifeboat and asked permission to accompany her, arguing that he wanted to protect her. Denied permission by the officer supervising the loading, he waved goodbye and busied himself with helping to fill another boat. He was later seen standing to attention as the ship began to sink. He was apparently not drowned but killed by flying debris. When his body was recovered, his pockets were found to contain gold and notes worth approximately £44,000 in current value.

[44] Astor, *Lightning Sketch*, p. 36.

Chapter Three: The Chase

[1] In this case Edith Cunard, wife of Gordon Cunard, later 4th baronet, brother of Sir Bache Cunard, lately retired as Master of the Fernie, whose wife was a famous hostess between the wars, and whose grandfather Samuel, a Canadian, had been raised to the baronetcy in 1859, on Lord Palmerston's recommendation, in recognition of the benefits his Cunard shipping line was bringing to the country. The soldier who offered to help Nancy to mount was General Holland, whose family's knowledge of Americans was increased by the Household Cavalryman Captain Tom Holland marrying the American Miss Pfizer.

[2] See Forbes. Lady Angela Forbes was considered to be somewhat of a virago, 'living life with great gusto and loving horses, her independence and her admirers in that order' (see Abdy and Gere, p. 180). She was half-sister to Daisy, Countess of Warwick, mistress of the Prince of Wales before he ascended the throne as King Edward VII; Angela Forbes was also a sister of Millicent, Duchess of Sutherland, and the beautiful Countess of Westmorland, both leading members of the Souls. Among those who turned out for I Zingari was the celebrated Bay Middleton, paramour of the Empress Elizabeth of Austria, one of the first women in the hunting field, whom Middleton used to 'pilot' when she hunted in Leicestershire.

[3] *The Queen, The Lady's Newspaper & Court Chronicle*, 14 January 1905.

[4] Astor Papers, University of Reading, MS 1416/1/6/86. The American

ambassador, Joseph Choate, was described at the time as a virile, unconventional Middle West American.

5 Astor, *Lightning Sketch*.
6 Astor Papers, University of Reading, MS 1416/1/7/17.
7 For a study of Baring Brothers, and Lord Revelstoke, see Philip Ziegler, *The Sixth Great Power, Barings, 1762–1929*, Collins, London, 1988.
8 Lord Revelstoke to Nancy Shaw, 30 March 1905, Astor Papers, University of Reading, MS 1416/1/4/79.
9 Astor Papers, University of Reading, MS 1416/1/6/86.
10 Lord Revelstoke to Nancy Shaw, 5 July 1905, Astor Papers, University of Reading, MS 1416/1/4/79. See MS 1416/1/4/79 for further Revelstoke letters to Nancy.
11 Astor Papers, University of Reading, MS 1416/1/6/86, and quoted in Sykes, p. 78.
12 *The Queen*, 28 October 1905.
13 Astor, *Lightning Sketch*.
14 Lord Elphinstone to Nancy Shaw, 27 November 1905, Astor Papers, University of Reading, MS 1416/1/4/40.
15 Astor Papers, University of Reading, MS 1416/1/4/40.
16 *The Queen*, 20 January 1906.
17 Astor Papers, University of Reading, MS 1416/1/4/40.
18 Lord Revelstoke to Nancy Shaw, 7 September 1905, Astor Papers, University of Reading, MS 1416/1/4/79.
19 Astor Papers, University of Reading, MS 1416/1/6/86.
20 Nancy Astor note, Astor Papers, University of Reading, MS 1416/1/6/86.
21 W. W. Astor, 'John Jacob Astor', *Pall Mall Magazine*, Vol. XVIII, May–August 1899.
22 Ibid.
23 'Silhouettes': William Astor's reminiscences from 1855 to 1885, Astor Papers, Hever, Kent. The young lady was Mary Hartpence, five years his junior, who later married Mahlon Day Sands and whose eldest daughter, Ethel, lived in Chelsea and became a friend of Walter Sickert and other artists of the day. Ethel Sands became a well-known artist herself.
24 William Astor's work for the Republican Party was rewarded by President Arthur, who appointed him US Minister to Italy, although he received no special instructions or objectives: 'Go and enjoy yourself, my dear boy,' said the Secretary of State. 'Have a good time.' With his wife and infant son, Waldorf, Astor took up his duties and set off for Rome. Having a great amount of money to spend, and little to do but entertain lavishly, he soon took to Italian life. Received in royal circles, his shy wife welcomed

at court, popular in the highest society, he blossomed among the European aristocracy and began a rapid education in the treasures of the Old World. Soon he was collecting on a formidable scale: paintings, sculpture, tapestries, furniture, china, glass and silver, as well as artefacts and stonework. Even the magnificent world-famous balustrade in the gardens of Rome's Villa Borghese, carved for Cardinal Scipio Borghese early in the seventeenth century, fell to his onslaught 'regardless of price'. Despite outrage in Italy and the government suing the Borghese family in an attempt to keep the balustrade *in situ*, it was dismantled piece by piece and sent to England, where it became famous in a new setting – Cliveden. Delighted by Rome, and recovering his long-subdued romantic urge, William also wrote the first of two novels about Italy, its hero modelled on Cesare Borgia – a man whose praises few others had sung. His happy experience of Italy convinced him that his talents were best suited to the older values of Europe, and added to his desire to break with America, where he had returned when a change of president brought his Roman holiday to an end.

[25] The society known as Pop; for many generations, election to its offices carried responsibility that few found in the wider world. As late as the 1960s a British prime minister recorded that he felt he had more to do as president of Pop than he did at the head of the government. Waldorf's intellectual achievements at Eton included editing the school magazine, the *Eton College Chronicle*, and becoming president of the Literary Society.

[26] In the following pages of this chapter, except where otherwise described, quotations from Waldorf's letters to Nancy during his courting of her in the early weeks of 1906 are taken from private papers held by the Astor family.

[27] The Sancy is a heart-shaped jewel comprising the finest-quality Indian diamonds. Found originally in India, it passed through the hands of six kings, and the stomach of a messenger, before disappearing during the French Revolution. From time to time during the nineteenth century it reappeared in exotic hands, at ever more exotic prices, and by 1865 was in the possession of the Demidoff family, who entrusted it to the diamond dealers Leverson, Forster & Co. for the purpose of making models in crystal and silver. In 1888 it was for sale in the London market at £20,000–£22,000 (£2.3m in 2011 prices), and in November 1889 Leverson, Forster bought it from the executors of Sir Jamsetjee Jeejeebhoy, the head of a family of Parsee merchants in India; in 1892 they certified the stone as weighing 55.23 carats. Shortly afterwards it was bought by William Astor.

[28] William Waldorf Astor to Mrs Amy Small Richardson, 16 December 1906, Astor Papers, Library of Congress, Washington DC.

[29] Waldorf to Nancy, Easter 1906, Astor Private Papers.

[30] Chillie Langhorne to Nancy, 9 March 1906, Astor Private Papers.

[31] Astor Papers, University of Reading, MS 1416/1/3/6.

[32] *The Queen*, 'Americans in London', 17 March 1906.

[33] Ibid., 25 March 1906.

[34] *Town Topics*, 1906.

[35] *Star*, 3 May 1906, Astor Papers, Library of Congress, Washington DC.

Chapter Four: Gilded Youth

[1] Nancy to Phyllis, 2 September 1908, Astor Papers, University of Reading, MS 2422/1. Princess Marie's letters to Nancy are in the Astor Papers, University of Reading, MS 1416/1/4/18.

[2] Pauline Shaw to Nancy Astor, 5 June 1906. Astor Papers, University of Reading, MS 1416/1/3/40.

[3] *The Queen*, 2 March 1907.

[4] Robert Tressell, *The Ragged Trousered Philanthropists*, edited with an introduction and notes by Peter Miles, OUP, 2005. See generally this book, first published in 1914 and set around the time when Waldorf and Nancy were converting Cliveden, for a description of the hardships of the life of manual labourers in Edwardian England.

[5] William Astor to Nancy Astor, 10 May 1907, Astor Papers, University of Reading, MS 1416/1/3/6.

[6] Adèle Grant, from Boston, had married George, Earl of Essex. Their story was to be sadly typical of the dramatic and swift change of fortune that befell so much of the top echelons of English society following the First World War, when political, social and financial upheaval almost entirely obliterated what had seemed only a few years previously to be set fair for ever. The Essex family had lived at Cassiobury, in Hertfordshire, for 300 years, but the post-war difficulties of making an estate pay, compounded by some unwise investments, forced George and Adèle Essex to abandon their heritage and sell up. Lady Essex was found dead in her bath a few weeks before the sale; it was thought she had died from a heart attack. The ancient parkland surrounding their stately home was sold off for housing, and the building of an air station between the wars, subsequently used by the RAF in the Second World War, finally extinguished all traces of the tranquillity of centuries. Consuelo Iznaga, later Duchess of Manchester, was born in Louisiana of a Cuban father and

an American mother, and became well known in New York society, where she met the future 9th Duke of Manchester.

7 In the opinion of some, Sir Bertrand Dawson's skill in diagnosis came second to his social aspirations. He did not, in the event, put Nancy 'quite right', which was one of the factors in due course leading her to embrace Christian Science. However, Dawson, later raised to the peerage, became physician to King George V, from whose deathbed he issued, in January 1936, the famous bulletin 'The King's life is drawing peacefully to its close' – a judgement in which, as became apparent long afterwards when the records were opened, he had every reason to feel confident, as he had just administered a fatal dose to 'ease the passing' of the King to another realm.

8 Nancy Astor, diary, Astor Papers, University of Reading.

9 Balsan, p. 204. Americans who became duchesses around the turn of the century had colourful but often sad lives. For example, the Duke of Marlborough's second wife had a liaison with a woman, Lady Colin Campbell. Such an affair was unusual in those days, but her needs may have reflected her unhappy life with the Duke; when he died, she threw herself upon his dead body and kissed him, crying out to her maid, 'He would never let me kiss him when he was alive.'

10 The masterly quintessential English butler in Kazuo Ishiguro's bestselling novel, *The Remains of the Day*, was in part-modelled on Edwin Lee. The quoted paragraphs are from Harrison, *Gentlemen's Gentlemen*, p. 110.

11 V. Sackville-West, *The Edwardians*, Hogarth Press, London, 1930.

12 Marquess Curzon of Kedleston, notes and letters to Nancy Astor, Astor Papers, University of Reading, MS 1416/1/4/39, and Colefax Papers, MS Eng.c.3166, Special Collections Dept, Bodleian Library, Oxford.

13 Sonia Keppel, *Edwardian Daughter*, Hamish Hamilton, London, 1958.

14 See also Eric Horne, *What the Butler Winked At*, T.W. Laurie Ltd, London, 1923.

15 Ethel ('Ettie') Fane (1867–1952) lost both her parents as an infant but was heiress to the fortune of her aunt and uncle, Earl and Countess Cowper, and became one of the most brilliant and scintillating of Edwardian hostesses. Having as a small child been patted on the head by Disraeli, she made a closer political connection when, aged nineteen, she married William Grenfell, a Liberal and then Conservative MP. Grenfell was supported by money from family tin mines in Cornwall, and was later ennobled as Lord Desborough, possibly partly as a result of special pleading by Ettie to the then Prime Minister, Arthur Balfour,

who, with Ettie, was at the core of the Souls. Willy Grenfell was nearly six and a half feet tall, and was immensely strong and athletic, twice swimming the pool at the base of the Niagara Falls. As a champion fencer, he represented England in the 1908 Olympic Games. Two of their sons, Julian and Billy, were killed in the First World War, and were symbolic of the 'lost generation' of England's golden youth. The death of so many friends would have grieved Balfour as much as any, although he was older than the many 'children of the Souls' who died. His warm heart and amused outlook on life lay beneath a rather cool and unemotional surface. At one dinner party his neighbour, Margot Asquith (then Tennant) challenged him, saying, 'You're quite cold; I don't believe you would care if we all died.' After a pause for reflection, Balfour graciously conceded, 'I should care if you all died on the same day.'

[16] *England*, 19 November 1892. For a good description of various members of the Souls, see *The Letters of Arthur Balfour and Lady Elcho, 1885–1917*, ed. Jane Ridley and Clayre Percy, Hamish Hamilton, London, 1992. Harry Cust was very much part of their company. He was, if not 'the ladykiller of the century', then fatally attractive to, and attracted by, women: the presence in many of England's nurseries where they did not properly belong of wonderful blue eyes remarkably suggestive of Harry Cust raised the possibility that some, at least, of the Souls were bound also by bodily ties. One of the most notorious scandals featuring Cust concerned Lady Londonderry and Lady de Grey, and resulted in Lord Londonderry not speaking to his wife in private for the rest of his life. On the other hand, the unworldliness of some of the Souls was illustrated in a small way by Balfour's particular friend Mary Elcho, who posted a letter in an envelope bearing the words 'Caution, Money Inside'. Lady Asquith, however, wife of Prime Minister Henry Asquith, was more au fait: her wit was exemplified many years later when the American film star and blonde bombshell Jean Harlow went up to her, without an introduction, at a party, and greeted her with, 'Say, Margotte, how're yer doin'?' receiving the icy reply, 'In *my* name, as in yours, the "t" is unpronounced.' Nor was she reticent about her family: at one party she advised Cimmie Mosley, wife of the future Blackshirt leader Sir Oswald, not to have another baby until she was strong enough, adding, 'Henry always withdrew in time: such a noble man.' See Oswald Mosley, *My Life*, Nelson, London, 1968. Asquith's friends were also amused to know that one of his relaxations consisted of retiring to bed and translating Kipling into Greek.

[17] Lady Hamilton diary, Liddell Hart Centre for Military Archives, Hamilton

20/1/2, and quoted in Richard Davenport-Hines, *Ettie: The Intimate Life and Dauntless Spirit of Lady Desborough*, Weidenfeld & Nicolson, London, 2008, p. 141.

[18] See Davenport-Hines, op. cit.

[19] Nancy Astor to Phyllis Brooks, 23 July 1908, Astor Papers, University of Reading, MS 2422/1. Mrs Keppel – chestnut hair, alabaster skin, turquoise eyes, Alma-Tadema beauty – was the King's mistress.

[20] Nancy Astor to Phyllis Brooks, 4 August 1907, Astor Papers, University of Reading, MS 2422/1.

[21] Nancy Astor to Marion McKearn, at Pride's Crossing, Massachusetts, 25 July 1907, Astor Papers, University of Reading, MS 1416/1/3/40.

[22] Nancy to Pauline Spender-Clay, 23 July, 1908, Astor Papers, University of Reading, MS2422/1.

[23] Nancy Astor to Phyllis Brooks, 21 August 1907, Astor Papers, University of Reading, MS 2422/1.

[24] *The Complete Works of George Orwell*, ed. Peter Davison; V. xix, 'It Is What I Think', Secker & Warburg, London, 1998, p. 376.

Chapter Five: New Adventures

[1] Astor, *Lightning Sketch*, p. 66. I am greatly indebted to Mr David Oldrey for information about the Cliveden stud and other racing details. See also *Ruff's Guide to the Turf, passim*, and, for an appreciation of Waldorf's contribution to racing, *The Bloodstock Breeders' Review, 1952*.

[2] Among the recommendations of the Royal Commission on Tuberculosis was the creation of a permanent medical research body. Legislative provision for medical research was first made by the National Insurance Act of 1911, which led to the establishment of a Departmental Committee on Tuberculosis. A Medical Research Committee was appointed in 1913, with the prime role of distributing medical research funds under the terms of the 1911 Act. Waldorf was chairman of the Departmental Committee on Tuberculosis in 1912–13 and of the Medical Research Committee from 1916 to 1920.

[3] Nancy Astor memoir, Astor Papers, University of Reading, MS 1416/1/6/86.

[4] Salisbury Papers, Hatfield House archive.

[5] London charities receiving money from William Astor included the National Refuges for Homeless and Destitute Children, and the training ships *Arethusa* and *Chichester*, used for the benefit of poor boys of good character; other beneficiaries included Guy's Hospital and the Society for the Prevention of Cruelty to Children. The gift to the SPCC was the

only one the society received from Astor, as, owing to an enormously foolish and expensive oversight, he was omitted from the list of guests at the opening of new premises constructed with his money. Being a man who placed a premium on courtesy, he was not pleased, and severed his relations with the charity.

6   William Astor to Nancy Astor, 1 December 1909, Astor Papers, University of Reading, MS 1416/1/3/6.

7   A situation that prevailed until the 1918 general election when, partly reflecting ongoing evolution in parliamentary representation and partly Boundary Commission changes, the constituency was divided into three: Plymouth Drake, Plymouth Devonport and Plymouth Sutton, the latter being won by Waldorf Astor, previously one of the two members returned for Plymouth *tout court*. The Conservative Party, founded in 1834, was the offspring of the Tory Party, which had its origins in the seventeenth century. In 1912, the Conservatives fused their organisation with that of the Liberal Unionists, i.e. the part of the Liberal Party opposed to Home Rule for Ireland, the merger forming the Conservative and Unionist Party.

8   Fox, p. 145.

9   Astor, *Lightning Sketch*, p. 51. St Just is a town a few miles west of Penzance, in Cornwall.

10   William Waldorf (House of Lords), Waldorf (House of Commons and Lords); Hon. J.J. Astor, Waldorf's brother (Commons); Nancy, William, Michael and John Jacob Astor (Commons); Col. Herbert Spender-Clay, Waldorf's brother-in-law (Commons); Lord Willoughby de Eresby, son-in-law (Commons). Also, Ronald Tree was MP for Harborough at the same time as being married to Nancy's niece Nancy, daughter of Lizzie.

11   Nancy to Phyllis Brooks, 25 September 1908, Astor Papers, University of Reading, MS 1416, 2422/1.

12   Harrison, *Gentlemen's Gentlemen*.

13   Nancy would not have appreciated that aspect of Belloc, exemplified by his intake when staying with Wilfred Blunt at Easter 1912: 'Belloc abstains in Lent. After mass into cellar (1) pint of brandy (2) beer at breakfast (3) Bott Saumur wine during the course of the morning (4) More beer at lunch (5) 1½ Claret (with Elodie) at dinner, port, sherry, Crème de Menthe. No apparent effect, except jollity.' Wilfred Blunt, General Memoirs, MS 11-1975, Fitzwilliam College, Cambridge. Elodie was Belloc's wife.

14   Daisy, Princess of Pless, *My Diary*, John Murray, London, 1931. Entry for Saturday 24 July 1909.

15   Winston Churchill, 28 March 1945, speech in the House of Commons following the death of Earl Lloyd George.

16 Nancy Astor diary, 9 February 1910, Astor Papers, University of Reading, MS 1416/1/6/78.

17 On Thursday 5 May 1910, the King had been upset by his ministers worrying him at a meeting, for which he had been inadequately briefed; he had lost his temper and had had a bad fit of coughing. The next day he conducted further business and had another fit of coughing, which got worse. 'They sent for the Archbishop of Canterbury but he did not see him and he smoked a cigar. Only once he said, "If this goes on much longer I shall be done for", and soon after he became unconscious, and never said another word.' Wilfred Blunt, Diaries, Fitzwilliam College, Cambridge, MS7-1975. The King died on Friday 6 May.

Chapter Six: Into Battle

1 *Hansard*, 28 February 1911, cols. 261, 265.

2 According to Walter Bagehot, one of the leading constitutional experts of the nineteenth century.

3 It is not clear who designed the house; it has been suggested that it was Giacomo Leoni, but the best evidence points to Edward Shepherd.

4 Quoted in Sermoneta.

5 Quoted in Desborough.

6 Waldorf to Nancy, 28 November 1911, Astor Private Papers.

7 Ibid.

8 Winterton note, 22 February 1913, Astor Private Papers. Earl Winterton, 1883–1962, was a descendant of Edward Turnour, MP for Bramber, in Sussex, who in 1766 was granted the earldom of Winterton, an Irish peerage such was at that time commonly granted to Members of Parliament, for services rendered, as of their nature they not exclude the holding of a seat in the Commons. The Winterton family seat was Shillinglee Park, in Sussex, which late in the nineteenth century became famous for its cricket matches; celebrated players of the day, such as Prince Ranjitsinghi and W.G. Grace, were often guests at the house.

9 Nancy to Phyllis, 8 March 1908, Astor Papers, University of Reading, MS 2422/1.

10 Earl Winterton, Diary, 15 August 1912, Winterton Papers, Bodleian Library, Oxford.

11 Waldorf to Nancy, August 1913, Astor Private Papers.

12 Astor, *Lightning Sketch*, p. 63. At that time the relative attractions of homeopathy, self-healing religions and orthodox medicine were less skewed in favour of the latter: the standard of medical science was low, and seemingly confident doctors made many mistakes. George Bernard

Shaw's 1906 play *The Doctor's Dilemma* touches on the matter, and was reportedly inspired by actual events.

[13] Ibid.

[14] Ibid., p. 64.

[15] Astor Papers, University of Reading, MS 1416/12/584 and MS 1416/1/3/35.

[16] Fox.

[17] Astor, *Tribal Feelings*, p. 156.

[18] Harrison, *Gentlemen's Gentlemen*, p. 117.

[19] Quoted in Fox, p. 227.

[20] According to Sir Robert Vansittart, Permanent Undersecretary of State for Foreign Affairs, 1930–38. During the 1930s Vansittart was a leading opponent of those who sought to appease the dictators; for him, therefore, Philip Kerr, by then Marquess of Lothian, was a bête noire. Quoted in *Lord Lothian and Anglo-American Relations, 1900–1940*, ed. Priscilla Roberts, Dordrecht, 2010, an in-depth and perceptive study of that subject.

[21] Philip Kerr to Nancy Astor, 3 December, 1912. Astor Papers, University of Reading, MS1416/1/4/45.

[22] Quoted in Fox, p. 224.

[23] Lionel Curtis, later founder of the Institute of International Affairs (subsequently Royal), was the paramount thinker among the group, and was affectionately known as 'the prophet', although he was regarded by others as 'a great bore, with his eternal reminiscences and lack of humour'. Edward Grigg, later Lord Altrincham, was originally a journalist and in 1913 became co-editor, with Philip Kerr, of the journal of the Round Table. In 1920 he became a private secretary to Lloyd George, before embarking on a career as a colonial administrator and subsequently member of Parliament. Geoffrey Dawson, whose surname was Robinson at that time and until he changed it on inheriting an estate in Yorkshire, was in the 1930s editor of *The Times*; John Buchan became Governor-General of Canada and achieved fame as a writer; Robert Brand, later Lord Brand, was an international banker with Lazard Brothers and in 1917 married Nancy's sister Phyllis; during the First World War he became closely associated with the financing of munitions and in 1917–18 was deputy chairman of the British War Mission in Washington. Philip Kerr, later Marquess of Lothian, assisted Lord Milner in the reconstruction of South Africa before returning to England in 1909. He became a private secretary to Lloyd George, and later Chancellor of the Duchy of Lancaster and Undersecretary of State for India. In 1939–40 he was British ambassador in Washington, dying in office in 1940. Nancy quite convinced him of the merits of Christian Science, but that did not prevent

him suffering a terrible shock when he was described as a renegade Roman Catholic by the priest at his mother's funeral. Also in Milner's Kindergarten was Patrick Duncan, later Governor-General of South Africa. Milner himself, a leading colonial administrator, was partly responsible for the outbreak of the Boer War. Upon his return to England after successfully completing his work of founding the Union of South Africa, he turned to business interests. Although he was strongly opposed to Lloyd George's political schemes, he joined Lloyd George's Coalition War Cabinet in December 1916.

[24] I am very much indebted to both Dr Alex May and Dr Priscilla Roberts for information and advice about members of the Round Table, and about the group's policies and achievements. See Dr May's thesis on the subject, at Rhodes House, Oxford, and the several published works of Dr Roberts, which throw an invaluable light upon the field of Anglo-American relations between the wars, and upon Philip Kerr. Priscilla Roberts is Associate Professor of History at the University of Hong Kong.

[25] Harrison, *Gentlemen's Gentlemen*, p. 117. Archduke Franz Ferdinand visited Cliveden on Sunday 25 June 1911.

[26] Astor, *Lightning Sketch*, p. 68.

[27] See R.L.Borden, *Robert Laird Borden: His Memoirs, Volume II*, Macmillan, Toronto, 1938, p. 933, quoted in *Nancy Astor's Canadian Correspondence, 1912–1962*, ed. Martin Thornton, Edwin Mellen Press, Lewiston, p. 16.

[28] Willard Straight Diary, Reel 12 (1908–November 1917), Cambridge University Library.

[29] *Nancy Astor's Canadian Correspondence*, op. cit., p. 12.

[30] Philip Kerr to Nancy Astor, Astor Papers, University of Reading, MS 1416/1/4/48.

[31] Astor, *Lightning Sketch*, p. 74.

[32] William Astor to Nancy Astor, 4 September 1914. Astor Papers, University of Reading, MS 1416/1/3/6.

[33] Astor Papers, University of Reading, MS 1416/1/4/42.

[34] Billy Grenfell to Nancy Astor, 14 and 28 July 1915, Astor Papers, University of Reading, MS 1416/1/4/42.

[35] de Courcy, p. 117; for a detailed description of the Ark see also Urquhart.

[36] Countess of Kenmare to Lady Desborough, 20 November 1918, Desborough Papers, Hertfordshire County Record Office, DERV C307/21.

[37] Asquith.

[38] Jones, *Whitehall Diary*.

[39] Thomas Jones Papers, Special Collections, Bodleian Library, Oxford.

[40] Willard Straight diary, 1915 January 1–3, Morgan Grenfell Papers,

Guildhall Library, London, MS 28259. I am much indebted to Dr Priscilla Roberts for information about Anglo-American relations and development during the First World War and in the inter-war years. Her various works on the subject contain much invaluable information. See, e.g., *Lord Lothian and Anglo-American Relations, 1900–1940*, Dordrecht, 2010, and 'The First World War as Catalyst and Epiphany: The Case of Henry P. Davison', *Diplomacy & Statecraft* (2007) 18: 2, 315–50. Julian Grenfell had gained the nickname 'the stalker' for a number of aggressive, fearless and successful escapades in no-man's-land and in and among the German trenches. For the story of someone possibly even more brave and bold than Julian Grenfell see A.O. Pollard, *Fire-eater, The Memoirs of a VC*, with a preface by J.E.B. Seely, Hutchinson, London, 1932. Seely, later Lord Mottistone, was from a similar mould, and once sent in a recommendation for a Victoria Cross for his batman on the basis that 'throughout the action he remained never more than twenty yards behind me'.

[41] See J.A. Turner's thorough study of the origins of Lloyd George's Garden Suburb, Turner, John, *Lloyd George's Private Secretariat, 1917–1918*, University of Oxford, Faculty of Modern History, 1976.

[42] Herbert Praed to Andrew Bonar Law, 5 June 1912. Bonar Law Papers, House of Lords Records Office.

[43] Nancy maintained that hereditary peerages were 'all wrong', descending to people who had never done anything at all and probably never would, exclaiming, 'You might as well have an hereditary cricket team.' Cf. the radical socialist politician Anthony Wedgwood-Benn, formerly Viscount Stansgate, who said in a speech in 2010, 'The hereditary principle is absurd. What am I to think if I go along to my dentist, who, standing above me with his drill at the ready, says "I'm not a dentist myself, of course, but my father was . . ."'

[44] Lord Astor to Nancy Astor, 7 January 1916, Astor Papers, University of Reading, MS 1416/1/3/6.

[45] The young diplomat, Harold Nicolson, later an MP and famous as a diarist, whose mother-in-law had an affair with William Astor, was occasionally invited for lunch, both at Hever Castle and at the secluded Regency house in Brighton to which William eventually moved. Nicolson left a record of his host's magnificence:

'. . . he lived in a large house packed with expensive and curious purchases and surrounded by intricate gardens. In the centre of his house stood his kitchen, and a chef from Dijon, and a patissier from Nancy. The essential meal occurred in the middle of the day; a peach only for breakfast; and for dinner, only a little broth. Then

there was his Swedish masseur, who created an appetite by banging
and beating the old gentleman across the stomach from eleven till
eleven-thirty; a little turn in the Dutch garden; and then . . . the
old man would stump into the enormous dining-room, and there,
beneath the Gobelins, he would sit (fee-fi-fo-fum) in an Italian
brocade chair; waiting for his soup . . . a lobster, rather shattered
and dissected, but still a lobster . . . a large dish of black potatoes,
which were in fact truffles . . . scarlet pepper-heads from Thessaly,
and pickled cucumbers from the Ukraine, spices from Bali and
Sumatra, a little silver nutmeg-grater, a little gold instrument for
crushing picatilloes, a little crystal mortar for grinding those locarto
beans which come from Marrakesh; the roots of a palmetto-bush;
olives from Ithaca.

I exaggerate a little, but I do not exaggerate very much . . .'
(Harold Nicolson, *Small Talk*, Constable, London, 1937.)

[46] Royal Archives, RA/PS/PSO/GV/C/J/1524/1.

[47] John Astor had been wounded in the hand in 1914 and had lost a leg in
1918; he later overcame these handicaps and became the Member of
Parliament for Dover. He was also for a time parliamentary squash champion, a remarkable achievement for a one-legged man, even as outstanding
a ball-player as he had been as a young man.

[48] Of the female candidates in the 1918 election, four were Liberal, four were
Labour, one was Conservative and two Sinn Fein. Seventy-three Sinn Fein
candidates were elected but all declined to sit in the House of Commons. In
that election Sinn Fein emerged victorious, in Irish politics, over the Irish
Parliamentary Party, which, although nationalist, was more moderate and
whose members were happy to sit in the House of Commons. In the aftermath of the 1918 election, the revolutionary assembly, Dail Eireann, was
convened, and became known as the First Dail. Those who had been elected
to the House of Commons sat in the Dail instead of going to Westminster.
Shortly afterwards civil war broke out in Ireland. Countess Markiewicz,
returned for the St Patrick's division of Dublin, and the only woman
elected in the 1918 election, was married to a Pole; her maiden name was
Constance Gore-Booth. In the Commons a hat and coat peg was reserved
for her, with her name above it, in the corridor in the oldest part of
the building, next to the small room where the death warrant of Charles I
was signed. Lady Markiewicz was reputed to have secretly entered the
precincts once, in order to have a look at her name plate. A year after
these events she became the first woman in Europe to hold government

office when she became Minister of Labour in the first republican Irish parliament.

[49] J.M. Barrie to Nancy Astor, Astor Papers, University of Reading.

[50] Nancy Astor to Plymouth Unionist Association, 27 October 1919, Astor Papers, University of Reading, MS 1416/1/7/1.

[51] Collected press reports of Nancy's campaign may be found in Astor Papers, University of Reading, MS 1416/1/7/31–6.

Chapter Seven: The Power of One

[1] See Lord Riddell, *Intimate Diary of the Peace Conference and after, 1918–1923*, Gollancz, 1935.

[2] Frances Stevenson, *Lloyd George, A Diary*, ed. A.J.P. Taylor, Hutchinson, London, 1971. In 1919 Stevenson was the Prime Minister's confidential secretary, a post with important and wide-ranging duties which she filled with great efficiency. She herself was a pioneer, becoming the first female principal private secretary to a Cabinet minister. She eventually married Lloyd George, having long been his mistress. It was said, rather surprisingly, that Nancy was the last person to know of the Prime Minister's liaison with his secretary. Eventually she tackled him, saying, 'What's all this I hear about you and Frances?' Lloyd George responded with 'Ah, but what about you and Philip?' Nancy angrily replied, 'Everybody knows that my relations with Philip are completely innocent and above board.' Lloyd George: 'Then you should be ashamed of yourself.' See Rowse Papers, Exeter University, EUL MS 113/3 Astor.

[3] *Daily Express*, 2 December 1919.

[4] See Sinclair, p. 325.

[5] Diary of Sir Robert Sanders, Sunday 30 November 1919, Bodleian Library, Oxford, Special Collections, Dep. d.752. Sanders, MP for Bridgwater and subsequently Wells, was a Conservative whip before moving to the Treasury. He later became Minister of Agriculture and Fisheries. He was ennobled as Lord Bayford.

[6] This warning came from Nancy's fellow MP Josiah Wedgwood, a scion of a famous Liberal family with a fortune based on pottery. He became a minister in the first Labour government, in 1924, and was to be an early critic of Hitler.

[7] Notes of Lady Astor's conversation, made by Barbara Strachey, the Women's Library Archive, London Metropolitan University, ref. 7BSH/5/1/1/0. Horatio Bottomley was a populist MP, representing Hackney South. His parliamentary career ended in 1922 when he was imprisoned for fraud arising out of selling to the public his own version

of Premium Bonds. He had been trusted by millions of people up and down the country. His magazine *John Bull* was to carry a number of attacks on Nancy. See, for example, Julian Symons, *Horatio Bottomley*, Cresset Press, London, 1955.

8 Nancy Astor, addressing the League of Women Voters on 'Women in Politics' at the Town Hall, New York, 9 April 1922. Astor Papers, University of Reading, MS 1416/1/7/7.

9 Quoted in Lady Dorothy Nevill, *My Own Times*, Methuen, London, 1912, pp. 132–3. Dorothy Nevill, herself the victim of a member of Parliament failing to do the decent thing after placing her in a compromising situation, went on to marry a cousin twenty years her senior, and later became a leading political and literary hostess, and horticulturalist.

10 Mrs Senior's ground-breaking appointment was applauded by, among others, Florence Nightingale. For treatment of the subject see Oldfield. Jeannie Senior was the sister of Thomas Hughes, author of *Tom Brown's Schooldays*. The first appointments of magistrates included that of the Prime Minister's wife, Megan Lloyd George, besides Lady Londonderry, Mrs Humphry Ward and Mrs Sidney Webb. The first woman barrister, Helena Normanton, was appointed in November 1922. In 1924, she also acquired the distinction of being the first married woman to be issued with a passport in her maiden name.

11 Lady Astor, interviewed by Stephen Black, BBC, 1954, British Library Listening Archive, CDA 24051/307928.

12 Dame Caroline Haslett, DBE, JP, electrical engineer and electricity industry administrator. The Electrical Association for Women pioneered such wonders as the 'All-Electric House' in Bristol in 1935. In the 1920s, few houses had electric light or heating, or electrical aids to housework.

13 See Musolf, *From Plymouth to Parliament*, p. 150.

14 Sidebotham.

15 H.A.L. Fisher, then President of the Board of Education. See *Hansard* Vol. 125, cols 1642–3. Fisher became a friend of Nancy until she took exception to a book he wrote about Christian Science, after which she no longer spoke to him.

16 Diary of Sir Robert Sanders, Sunday 29 February 1920, Bodleian Library, Oxford, Special Collections, Dep. d. 752.

17 The *Morning Post*, quoted in Sinclair, p. 327.

18 A. Beverley Baxter MP, in *The Strand Magazine*, Vol. CIV, no. 625, January 1943, p. 33.

19 Notes of Lady Astor's conversation, made by Barbara Strachey, the Women's Library Archive, London Metropolitan University, ref. 7BSH/5/1/9. Baroness Willoughby, Nancy's granddaughter, in

conversation with author; author's conversation with Mr Freddie Knox, for many years Nancy's friend and unofficial agent in Plymouth. Nancy often spoke graphically to Mr Knox about how acutely unpleasant were many aspects of her first two years in Parliament.

20 See *The Saturday Review*, 6 December 1919, p. 527.

21 *Hansard*, 1920, Vol. 127, cols 1792–5.

22 Nancy Astor interview with Mary Stocks, BBC *Woman's Hour*, 1956.

23 See *The Westminster Gazette*, 25 March 1920.

24 Notes of Lady Astor's conversation, made by Barbara Strachey, the Women's Library Archive, loc. cit. In May 1920, Margaret Bondfield, later to be the first female Cabinet minister, lost a by-election in Northampton, and Susan Lawrence, a former Conservative who in due course became a Labour MP, lost in Camberwell

25 Astor Papers, University of Reading, MS 1416/1/7/15.

26 Ibid.

27 The court is still in use today, as part of the Naval and Military Club, which has leased the Astors' former house.

28 Lady Astor annual reports to Plymouth Conservative & Unionist Association, Astor Papers, University of Reading. For discussion of Nancy's administrative support, and for a comprehensive appraisal of her contributions to parliamentary debate, see particularly Harrison, *Prudent Revolutionaries*.

29 Lady Astor annual reports to Plymouth Conservative & Unionist Association, loc. cit.

30 Quoted in Barbara Strachey, *Remarkable Relations*, Gollancz, London, 1980. The enthusiastic and highly efficient Ray Strachey had married a civil servant, the elder brother of Lytton Strachey, whose company Nancy was greatly to enjoy. She wrote a seminal work on the development of women's political role, *The Cause*, published in 1928. By 1921, she was closely involved in League of Nations work with Lord Robert Cecil, a major champion of the League and a friend of Nancy, who greatly admired him.

31 Bunny Benningfield to Nancy Astor, quoted in Michael Carney, *Stoker: The Life of Hilda Matheson, OBE*, Michael Carney, Llangynog, 1999. Matheson in due course left Nancy's service and became director of talks at the BBC.

32 See 'Nancy Astor: Myth and Woman', *North American Review*, Vol. 227, no. 4. Sometimes the crush of people was confusing to one and all: one guest recounted saying to an attractive lady standing next to her, 'I don't know anyone here.' 'Nor do I,' came the reply. 'Well, tell me who *you* are, as a start.' 'The hostess!'

33 Astor Private Papers.

34 Waldorf to Bobbie Shaw, 6 January 1921, MRL Astor Papers.

35 For the work of Rachel and Margaret McMillan, see G.A.N. Lowndes, *Margaret McMillan, 'The Children's Champion'*, Museum Press, 1960; McMillan; Bradburn.

36 See, e.g., Andrew McDonald, 'The Geddes Committee and the Formulation of Public Expenditure Policy, 1921-1922', *Historical Journal*, 32, 2 (1989), pp. 643-74.

37 Waldorf Astor, 1922 US diary, 18 April–23 May 1922, Astor Papers, University of Reading, MS 1416/ 2/16; see also press reports in MS 1416/1/7/7.

38 Ibid.

39 Robin Barrington-Ward, diary, 7 November 1922, private collection. Barrington-Ward was a frequent guest at Cliveden, and fell much under Nancy's spell: 'She has the pluck and vitality of twelve men,' he wrote, 'great charm, wit, a very good heart, and a very quick feminine intelligence – not the blue-stocking kind, man-made at Somerville and Girton.' He was amused when she told him that his golf was like the Prime Minister, Lloyd George: 'strong but crooked'.

40 Kenneth Rose to author. Rose, however, said that he had received the account from a lady close to both Nancy and Winterton but who was a gossip and a troublemaker. On the other hand, Winterton's own diary for 12 December 1918 reads: 'Dance for the nurses at the hospital in the evening. Nancy, with whom earlier in the evening I had a violent quarrel over military service during the war, which actually ended in blows and was as quickly made up, was in her element. She & Waldorf have a great sense of public service in these matters.' In 1917, Winterton, as a major, had commanded a battalion of the Imperial Camel Corps, based in Palestine and part of the Egyptian Expeditionary Force.

41 MRL Astor Papers.

42 *Hansard's Parliamentary History*, (1741–3), Vol. XII, cols 1206–7.

43 *Hansard*, 13 July 1923, Vol. 166, col. 1773.

44 *Observer*, 4 June 1922.

45 *Daily Express*, 4 November 1922.

46 Edith Summerskill, *A Woman's World*, Heinemann, London, 1967, pp. 59, 60.

47 See the article on Ellen Wilkinson MP, *Liverpool Express*, 20 April 1926.

48 Summerskill, *op. cit.*

Chapter Eight: Centre Court

1 Cazalet-Keir.

2 Turbervill. Edith Picton Turbervill was MP for the Wrekin from 1929 to 1931.

3 See Adam.

4 A.P. Herbert, *Tantivy Towers*, Methuen, London, 1932. Herbert, a noted humorist – which largely prevented him achieving a successful career as an MP – was reflecting the sort of dogmatic utterances, serious or humorous, that Nancy frequently uttered in public, and which continued to provide good copy for the press. An example, typical in being both amusing and unfounded, was her claim that the Australians had defeated England in the 1931 Test series because they did not drink – which irritated the English team but greatly annoyed the Australians, who fancied themselves as much with the bottle as with bat and ball.

5 Sir Philip Sassoon, Bt (1888–1939), scion of a famous Parsee family, exotic, rich, noted art collector and confirmed bachelor. MP for Hythe, he was Parliamentary Private Secretary to Lloyd George in 1920, Undersecretary of State for Air, 1931–7 and First Commissioner of Works, 1937–9. He was a man of unusual taste, expressed in his houses at Trent Park and Port Lympne, and as Commissioner of Works he conceived the idea of sowing wild flowers around the trees in London's parks, which enhances their attraction to this day. Sir Henry Channon (1897–1958), MP for Southend, was a leading host in London society between the wars. For a portrait of Channon see Adrian Fort, *Archibald Wavell: The Life and Times of an Imperial Servant*, Jonathan Cape, London, 2009, and *Chips: The Diaries of Sir Henry Channon*, ed. Robert Rhodes James, Weidenfeld & Nicolson, London, 1967.

6 Joyce Grenfell Papers, LP9/1-3, Archive Department, Lucy Cavendish College, Cambridge.

7 The flavour of a hostess's mentality may be found in the papers of Lady Colefax, Special Collections Dept., Bodleian Library, Oxford; also more generally see Kirsty McLeod, *A Passion for Friendship, Sibyl Colefax and Her Circle*, Michael Joseph, London, 1991, and Brian Masters, *Great Hostesses*, Constable, London, 1982.

8 Notes by Lady Astor, the Women's Library Archive, London Metropolitan University, ref. 7BSH/5/1/1/01.

9 Lady Astor, Impressions of English Politics, the Women's Library Archive, loc. cit., ref., 7BSH/5/1/1/11/38.

10 Neville Chamberlain to his sister Ida, 11 May 1924, quoted in Self.

11 19 July 1925, quoted in Self.

12 Lady Astor to Sean O'Casey, 8 November 1935, Astor Papers, University of Reading, MS 1416/1/4/77.

13 Joyce Grenfell Papers, LP9/1-3, loc. cit.

14 *Shaw, Interviews and Recollections*, ed. A.M. Gibbs, Macmillan, Basingstoke, 1990, p. 492.

15 Eugene Lyons, *Assignment in Utopia*, Harcourt Brace, New York, 1937. Lyons, a communist fellow traveller, was a journalist based in Moscow, working for the American news agency UPI.

16 Astor Papers, University of Reading, MS 1416.

17 Lady Astor, telephone interview with the BBC, 14 January 1952.

18 In 1930, Philip Kerr became the 11th Marquess of Lothian, inheriting the title from a cousin. Where he appears in the following pages it will be by that name.

19 Lord Lothian to Lady Astor, 6 November 1936, Astor Papers, University of Reading, MS 1416/1/4/55.

20 Later 7th Earl of Longford, KG, and a well-known philanthropist.

21 Lady Astor to Lord Beaverbrook, Beaverbrook Papers, BBK/H/158.

22 Joyce Grenfell to Nora Flynn, 4 July 1933, Joyce Grenfell Papers, LP9/1–3, loc. cit.

23 Wissie's fiancé was at that time MP for Rutland and Stamford, and Ronald Tree represented Harborough, in Leicestershire. The Prince of Wales was Edward, who became King in 1936 and abdicated in the same year. Nancy had lost to him in the semi-final of a parliamentary golf contest at Sandwich. The house next to the Astors' in St James's Square had been put up for sale, having previously been bought by speculators who had subsequently run short of money. Had Waldorf bought it, it would in the long run have proved as successful an investment as those his forebears had so often made in New York. In the event the house was demolished and a tall new building erected, of which the first tenants were the National Sporting Club, whose members were occasionally to overlook Nancy in the adjoining garden doing her exercises or practising her speeches. Lord Willoughby de Eresby, Wissie's husband-to-be, was due eventually to become Earl of Ancaster. Nancy, like Bernard Shaw, had been sculpted by the Hungarian Zsigmond Strobl; it seems that Lawrence preferred Jacob Epstein. At Cliveden there was also a bust of Nancy sculpted by an American, Joe Davidson, in 1930.

24 Quoted in Jeremy Wilson, *Lawrence of Arabia: The Authorised Biography of T.E. Lawrence*, Heinemann, London, 1989. Geoffrey Dawson, at that time editor of *The Times*, had long been a close friend of Nancy and Waldorf.

25 Jones, *A Diary with Letters*, p. 15, 6 October 1931.

26 Strachey MS notes, the Women's Library Archive, London Metropolitan University, ref. 7BSH/5//1/1/01.

27 Waldorf to Nancy, 20 January 1931. Astor Papers, University of Reading.

Dropmore, Taplow and Hedsor were nearby big houses; Hopkins was the Astors' chauffeur.

Chapter Nine: Downhill

[1] See Astor, *My Two Countries*.

[2] Wilhelm Frick was a member of Hitler's first Cabinet; a lawyer, he played an important part in creating the legal structure that enabled the Nazi Party to take power in Germany with a semblance of legality; he was later instrumental in the promulgation of the Nuremberg Laws. After the Second World War he was tried for war crimes, convicted and hanged.

[3] Abyssinia was at that time beginning also to be known by its present-day name of Ethiopia. The League of Nations' failure to achieve a unanimous, or even a majority opinion on how to constrain Italy or help Abyssinia in the crisis that in 1935 erupted between the two countries was final confirmation of its lack of effectiveness. For many in England, troubles in east Africa were far away, of little consequence and certainly not worth a war. Even members of the government who were dismayed by the failure to 'do the right thing', in the proper British way, seemed unsure of their facts. During one lengthy discussion of the subject at a Cabinet meeting, a minister complained that it was 'all very well spending time in talking about Ethiopia when the real problem to which we should address our attention is Abyssinia'. Despite widely published accounts of Italian atrocities, including the use of gas bombs, Abyssinia's subjugation did not cause much stir in England. A typical example of the lack of impact made on MPs by faraway countries was recorded by Lord Winterton, whose diary for 3 May 1936 read, 'The blow has fallen. Haile Selasse has fled the capital & there is looting and rioting there. Pleasant day; over to Aldbury to play tennis . . .'

[4] See Schweppenburg.

[5] See Jones, *A Diary with Letters, 1931–1950*.

[6] *Hansard*, 10 March 1936, Vol. 309, col. 1999.

[7] Ibid., 6 April 1936, Vol. 310, col. 2482.

[8] See Richard Griffiths, *Fellow Travellers of the Right*, Constable, London, 1980.

[9] Ribbentrop had established, with Hitler's blessing, an 'alternative Foreign Office' in Berlin, more or less opposite the established Foreign Office, which regarded Ribbentrop and all his works with suspicion and distaste. In August 1936 he became ambassador to Britain, and in February 1938 he was appointed Foreign Minister, masterminding the Nazi–Soviet Pact of 1939. He was tried at Nuremberg after the war and hanged in October

1946. The Anglo-German Fellowship in time gained a controversial reputation; many of its members, some of them leading figures in the City and industry, came to be seen as overtly pro-German. See, for example, Tennant.

[10] Joyce Grenfell papers, LP9/1–3, Archive Department, Lucy Cavendish College, Cambridge.

[11] E. Phillips Oppenheim, a popular novelist of the day, noted for spy adventures.

[12] Jones, *A Diary with Letters*, 2 and 3 June 1936, pp. 215–17. 'PT' refers to the Pilgrim Trust, a charitable organisation founded in 1930 by Edward Harkness, an American philanthropist, son of one of the original partners in John D. Rockefeller's Standard Oil. The trust used its endowment broadly to further the preservation of England's heritage. Stanley Baldwin was the first chairman, and at the time of Ribbentrop's meeting at Rest Harrow Jones was its secretary.

[13] Harold Nicolson, *Diaries and Letters, 1930–1939*, ed. Nigel Nicolson, Collins, London, 1966, entry for 20 September 1936.

[14] *Time and Tide*, 4 July 1936.

[15] Astor Papers, University of Reading, MS 1416/1/1180.

[16] Ibid.

[17] The Women's Library Archive, London Metropolitan University, ref.7BSH 5/1/1/01.

[18] Nancy Astor to Lady Hildyard, 16 December 1936, private collection.

[19] Astor Papers, University of Reading, MS 1416/1/7/76.

[20] See Robert Rhodes James, *Victor Cazalet: A Portrait*, Hamilton, London, 1976.

[21] Quoted in Sykes, p. 406.

[22] Lady Astor to Six Point Group, 11 March 1937, Astor Papers, University of Reading, MS 1416/1/1/1483.

[23] Von Ribbentrop to Lady Astor, April 1937, Astor Papers, University of Reading, MS 1416/1/1/1483.

[24] *Manchester Guardian* and *Morning Post*, 16 July 1937.

[25] Margesson Papers, MRGN/5, 'Neville Chamberlain, A Candid Portrait', Churchill Archives Centre, Churchill College, Cambridge.

[26] Jones, *A Diary with Letters*, 24 October 1937.

[27] Von Ribbentrop to Hitler, 28 December 1937, Politisches Archiv des Auswärtigen Amt, R28895a, 'Das deutsche-englische Verhaltnis . . .', para. VIIB.

[28] *Oxford Magazine*, 23 February 1939.

[29] *Sunday Chronicle*, 5 March 1939.

[30] Joyce Grenfell Papers, loc. cit. The Game is an acting game, similar to

charades. Battleship was an American-bred horse which won the 1938 Grand National, at a starting price of 40–1; it had also won the American Grand National.

[31] Lady Astor speaking in Plymouth, 20 February 1938, Astor Papers, University of Reading, MS 1416/1/7/77.

[32] Neville Chamberlain to Ida Chamberlain, 15 May 1938, Self, p. 322. Joseph Kennedy, at that time the American ambassador in London, was to become a friend of the Astors, and to court controversy for his defeatist attitude about Britain's prospects if she went to war with Germany.

[33] Neville Chamberlain writing from Wilton House to his sister, 25 June 1938.

[34] Viscountess Astor, Personal Explanation to the House of Commons, 27 June 1938, *Hansard*, Vol. 337.

[35] *Hansard*, 28 November 1938, Vol. 342, col. 108.

[36] Viscount Astor, letter to *The Times*, 5 May 1938.

[37] *Saturday Evening Post*, 4 March 1939.

[38] Sir Thomas Inskip, diary, 13 and 14 September 1938, Inskip Papers, INKP1, CAC, Churchill College, Cambridge.

[39] Note of a talk between President Roosevelt and Josephus Daniels, at the White House, 14 January 1939. Josephus Daniels Papers, President's Personal File, PPF 86, Hyde Park Presidential Library, Hyde Park, NY.

[40] For the recollections of Anne Lindbergh, see Anne Morrow, *The Flower and the Nettle: Diaries and Letters of Anne Morrow Lindbergh, 1936–1939*, Harcourt Brace Jovanovich, New York, *c.* 1976.

[41] Quoted in David Faber, *Munich*, Simon & Schuster, London, 2008.

[42] *Hansard*, 5 October 1938, Vol. 339, col. 360.

[43] Memoranda of the Foreign Policy Committee, 21 November 1938, National Archives, CAB 27/627. Bill Astor had been elected MP for East Fulham in 1935, in the general election that confirmed in power a National Government with an overwhelming Conservative majority. Two years earlier there had been a sensational by-election in East Fulham, when Labour won the hitherto safe Tory seat. The then Conservative leader, Stanley Baldwin, cited the result as a reason for not prioritising expenditure on defence, interpreting the country's mood as pacifist. However, the majority of canvassers in the constituency said that defence was only of secondary interest to the electors, and that their chief concern was the appalling state of housing in the area, as a result of which the incumbent Conservative was defeated.

[44] Balsan.

[45] Spitzy. Edouard Benes was the Czechoslovakian president at the time of Munich.

[46] Marquess of Lothian to Sir Ronald Lindsay, 31 March 1939, Lothian Papers, National Archives of Scotland, GD 40–17. Lindsay was Lothian's predecessor as British ambassador in Washington. A month later Lothian wrote to Roosevelt elaborating his belief that peace depended on the dictators realising that the democracies firmly controlled the seas, but adding that Britain could no longer establish that control without American help. See Lothian, Lord Philip H.K., President's Personal File PPF 5731, Hyde Park Presidential Library, Hyde Park, NY.

[47] FDR to Roger Merriman, 15 February 1939, President's Secretary's File (PSF) 46, Library of Congress, Washington DC, and see David Cannadine, 'Historians as Diplomats?: Roger B. Merriman, George M. Trevelyan, and Anglo-American Relations', *New England Quarterly*, Vol. 72, no. 2, June 1999, pp. 207–31.

Chapter Ten: War on Two Fronts

[1] Dowager Marchioness of Salisbury to author.

[2] Ibid.; cf. Harrison, *Gentlemen's Gentlemen*.

[3] Nancy Astor to Pem Shaw, 18 December 1939, Astor Papers, University of Reading, MS 1416/1/3/38.

[4] *Hansard*, 11 April 1940, Vol. 359, col. 760.

[5] Nancy Astor to Pem Shaw, 5 June 1940, Astor Papers, University of Reading, MS 1416/1/3/38. The BEF was the British Expeditionary Force, sent to France at the beginning of the war, but forced back on to the beach at Dunkirk.

[6] Billy Butlin went on to make a successful career out of holiday camps, opening his first 'fairground' camp in 1936, in Skegness, famously advertised on the railways with placards inviting passengers to 'come to Bracing Skegness'. Eventually he retired, rich and famous, to the Channel Islands.

[7] See the *Western Morning News*, anniversary report, 20 March 1951.

[8] Queen Elizabeth to Lady Astor, 23 March 1941. Astor Papers, University of Reading, MS 1416/1/3/38.

[9] Plymouth and West Devon Record Office, Astor Papers, news-cutting scrapbooks, MS 186/18/64–5.

[10] *Western Morning News*, 7 April 1941. For a description of local aspects of Plymouth during and after the Blitz, see also Veronica Norman, *Sunshine of Plymouth*, Joseph Louci, Plymouth, 2009.

[11] Cole Lesley, *The Life of Noel Coward*, Jonathan Cape, London, 1976, p. 219.

[12] Plymouth and West Devon Record Office, Astor Papers, news-cutting scrapbooks, MS 186/18/64-5.

13 *Western Evening Herald*, 6 June 1941. Hoe means 'height'.

14 Plymouth and West Devon Record Office, Astor Papers, news-cutting scrapbooks, MS 186/18/64-5.

15 Harrison, *Gentlemen's Gentlemen*, pp. 184-5.

16 Franklin D. Roosevelt to Nancy Astor, 4 September 1918, Astor Papers, University of Reading, MS 1416/1/4/1114.

17 President Roosevelt to Nancy Astor, 19 February 1941, President's Personal File (PPF), 192, Astor, Lord and Lady Waldorf, Hyde Park Presidential Library, Hyde Park, NY.

18 Nancy Astor to Pem Shaw, 20 June 1942, Astor Papers, University of Reading, MS 1416/1/3/38.

19 Ben Robertson, *I Saw England*, Jarrolds, London, 1941. Robertson was a reporter for the *New York Herald Tribune*, to whose London office he was on his way in 1943 when he was killed in an aeroplane crash near Lisbon.

20 Sykes, p. 459.

21 Viscount Astor, introduction to H.P. Twyford, *It Came to Our Door*, Underhill, Plymouth, 1946.

22 Harrison, *Gentlemen's Gentlemen* pp. 192-3. Rose Harrison was an invaluable help to Nancy in her domestic arrangements, and it was lucky for her mistress that she was not called up for war work; although in 1942 she was asked by the relevant committee to give reasons as to why she should not be called up in some capacity, she was allowed to continue with Nancy. 'I am very relieved for your sake, my lady,' she wrote afterwards, 'as I could not visualise how on earth you would get along, as living with you for fourteen years I have learnt your ways, what to do and when to do it. Life is hard enough for a public person like you without having help taken away from you . . .' Astor Papers, University of Reading.

23 Mrs Churchill to Lord Astor, 27 June 1941, Plymouth and West Devon Record Office, Lord Mayor's Secretary's Files, 1495/57.

24 'Blitzed Plymouth Plans A New City', transcript of a broadcast to the USA by the North American Service, by William Holt and Viscount Astor, Plymouth and West Devon Record Office, 3642/1707. After consultation with Waldorf, the council had engaged Professor Patrick Abercrombie as consultant planning surveyor for the new Plymouth, to work in harness with J. Paton Watson as city engineer and surveyor.

25 *Observer*, 2 August 1942.

26 Quoted in Peter Stanford, *Bronwen*, HarperCollins, London, 2000, p. 162.

27 *Hansard*, 20 May 1941, Vol. 371, cols 1440-3.

28 See correspondence in PPF 192, Hyde Park Presidential Library, Hyde

Park, NY: Nancy Astor to President Roosevelt, 2 April 1942, and Ambassador Bingham to President Roosevelt, 2 May 1942.

[29] FDR to Sumner Welles, 19 May 1942, PPF 192, loc. cit.; and see *FDR, His Personal Letters 1928–1945*, ed. Elliott Roosevelt and Joseph P. Nash, Duell, Sloan and Pearce, New York, 1950.

[30] Dr Thomas Jones to Lady Astor, 10 August 1942, Thomas Jones Papers, Class Q, Vol. 2, National Library of Wales.

[31] *Hansard*, 18 March 1943, Vol. 387, cols 1384–8.

[32] Lady Astor to Mrs Loth, 8 August 1944, private collection.

[33] Angus McDonnell to Nancy Astor, quoted in Alice Winn, *Always a Virginian*, J.P. Bell, Lynchburg, 1973.

[34] Press report, 13 February 1944, Plymouth and West Devon Record Office, 186/18/72–3, Astor news-cutting scrapbooks, 1 January–30 June 1944.

[35] David Astor to Dr Thomas Jones, 23 May 1944, Thomas Jones Papers, Class Q, Vols 3 and 6, National Library of Wales, quoted in Cockett. Richard Cockett's book is a paramount source of information about these matters. In fact, within seven years David Astor's editorship was to help increase the circulation of the *Observer* by about 200 per cent.

[36] Waldof to Nancy, Astor Papers, University of Reading, MS 1416.

[37] Notice to Plymouth newspapers, 1 December 1944, Plymouth and West Devon Record Office, Astor Papers, 186/18/72.

Chapter Eleven: Aftermath

[1] Waldorf to Nancy, 5 May 1945, Astor private papers.

[2] Waldorf to Nancy, 1 July 1945, Astor private papers.

[3] Dame Edith Lyttelton to Lady Astor, 25 April 1945, Astor private papers.

[4] Press cuttings 3/7/1945-23/7/1949, Box 84, Astor Papers, University of Reading, MS 1416.

[5] US press reports, 4 July 1946, Box 84, Astor Papers, University of Reading, MS 1416.

[6] Bobbie Shaw to Nancy Astor, June 1947, Astor Papers, University of Reading, MS 1416/1/3/11.

[7] Waldorf to Nancy, 11 June 1947. Astor Papers, University of Reading, MS 1416/1/3/11.

[8] Quoted in Langhorne.

[9] Waldorf to Nancy, 31 August 1951, Astor private papers.

[10] Mrs Thomas Baring, formerly Viscountess Astor, to author.

[11] Nancy Astor to the Marchioness of Salisbury, 4 April 1944, Astor Papers, University of Reading, MS 1416/1/4/84. A month later, Kathleen ('Kick') Kennedy, daughter of the former United States ambassador Joe

Kennedy, and sister of the future president, married the Marquess of Hartington, who was later killed in action. Nancy was one of the few guests at their marriage, which was a civil ceremony and restricted in size, because of the religious complications.

[12] Mrs Helen Mildmay-White, diary, private collection.

[13] Waldorf to Nancy, 7 May 1947, Astor Papers, University of Reading, MS 1416/1/3/11.

[14] Waldorf to Nancy, 17 June 1947, Astor Papers, University of Reading, MS 1416/1/3/11.

[15] Albert Roux to author.

[16] See *Shaw: Interviews and Recollections*, ed. A.M. Gibbs, Macmillan, 1990. Subsequently, commenting in a lighter mood on Shaw's death, Nancy had said, 'No one remembers politicians after their deaths and my one chance of immortality is to be mentioned in his will. Besides, I need the money.'

[17] Nancy Astor to Dr Thomas Jones, 23 October 1952, Thomas Jones Papers, Class Q, Vol. 2. An olive branch was also extended by Churchill, who wrote to Nancy, 'I know how vain words seem but I felt that you will not mind my expressing my sorrow.'

[18] In later years there were several occasions on which upon opening up the drawing room in the morning cushions appeared to have been thrown around during the night. At a twenty-first birthday party given by the subsequent occupants, one of the guests was the Duchess of Beaufort, who at that time looked very like Nancy. Two of those present remarked to the hosts that it was 'very nice to see Mary Beaufort again' and that they would go and talk to her shortly. The hosts replied that the Duchess had earlier telephoned to say that she could not come to the party. 'But she's there,' said the guests, 'sitting in the armchair at the far end, with that stick she always has, the ebony one with the silver top – looking rather disapproving, for some reason!' On investigation she was not there, and had never come to the party.

[19] R.F. Wilson to author.

[20] Conversation between author and Cyril Whiting, whose grandfather, Fred Whiting, had established a family caddie operation, succeeded by his son Albert and then by Cyril. Fred Whiting had been the favourite caddie of the Prince of Wales, who often used to fly himself down to play at St George's in the early 1930s.

[21] Joyce Grenfell to Virginia Graham, 12 October 1955. Joyce Grenfell Papers, LP9/1-3, Archive Department, Lucy Cavendish College, Cambridge.

[22] Nancy Astor to Harold Macmillan, 22 February 1954, Macmillan Papers, C519, Bodleian Library, Oxford. Macmillan's later ill-disposition towards

the Astors was increased by what he perceived as their stance over the Suez affair. Near the end of his life, when a friend asked him for his reaction to the news that Cliveden was being turned into a hotel, he replied, 'But, my dear boy, it always has been!'

[23] Maurice Collis, *Nancy Astor*, Faber and Faber, London, 1960, p. 229.

[24] Mrs Thomas Baring (Viscountess Astor) to author.

[25] Ibid.

[26] Earl of Gowrie to author.

[27] Ibid.

[28] Conversation between author and Harold Hickson, gardener at Rest Harrow in the 1950s and 1960s.

[29] Conversation between author and Lottie Barton, housemaid at Rest Harrow in the 1950s and 1960s.

[30] Michael Astor, diary, Astor Papers.

Abdy, Jane, and Gere, Charlotte, *The Souls*, Sidgwick & Jackson, London, 1984

Adam, Ruth, *A Woman's Place, 1910–1975*, Chatto & Windus, London, 1975

Amory, Cleveland, *The Last Resorts*, Harper & Brothers, New York, 1952

Asquith, Cynthia, *Remember and Be Glad*, James Barrie, London, 1952

Astor, Michael, *Tribal Feeling*, John Murray, London, 1963

Astor, Nancy, *A Lightning Sketch*, Wilton 65, Winkfield, 2003

Astor, Nancy, *My Two Countries*, Heinemann, London, 1923

Baker, Arthur, *The House Is Sitting*, Blandford Press, London, 1958

Balsan, Consuelo, *The Glitter and the Gold*, Harper, New York, 1952

Becker, Robert, *Nancy Lancaster*, Alfred A. Knopf, New York, 1996

Bradburn, Elizabeth, *Margaret McMillan*, Routledge, London, 1989

Brookes, Pamela, *Women at Westminster*, P. Davies, London, 1967

Cazalet-Keir, Thelma, *From the Wings*, Bodley Head, London, 1967

Clayton, Michael, *Foxhunting in Paradise*, John Murray, London, 1993

Cockburn, Claud, *In Time of Trouble*, Hart-Davis, London, 1956

Cockett, Richard, *David Astor and the Observer*, Deutsch, London, 1991

Collis, Maurice, *Diaries, 1949–1969*, ed. Louise Collis, Heinemann, London, 1976

Curzon, Grace, *Reminiscences*, Hutchinson, London, 1955

de Courcy, Anne, *Circe: The Life of Edith, Marchioness of Londonderry*, Sinclair-Stevenson, London, 1992

Desborough, Ethel, *Pages From a Family Journal, 1888–1915*, Spottiswoode, Eton, 1916

Downey, Fairfax, *Portrait of an Era, as drawn by C.D. Gibson*, Life Publishing Co., Charles Scribner's Sons, New York, 1936

Ervine, St John, *Bernard Shaw: His Life, Work and Friends*, Constable, London, 1956

Fane, Lady Augusta, *Chit-Chat*, Butterworth, London, 1926

Forbes, Lady Angela, *Memories and Base Details*, Hutchinson, London, 1921

Fort, George Seymour, *Dr Jameson*, Hurst & Blackett, London, 1908

Fox, James, *The Langhorne Sisters*, Granta Books, London, 1998

Gibson, Langhorne, *The Gibson Girl: Portrait of a Southern Belle*, Commodore Press, Richmond, 1997

Hamilton, Mary Agnes, *Remembering My Good Friends*, Jonathan Cape, London, 1944

Harrison, Brian, *Prudent Revolutionaries*, Clarendon Press, Oxford, 1987

Harrison, Michael, *Rosa*, P. Davies, London, 1962

Harrison, Rosina, *Gentlemen's Gentlemen, My Friends in Service*, Arlington Books, London, 1976

Hesse, Fritz, *Hitler and the English*, ed. F.A. Voigt, Allan Wingate, London, 1954

Hopper, Trevor, *Robert Tressell's Hastings*, Hopper Books, Brighton, 1999

Horner, Frances, *Time Remembered*, Heinemann, London, 1933

Jacobsen, Hans Adolf, *The Nazi Party and the German Foreign Office*, Routledge, London, 2007

Jones, Thomas, *A Diary with Letters*, OUP, Oxford, 1954

Jones, Thomas, *Whitehall Diary*, ed. Keith Middlemas, OUP, Oxford, 1969–1971

Kavaler, Lucy, *The Astors, A Family Chronicle*, Harrap, London, 1966

Langhorne, Elizabeth, *Nancy Astor and Her Friends*, Arthur Baker, London, 1974

MacKenzie, Jeanne, *Children of the Souls*, Chatto & Windus, London, 1986

McMillan, Margaret, *The Nursery School*, J.M. Dent, London, 1919

Mitchell, David, *Women on the Warpath*, Jonathan Cape, London, 1966

Musolf, Karen J., *From Plymouth to Parliament*, Macmillan, Basingstoke, 1999

Newnham-Davis, Nathaniel, *The Gourmet's Guide to London*, Grant Richards Ltd, London, 1914

O'Connor, Harvey, *The Astors*, A. Knopf, New York, 1941

Oldfield, Sybil, *Jeanie, An Army of One*, Sussex Academic Press, Brighton, 2008

Picton–Turbervill, Edith, *Life Is Good*, F. Muller, London, 1939

Pless, Fürstin von, *What I Left Unsaid*, Cassell, London, 1936

Pugh, Martin, *Women's Suffrage in Britain, 1867–1928*, Historical Association, London, 1980

Rhondda, Viscountess, *Notes on the Way*, Macmillan, London, 1937

Richardson, Mary, *Laugh a Defiance*, George Weidenfield & Nicolson, London, 1953

Schweppenburg, Freiherr Geyr von, *The Critical Years*, Wingate, London, 1952

Schwerin, Detlef Graf von, *Dann sind's die besten Köpfe, die man henkt*, Piper, Munich, 1991

Seidel, Kathryn Lee, *The Southern Belle in the American Novel*, University Presses of Florida, Tampa, 1985

Self, Robert C., ed., *The Neville Chamberlain Diary Letters*, Aldershot, Ashgate, 2000

Sermoneta, Duchessa di, *Things Past*, Hutchinson, London, 1929

Sidebotham, Herbert, *Political Profiles from British Public Life*, Houghton Mifflin, Boston, 1921

Sinclair, David, *Dynasty: The Astors and Their Times*, J.M. Dent, London, 1983

Smith, Truman, *Berlin Alert*, Hoover Institution Press, Stanford, 1984

Spargo, John, *The Bitter Cry of the Children*, Macmillan, New York, 1906

Spitzy, Reinhard, *How We Squandered the Reich*, tr. G.T. Waddington, Michael Russell, Wilby, 1997

Stocks, Mary, *My Commonplace Book*, Peter Davies, London, 1970

Strachery, Ray, *Our Freedom and its Results*, Hogarth Press, London, 1936

Sykes, Christopher, *Nancy: The Life of Lady Astor*, Collins, London, 1972

Tennant, Ernest, *True Account*, Max Parish, London, 1957

Turner, John, ed., *The Larger Idea*, The Historians' Press, London, 1988

Urquhart, Diane, *The Ladies of Londonderry*, Tauris, London, 2007

Watt, Donald Cameron, *Personalities and Appeasement*, Harry Ransom Humanities Research Center, University of Texas, Austin, 1991

Willoughby de Broke, Lord, *The Passing Years*, Constable, London, 1924

INDEX

(the initials CL refer to Chiswell Dabney Langhorne; NA to Nancy Astor; WA to Waldorf Astor; WWA to William Waldorf Astor)

www.vintage-books.co.uk